# SHADOW WARRIORS

A HISTORY OF THE US ARMY RANGERS

# SHADOW
# WARRIORS

## A HISTORY OF THE US ARMY RANGERS

# MIR BAHMANYAR

First published in Great Britain in 2005 by Osprey Publishing, Midland House,
West Way, Botley, Oxford OX2 0PH, United Kingdom.
443 Park Avenue South, New York, NY 10016, USA.
Email: info@ospreypublishing.com

A CIP catalog record for this book is available from the British Library

ISBN 1 84176 860 X

Mir Bahmanyar has asserted his right under the Copyright, Designs and Patents
Act, 1988, to be identified as the author of this book.

Index by Alison Worthington
Line drawings by John Richards
Originated by PPS Grasmere, Leeds, UK
Printed in China through Bookbuilders.

05 06 07 08 09    10 9 8 7 6 5 4 3 2 1

For a catalog of all books published by Osprey please contact:

NORTH AMERICA
Osprey Direct, 2427 Bond Street, University Park, IL 60466, USA
E-mail: info@ospreydirectusa.com

ALL OTHER REGIONS
Osprey Direct UK, P.O. Box 140, Wellingborough, Northants, NN8 2FA, UK
E-mail: info@ospreydirect.co.uk

www.ospreypublishing.com

Front cover image: © Corbis

# CONTENTS

# Acknowledgments

It is customary to thank people and so shall I. First and foremost, SOvV and her three beautiful children. Marcus Cowper and Nikolai Bogdanovic, now Ilios Publishing, gave me my first break in writing. They are regretting it as I write these words. No person can be found with greater patience and patience and more patience coupled with a great personality than Anita Baker at Osprey Publishing – you may curse loudly at me now. Particular thanks must also go to Ruth Sheppard at Osprey for letting me pick on her regularly.

Many Ranger and Special Operations Forces (SOF) types helped out over the years with pictures, interviews, and source material. Among them are James Altieri, Phil Stern, Carl Lehman, Gino Mercuriali of Darby's Rangers, and Phil Piazza, a most noble man and leader of those marauders that filled the ranks of Galahad – 5307th Composite Unit Provisional (CUP). Thanks also to Roy Boatman, Special Forces – we won't hold it against him – and Ranger NCO of too many years, for his excessive knowledge on Vietnam. Tim Abell, 2nd Battalion, 75th Ranger Regiment, now an actor and star of my film *Soldier of God*, for his right-wing points of view that allow for hours of browbeating, and Sean Naylor, a critic and journalist *par excellence*, for answering many questions even when inconvenient.

I should also thank Kimberly Laudano, Public Affairs 75th Ranger Regiment, who more than once would have liked to have strangled me, Carol Darby of the US Army Special Operations Command, Public Affairs Office (USASOC PAO), for tolerating me over the years, and Kenneth Finlayson, Historian USASOC, who went above and beyond.

# Introduction

Rangers: not the Forest Park Rangers, not the Law Enforcement Texas Rangers and most certainly not the baseball Texas Rangers. No, indeed there is only one kind of American Ranger – the killing kind.

Their names are many: Rogers' Rangers, Darby's Rangers, Airborne Rangers or Army Rangers... but then there are also others called Rangers – Merrill's Marauders, Mars Task Force, the 475th, Long Range Reconnaissance Patrollers (LRRP), Long Range Patrollers (LRP), Ranger Rangers, and even Vietnamese Rangers advised by American Rangers.

No person can claim to write a complete history of any unit, much less of one that has painted the canvas of war blood-red so often and on so many occasions. One Ranger officer serving during the Global War on Terrorism calls Rangers that "Pantheon of Heroes." Certainly appropriate, as no sane individual joins an outfit that usually advertises with such succinct bulletins as "volunteers wanted for dangerous and hazardous missions... 80% casualties expected." However, one little secret people don't know about is that, in general terms, a soldier serving during war time has a better chance of surviving with an elite unit – an outfit that has high standards and excellent training. The old adage of "the more you sweat in battle the less you bleed on the battlefield" is apt... but when things go wrong, they go dreadfully wrong, as we will see throughout the Rangers' history.

Many Ranger books are excellent historical records of the men they cover, but many also do not discuss the more problematic issues such as race relations, drug abuse, failure in combat, or even bad morale. Most of those issues fall outside of the parameters of this book as well and I can only offer a cursory review of some of the Ranger histories, focusing instead on the modern Rangers from 1974 to 2005. This is not to belittle other Rangers; some don't even receive a mention, simply because there is only so much that can be covered within these pages (just to note one such example, there were hundreds of Ranging-type units during the American Civil War). The official lineage and honors of today's 75th Ranger Regiment only begin with William O. Darby's 1st Ranger Battalion founded in 1942. Colonial and Civil War Rangers are excluded, though often mentioned in an historical context. Suffice it to say that this book offers merely a glimpse into Rangers and their history. I apologize in advance for the cursory coverage, particularly to those outstanding Long Range Patrollers from World War II and the parent unit of the modern Regiment, the 5307th Composite Unit Provisional (CUP), commonly known as Merrill's Marauders. They are the founding fathers of our current Rangers. It is almost criminal not to have covered in detail the all-black 2nd Airborne-Ranger Company of the Korean Conflict – a great outfit deserving of a more detailed painter for their contribution to Ranger history. Equally dissatisfied, the Long Range Patrollers and Rangers of Europe and Vietnam.

The focus of this book is on the modern Airborne Rangers from 1974. The reason for this is simple; plenty of books detail Ranger exploits, particularly during the French and Indian War, with Rogers' Rangers as the shining example. The Civil War has enough literature to keep most people happy for years to come. World War II has experienced a sensational explosion of material ever since the well-received film, *Saving Private Ryan*. The Korean War had about 700 Rangers and thus represents the smallest force – but it does have several fine histories despite that fact. Vietnam has dozens upon dozens of volumes of varying quality. I have recommended a number of these books in the Bibliography and Further Reading section on page 317.

There are many myths surrounding Rangers and their combat record. Colonial Rangers made mistakes and were killed, they scalped people, and their leader owed his men money and went to jail. Mark Twain recalls his misadventures as a Ranger during the Civil War and the Rangers don't come out looking good. World War II has its share of myths as well. The 2nd Ranger Battalion was not the first American unit on top of Pointe du Hoc during D-Day – elements of the 116th were. Although some Darby's Rangers fought valiantly at Cisterna, most surrendered, the majority of casualties being suffered by the 4th Ranger Battalion while attempting to relieve their trapped comrades. On the other hand, Vietnam-era patrollers and Rangers were by and large professional and provided the NCO core for the future Rangers that reactivated the 75th Infantry in 1974. A huge debt is owed to them.

Most importantly, this book is not about the Tab wearer, the Ranger School graduate, no, he only attended a two-month school. Indeed this book is about the men who chose and are still choosing to lead a lifestyle that usually is extremely difficult, fraught with physical and mental hardships. Those are the real Rangers – the Rangers that wore and are wearing the highly coveted Ranger Scroll, their unit patch, their way of life and death.

Mir Bahmanyar
City of Angels

# PART I
# THE RISE OF THE RANGERS

# Colonial Rangers

Fleeing one empire to start another

As people were fleeing the yoke of "old Europe," as Secretary of Defense Donald Rumsfeld likes to say, a great many men were waging a campaign to carve out a new country, disposing of the previous inhabitants over the next two hundred years, and in the process creating a new type of soldier, one that could range to and fro, live off the land, and adopt some of the fighting techniques and tracking skills the Native Americans had developed in their culture.

As the English and Scots grew in numbers, more and more settlements were built. As these encroached on the natives, war broke out with some regularity and this led to the English settlements establishing small immobile garrisons along the major approaches as a defense against those Native American attacks. This protection soon proved inadequate, as the enemy would raid the settlements through various routes and retreat before the militia could respond. Thus each colony needed to establish a foot patrol to guard against the enemy's approach, and give the militia enough time to assemble and march.

The action of these soldiers patrolling an area was described as ranging, and the soldiers who ranged were called Rangers. René Chartrand in his book *Colonial American Troops 1610–1774* argues that men assigned to patrols or "ranger" duties were called Rangers as early as the 14th century in England.[1]

In a public affairs document released by the 75th Ranger Regiment in 1999, "Rangers served the English King in his forest districts during the Middle Ages. For example, in 1371, Henry Dolyng was a Ranger of the New Forest and Thomas of Croydon was a Ranger in Waltham."[2] The primary purpose of these woodsmen was to protect the animals of his Lord's forests as well as to serve as a deterrent to the occasional brigand on the prowl around the local areas.

It further states that in the American colonies, "in 1634 through 1635, Edward Backler was hired as a Ranger for Kent Island, a Virginia plantation in the upper Chesapeake Bay (now Maryland), and assigned with the task of the guarding against the approach of Native Americans who had been

## STANDING ORDERS, ROGERS RANGERS
### MAJOR ROBERT ROGERS•1756

1. Don't forget nothing.
2. Have your musket clean as a whistle, hatchet scoured, sixty rounds powder and ball, and be ready to march at a minute's warning.
3. When you're on the march, act the way you would if you was sneaking up on a deer. See the enemy first.
4. Tell the truth about what you see and what you do. There is an army depending on us for correct information. You can lie all you please when you tell other folks about the Rangers, but don't never lie to a Ranger or officer.
5. Don't never take a chance you don't have to.
6. When we're on the march we march single file, far enough apart so one shot can't go through two men.
7. If we strike swamps, or soft ground, we spread out abrest, so it's hard to track us.
8. When we march, we keep moving till dark, so as to give the enemy the least possible chance at us.
9. When we camp, half the party stays awake while the other half sleeps.
10. If we take prisoners, we keep 'em separate till we have had time to examine them, so they can't cook up a story between 'em.
11. Don't ever march home the same way. Take a different route so you won't be ambushed.
12. No matter whether we travel in big parties or little one, each party has to keep a scout 20 yards ahead, twenty yards on each flank and twenty yards in the rear, so the main body can't be surprised and wiped out.
13. Every night you'll be told where to meet if surrounded by a superior force.
14. Don't sit down to eat without posting sentries.
15. Don't sleep beyond dawn. Dawn's when the French and Indians attack.
16. Don't cross a river by a regular ford.
17. If somebody's trailing you, make a circle, come back onto your own tracks, and ambush the folks that aim to ambush you.
18. Don't stand up when the enemy's coming against you. Kneel down, lie down, hide behind a tree.
19. Let the enemy come till he's almost close enough to touch. Then let him have it and jump out and finish him up with your hatchet.

The Standing Orders. The origins of it are disputed, but it was probably written by someone in the Ranger Training Detachment in the 1950s. (Author's collection)

harassing the settlement."[3] The private use of small parties of military Rangers by plantation owners in Virginia and Maryland was apparently common and would continue throughout the coming century. Much like his Old World counterpart, the colonial Ranger was tasked with combat and reconnaissance patrols – to ambush the dreaded, marauding Indians whenever and wherever possible.

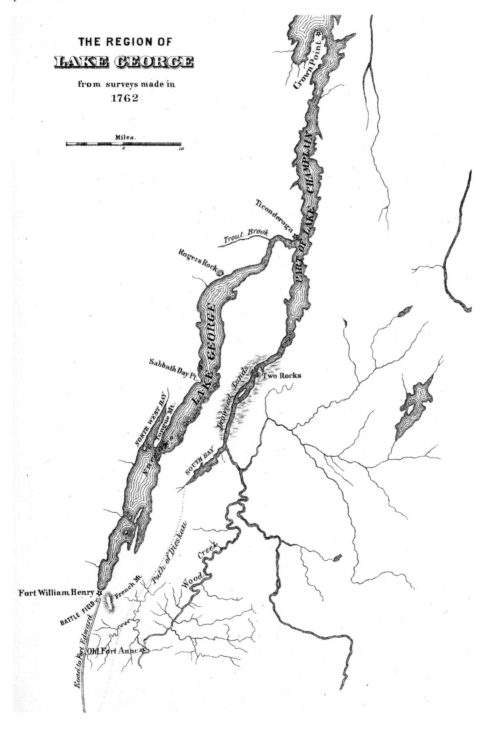

The primary battlefield of Roger's Rangers between 1755 and 1759: the rivers, lakes, islands, swamps, and forested mountains of the northern New York war front. (Gary Zaboly)

## THE EARLY RANGERS

Extract from *Reminiscences of the French War: Robert Rogers' Journal* (The Freedom Historical Society, New Hampshire, 1898) preface xvi–vxii:

The British Generals [were convinced] of their utter inability to operate in America, without the aid of a strong corps of Rangers, composed of the natives of the country, whose knowledge of Indian warfare, would enable them to prevent a similar surprise and overthrow. A commission was accordingly issued to Major Rogers, the author of this Journal, to enlist and discipline the corps; and his details may be relied upon as being substantially correct; and the rules established by him for the ranging service, may be of some benefit to future partisans, should wars with the Indians render such services necessary.

The Rangers were raised principally in New Hampshire, were regularly paid by the Crown in the same manner as troops of the line, and officered by the most hardy, intelligent, and enterprising partisans of that day, many of whom, were afterwards distinguished in the Revolutionary war. The hardy character of the Rangers and the experience acquired by their hunting excursions and intercourse with the Indians, enabled them to discharge the arduous duties in which they were employed. These were to scour the woods, and ascertain the force and position of the enemy; to discover and prevent the effect of his ambuscades, and to ambush him, in their turn; to acquire information of his movements, by making prisoners of his sentinels, who were frequently taken and brought away from the gates of Crown Point and Ticonderoga, by these daring woodsmen; to clear the way for the advance of the regular troops, and lastly, to fight the enemy according to his own fashion, and with his own weapons, whenever circumstances required. If on these occasions, they sometimes deviated from the usages of civilized warfare, in making use of the scalping knife, the barbarity of the enemy, the law of retaliation, and the emergency of the times must be their apology. They were compelled to fight Indians upon their own terms.

Their expeditions were confined to no particular season. Summer or winter, it was the same to them. They frequently made long and fatiguing marches through the snow, by the use of snow shoes, and were often obliged to encamp in the forest without fire, for fear of being discovered by the vigilance of the enemy; and with no other food, than the game they had killed on the march. They frequently penetrated 500 miles into the enemy's country, destroying French settlements, and Indian villages. They were in fact, the most formidable body of men ever employed as partisans in the wars of this country; and in every regular engagement proved themselves not inferior to the British Troops. The description and character of the scout in the Last of the Mohicans, is not inapplicable to those of one of Rogers' Rangers.

Virginia used Rangers as early as 1676 and at times coordinated operations with the colony of Maryland. Other southern colonies eventually followed suit and continued to use Rangers during those periods when Native American raids appeared likely.

Much like the sister colonies in the south, the northern colonies – which ultimately saw more action during the French and Indian War than their neighbors – started forming Ranger units to protect against raids during the 17th century. "In 1670, the colony of Plymouth (in modern-day Massachusetts) maintained a Ranger unit under Thomas Willet."[4]

During King Phillip's War (1675–76), also known as the Metacomet War, the colonies of Plymouth and Massachusetts formed ranging units. One of the interesting aspects of colonial Rangers is that they also included other races, including blacks and friendly Native Americans who were organized into independent ranging companies. One of these units was the one commanded by Benjamin Church (1639–1718) whose Rangers adapted very well to this new breed of war fighting – raiding and skulking in the woods. Gary Zaboly points out in *American Colonial Ranger: The Northern Colonies 1724–64* that battles with Native American warriors in the early 17th century had demonstrated the virtual uselessness of European armor, pikes, cavalry and maneuvers in the dense New World forests. And that not until the early 1700s were the colonists finally capable of producing hearty men who could penetrate deeply into uncharted Indian territory.[5] Ranger Church is credited not only with combining colonists with friendly Natives and thereby creating a deadly ranging force, but also with the creation of the first American military manual, when one of his sons published Benjamin Church's memoirs in 1716.[6]

During much of the 18th century, most of the other northern colonies used Ranger units to screen and protect their frontiers. In Nova Scotia, New York, and Georgia, Rangers were active during the War of Jenkins' Ear (1739–42) and King George's War (1739–48), fighting against the French, Spanish, and their Native American allies.

The European portion of the Seven Years' War (1755–63), unlike the portion fought in America known as the French and Indian War, was fought by pitting columns of drilled soldiers against one another. With lines of soldiers standing facing each other, and firing volley after volley at each other's immobile lines, 18th-century European warfare was nothing like the new style of warfare developed in the North American colonies during the French and Indian War.

In North America, the British Army formed companies of Rangers, including the Ranger Company of the New Hampshire Provincial Regiment, founded in 1756 and later known as His Majesty's Independent Company of American Rangers. This unit is more commonly known as Robert Rogers' Rangers.

The first Ranger company formed by the British Army was founded on March 23, 1756, and was composed of 50 privates, three sergeants, one ensign, one lieutenant, and one captain. The enlisted men needed the qualifications of being rugged and experienced in traveling and hunting, as well as having the qualities of courage and loyalty. As British Army soldiers, the Rangers were subject to military discipline and the Articles of War, and their mission was to annoy, raid, destroy, and distress the enemy whenever possible.

These whaleboats were used by Rangers. Note the marking on the front one – Major Rogers Comp 1. (Gary Zaboly)

Major Robert Rogers raised ten companies to fight the French and their Native American allies. Reconnaissance, ambushes, raids, and prisoner snatches were the main tactics of the colonial Rangers, and when they found themselves outnumbered, the Rangers would disperse and re-form later, traits which are true of today's Rangers. It was Robert Rogers who put the Ranger training and standard operating procedures (SOPs) onto paper. The Standing Orders (of disputed origin but probably based on Kenneth Roberts' *Northwest Passage*) and the Rules of Discipline have remained unchanged and are to this date taught to new Rangers, the rules just as applicable today as they were 250 years ago.

Despite the emphasis on discipline and rules, Rangers and their officers tended to be a little wild, which tended to strain their relationships with regular troops. It was, however, this wildness of character that made them uniquely suited for duty with Ranger companies. Unorthodox men with an unorthodox fighting style also required an unorthodox leader – a role well filled by Robert Rogers. Rough and tough and generally at odds with his superiors, Rogers was an ideal leader for such troops. The unique challenges inherent in the system of irregular fighters functioning within the hierarchical structure of a regular army would continue to trouble future Ranger units. In his book, *A True Ranger*, Gary Zaboly notes:

> His checkered historical reputation must lay at his own feet; and part of the tragedy is that he seemed unable to completely shake off the dirty moccasin from one of those feet. He was cautious but also impulsive. He was princely at times, but shameless at others. He was the type of man who could accept the surrender of the last major fort in French Canada, yet also be capable of wrecking an English tavern in a drunken brawl. He could

War fighting between the opposing forces was nasty and brutish – Rangers did take scalps. (Gary Zaboly)

romance and proudly wed the fair daughter of a prominent New England minister, but on his many travels fall prey to infidelity and whoring. He could foil and collar an English highwayman during a robbery attempt... but also keep jolly company with scoundrels, rakes and wanted men.

He was put through trials as an accused counterfeiter and debtor. The British had him court-martialed for high treason. Washington ordered him arrested as a spy. Creditors constantly hounded him. He was often jailed, and once had his legs so tightly shackled that the marrow oozed from a split shin bone. On another occasion he barely escaped getting his ears cropped, and possibly even being executed. And the day came, almost inevitably, when he began to drink heavily. Gambling also became a very costly addiction, while divorce removed him forever from his only son.

Such a stormy life was generally a breeding ground for rumors, and his was rife with them. Time and again he was reported captured, killed or missing in combat. Once it was said that he had staged his own kidnapping. The French, constantly bedeviled by him, imagined he had built a secret fort somewhere high in the Adirondacks to use as a base for his operations. He was thought to have donned Indian garb and paint several times in order to casually infiltrate enemy villages and camps. During a pursuit in wintertime, it was said that he barely escaped capture by sliding down a fearfully steep mountain slope some 700 feet in length. In his forties, he claimed to have fought in the Sahara Desert, in the service of the Ottomans. At the start of the Revolution, a report circulated that hundreds of Indians had formed an army under his leadership to join the American cause. Insinuations of adultery, of formulating nefarious schemes to create autonomous western empires, of plotting to sell his services to this government or that, all colored and shook his passage through this world.

That some of these rumors eventually proved true probably surprised no one. For Robert Rogers was a man apart, one who was forever demonstrating that he was capable of anything. His was a life filled with enough fame and turmoil, glory and trouble, accomplishment and tragedy for a dozen active men.[7]

In response to the Ranger tactics, the French and Native Americans formed special anti-Ranger companies, which would later be strikingly called to mind by the North Vietnamese reaction forces formed against Ranger (LRRP/LRP) teams in 20th-century Asia.

Rangering or ranging in northeastern winters required hardened men who were experts at wilderness survival and crack shots with their rifles. Their missions were always high risk, and many Rangers were killed, wounded, captured, or died of exposure or starvation. Rogers' Rangers would develop another tactic still used by modern Rangers – the deep raid – and striking at the enemy in their own area of operation became a Ranger trademark. Rangers from their beginning have excelled at terrifying their opponents by striking where and when least expected.

In October 1759, Rogers and his unit of 200 men raided the Abenaki tribe at St Francis, traveling hundreds of miles across land and water, battling harsh elements for nearly a month. The raid was successful, although the Rangers were attacked and took many casualties on the way back from pursuing French and Native American irregulars. By showing that they could achieve the seemingly impossible, the Rangers greatly enhanced their prestige and reputation with the St Francis raid. Most people only casually acquainted with the St Francis raid do not realize that the village was not only a polyglot of different tribes, captives and whites who had been amalgamated into the host tribe but also an established settlement, rather than a native village per se. A description of it comes from "a military engineer who visited St Francis in 1752 [who] counted more than 50 houses made of squared timbers covered with bark or boards. Another dozen homes were built in the French style, possibly of frame construction. Two years later St Francis boasted near 40 buildings of all sorts, including some built of stone."[8]

Rogers' Rangers also participated in the Montreal Campaign of 1760, and the western campaign, reclaiming posts as far as Detroit and Shawneetown. In the west in 1763, Rogers Rangers performed with distinction in the battle of Bloody Ridge.

# MAJOR ROBERT ROGERS' RULES OF DISCIPLINE

These volunteers I formed into a company by themselves, and took the more immediate command and management of them to myself; and for their benefit and instruction reduced into writing the following rules or plan or discipline, which, on various occasions, I had found by experience to be necessary and advantageous, viz.

I.       All Rangers are to be subject to the rules and articles of wars to appear at roll-call every evening on their own parade, equipped each with a firelock, sixty rounds of powder and ball, and a hatchet, at which time an officer from each company is to inspect the same, to see they are in order, so as to be ready on any emergency to march at a minute's warning; and before they are dismissed the necessary guards are to be drafted, and scouts for the next day appointed.

II.      Whenever you are ordered out to the enemy's forts or frontiers for discoveries, if your number is small, march in a single file, keeping at such a distance from each other to prevent one shot from killing two men, sending one man, or more, forward, and the like on each side, at the distance of twenty yards from the main body, if the ground you march over will admit of it, to give the signal to the officer of the approach of an enemy, and of their number etc.

III.     If you march over marshes or soft ground, change your position, and march abreast of each other, to prevent the enemy from tracking you (as they would do if you marched in a single file) till you get over such ground, and then resume your former order, and march until it is quite dark before you encamp, which do, if possible on a piece of ground that may afford your sentries the advantage of seeing or hearing the enemy at some considerable distance, keeping one half of your whole party awake alternately through the night.

IV.      Some time before you come to the place you would reconnoiter, make a stand, and send one or two men in whom you can confide, to look out the best ground for making your observations.

V.       If you have the good fortune to take any prisoners, keep them separate till they are examined, and in your return take a different route from that in which you went out, that you may the better discover any party in your rear, and have an opportunity, if their strength be superior to yours, to alter your course, or disperse, as circumstances may require.

VI.      If you march in a large body of three or four hundred, with a design to attack the enemy, divide your party into three columns, each headed by

Rogers meets General William
Johnson. Note the uniforms
of the Rangers. (Gary Zaboly)

a proper officer, and let these columns march in single files, the columns
to the right and left keeping at twenty yards distance or more from that
of the center, if the ground will admit, and let proper guards be kept in
the front and rear, and suitable flanking parties at a due distance as
before directed, with orders to halt on all eminences, to take a view of
the surrounding ground, to prevent your being ambushed, and to notify
the approach or retreat of the enemy, that proper dispositions may be
made for attacking, defending, etc. And if the enemy approach in your
front on level ground, form a front of your three columns or main body
with the advanced guard, keeping out your flanking parties as if you
were marching under the command of trusty officers, to prevent the
enemy from pressing hard on either of your wings, or surrounding you,
which is the usual method of the savages, if their number will admit of
it, and be careful likewise to support and strengthen your rear guard.

VII.    If you are obliged to receive the enemy's fire, fall, or squat down, til it is
over, then rise and discharge at them. If their main body is equal to yours,
extend yourselves occasionally; but if superior, be careful to support and
strengthen your flanking parties, to make them equal with theirs, that if
possible you may repulse them to their main body, in which case push
upon them with the greatest resolution, with equal force in each flank
and in the center, observing to keep at a due distance from each other,

and advance from tree to tree, with one half of the party before the other ten or twelve yards, if the enemy push upon you, let your front fire and fall down, and then let your rear advance thro' them and do the like, by which time those who before were in front will be ready to discharge again, and repeat the same alternately, as occasion shall require; by this means you will keep up such a constant fire, that the enemy will not be able easily to break your order, or gain your ground.

VIII. If you oblige the enemy to retreat, be careful, in your pursuit of them, to keep out your flanking parties, and prevent them from gaining eminences, or rising grounds, in which case they would perhaps be able to rally and repulse in their turn.

IX. If you are obliged to retreat, let the front of your whole party fire and fall back, till the rear has done the same, making for the best ground you can; by this means you will oblige the enemy to pursue you, if they do it at all, in the face of a constant fire.

X. If the enemy is so superior that you are in danger of being surrounded by them, let the whole body disperse, and every one take a different road to the place of rendezvous appointed for that evening, which must every morning be altered and fixed for the evening ensuing, in order to bring the whole party, or as many of them as possible, together, after any separation that may happen in the day; but if you should happen to be actually surrounded, form yourselves into a square, or if in the woods, a circle is best, and, if possible, make a stand till the darkness of the night favours your escape.

XI. If your rear is attacked, the main body and flankers must face about to the right or left, as occasion shall require, and form themselves to oppose the enemy, as before directed, and the same method must be observed, if attacked in either of your flanks, by which means you will always make a rear of one of your flank-guards.

XII. If you determine to rally after a retreat, in order to make a fresh stand against the enemy, by all means endeavor to do it on the most rising ground you can come at, which will give you greatly the advantage in point of situation, and enable you to repulse superior numbers.

XIII. In general, when pushed upon by the enemy, reserve your fire till they approach very near, which will then put them into the greater surprise and consternation, and give you an opportunity of rushing upon them with your hatchets and cutlasses to the better advantage.

XIV. When you encamp at night, fix your sentries in such a manner as not to be relieved from the main body till morning, profound secrecy and silence being often of the last importance in these cases. Each sentry, therefore, should consist of six men, two of whom must be constantly alert, and when relieved by their fellows, it should be done without noise; and in case those on duty see or hear anything, which alarms them, they are not to speak, but one of them is silently to retreat, and acquaint the commanding officer thereof, that proper dispositions may be made and all occasional sentries should be fixed in like manner.

XV.    At the first dawn of day, awaken your whole detachment that being the time when the savages choose to fall upon their enemies, you should by all means be in readiness to receive them.

XVI.   If the enemy should be discovered by your detachments in the morning and their numbers are superior to yours, and a victory doubtful, you should not attack them till the evening, as then they will not know your numbers, and if you are repulsed, your retreat will be favoured by the darkness of the night.

XVII.  Before you leave your encampment, send out small parties to scout round it, to see if there be an appearance or track of an enemy that might have been near you during the night.

XVIII. When you stop for refreshments, choose some spring or rivulet if you can, and dispose your party so as not to be surprised posting proper guards and sentries at a due distance, and let a small party waylay the path you came in, lest the enemy should be pursuing.

XIX.   If, in your return, you have to cross rivers, avoid the usual fords as much as possible, lest the enemy should have discovered, and be there expecting you.

XX.    If you have to pass by lakes, keep at some distance from the edge of the water, lest, in case of an ambuscade, or an attack from the enemy, when in that situation, your retreat should be cut off.

XXI.   If the enemy pursue your rear, take a circle till you come to your own tracks, and there form an ambush to receive them, and give them the first fire.

XXII.  When you return from a scout, and come near our forts, avoid the usual roads, and avenues thereto, lest the enemy should have headed you, and lay in ambush to receive you, when almost exhausted with fatigue.

XXIII. When you pursue any party that has been near our forts or encampments, follow not directly in their tracks, lest you should be discovered by their rear guards, who, at such a time, would be most alert; but endeavor, by a different route, to head and meet them in some narrow pass or lay in ambush to receive them when and where they least expect it.

XXIV.   If you are to embark in canoes, bateaux, or otherwise by water, choose the evening for the time of your embarkation, as you will then have the whole night before you, to pass undiscovered by any parties of the enemy, on hills, or other places, which command a prospect of the lake or river you are upon.

XXV.    In paddling or rowing, give orders that the boat or canoe next the sternmost, wait for her, and the third for the second, and the fourth for the third, and so on, to prevent separation, and that you may be ready to assist each other on any emergency.

XXVI.   Appoint one man in each boat to look out for fires, on the adjacent shores, from the numbers and size of which you may form some judgment of the number that kindled them, and whether you are able to attack them or not.

XXVII. If you find the enemy encamped near the banks of a river, or lake, which you imagine they will attempt to cross for their security upon being attacked, leave a detachment of your party on the opposite shore to receive them, while, with the remainder, you surprise them, having them between you and the lake or river.

XXVIII. If you cannot satisfy yourself as to the enemy's number and strength, from their fire, etc. conceal your boats at some distance, and ascertain their number by a reconnoitering party, when they embark, or march, in the morning, marking the course they steer, etc. when you may pursue, ambush, and attack them, or let them pass, as prudence shall direct you. In general, however, that you may not be discovered by the enemy on the lakes and rivers at a great distance, it is safest to lay by, with your boats and party concealed all day, without noise or show, and to pursue your intended route by night; and whether you go by land or water, give out parole and countersigns, in order to know one another in the dark, and likewise appoint a station for every man to repair to, in case of any accident that may separate you.[9]

# The Revolutionary War
## Don't Tread on Me!

In Congress, July 4, 1776
The unanimous Declaration of the thirteen united States of America,

When in the Course of human events, it becomes necessary for one people to dissolve the political bands which have connected them with another, and to assume among the powers of the earth, the separate and equal station to which the Laws of Nature and of Nature's God entitle them, a decent respect to the opinions of mankind requires that they should declare the causes which impel them to the separation.

We hold these truths to be self-evident, that all men are created equal, that they are endowed by their Creator with certain unalienable Rights, that among these are Life, Liberty and the pursuit of Happiness.--That to secure these rights, Governments are instituted among Men, deriving their just powers from the consent of the governed,--That whenever any Form of Government becomes destructive of these ends, it is the Right of the People to alter or to abolish it, and to institute new Government, laying its foundation on such principles and organizing its powers in such form, as to them shall seem most likely to effect their Safety and Happiness.

Americans... [10]

The British Empire was vast; the Americans also had vast amounts of land, mostly unexplored, and much like the British Empire it would require the establishment of a regular army to create and maintain the newly announced republic – to not only combat the European troops employed by the Crown who sought to quell the colonial rebellion but to also subdue any other resistance domestic or foreign. The Empire, however, would not go quietly – it would fight for nearly a decade (1775–84) to retain its colonies in America. As one empire was showing her age and was beginning to crumble like a weathered face, another one was born.

Although the official 75th Ranger history stipulates that "during the American Revolution the individual states as well as the continental government made widespread use of Rangers and that on June 14, 1775, with the threat of war looming, the Continental Congress mandated the immediate formation of ten companies of expert riflemen – six in Pennsylvania, two in Maryland, and two in Virginia and by 1777, this force was commanded by Daniel Morgan, and was christened by George Washington, the Corps of Rangers,"[11] it would be far more accurate to argue that Rangers and ranging-type units were more or less used to patrol local frontiers and arguably unimportant to the war as a whole. Indeed a US Army abstract on colonial and revolutionary Rangers concludes:

> Ranger veterans played a major role in the Continental Army during the Revolution, including Major General Israel Putnam and Brigadier Generals John Stark and Moses Hazen. [But] the traditional ranger usage had only limited application during that later war. Various state governments did

This representation of an 18th-century American Ranger is part of an exhibition at the Infantry Museum, Fort Benning, Georgia, covering Rangers from Rogers to the present day. (Author's collection/Camera 1)

employ such units for local frontier security, but the Continental Army formed very few, in part because George Washington considered frontier security to be a local responsibility and focused national military forces on opposing regular British and German units in a formal battlefield context.

Contrary to myth, the light troops in the Continental Army overwhelmingly followed European doctrinal concepts. Light infantry companies added to the regimental organization of each Continental Army infantry regiment in 1778 also had European roots. The American leadership stressed the ideas of Maurice, comte de Saxe and the comte de Guibert, two leading French military theorists, which advocated cross-training every soldier to perform both line or light infantry roles to allow mission flexibility. Light companies normally assembled into provisional battalions at the start of each year's campaign and acted as a special strike force in traditional battlefield roles, not as a reconnaissance element.

The Continental Army's other light troops sprang from a relatively new European concept not the native American ranger tradition. During the Seven Years' War most European armies developed partisan corps (also called Frei Korps). Originally fielded by the French to counter Austrian irregulars recruited in the Balkans, they filled a unique niche by providing deep security around an army in the field or carried out raids behind enemy lines. The Continental Army authorized several of these formations in 1777 and 1778, primarily as a vehicle to employ European volunteers who could not be inserted into existing regiments without provoking major arguments over rank, or because of language barriers. "Light Horse Harry" Lee of Virginia (the father of Robert E. Lee) raised the only American-born unit under this concept.

None of the light units employed by the Continental Army carried out a training role as Rogers' Rangers had during the French and Indian War.[12]

There can be little doubt that Colonel Daniel Morgan and his riflemen were good soldiers, dressed more or less in frontier garb, and that these Americans were familiar with unconventional fighting and expert marksmen. Morgan's unit served for six years from 1775 to 1781, and participated in one of their most famous battles at Freeman's Farm during September 1777 and the battle of Cow Pens [Cowpens] during January 1781. "The British General Burgoyne called the crack shots of Morgan's Riflemen the most famous corps of the Continental Army."[13]

Another Ranger-type commander, Francis Marion, commonly known as the "Swamp Fox," organized Marion's Partisans. Marion's Partisans were loosely organized and their numbers ranged from a dozen to a few hundred. They conducted mostly independent operations in the Carolina swamps, harassing British communication lines and terrorizing many loyalists. Freedom in the new republic was certainly not open to subjects loyal to the crown, even if they did not participate in the fighting. Historian Christopher Hibbert said that Marion was "a wily and elusive character, very active in the persecution of the Cherokee Indians and not at all the sort of chap who should be celebrated as a hero. The truth is that people like Marion committed atrocities as bad, if not worse, than those perpetrated by the British."[14] The official 75th Ranger Regiment history makes no mention of it. "On occasion Marion's brigands operated with the Continental Army. Marion's unit served from 1775 to 1781 and participated in the capture of Fort Johnson and the victory of Charleston in 1775. Reactivated in 1780, Marion's Partisans played an instrumental part in the capture of Fort Watson and Fort Motte, South Carolina, in 1781. The loss of Fort Motte, on the line of communication between Camden and Charleston, was a great blow to the British cause. Marion's men also commanded the first line at the battle of Eutaw Springs, one of the decisive battles of the Revolutionary War." Indeed the author(s) of the official history argue that "the British commanders regarded Marion's style of fighting with disdain. Their plans for securing their possession of the southern country with the establishment of military posts throughout North and South Carolina were foiled. The rapid movements and secret expeditions of Marion's Rangers cut off communication between posts and threw the British system of government and military surveillance into confusion, providing a substantial boon to the Revolutionary cause." And the prestigious Ranger Hall of Fame's induction citation reads:

> Brigadier General Francis Marion is inducted into the Ranger Hall of Fame for his distinguished service as a Ranger leader during both the French and Indian War and the American Revolution. During the French and Indian War, he fought against hostile Cherokee Indians who were making raids on frontier settlements in South Carolina. He and his men adopted many tactics used by the Indians and used them to their advantage. In the American Revolution, Brigadier General Marion directed Ranger-type operations against the British throughout the southern colonies. Marion's men conducted raids on British encampments and ambushes on their supply lines. The South Carolinians once captured a British prisoner of war camp freeing 150 Colonial survivors of the Battle of Camden. It was during this time that Brigadier General Marion earned the nickname the "Swamp Fox" because of his ability to use the cover and concealment of the swamps to strike British and Loyalist forces at will. The operations conducted by Francis Marion were key in preventing the British from securing the southern colonies. Brigadier General Marion brought great credit upon himself, the state of South Carolina and the United States Army. His actions and outstanding service to the United States of America truly exemplify what it means to be a Ranger.[15]

Ultimately, however, the victor writes history, and the phrase "one man's terrorist is another man's freedom fighter" applies aptly to the legendary Francis Marion.

Thomas Knowlton's Connecticut Rangers were another Revolutionary ranger unit. Their mission was primarily reconnaissance in nature and the force never surpassed 150 soldiers. Knowlton did not survive the war, and like any good Ranger commander should if he has to, he died leading his men in battle.

The British Army employed loyalist Ranger units, like John Butler's Corps of Rangers, in raiding and ambushing Americans along the frontier and Butler's Rangers proved to be the most successful of all. Raised along the New York and Canadian border this unit ultimately rose to 10 companies and included two field pieces. These Rangers were disbanded in June 1784 in Canada.[16] In a few instances, the American and British Rangers engaged one another in combat.

Another interesting unit that bore the Ranger title was another British outfit called the Jamaica Rangers; this black corps constituted of three battalions and was initially raised in 1779.[17] The following is an extract of a letter dated June 5, 1782, authorizing the formation of additional battalions:

> I have much satisfaction in communicating to you His Majesty's Royal pleasure that you shou'd accept the offer [of] raising two Battalions of Free Mulattoes and Blacks, if you continue to be of Opinion that "many advantages will result from it to Government"...especially by affording a means of removing the Regular Troops to more healthy Stations, by which a number of very valuable lives may be preserved.[18]

The British government as it had previously done during the French and Indian War, enlisted the aid of Native American tribes during the War of 1812 (1812–15). As a result of it, the United States, as part of the regular army, as well as frontier states raised Ranger-type units who patrolled and skirmished with the enemy mostly on the frontiers.

# THE REST OF THE BUNCH

The federal government of the United States as well as several frontier states continued using Rangers as protection against hostile Native Americans. "During 1832–33, a 600-man battalion of Mounted Rangers patrolled the prairies and plains of the western frontier, defending against Native American war parties, and employed by the US Army, and in 1835 Texas began using Rangers to defend its frontier."[19]

Although no Rangers have excelled the legendary stature of Robert Rogers, the 18th and 19th centuries created other well-known Rangers. Among them was Daniel Boone, who was briefly a North Carolina Ranger, probably around 1759. Three of his sons commanded Ranger companies during the War of 1812.[20] Nathan Hale, also inducted into the Ranger Hall of Fame, commanded a company in Thomas Knowlton's battalion of Connecticut Rangers during the Revolutionary War where his intelligence/spy gathering mission turned tragic and resulted in his execution by the British on September 22, 1776. One of the most interesting people who joined ranging-type units was the future President of the United States, Abraham Lincoln, who in Illinois during the Black Hawk War of 1832, was a member of Elijah Illes' company in the State Frontier Guard whose primary task was to patrol against Native Americans. Lincoln served from May 29 to June 16, 1832 and subsequently reenlisted in Jacob Early's company from June 20 to July 10, 1832. His induction citation reads:

> Abraham Lincoln is inducted into the Ranger Hall of Fame for his outstanding service to the United States of America, culminating with his service as President (1861–65). Early in 1832 he was elected captain of a company of the 4th Illinois Regiment, which served during part of the

Black Hawk War (1832). When his company was discharged, Lincoln volunteered as a private in a company of the Illinois frontier guard, whose soldiers were known as Rangers, scouts, and spies. For two and one-half weeks during the late spring of 1832 he patrolled the northwestern frontier of Illinois with his company, on the lookout for Indian war parties. When the company's Rangers were discharged, Lincoln immediately reenlisted in another company of the frontier guard. He and the company served a three week tour of duty during the early summer by scouting in advance of the army as it moved northward into Wisconsin. After his military service Lincoln became a prominent Illinois attorney, a popular political leader, and President of the United States. His strong, successful leadership as the Union's President during the War Between the States (1861–65) made him a great American folk hero. He is often considered the best example of the greatness that can be produced by a democracy.[21]

The interesting aspect of Lincoln's induction to the Hall of Fame is that in today's Ranger Regiment a hierarchy exists which dismisses Rangers that served for short periods of time and/or did not attend Ranger school and these Rangers stand little chance of being inducted. Yet, throughout the history of Rangers it is indeed these short timers and non-school graduates that have created Ranger history from the early colonial days through today and seemingly someone thought that Lincoln's contribution of a few days merited an induction.

# The Civil War

## Brother against brother

According to the official history of the 75th Ranger Regiment, in 1862, the second year of the Civil War, the Confederate government authorized the formation of Partisan Ranger bands to infiltrate Union lines to conduct raids and ambushes, and gather information. Units were formed throughout the South, and some made significant contributions toward the Southern effort. John McNeill's Company of Partisan Rangers, out of Virginia, captured two Union generals.

John Singleton Mosby was the most famous Ranger during the Civil War. Enlisting in the Confederate Cavalry in 1861 where he served on General Jeb Stuart's staff, he began his independent Ranger activities in 1863. His fame grew out of his raids on Union camps and bases, and his native region of North-Central Virginia soon became known as Mosby's Confederacy. Mosby was greatly influenced by Francis Marion and used many of his tactics. One central maxim was that aggressive tactics toward the larger opponent would force the opponent to commit his efforts to a defensive guard. Mosby's forces would then attack one of their weakest areas, a tactic that frequently worked. A classic Mosby strike would be to insert his men far behind Union lines and snatch a general officer from amidst his own troops. His scouts were so thoroughly trained and familiar with the land, that he would mount them on thoroughbred horses, borrowed from his officers, in order to conduct night raids, a type of operation that was not a standard tactic during the Civil War.

The first big success that Mosby's Rangers experienced was at Fairfax Courthouse, Virginia, located well within the Union stronghold. Knowing that the officer in charge was Colonel Perry Wyndham, a British soldier of fortune fighting for the Union cause, Mosby made an ostentatious plan: to infiltrate the Union lines and abduct the officer, despite the fact that thousands of Wyndham's troops were protecting the roads west of Washington. He explained his hope for success with the theory that to all appearances it was impossible.

Under cover of darkness, Mosby and 29 of the raiders infiltrated the Union line in the woods of North Centerville, Virginia. As Mosby had hoped, the Union headquarters was quite confident of its safety, being positioned so far behind the lines. Mosby and some of the raiders proceeded to what they thought to be Wyndham's headquarters. It was the wrong house. Mosby learned that a Union soldier they had captured was one of the guards at the headquarters of Brigadier General Edwin H. Stoughton. Directing some of his men to Wyndham's quarters, Mosby took several others and set out to capture General Stoughton. Posing as Union couriers, they gained entrance into the general's quarters and captured the sleeping officer. The men who had been detailed to capture Wyndham reported that the colonel had gone to Washington the day before, but they still salvaged some success as the raid on his quarters resulted in the capture of the captain who was his assistant adjutant general. By the end of the mission, they had captured a general, members of his staff, and more than 100 soldiers, as well as a large number of horses.

In March 1863, Mosby and his Rangers defeated a much larger force of Union troops near the town of Chantilly, Virginia. When the original plan of their attack

Colonel John Singleton Mosby.
(Topfoto.co.uk)

miscarried, and a strong Federal cavalry unit issued pursuit, the men took cover in a half-mile stretch of woods. From their concealed positions, they delivered deadly carbine and pistol fire into the front and flanks of the Union troops, killing five and wounding several others. One officer and 35 men, as well as a large number of horses, were captured, while no Ranger casualties were incurred.

General John Hunt Morgan organized and led another prominent Ranger unit. Morgan and the men of his calvary squadron executed the first of their famous attacks in December 1861 in Lebanon, Kentucky, 60 miles distance from Morgan's camp. During the raid they destroyed large quantities of stores and captured several prisoners. They additionally destroyed a railroad bridge of military importance, delaying the movement of Union supplies to the front.

One of Morgan's most successful raids was in the summer of 1862. The 800-man strong Morgan's Rangers left Knoxville and headed west toward Sparta, Tennessee, encountering only a few scattered enemies along the way. Turning north at Sparta, Morgan crossed into Kentucky and captured a small garrison, taking 400 prisoners and valuable stores, including enough rifles to equip most of his unarmed men. The raiders then moved on to Glasgow and captured that garrison, destroying more public stores. These two incidents were typical of the raids Morgan conducted throughout his two-and-a-half week march behind Union lines. During this time the number of men in the ranks increased to 1,200, the result of recruiting en route. The Rangers marched more than a thousand miles, capturing 17 towns, destroying millions of dollars' worth of Union stores, dispersing many of the Home Guard, and bolstering Confederate morale. Total casualties incurred by the Ranger force numbered fewer than 90.

Morgan's Rangers' most famous raid started in July 1863. With a command of 2,400 men, Morgan attacked Green River Bridge, Kentucky, where the Rangers were forced to withdraw after a severe fight. They continued to Lebanon, Kentucky where they captured the garrison. Continuing to the Ohio River near Brandenburg, they crossed the river on two captured steamers having successfully dispersed the hostile troops on the far side. They encountered more Union militia at Corydon, Indiana, which they quickly scattered, and captured the town. By this time, the whole countryside had risen in arms against them. Newspapers proclaimed an "Invasion of Indiana." Reinforcements and gunboats were brought in to intercept the Confederate marauders. Following a course roughly parallel to the Ohio River and going around Cincinnati, Morgan's men achieved the deepest penetration of any Confederate force during the war. However, close on their heels was a Union cavalry force. Near the end of July, near the town of Liverpool, Ohio, Morgan was forced to surrender.

In spite of Morgan's surrender, the raid was successful. It occupied some of the forces that might have harassed Bragg's retreat from middle Tennessee, and which might have helped Rosencrans at the battle of Chickamauga later on. Colonel MacGrown, a Union soldier, said Morgan's raid redefined military operations in Tennessee and Kentucky in the summer and fall of 1863. Had Morgan not diverted and delayed Burnside's movement upon Knoxville and East Tennessee, Virginia, as well as the Georgia railroad, Burnside and his command of 28,000 men would have joined Rosencrans three weeks before the Battle of Chickamauga was fought.

Also noteworthy are the Rangers led by Turner Ashby. The Rangers of Morgan, Mosby, and Ashby did great service for the Confederate war effort. Through their intrepid feats of scouting, harassing, and raiding, they embodied a constant and ever-present threat to Union troops.

The United States Army, in contrast to the Confederacy, made only minor use of Ranger units during the Civil War. However, as Native American unrest soared in the West during the war, and with the decrease in availability of Union troops, who were occupied with the war, several states formed Ranger units for frontier defense. The First Regiment of Mounted Rangers, a Minnesota unit with 12 companies tasked with ranging the frontier, and who helped defeat the Santee Sioux in 1862–63, was one of the most active.

After the Civil War, Rangers continued to guard the Texan frontier. In 1881, after they had fought their last battle against Native Americans, their primary mission evolved into one of law enforcement. Today, the unit's lineage can be traced down to the small companies of Rangers who are part of the Texas State Police.[22]

# Ranger Battalions of World War II

## Lead the way, Rangers!

Rangers were noticeably absent after the Civil War and it would take a world war to reactivate them. Adolf Hitler adorned the pages of *Time* magazine as "The Man of the Year of 1938" and had many American friends despite his desires for a greater Germany and his dislike of Jews. Shortly after the attack on Pearl Harbor on December 7, 1941, the United States entered the world's largest and most destructive war, joining a world already torn apart by conflict.

The first World War II Rangers were created in 1942 and led by Major William O. Darby. They trained in Scotland with the British Commandos and ultimately earned the highly coveted title of Ranger. Few people are aware that these Darby Rangers were supposed to be trained, and bloodied if possible, then returned to other units as cadre. Ultimately the need for a specialty unit outweighed the other advantages and thus the first Ranger battalion stayed active and was only disbanded after approximately two years of continuous fighting, culminating in their disintegration as a fighting force in Cisterna, Italy, in 1944. The 1st Ranger Battalion was organized and activated in Carrickfergus, Northern Ireland, on June 19, 1942. It drew its recruits from the volunteers of the 1st Armored and the 34th Infantry divisions, as well as V Corps. A handful of Rangers participated in the raid on Dieppe and were thus the first men to experience combat in the European Theater of Operations.

Later on, the 3rd and 4th Ranger Battalions were activated and trained by Colonel Darby's Rangers – their cadre made up of the "old boys." The 1st, 3rd, and 4th Battalions formed the Ranger Force. They began the tradition of wearing the scroll shoulder sleeve insignia when Darby Ranger Anthony Rada won a competition for his design.

# 1ST RANGER BATTALION – EXPERIENCING A SPOT OF TEA

In 1942 the world landscape had been transformed into a maelstrom of death and destruction. Everywhere there was fighting, and Allied forces were pushed back by their better-trained and better-led opponents. Unprepared for the war it was entering, the US Army still needed to gain the confidence of the people back home. Positive action was needed in order to restore the morale of the citizens of the remaining, and ever-shrinking, free world. In the United States, President Roosevelt sought to create commando-style units to do just that – strike back at the enemy and restore confidence in the American military.

In the spring of 1942, General George Marshall, Chief of Staff of the US Army, sent Colonel Lucian K. Truscott Jr to England to coordinate training between the inexperienced US troops and the already battle-proven British Commandos. On June 1, 1942, General Marshall, impressed with his visit to the British Commando Training Depot, ordered the creation of an American commando unit. This unit became known as the Rangers, so-called after the famous 18th-century Rangers of the French and Indian War. Initially, the Ranger unit was formed for the specific purpose of training soldiers in commando skills and then reassigning them to other units, thus providing a well-trained core for the newly forming American units.

The 1st Ranger Battalion, founded on June 7, 1942, and commanded by Major William O. Darby, originally consisted of a headquarters company of seven officers and 72 enlisted men as well as six companies of three officers and

William O. Darby, 1942, Scotland. The first Ranger commander of World War II. (US Army)

59 enlisted men each. The size of these companies was determined by the need to accommodate the small landing crafts used by the British Commandos. The original Darby Rangers were a varied lot: the youngest man was 17 and the oldest 35. The average age was 25. Sixty percent of the Ranger enlistees came from the 34th Division, 30 percent joined from the 1st Armored Division, and the remaining 10 percent were from medical, quartermaster, and signal troops from the V Corps.[23] The Ranger officers did not field one regular Army officer with the notable exception of Darby himself. All others were guardsmen or reservists. Although some enlisted personnel came from regular Army units, the majority were draftees who volunteered for the new Ranger unit.

On June 28, Darby's 1st Ranger Battalion moved to the Commando Training Depot at Achnacarry Castle, Scotland. Here the Americans were introduced to the man tasked with guiding the training of the Rangers, Lieutenant Colonel Charles Vaughan, a ruddy-cheeked, husky British officer who radiated enthusiasm and good will.

Darby recalls in *Darby's Rangers: We Led the Way*:

> The tremendous personality of Colonel Vaughan pervaded the atmosphere of the Commando Depot. A former Guards drill sergeant and an officer in World War I with later experience in commando raids in World War II, he was highly qualified for his job. He had served with distinction during the commando raids against Vaagso and the Lofoten Islands in Norway. A burly man, about six feet two, strongly built and of ruddy complexion, he had a face which at times showed storm clouds and at other times, warm sunniness. A man of about 50 years of age, he was in excellent physical condition and was remarkably agile. He was constantly in the field, participating in, observing, and criticizing the training of the men. During it all he was highly enthusiastic. Observing a mistake he would jump in and

British Commandos training Rangers in the rudimentary skill of shooting. Americans tended to be excellent shots. (75th RR)

personally demonstrate how to correct it. He insisted on rigid discipline, and officers and men alike respected him. He was quick to think up means of harassing the poor weary Rangers, and as he put it, "To give all members the full benefit of the course." The British Commandos did all in their power to test us to find out what sort of men we were.

Then, apparently liking us, they did all in their power to prepare us for battle. There were British veterans who had raided Norway at Vaagso and at the Lofoten Islands, men who had escaped from Singapore, and others who had slipped from the Italians in Somaliland. As instructors at the depot, these men were a constant source of inspiration to my Rangers and, at the same time, a vivid reminder of the difficulties of the job ahead. At the beginning of the training, in the presence of the commanding officer of the Commando Depot, I told the Ranger officers that they would receive the same training as their men. Furthermore, the ranking officer present was to be the first to tackle every new obstacle, no matter what its difficulty. I included myself in this rule, believing deeply that no American soldier will refuse to go as far forward in combat as his officer.[24]

The 1st Ranger Battalion moved to Argyll, Scotland, on August 1 for amphibious training with the Royal Navy. On August 19, 1942, 50 Rangers were attached to a 1000-strong Canadian/British force for a large-scale raid on the French coastal town of Dieppe. Forty Rangers were attached to No. 3 Commando, six to No. 4 Commando, and the remaining four Rangers were attached to the Canadians. Ranger losses from these engagements included six killed, seven wounded, and four captured. The casualties suffered by the Canadian/British troops were horrific. Dieppe provided the Rangers with invaluable lessons to be applied to future Ranger actions. The importance of detailed intelligence and reconnaissance was fully realized by the Ranger staff. In addition, Darby understood the value of discipline and training. These were necessary qualities to manage and overcome the fear and the subsequent paralysis inherent in battle.

The following is a revealing contemporary report on the development of the World War II Rangers and their part in the Dieppe raid:

SUBJECT: Report on Ranger Detachment.

TO: C.O. 1st Ranger Bn.

1. August 1, 1942, Lt. Leonard F. Dirks, six men from A Company, and six men from D Company, part of a detachment of Rangers under the command of Captain Roy Murray, were attached to 3 troop of 3 Commando. The group of 12 men were divided among the troop, 3 men assigned to each sub-section, the officer assigned to troop HQ. The troop was billeted together and the men from the Rangers stood all parades.

2. The training program consisted mainly of exercises over ground very similar to that which was to be covered in the actual raid. The first exercise was made during daylight hours on the Isle of Wight, these that followed

took place at night. 3 troop was the right flank on all exercises and had the 3rd mortar section attached. The objective in all exercises was the same, that is the elimination of a battery of coast and A.A. guns. The troop for these exercises was broken down into boat-lead groups, each boat with an officer or N.C.O. in charge of the men in the boat. The boat group was made up for L.C.P. boats (R boats) and varied from 19 to 22 men. These groups were not changed except for minor details. There were 5 boats for 3 troop and the mortar section. Several exercises were carried out without the use of boats over different ground but with the same objective in mind and the same principles involved. In these cases the men marched to the point designated as the beach in boat lead groups. These exercises usually terminated several hours after daylight and the troops returned to their billets, cleaned weapons and equipment and rested. Training during the time we were not on exercises consisted of weapons training, cliff scaling, fieldcraft and some range work. Cliff scaling was done with the aid of scaling ladders which are made of tubular metal, very light and about 6 inches wide. They are made up in sections about 5 feet long. These sections can be locked together to make a ladder of the necessary length. For using to enter buildings or getting over walls a hook can be locked on one end. A great deal of time was spent in swimming and a swimming class held for all nonswimmers every afternoon. Fieldcraft, including cover through buildings and streets, was conducted as a troop exercise, one section working against the other. Troop orders were posted on the bulletin board every morning giving the program and orders for the day. Before each exercise the troop C.O. had a conference with the Officers and N.C.O.s and everything was covered in detail. Maps were studied and ammunition leads decided upon. 3 troop's problems were complicated in that the 3" mortar section was attached, and one of the officers of 3 troop was to command it. The ammunition lead for the 3" mortar consisted of 42 rounds of smoke and 72 rounds of H.E. for the two mortars. This meant that 3 troop had to assist in getting 114 rounds of mortar shells ashore in addition to their usual ammunition load. The disposal of 3 troop ashore will show how this was taken care of.

3. Once 3 troop landed, one section (platoon) made their way along the approach route immediately. Troop HQ, made up of the 2" mortar section, AT rifle, radio man, and Sgt Major and runners, followed immediately. The remaining section was left to assist in bringing the mortar ammunition to the mortar site, dumping it there and then follow the leading section. The beach party with an N.C.O. with a Thompson sub-machine gun, a Bren gunner and a number two man, and one rifle man. This group was made up out of the second section and placed on the beach in a position to give covering fire for the 3" mortars and to give covering fire for the withdrawal. This was a last minute change to utilize the L.M.G. as they did not arrive until the day before the actual raid. The L.M.G. and the ammunition was handled by the three men. 2000 rounds were carried on the boat. As soon as we landed these men were to unload all ammunition

and to proceed to their position with 1000 rounds, the third man coming back to bring up the balance of the ammunition. The troop assembled in a defensive position previously decided on, waiting for the assault, the assault to follow the mortar barrage. The time for the barrage was Zero plus 55 to Zero plus 63, the last 3 minutes being smoke. The assault for three troop made up of two waves, one section followed by troop HQ and the balance of two sections. 4 troop was to land from the Flak ship in L.C.P.s and make up the reserve. The withdrawal was set at Z plus 120, Zero being the time of landing. Except for the use of the L.M.G. everything was done in the exercises.

4. The actual raid, however, turned out quite differently. Sunday, August 16, 3 Commando was confined to billets, except for necessary trips for supplies. Monday preparations began. Maps were brought down from Commando HQ and studied, ammunition and demolitions drawn, aerial photographs and a relief map, made of plaster paris and colored, was studied. The Officers and N.C.O.s went through the entire thing then the men were brought in and they studied the maps and photographs. Demolitions ops were distributed, the whole troop was then formed completely dressed ready to go, the troop C.O. then checked everybody. At 5:00 P.M. we boarded buses and trucks and went to the harbor. There we had about an hour's wait and then 3 troop beared its five L.C.P.s. At the last moment, I was placed in boat 17, boat 16 was carrying troop HQ. I was the only Ranger in 17. We left the harbor and started towards our objective along with the rest of the fleet. We were to reach our beach on the left flank of the main landing party at 4:50. Between 3:45 and 4:00 we contacted a group of enemy E boats numbers unknown, and were fired upon. We were at this time about ten miles from shore as I found out later. We were under fire from that time on. Our boat officer did not know his location because we had dispersed trying to duck the enemy fire. When we did get straighten around it was getting daylight, when we started ashore we were fired upon by coast guns and machine guns. We did not get ashore and I don't know what beach we were headed for when we started. Then we went to Dieppe proper. This was about 6:00 A.M. We were at Dieppe until 11:30 when we started back to England. Our boat broke down about 12:30 after some time we were picked up by an ML. At 9:45 P.M. we were back in England.

5. Ammunition leads – Each man armed with a rifle carried 100 rounds and two 36 grenades and one 68 grenade. Rangers carried 80 rounds in their belts and two bandeliers and total of 176 rounds, in addition they had one bandelier which was left on the boat for AA use on the return trip.

Demolitions – 20 lbs of assorted charges were made up by the HQ demolition section. In addition to this, four sections of bangler [Bangalore] torpedoes were carried. The ends of these torpedoes were plugged with plastic and detonators carried. The demolitions were split in ten groups, packed in U.S. canvas field bags and distributed. Most of the demolitions were 1½ lbs. Charges of plastic with tape to fasten them to the coast guns.

Dress – Commandos wore denim trousers with wool battle dress jacket. No leggings were worn. Rangers wore denim and no leggings. One problem with the Rangers was to carry the grenades. This was solved by a number of men who took their meat can pouch off their pack and tied it to their belts. The canvas field bag worked very well for the demolition kits.

6. The conduct of the men was of the highest type, both under fire and in the normal course of training. A very friendly spirit exists between the men of 3 Commando and the Ranger Bn.

Leonard F. Dirks
1st Lt, 1st Ranger Bn.

One of the Old Guys, Ranger Gino Mercuriali, remembers Dieppe as well – only not as glorious – in a 2002 interview:

There were only 50 American Rangers who participated in the Dieppe Raid, so I will account for my part in it. To give some insight as to the differences in the U.S. soldier as opposed to the British.

Ready for Dieppe, although we knew nothing about our assignment.

A Ranger company consisted of about 70 men and six men from each company were chosen to train with a British commando company. There were six Officers. Eight more GIs were attached to Canadians.

As I look back, while we were somewhat in awe of these veterans, and were friendly with them, I don't believe we (my Company) established any personal rapport that we well may have done, probably due to our tenuous state in their unit and our desire to spend our free time in a free spirited way as you may all imagine. We were housed in an empty house, laid out our blankets on the bare floor, and ate many additional meals in town as the British ration was not to our liking.

I remember confronting the Co. Commander for the lack of utensil cleaning and he did make provisions for us by adding a garbage pail and we were given a tub of hot water for cleaning our utensils. Still, we liked the people very much and understood them and their ways to a degree.

Our training here as such like that of Achnacarry, with some emphasis, I assume, in the British's purpose to learn about the American "staying power" as much of the training included long, enduring marches. The British do sing on these marches, you know. We also learned to use a 20mm gun from the hip, using a rope sling. And of course, some of the accounts of the experienced Commandos were very interesting.

Before we were picked for this assignment, there had been a few people, earlier on, picked from the Rangers for this special raid. We did not at the time know that, but later learned they returned to our unit while in Scotland because the Raid had been postponed and jeopardized. I remember going to the Guard house with someone and talked to a Canadian that told us he was accused of talking about the upcoming event.

We did know we were there for some type of a mission and sometime during our stay we were briefed and trained by making landings on the Isle of Wight. One significant lesson we learned was not to hang grenades from our belts. We were to study the terrain from a mock-up of the coast line and supposedly precise gun locations, etc. just as we did later for the Algerian Invasion. The British had a superior intelligence unit at least at that time, in my opinion.

There is an account of the Dieppe Raid in the World War II mag – May/86 which describes things we would not be aware of. Our company and I assume most if not all others were loaded into a landing craft, not a LCP as we know them but a boat with a red wing engine, I believe it was called an Eureka, housed in the center of the boat and a ramp around the sides which provided you a place to sit. You might also crawl under the ramp but I don't recall that anyone did. We experienced the E-Boat's attack, but fortunately did not lose any personnel in our craft that I'm aware of. The flaming "onions" from their guns was a sight to behold, as they appeared to be aimed to hit between the eyes. The Germans were chased off by the British ships.

The boat pilot must have gotten too excited as I understand. He attempted to back up to swivel the boat nose in another direction and it flooded the engine. We then had to evacuate, probably due to the lag in time during the evasive actions required by the E-boat attack, but this was a blessing as we would otherwise be sitting ducks, if not already so.

Our evasive action threw our timing, so we were directed to congregate with the Mother ship in the Dieppe Harbor. This was an experience not unlike the WWI as far as the dog fights were concerned. Numerous parachutists were observed and many times it could not be determined who was who. Some of these planes and pilots were American. Of course, we were in shelling distance from land, could see the Buffors [bofors] and POM-POMs being fired from the Mother Flag ship's deck and the tanks trying to make their landing in the harbor area. Yet, we were relatively safe, surely not envious of the Canadian troops trying to get to shore. The Canadian tanks were disabled on the beaches and the men were in a terrible position to survive. It was truly a sad sight. On this occasion as with later ones, my composure, I would say was very good. I always seemed to be engaged enough that things weren't so scary during they were happening, but at some time later when recalled to mind, you are scared out of your pants at times.

After returning to our base in England, Sgt. Kavanaugh and myself went to a place much like our USO and were asked the question – "what do you think of the Raid – Yank?" Them not realizing we were a part of it. We never let on that we were and wouldn't intrude on their elation for anything. In contrast, we would later learn of the news about the Raid in the U.S. newspapers and you would think it was a U.S. operation! The British and Canadians didn't much appreciate this. Quite understandable!

The fact that many of us that were assigned to this raid did not have the opportunity to actually land is frustrating for us. In truth, we are fortunate to come off it untouched. The Raid was an extreme failure as a battle though the lessons learned from it helped the British and may have made it seem worthwhile.

After everything, I think of the various countries, Northern Ireland, Scotland including far north and billeting in civilian homes in Dundee, Scotland, then England, including London and Brighton, the trip through the Mediterranean Sea, Algeria and Tunis and North Africa, Sicily including Palermo, and Italy including Naples and Mt Vesuvius. I think it's great. Sadly I'll never have grandchildren to pass any of this down to them.

Shortly after the raid on Dieppe, the battalion moved to Dundee for coastal raiding training. The Rangers practiced attacking pillboxes, gun batteries, and other coastal defenses. In Dundee, the Rangers stayed with families in town as there were no barracks available to them. To this date, there is a close relationship between the Rangers and their adoptive families.

It was also during this time that one of the most beloved and colorful characters joined the Rangers. Father Albert E. Basil, a chaplain captain, who was attached to the British Special Service Brigade, first met the Rangers when he arrived to conduct the funeral of a Ranger killed during a training exercise. Ranger Darby recalled fondly:

> I asked if he could be permitted to stay with us until after we had landed in North Africa. In fact he stayed on with us through the Tunisian campaign until the British Army discovered they had one missing chaplain. Unfortunately for us, Father Basil was then returned to the British Army. During his nine months with the Rangers, he was a constant source of inspiration and comfort to us. Slight of build, about medium height, with large horn-rimmed spectacles punctuating a very sharp-featured, intelligent, and happy face, he became a familiar sight as his uniform began to look like that of the Rangers. His one unfailing exception to complete Americanization was his insistence on wearing the Commando's Green Beret and shoulder patch.

The Rangers left Dundee for Glasgow on September 24, 1942, and were attached to the 1st Infantry Division. They continued training until the end of October when they boarded the *Ulster Monarch*, the *Royal Scotsman*, and the *Royal Ulsterman*, launching the North African campaign. The Rangers had undergone intense training for many months, ranging from basic infantry skills to advanced amphibious assaults. Men were killed during training and in raids. The Rangers had become a hardened, well-trained, well-led, and close-knit unit. They were highly trained American infantrymen able to operate in any kind of warfare.

# NORTH AFRICA AND ITALY

The Ranger unit was given an important job during Operation *Torch*, the invasion of North Africa. The Rangers, attached to General Terry Allen's 1st Division, had to conduct difficult nighttime amphibious landings in order to seize batteries that threatened the Arzew beachheads. En route to Tunisia, the Rangers continuously reviewed their plans to seize the gun batteries. Plaster-paris models plus maps and intelligence reports were analyzed to find any flaws in their operation's order. Every section and platoon reviewed its mission. The Rangers had learned that proper planning had to be based on timely intelligence and reconnaissance reports in order to avoid any mishaps.

There were two coastal batteries at Arzew, and the Rangers decided that a simultaneous attack was the best way to execute their mission. The Dammer Force, named after Darby's right-hand man Herman Dammer of German descent, consisted of A and B Companies and seized the smaller gun battery at Fort de la Pointe. The rest of the Rangers, codenamed the Darby Force, landed 4 miles northwest and secured the larger gun emplacements of Batterie du Nord from behind. These operations were executed with few casualties. Proper planning and training had prepared Darby's Rangers very well. Some companies assisted in continued mop-up operations of nearby towns.

Training continued to keep the men sharp. They were attached to the 5th Infantry Training Center at Arzew to act as a demonstration unit for the new amphibious-assault depot. January 1943 saw the formation of G Company – its intended purpose was to train replacements for the Rangers. D Company, which had been reorganized temporarily as an 81mm mortar unit in Dundee, divested itself of its mortars and returned to its original function as an assault company.[25]

On February 11, 1943, A, E, and F Companies set out to raid the Italian positions at Station de Sened, which were defended by the Centauro Division and the elite Bersaglieri mountain troops. With eight miles of rough terrain to cover, the Rangers carried no packs, traveling light with a canteen of water, a C ration, and a shelterhalf each. The raid was carefully planned and exceeded all expectations. Ranger Darby recalls one incident when he was in radio communication with Captain Max Schneider, future commander of the 5th Ranger Battalion:

> During the action I called Captain Max Schneider to find out how many prisoners he had taken. The captain replied, "I think I have two, sir." The field radio connection was bad, and I asked for a repeat. The two Italians tried to pull a getaway, and the captain fired two quick shots, answering in the same breath, "Well, sir, I had two prisoners."[26]

The raid resulted in at least 50 Italian dead and 11 prisoners from the famed 10th Bersaglieri Regiment. The fighting was very close and personal. One Ranger recalls, "There was some pretty intense in-fighting there, but a man doesn't talk about what he does with a bayonet." Five officers and nine enlisted men were awarded the Silver Star for their part in the Sened raid.

The Rangers continued to conduct numerous combat patrols. It was during this time that the 7th Regiment Tirailleurs Algeriens inducted the 1st Ranger Battalion as honorary members of their regiment.

During the large German attack through the Kasserine Pass, the battalion fought a rearguard action through Feriana to the Dernaia Pass, where the enemy was stopped. From March 19 through March 27, the Rangers assisted in the El Guettar attacks, and then held their positions against a series of enemy counterattacks. After March 28, the battalion maintained outposts at Nogene El Fedge, and then moved to Gafsa and Nemours where it provided men for the 3rd and 4th Ranger Battalions, and helped train these new units.

On July 9, the men of the 1st Battalion made an assault landing at Gela, Sicily, and captured part of the city against heavy German resistance. After fighting off enemy counterattacks, the Rangers moved inland where they stormed the city of San Nicola and captured and held the fortress of Butera. Following the battle, the Rangers trained and also guarded enemy prisoners and war stores.

Earl Morris, Headquarters 4th Ranger Battalion, Darby's Rangers, 1944–45, recalls in a 1999 personal interview:

> A Lt. Marshner came to our outfit somewhere in Sicily. He was assigned as our communications officer. I think he had some training with either the 2nd or 5th Ranger Bn in England. I'm not sure. We had pulled back from the front and the 36th Division moved on ahead towards Naples, while we bedded down on a hillside in a big olive grove. Well, our new Lt. Marshner and a Ranger named Stewart got into one hell of a hassle. They both

claimed the same sleeping spot. To tell the truth, Stewart had it first. I was there and I know. When Stewart left the area the Lt. moved Stewart's equipment and took the spot. That Lt. should have gotten more training because he sure as hell didn't know Rangers.

Later Stewart came back from wherever and saw what had happened. He tore down Lt. Marshner's setup, kicked his stuff around, said something about repossessing territory, rolled out his own bedroll and went to sleep, I think. When Marshner came back, he almost had a heart attack. To think an enlisted man could do this to him. It freaked him out. He went to Col. Darby, and they say, almost "demanded" (and maybe rightfully so) that Stewart be court martialed for insubordination refusing a direct order & etc... Well one of our officers came down, disarmed and put old Stewart under arrest and guard. After that we had to build a stockade. Simple we just strung three strands of barbed wire around four different tree trunks, let old Stewart crawl in and that was that. Then we got to wondering what would happen to old Stewart. Someone suggested that he could even be shot, and maybe he could have, being in a combat situation and all that B.S. From here on no one explains anything. No pre-op or later post-op briefings, no nothing. But the same night or the next we got an alert with orders for everyone to pack up with everything ready to move out A.S.A.P.

D-Day – I Anzio Beachhead. CPT George C. Nunnelly, Georgia Ranger, left, CPT James Lavin, 4th Battalion Adjutant, and LT James Altieri, center, embark on ships (LCIs) destined to land them on the beaches of Anzio, January 22, 1944. (Jim Altieri collection)

Shortly afterwards, we loaded up on great big ass earth moving trucks belonging to the combat engineers. How we ever came by them is still a mystery. But leave it to Darby. He could do anything. We could have used a cherry picker and a parachute to get on and off those damn trucks. We moved out, no one knew where or why. The best I can remember we rode around most of the night. It wasn't a joy ride. At one time we could smell sulphur burning from sulphur pits that dated back to Biblical times, I'm told. Hours later we off loaded, exactly where we started from. Same spot. When we got the alert Stewart was given back his side arms, and turned back to duty with his unit. After the joy ride (we named it) nothing was ever said about Stewart's court martial. We were given the understanding that by rearming and turning Stewart back to duty, it nullified the pending court martial. Anyway it didn't happen. And there's not a Ranger who was there, who will ever believe anything other than Col. Darby initiated this joy ride to save old Stewart's ass from a court martial.

Almost forgot! Stewart kept his sleeping spot. We built his stockade around it.

Map detailing the expansion of the Anzio beachhead. The Rangers were pushing toward Cisterna when they became surrounded and wiped out as a fighting unit. (US Army)

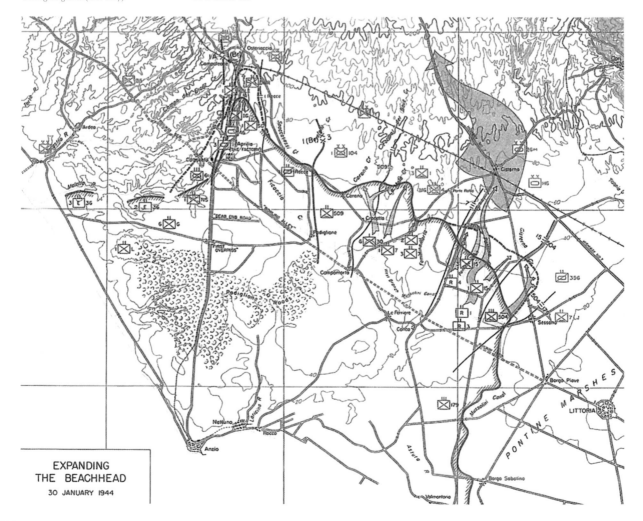

EXPANDING
THE BEACHHEAD
30 JANUARY 1944

On September 9, the battalion made another assault landing at Maiori (several miles north of Salerno) on the Italian mainland and pushed inland to seize Chiunzi Pass in a surprise attack. The Rangers held the pass against great odds until September 23, and fought off seven major counterattacks before joining in the advance on Naples. After a brief rest, the battalion was assigned to the Venafro Sector. After two weeks of bitter mountain fighting against a well-emplaced enemy force, they captured the heights and beat back several counterattacks before being given a rest on December 15.

## FALLSCHIRMJÄGER LEHR-REGIMENT VERSUS THE RANGERS

German points of view of the battle around Cisterna from *The Green Devils* by JeanYves-Nasse:

> In Winter 1943, Fallschirmjäger Lehr-Battalion was deployed at Terracina, to the south of Rome. In January 1944 the unit was expanded into a regiment while based at Citta di Castello to the north of Perugia. During the Anzio-Nettuno landings, it was part of Kampfgruppe Herrmann which fought in the Cisterna sector in late January.
>
> Recently promoted to the rank of Oberjäger Hermsen recalls: "Our unit was being restructured when the Allies landed at Anzio-Nettuno. We were deployed in that sector to keep the enemy forces away from via Appia. We checked them near Cisterna. Our regiment was highly praised for its achievements, particularly, Feldwebel Kempe who destroyed several tanks with his gun. But these successes were dearly paid for as of a 750-man force, only 52 survived. I was among the wounded."
>
> Here is the account of Oberleutnant Opel, one of the regiment's company commanders: "We had no heavy weapons, only FG 42 submachine-guns. We were deployed to protect the counter-attacks of our tanks. I only remember one episode of these actions. To check a force of Rangers who had thrust into the positions held by a neighbouring company, I launched a counter-attack at one of their flanks, thus cutting off a large number of Americans from their unit. About 4–500 Americans fell into our hands. However others had escaped and entrenched themselves in surrounding farms. They surrendered after a heroic stand. During this action, I was shot twice, but kept on fighting until relieved by reinforcements."
>
> But matters were different for Lt. Wolter, one of 2nd Company's squad leaders: "The composition of our force was that of a standard paratroop company. My squad, organised into three groups, was armed with six MG 42s, a few submachine-guns and one mortar. A couple of Paks may have also been issued at battalion level. Artillery support was provided by a neighbouring Heer [army] unit. We had no details about the direction of the thrust, as the operation was primarily aimed at keeping the enemy from outflanking us.
>
> On 10 February 1944, at night, while opposing a frontal raid by American Rangers, I was captured along with two comrades."[27]

On January 22, 1944, the men of the battalion made their fourth combat assault, on Anzio, and assisted in widening the beachhead into a salient flanking the Carrocetra-Aprilla factory area.

On January 30, 1944, Darby's Rangers ceased to exist as a fighting force. Although the 4th Ranger Battalion was not deactivated until a few months later, it was never the same after two of its battalions were captured near Anzio, Italy, in the town of Cisterna.

As part of Operation *Shingle*, Darby commanded Ranger Force 6615, which included three Ranger battalions plus Headquarters, the 83rd Chemical Mortar Battalion, the 509th Parachute Battalion, and a company of the 36th Engineers. This force was tasked with the capture of Anzio and Nettuno. This was done successfully, although some of 83rd Chemical Company's landing crafts hit several mines, which resulted in hundreds killed. Darby landed almost directly in front of the main landmark, the casino at Anzio. Another successful amphibious landing for the Rangers.

Subsequently, Darby was tasked with a night infiltration into the town of Cisterna. The 1st and 3rd Battalions were assigned with the mission while 4th Battalion was held in reserve just below the hamlet, Conca. The advance roughly

Rangers at Pointe du Hoc. The 116th were the first Americans to seize the area. (Carlisle Barracks)

followed the Conca–Cisterna road across the Mussolini Canal. On January 30, the two battalions moved ahead, eventually using a large ditch to mask their movement. When the ditch ended, the Rangers traversed a large open area, as daylight was just starting. Along with some sentries, a German company was encountered and eliminated. German resistance stiffened immediately, and veterans of the Herman Göring Division and the Lehr Parachute Battalion surrounded and captured the 1st and 3rd Ranger Battalions after several hours. Of the 767 Rangers near Cisterna, 12 men were killed, six escaped to Allied lines and over 700 were captured to be filmed later on for propaganda purposes. The 4th Ranger Battalion tried desperately to reach the trapped sister units but was stopped, taking the majority of the Ranger casualties during the day.

There are several reasons why the Rangers were unsuccessful in their mission. A large number of their replacements were not well trained, but there were far more significant factors. The command failed to provide proper air cover and artillery support. Virtually non-existent communication hampered coordinations between the various units. However, singularly the greatest failure to be borne by the commanders, including William Darby, was the lack of proper intelligence. The Rangers unknowingly entered an area that had become heavily reinforced by veteran German units. Lightly equipped Rangers without proper support were no match for experienced battle-hardened mechanized German units. It was an unfortunate ending to one of the great fighting forces of World War II.

The few survivors of the 4th Ranger Battalion remained at Anzio, assigned to guard and reserve duties, until March 25, 1944, when the veterans of the earlier campaigns were ordered to return to the United States. Other Rangers joined the 1st Special Service Force Brigade, though this was not always a happy marriage, and continued the fight until 1945.[28]

The 1st and 3rd Ranger Battalions were disbanded on October 24, 1944, at Camp Butner, North Carolina. The 4th Rangers followed suit on October 26.

Rangers in England during the build-up for the invasion of Normandy. (US Army)

# 2ND AND 5TH RANGER BATTALIONS

The 2nd and 5th Ranger Battalions, who originally wore the Sunoco patch (see page 59), participated in the June 6, 1944, D-Day landings at Omaha Beach, Normandy – the invasion of France.

The 2nd Ranger Battalion, activated on April 1, 1943, at Camp Forrest, Tennessee, was trained and led by Lieutenant Colonel James Earl Rudder. Three companies, D, E, and F, assaulted the cliffs of Pointe du Hoc under intense machine-gun, mortar, and artillery fire and destroyed a large gun battery that would have wreaked havoc on the Allied fleets offshore. For two days and nights they fought without relief until the 5th Ranger Battalion linked up with them.[29]

After the successful landings in Normandy the two non-Darby Ranger units launched attacks against the German fortifications around Brest in the La Coquet peninsula. The Rangers of the 2nd Battalion fought through the bitter Central Europe campaign and won commendations for their heroic actions in the battle of Hill 400 where the fighting was up close and personal and almost destroyed the battalion's combat prowess. The 2nd Rangers earned the Distinguished Unit Citation and the Croix de Guerre. The 2nd Ranger Battalion was inactivated at Camp Patrick Henry on October 23, 1945.

The 5th Ranger Battalion was activated on September 1, 1943, at Camp Forrest; it was commanded by Lieutenant Colonel Max Schneider, former executive officer of the 4th Ranger Battalion, and was part of the provisional Ranger Assault Force commanded by Colonel Rudder. Three companies of the 2nd Battalion, A, B, and C, landed where elements of the 116th Regiment of the 29th Infantry Division were pinned down by the effective German cross-fire from above.

One of the public affairs histories generated by the 75th Ranger Regiment recounts the actions as follows:

Rangers, one of them wearing the unpopular Sunoco Ranger patch, sometime after the capture of Pointe du Hoc. (Carlisle Barracks)

The Fifth Battalion Rangers broke across the sea wall and barbed wire entanglements, and up the pillbox-rimmed heights under intense enemy machine-gun and mortar fire and with A and B Companies of the 2nd Battalion and some elements of the 116th Infantry Regiment, advanced four miles to the key town of Vierville, thus opening the breach for supporting troops to follow-up and expand the beachhead. Meanwhile C Company of the 2nd Battalion, due to rough seas, landed west of the Vierville draw and suffered 50% casualties during the landing, but still scaled a 90 foot cliff using ropes and bayonets to knock out a formidable enemy position that was sweeping the beach with deadly fire.

The Fifth Battalion with elements of the 116th Regiment finally linked up with the beleaguered 2nd Battalion on D+3, although Lt. Charles Parker of A Company, 5th Battalion, had penetrated deep behind enemy lines on D Day and reached the 2nd Battalion with 20 prisoners. Later, with the 2nd Battalion the unit distinguished itself in the hard-fought battle of Brest. Under the leadership of Lt. Colonel Richard Sullivan the Fifth Ranger Battalion took part in the Battle of the Bulge, Huertgen Forest and other tough battles throughout central Europe, winning two Distinguished Unit Citations and the French Croix de Guerre. The outfit was deactivated October 2 at Camp Miles Standish, Massachusetts.[30]

A most important aspect of the modern Rangers is their saying of "Rangers Lead The Way!" This saying – the official motto of the modern Rangers is *Sua Sponte* (Of their Own Accord) – has its roots during the intense fighting along the beaches. As the situation became critical on Omaha Beach, Brigadier General Norman D. Cota, Assistant Division Commander of the 29th Infantry Division, stated that the entire assault force must clear the beaches and advance inland or die. It is interesting to note the discrepancy between the official history and the following quotation from Stephen Ambrose's book, *D-Day*, regarding the 116th assault at Pointe du Hoc, and the origins of the Ranger saying:

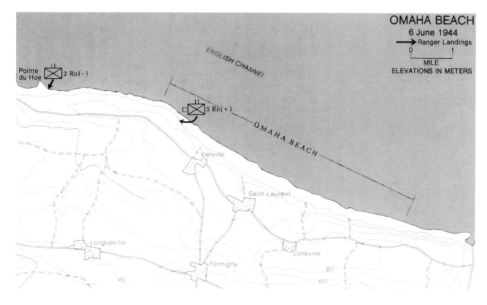

Map detailing the attacks of the 2nd and 5th Ranger Battalions on D-Day. (US Army)

German prisoners of war being escorted by American troops. (Jim Altieri collection)

General Cota came down the beach. In the Hollywood version, he calls out "Rangers lead the way!" and off they charged. In the real thing, the battlefield noise was such that he couldn't be heard ten feet away. What he did was move from group to group...

Cota started encouraging individuals and small groups to move out on their own, saying, "Don't die on the beaches, die up on the bluff if you have to die, but get off the beaches or you're sure to die." To [Captain] Raaen [Dcr HQ, 5th Rangers], he said, "You men are rangers and I know you won't let me down."

Cota found Schneider at his CP. Cota remained standing; Schneider stood upright to converse. According to one witness, Cota said, "We're counting on you rangers to lead the way." Sergeant Fast, Schneider's interpreter, remembered Cota saying, "I'm expecting the rangers to lead the way."

Whatever Cota's exact words, the motto of the Rangers became "Rangers lead the way." It is a valid motto, well earned, but insofar as it implies that it was necessary for the rangers to be inspired to lead, it needs some correcting.

British Commandos training the 29th Rangers. This unit saw a little bit of action, but was disbanded in 1943, and its members dispersed to the 29th Division. (US Army)

The rangers did not feel that they needed a kick in the butt from Cota. "There was little or no apprehension about going through the wire and up the hill," Cpl. Gale Beccue of B Company, 5th Rangers, remembered. "We had done that in training so many times that it was just a matter of course." He and a private went about their business; they shoved a bangalore torpedo under the barbed wire and blew gaps, then started up. They encountered little opposition: "The German forward positions had been pulling back to prepare rear positions." Meanwhile, German artillery was concentrating on the follow-up landing craft, making it "a lot worse on the beach than when we had landed."

As for the implication in the Ranger motto that it took rangers to lead the 116th off the beach, the fact is that the first organized company to the top at Vierville was Company C, 116th. By the time the rangers landed, many other individuals from the 116th had gone up. They preceded the rangers. The members of the 116th still at the seawall came from those companies that had been decimated in the first wave.[31]

# 29TH RANGER BATTALION

The 29th Ranger Battalion was formed on December 20, 1942, with volunteers from the 29th Infantry Division then stationed in England and commanded by Major Randolph Milholland, a Maryland National Guardsman. "The new unit consisted of a tiny cadre from Darby's original group and volunteers from the 29th Infantry Division, an inexperienced National Guard formation from Maryland and Virginia."[32] The volunteers trained for five weeks at Achnacarry, Scotland, the earlier training home for Darby's Rangers, and were attached to Lord Lovat's No. 4 Commandos.

Colonel Henry Mucci, fabled commander of the 6th Ranger Battalion. (US Army)

The official history of the 29th Division records this history of its Rangers:

On December 20 the 29th Provisional Ranger Battalion, composed principally of members of the 29th Division, was formed at Tidworth Barracks in compliance with a directive from ETO Headquarters. The 1st Rangers, until then the only U.S. Ranger battalion in ETO, had left in October with the 1st Division for the North Africa invasion, this move leaving no specially trained American troops for necessary raiding and reconnaissance missions on north European coasts. The 29th Provisional Ranger Battalion was designed to fill this need, and also to provide actual combat experience to its members, who would, in time, be returned to their original units. The directive issued in September provided that it be organized with a cadre of three officers and fifteen enlisted men from the 1st Ranger Battalion, and the remainder principally from the 29th Division. Major Randolph Millholland, who had returned from a term at the British GHQ Battle School, in Durham, was placed in command of the new battalion, an entirely volunteer organization. Its members were accepted only after strict physical examinations and personal interviews had disclosed that they possessed the physical requirements and the aggressive temperament necessary for this type of soldier. From December to February the Rangers engaged in preliminary training in the Division area near Tidworth and then moved to the British Commando depot at Achnacarry House at Spean Bridge, Scotland, for a five weeks' course under Commando instructors. After completing this course the Rangers were attached to Lord Lovat's No.4 Commando and worked with these

British troops in training and in practice raids on the southern England coast near Dartmouth. It was during this period that the battalion participated with the British in three daring raids on the coast of Norway.

The object of the first raid was to destroy a bridge over a fjord near a harbor on the west coast of Norway. Loss of the surprise element was responsible for the failure of this raid. After silent British MTB boats had put the party ashore the raiders moved quickly and silently down a concrete quay toward the bridge. Leading the group was a Norwegian guide, carrying a submachine gun, whose magazine had not been inserted securely. As the group ran silently down the quay in the dark the magazine became loose in the receiver and dropped to the concrete with a loud "clack!" A German called "Halt!" and on receiving no answer, opened fire. Other German machine guns in the area also opened up. The Commando and Ranger raiders returned the fire and then ran back down the road half a mile to the water, where MTB boats were waiting for them.

The second raid was a straight reconnaissance mission. Rangers joined with No.4 Commando personnel in a three-day close-in reconnaissance of another Norwegian harbor, where they remained unobserved, watching the harbor shipping and movements of troops on the docks. One hundred and eight men were involved in the third raid, which was to destroy a German command post on Norway's west coast. After a successful landing the raiders discovered that the CP had been moved. No Germans were in the area.

After six weeks with No.4 Commando the 29th Rangers returned to the Division area at Tidworth.[33]

Headquarters, 29th Infantry Division, issued General Orders disbanding the unit on October 18, 1943. The Rangers returned to the 29th Division.

# 6TH RANGER BATTALION

The 6th Ranger Battalion was organized on September 25, 1944, when the 98th Field Artillery Battalion was redesignated while stationed in New Guinea. The majority of the missions the 6th Ranger Battalion conducted tended to involve small numbers of men, usually platoon or company size. Most of the time they operated behind enemy lines conducting missions such as reconnaissance, long-range combat patrols, and direct-action raids.

The 6th Ranger Battalion holds the distinction of being the first American unit to return to the Philippine Islands where it was tasked with the job of knocking out coastal defense guns and radio and radar stations. "On A-Day minus three, October 17, 1944, the 6th Ranger Battalion was landed from fast attack-type converted destroyers, in the midst of a storm, on Dinagat, Suluan, and Homonohan Islands in Leyte Bay."[34] During the remaining days of October and the whole month of November the Rangers conducted aggressive combat patrols, searching for, and when encountered eliminating, pockets of resistance.

On January 10, 1945, Rangers were involved in the Lingayen Gulf invasion. Sadly, the Rangers had to perform guard duties for the Sixth Army headquarters and two companies were sent to establish a radar station on an island.

Former prisoners and members
of the 6th Ranger Battalion
after the successful raid at the
Japanese prison camp near
Cabanatuan. (US Army)

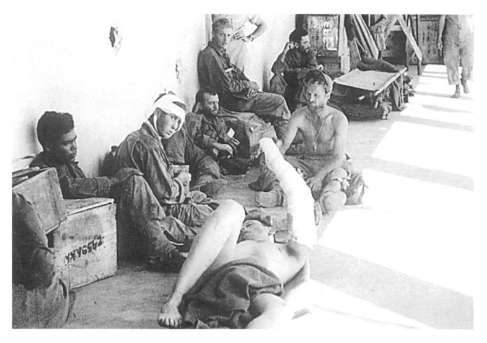

The 6th Ranger Battalion's most celebrated accomplishment was the liberation of prisoners of war, when a reinforced Ranger Company along with Filipino guerrillas, made short work of the Japanese prison camp at Cabanatuan, the Philippines, in January 1945. Ranger losses were two killed and ten wounded.

On July 1, 1945, the 6th Ranger Battalion, the only one serving in the Pacific Theater of Operations, was relieved of combat duties after having participated successfully and with distinction in three campaigns and one combat assault. "On September 15, 1945, the battalion embarked for occupation duties in Japan, and was stationed in the Kyoto area when it was inactivated on December 30, 1945."[35]

The Rangers of the 6th Battalion also wore the red, white, and black scroll invented by Darby's Rangers, and proudly worn by all five battalions in Europe.

# MERRILL'S MARAUDERS – PARENT OF THE 75TH RANGER REGIMENT

The following is an historical account provided by the 75th Ranger Regiment Public Affairs Office in a document entitled *Rangers Past and Present* and draws heavily on a 1962 Field Manual 21-50, *Ranger Training and Ranger Operations*, Headquarters, Department of the Army, Appendix XVII, as well as information provided by the Merrill's Marauders Association:

Merrill's Marauders, a Ranger type outfit, came into existence as a result of the Quebec Conference of August, 1943. During this conference, President Franklin D. Roosevelt, Prime Minister Winston Churchill of England, and other allied leaders conceived the idea of having an American ground unit spearhead the Chinese Army with a Long Range Penetration Mission behind enemy lines in Burma. Its goal would be the destruction of

Frank D. Merrill and Joseph W. Stilwell – arguably the two most influential men regarding the Marauders. (US Army)

## 5307TH COMPOSITE UNIT (PROVISIONAL)

Commanding General
BG Frank D. Merrill

Second in Command
COL Charles N. Hunter

**Command Post Group**
Executive Officer
MAJ Louis J. Williams

**Rear Base Supply Officer**
MAJ Edward T. Hancock

**1st Battalion**
Commanding Officer
LTC William L. Osborne

**2nd Battalion**
Commanding Officer
LTC George A. McGee, Jr.

**3rd Battalion**
Commanding Officer
LTC Charles E. Beach

**Red Combat team**
Commanding Officer
*MAJ Edward M. Ghiz
CPT Tom P. Senff

**Blue Combat team**
Commanding Officer
MAJ Richard W. Healy

**Orange Combat team**
Commanding Officer
**MAJ Lawrence Lew
MAJ Peter A. Petito

**White Combat team**
Commanding Officer
MAJ Caifson Johnson

**Green Combat team**
Commanding Officer
CPT Thomas Bogardus

**Khaki Combat team**
Commanding Officer
MAJ Edwin J. Briggs

\* Commanding Officer to 6 April 1944
\*\* Commanding Officer to 4 April 1944

## ORGANIZATION OF THE 5307TH COMPOSITE UNIT (PROVISIONAL) TO APRIL 27, 1944*

| | Battalion Headquarters | Combat teams No. 1 | No. 2 | Total |
|---|---|---|---|---|
| Officers | 3 | 16 | 16 | 35 |
| Enlisted men | 13 | 456 | 459 | 928 |
| Aggregate | 16 | 472 | 475 | 963 |
| Animals (horses and mules) | 3 | 68 | 68 | 139 |
| Carbines | 6 | 86 | 89 | 181 |
| Machine guns, Heavy | | 3 | 4 | 7 |
| Machine guns, Light | | 2 | 4 | 6 |
| Machine guns, Sub | 2 | 52 | 48 | 102 |
| Mortars, 60mm | | 4 | 6 | 10 |
| Mortars, 81mm | | 4 | 3 | 7 |
| Pistols | | 2 | 2 | 4 |
| Rifles, Browning Automatic | | 27 | 27 | 54 |
| Rifles, M-1 | 8 | 306 | 310 | 624 |
| Rockets (bazookas) | | 3 | 3 | 6 |

General Composition of each Combat Team:
Headquarters Platoon
Intelligence and Reconnaissance Platoon
Pioneer and Demolition Platoon
Medical Detachment
Communications Platoon
Heavy Weapons Platoon (3 heavy machine guns, 4 81mm mortars)
1½ Rifle Companies
½ Company Headquarters
*This Table of Organization does not include supply detachment at Dinjan

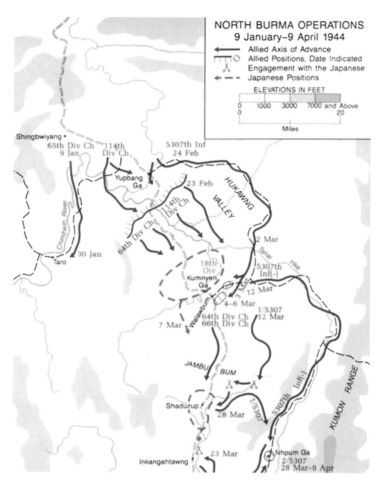

NORTH BURMA OPERATIONS
9 January–9 April 1944

Map detailing the long and arduous campaign fought by the 5307th in Burma in early 1944. (US Army)

Japanese communications and supply lines and generally to play havoc with enemy forces while an attempt was made to reopen the Burma Road.

A Presidential call for volunteers for "A Dangerous and Hazardous Mission" was issued, and approximately 2,900 American soldiers responded to the call. Officially designated as the 5307th Composite Unit (Provisional) code name "Galahad" the unit later became popularly known as Merrill's Marauders, named after its leader, Brigadier General Frank Merrill. Organized into combat teams, two to each battalion, the Marauder volunteers came from a variety of theaters of operation. Some came from Stateside cadres; some from the jungles of Panama and Trinidad; and the remainder were battle-scarred veterans of Guadalcanal, New Georgia, and New Guinea campaigns. In India some Signal Corps and Air Corps personnel were added, as well as pack troops with mules.

After preliminary training operations undertaken in great secrecy in the jungles of India, about 600 men were detached as a rear echelon HQ to remain in India to handle the soon-to-be vital air-drop link between the six Marauder combat teams (400 to a team) and the Air Transport Command. Color-coded Red, White, Blue, Green, Orange and Khaki, the remaining 240 Marauders began their march up the Ledo Road and over the outlying ranges of the Himalayan

Mountains into Burma. The Marauders, with no tanks or heavy artillery to support them, walked over 1,000 miles throughout extremely dense and almost impenetrable jungles and came out with glory. In five major and thirty minor engagements, they defeated the veteran soldiers of the Japanese 18th Division (conquerors of Singapore and Malaya) who vastly outnumbered them. Always moving to the rear of the main forces of the Japanese, they completely disrupted enemy supply and communication lines, and climaxed their behind-the-lines operations with the capture of Myitkyina Airfield, the only all-weather airfield in Burma.

For their accomplishments in Burma, the Marauders were awarded the Distinguished Unit Citation in July, 1944. However, in November, 1966, this was redesignated as the Presidential Unit Citation which is awarded by the President in the name of Congress. The unit was consolidated with the 475th Infantry on August 10, 1944. On June 21, 1954, the 475th was redesignated the 75th Infantry. It is from the redesignation of Merrill's Marauders into the 75th Infantry Regiment that the modern-day 75th Ranger Regiment traces its current unit designation.

# THE HISTORY OF THE WORLD WAR II RANGER BATTALION INSIGNIA

By 1st Lieutenant William D. Linn II

Ranger insignia of World War II has a history with characteristics much like the men who wore it. Ranger insignia was born out of personal initiative and unit pride; sometimes manufactured locally in the foreign lands where Rangers trained, fought, and died. The following history summarizes my research on the subject. I have obtained my information from primary source documents as well as correspondence and personal interviews with Rangers of that era.

Fifty American Rangers of the 1st Battalion participated in the Dieppe Raid of August 1942; an unsuccessful but highly publicized first Allied aggression against "Fortress Europe." American soldiers in England, attempting to capitalize on raid publicity, bragged in the pubs that they were Rangers in order to win favor with local women. Fights ensued with such frequency between Rangers and the imposters that something had to be done. Captain Roy Murray, the senior Ranger at Dieppe, recommended that Rangers be authorized their own shoulder insignia. Colonel William O. Darby requested authorization for a patch through Brigadier General Lucian Truscott and Major General Clark on August 28, 1942, based on the following reasons:

> 1. Tremendous boost to morale.
>
> 2. Soldiers all over UK are spreading stories about the recent raid and pretending to be Rangers.

Once the request was approved, on October 8, 1942, Colonel Darby organized a battalion-wide contest for the best design and a prize for the winner. Sergeant Anthony Rada of Headquarters and Headquarters Company (HHC), a native of Flint, Michigan, won with his design of a red, white, and black scroll patch that resembled the British commando insignia worn by the Ranger training cadre. The Army officially recognized the new scroll on October 8, 1942, and a supply of them were made locally in England. Though General Truscott intended them only to be worn on the service coat (dress uniform), 1st Battalion Rangers wore them proudly into battle. In May and June of 1943, 3rd and 4th Battalions were formed in Africa from men selected out of Darby's original battalion. Soon after the three-battalion task force arrived to take part in the fighting in Italy, Rangers obtained crude scrolls from local Italian sources. These examples had no uniform composition, being made of remnant cloth, wire bullion thread, and sometimes featuring irregular and reversed letters. As American Rangers and other allied units made their way up the Italian peninsula, Axis Sally began to broadcast threats to the Rangers over Radio Berlin. Glenn Hirchert, a sniper in C Company, 1st Ranger Battalion, recalls that every Ranger believed German policy dictated no quarter be given to Rangers who surrendered in combat. Once surrounded at Cisterna and with capture imminent, Hirchert watched Rangers draw their fighting knives and quickly remove and destroy their scrolls in hopes that they would be spared execution. The brutal German policy proved to be just effective propaganda. Ed Furru, a 1st Battalion Ranger wounded at Dieppe, was captured together with several members of the British 3 Commando. Since Rangers had no insignia at the time, he spent the whole war erroneously segregated as a British POW. As the war progressed and Rangers from other battalions were captured and brought to camp, Furru learned about the Ranger scroll. None were available in the camp, so he wore a crude 3 Commando tab made from bed ticking given to him by a member of that unit. He eventually purchased a scroll in the United States after being repatriated. He could not find a 1st Battalion scroll in the PX so he converted a 4th by removing thread from the "4th" to make a "1."

Task Force Ranger and its three battalions were disbanded following the disaster at Cisterna just about the time 2nd Battalion formed at Camp Forrest, Tennessee. During their train-up period, the Army approved a shoulder sleeve insignia for all Ranger units based on the design submitted by a 2nd Battalion Ranger. On July 16, 1943, the blue diamond patch with the word "RANGERS" in gold became the official Ranger insignia. The patch was not well received by the men and soon earned the nickname "Sunoco" since the patch resembled the logo of the Sun Oil Company. The 2nd Battalion received their diamond patches in September or October of 1943 at Fort Dix, New Jersey while they were en route to England. Prior to D-Day, as recalled by 1st Sergeant Len Lomell (D Company) and Captain Frank Kennard (HQ), all patches were removed for operational security. By midsummer of 1944, however, the men were again wearing the patch. Kennard recalls that in early August of 1944, during the siege of Brest, men of the 2nd heard of a scroll patch being worn by other Ranger units. William Kennard, Frank's father, was in the textile business in New York City and agreed to help secure insignia for his son's battalion. Captain Kennard drafted a purchase order, which Colonel Rudder signed, and the document was received on August 24 along with a 1st Ranger scroll to use as a pattern. William Kennard had 2,500 scrolls made for the battalion but found he could not send bulk commercial property through the military mail. Fifty men from the 2nd Battalion had to write individual letters to Mr Kennard whom, in return, could send them a set limit of 50 scrolls. All 2,500 examples arrived piecemeal with the battalion while in the field in Arlon, Belgium, in late September 1944. This allowed each man to receive two to four examples of the new insignia and the rest to remain in supply to outfit replacements as they arrived.

The men of the 5th Ranger Battalion arrived at Camp Forrest, Tennessee just as the 2nd Battalion were on their way out. It was during their stay at Camp Forrest that they learned of the approved diamond patch from an Army manual containing only a brief description, but no illustration. No Rangers from the 5th had ever seen one of the new patches and Army supply channels failed to yield diamond patches for the 5th, so the battalion took measures to have them locally made. Major General John Raaen, then commander of Headquarters Company, remembers having approximately 3,000 patches made and issued to the men. When the 5th arrived in England, they saw the approved patch for the first time being worn by their Ranger brothers in the 2nd Battalion. They found that their version of the patch was considerably smaller, lacked a single gold border, and featured the word "RANGER" not "RANGERS." They quickly discarded this version and acquired what they needed through supply channels in the UK. Unlike the 2nd, the 5th Battalion wore diamond Ranger patches ashore at Normandy. They continued to wear their patches until they saw the 2nd Rangers wearing their new US-made scrolls. The first man to acquire a scroll for the 5th Battalion was General Raaen who had returned to the United States after sustaining injuries in a jeep accident. In November 1944 he went to see an old family friend, Morrie Luxembourg, a prominent haberdasher in New York City. Luxembourg made 12 scrolls for General Raaen as a favor at no charge and then another modest batch not long afterwards. Some of these scrolls made their way back to the European Theater of Operations and to the men of

BELOW

Official uniform of the 5307th CUP. Note the Marauder's patch. (Author's collection/Camera 1)

BELOW RIGHT

Display of the 475th Infantry at the Infantry Museum. (Author's collection/Camera 1)

the 5th Rangers. When the Battalion found itself in Germany, some Rangers procured a batch of scrolls locally made by Bavarian nuns that were almost too large to wear on the uniform sleeve. These over-sized scrolls were similar in construction to previously made examples. They paid for the insignia using funds taken from a German Army paymaster.

The 6th Ranger Battalion had known from the beginning of their existence that their brother Rangers in Europe wore a unique scroll insignia. The scroll design had been a symbol used on letterheads and signposts since the 6th Battalion formed in September 1944. However, due to the primitive conditions in the Pacific Theater, insignia was difficult to come by. Private First Class Alvie Robbins (C Company) recalls that it was not until after the successful raid at Cabanatuan in January 1945 that 6th Rangers wore scrolls. The 6th acquired locally made examples while in the Philippines, but they tended to be crude in design. Another design that was common in the battalion area was a crest that featured a trench knife, lightning bolt, and sunset topped by the word "Rangers." In rare cases this design was embroidered onto scarves or worn as an unofficial pocket patch. In December 1945, most of the "high points" men shipped from the Philippines to California while the rest sailed for Japan to serve as an honor guard. As the men rotated home, they received a new uniform issue and are thought to have also received some US-made 6th scrolls. Certainly there were sources for all types of military insignia in San Francisco, where the men came into port. American insignia manufacturers nationwide catered their huge stocks to the demands of patch collectors and returning veterans.

In conclusion, it is interesting to note that the Army abolished the blue diamond Ranger patches in 1947 leaving no authorized insignia for Ranger units who fought in the Korean or Vietnam conflicts. Not until 1983, when the 1st and 2nd Ranger Battalions participated in the invasion of Grenada did the Army finally approve the red, white, and black scroll.

The memorial for the World War II Ranger battalions at Fort Benning, Georgia. (Author's collection/Camera 1)

# The Postwar Years: Korea and Vietnam

## The Cold War heating up

## THE RANGER INFANTRY COMPANIES (AIRBORNE) OF THE KOREAN WAR

During the Korean War (1950–53) specialized units were needed to conduct difficult missions beyond the capability of conventional infantry. This led to the creation of Airborne Ranger Companies. During World War II the Ranger battalions were used primarily as shock troops. The Korean era Airborne Ranger Companies were to perform missions closer to those envisioned by Major Rogers in the 1750s, including reconnaissance and raids. These Rangers would be the first airborne-qualified units. (See Appendix A for details of the Korean War Era Ranger Infantry Companies (Airborne).)

However, the Airborne Rangers were attached to larger, more conventionally minded forces. Many commanders ignored their specialized capability and deployed them as a spearhead for traditional infantry tasks, especially defensive operations. As a result, the Airborne Ranger Companies of the Korean War suffered up to 90% losses. One 112-man company of Rangers was attached to each 18,000-man infantry division.

In addition to these Airborne Ranger companies, an 8th Army Ranger Company was founded in Japan and was the first Ranger unit deployed to Korea.

In September 1950, with the Cold War heating up, particularly in Korea, Colonel John Gibson Van Houten, then in charge of the Ranger training program at Fort Benning, Georgia, was informed that training of the Ranger-type units was to begin shortly. Training was to start on October 1, 1950, and was scheduled for six weeks, with the initial requirements of a headquarters detachment and four

Korean Airborne-Rangers preparing for nighttime combat patrol. These were the first airborne-qualified Rangers. Prior to Korea all Ranger units were infantry units. (US Army)

Ranger infantry companies (Airborne). Orders were issued, and the selected volunteers relocated to Fort Benning. Among other recruits, starting on October 9, 1950, former members of the 505th Airborne Infantry Regiment, eventually known for smoke jumping in the Pacific Northwest, and the 80th Antiaircraft Artillery Battalion of the 82nd Airborne Division also started Ranger training. Initially designated the 4th Ranger Company, they would soon be redesignated as the 2nd Ranger Infantry Company (Airborne), the only all-black Ranger Unit in the history of the United States Army. Unlike prior colored units, which were officered by whites, its officers and enlisted were black.

Training, conducted during daytime hours and at night, included amphibious and airborne operations, demolitions, close combat as well as other infantry skills.

> The 1st Ranger Infantry Company (Airborne) left Ft. Benning on November 15, 1950, and arrived in Korea on December 17, 1950, where it was attached to the 2nd Infantry Division. The 2nd Ranger Company was attached to the 7th Infantry Division where it initially was not welcomed. The 4th Ranger Company served both Headquarters, Eighth US Army, and the 1st Cavalry Division. Tasks included scouting, patrolling, raids, ambushes, spearheading assaults, and as acting as counterattack forces to reclaim lost positions.
>
> The 1st Ranger Infantry Company (Airborne) executed a night raid 9 miles behind enemy lines to destroy an enemy complex, the 12th North Korean Division, and participated in the battle of Chipyong-Ni. The 2nd and 4th Ranger Companies parachuted into combat at Munsan-Ni. Rangers were the first unit to cross the 38th parallel on the second drive north.[36]

Of the 18 Ranger companies formed during the Korean War, 17 were certified Airborne and seven actually participated in combat. In October of 1951 the Ranger Training Command was redesignated as the Ranger Department. Its mission was to train soldiers in Ranger techniques. All the Ranger companies of the Korean War were deactivated by the end of 1951.

The Company Commander and Executive Officer of the 2nd Airborne-Ranger Company are inducted into the Hall of Fame:

## MAJOR JAMES C. QUEEN

Major James C. Queen is inducted into the Ranger Hall of Fame for his valiant actions while serving as a Ranger leader in the Korean War. While serving with the 4th Ranger Infantry Company (Airborne) (redesignated the 2nd Ranger Infantry Company (Airborne) Major Queen led numerous patrols and controlled the company heavy weapons. He made the combat jump with the company at Munsan-ni and saw action at Tangerine Pass. In May of 1951 Major Queen led the company on a mission to take Hill 581. During this operation he acted as the Company Commander for the 2nd Ranger Company. They moved as the lead element for the 7th Infantry Division and with only 65 men came into contact with a battalion of Chinese regulars. Major Queen immediately called for artillery fire and led his men into battle. They fought the enemy for three hours but after taking 50% casualties the company fell back to the 7th Division lines. At dawn the following day, Major Queen led the remainder of his company in a counterattack on the Hill. After nearly one hour of intense fighting, the Rangers pushed the Chinese back and retook the Hill. Major Queen's leadership ability and courageous actions are in the finest traditions of the Rangers and the United States Army.

## MAJOR WARREN E. ALLEN

Major Warren E. Allen is inducted into the Ranger Hall of Fame for his exceptional leadership and valor while serving as company commander of the legendary 2nd Ranger Infantry Company (Airborne) during the early part of the Korean War. Major Allen led America's only black Ranger unit from the front in several highly successful engagements, including the first Ranger parachute assault in history. He earned the Silver Star while leading his Rangers against a nearly overwhelming enemy attack. Although wounded in that intense exchange, he led his company in a successful fighting withdrawal. As a Ranger commander, Major Allen displayed great leadership, valor, and compassion for his men. Casualties within his ranks were exceptionally low, considering the precarious assault missions his company was assigned. Simultaneously his unit's rate of success was notably high. His life, both as an active duty Ranger and as a retired soldier, serves as an inspiration for all Americans. His character, based on a belief in hard work, persistence in achieving goals, and reliability are in the finest traditions of the Rangers and the United States Army.

# HOW THE LRRPS WERE ONE

The following, provided by the VII Corps LRRP Company (ABN) Association, is an excerpt from an interview conducted, on May 25, 2002, with Colonel Edward V. Maltese (Ret), the "Father of the LRRPs."

In 1960–61, I was in Fort Monroe, VA, working for Gen. Watters as head of the airborne test sections and so forth, and I was asked to extend there for another year – and it was sent back, disapproved. General Watters said he didn't understand why they disapproved my extension, so I went up there (to the placement office) and they said there are two places they wanted me to send me, one was Hawaii, so I said, "Yeah, I wouldn't mind that," and the guy said, "You can't go there, because I'm going there", and the other was back to Korea. So I called General Watters and told him I was being assigned to Korea, and he said, "I've just been assigned to VII Corps over in Germany. Why don't you come there with me?" I didn't end up there with him, but I was sent to 7th Army instead, under General Mel Zais, a tremendous airborne soldier. He was Gavin's brother in law – a good man. He was G-3 of 7th Army. He wanted me to go to work for him at 7th Army HQ, but I ended up instead as 7th Army Operations Officer with the G-2 division.

## THE VISION

I had never been a G-2 in my doggoned life. I had these two captains in there, and I'm Operations Officer. We got to talking one day and one of them said, "You were in the Special Forces, what did you think of them?" "Well," I said, "the trouble with Special Forces is that they were reactive to the Army, they were more of the theater concept." And he said, "That's what I've been thinking. We need some sort of means to find targets in the Army's sphere of influence," and I agreed. And they are the ones that really put the idea into my mind.

I said "OK, let's get to working on it." So they got to working on what we should do and shouldn't do, and I was up there fighting the battle with 7th Army headquarters – in my own way – and the G-2 wanted no part of it, of course, but Mel Zais was the one I had to convince.

The 2nd Airborne-Ranger Company was an all-black unit. Two of its officers, Allen and Queen, are inducted into the Ranger Hall of Fame. (US Army)

He finally agreed with me, said, "I'll support you. Now, Ed, what we have to do is find the spaces." To this day I'll never understand where he got the spaces. And I never asked.

But we finally got through 7th Army, approved for the two companies (V Corps and VII Corps) at the same time. Then Zais said, "Now you need to get USAREUR approval." It was just the two captains and myself – I wish I could remember their names – so we worked on that. One day I got a call from USAREUR Headquarters. They had some concerns from some special planner up there, and they said "Ed, we notice you've got a major as commander there," and I said, "Yeah, what of it?" They asked why, and I said, "It's because I'm going to command one of them, that's why! And I'm a major, that's why I've got a major commanding them, and that's the only reason I've got a major there." Well, they said, "that's reason enough for us," and that's how they approved it.

I got a call from the G-2 at VII Corps the day they approved it, and they asked, "Will the G-2 at 7th Army release you?" I said, "Probably not," and with that the Corps Commander got me on the phone, Colonel Oaks, and he said, "How about you come in and I'll do it?" and I said, "OK." And that's how I got there.

## THE MEN

The one that helped us most was the assignments NCO at VII Corps, who would call me every month and say, "I've got a list of people you might be interested in." So every month I would go over that list, and pick out the ones I wanted, and out they'd come. As far as qualifications, what mattered to me was what they had done, that's the only thing I ever cared about, if it looked like they had been in the Army.

This photograph, part of the Marshall Collection, was taken during a firefight. (Carlisle Barracks)

We had a full company – it really filled up well. We got permission to recruit – most of them came from the 505. I remember old Herb something from B Co 505, he tried to discourage them, called us a bunch of candy-asses, so I went up there – hell, I'm about forty-one years old, but in pretty good shape, and I said, "I'll take you out and we'll see who comes back." That was the end of that discussion.

The company was heavy with NCOs, by design. One day, McNeeley was out there cleaning with another NCO who was complaining, and McNeeley said, "Well, would you rather clean it as a Sergeant or as a private?" And that was the end of that. "Respect your NCOs," I always told my men, "If you don't, we don't want you."

## TRAINING

The training schedule was written by me, Captain Frank Garbers, Lt Jack Conlon, Sgt McNeeley and Sgt Darrell Daugherty. Daugherty did almost all the work. And I've got to give 7th Army credit. They let us alone, and we could do whatever we wanted. No one ever came out and said, "Don't do this, don't do that." For instance, we wanted to take ski training at Garmisch, we went to Garmisch, and the Army paid for all the facilities and we did whatever we wanted to do, even swimming at Garmisch in the summer.

They worked hard, they played hard. I always believed in training, for others and myself. Every one we sent to jump school when I was there came out as number one in his class. Had to be, they were in the best shape of anybody. There's no doubt about that. Hell, I was forty-two years old, and I'll bet you for a forty-two year old man I was in the best physical shape anybody's ever been in. I ran every morning, did rifle PT in the afternoon.

## SUPPORT

Our biggest problem was with helicopter support. Some of them didn't want to fly, but I'd have them out there flying in all kinds of weather and they'd say, "You're trying to kill us." But in general, we had good support. Initially we had some problems with VII Corps Aviation until the Corps Commander came out one day and had a few words with the Garrison Commander. The Corps Commander turned to me and said that he understood from the Garrison Commander that I really didn't cooperate with him. What the Garrison Commander was talking about, was KP! I said, "I told him NCOs don't pull KP, and we're not going to send any

### LRRP CO (ABN) TRIVIA

Although referred to as V Corps LRRP Company (ABN) and VII Corps LRRP Company (ABN), the two LRRP Companies (ABN) were both originally called USA LRRP Co (ABN). The only distinction was that one was attached to V Corps at APO 26 (Wildflecken), and one to VII Corps at APO 46 (Nellingen).

troops to pull KP." And the Corps Commander said, "I agree." Then he said, "Are there any other problems?" I said, "Yeah, come on in the office," and I showed him pictures on the wall of all sorts of aircraft. He asked, "Have you jumped all those planes?" I said, "Every plane on that wall. I was a parachute test officer, every one on that wall, every helicopter, otters, I worked on the caribou, etc. I jumped every one of them – but not in *this* Corps." He asked what I meant, and I said, "Your Operations Officer won't let us use them." "He will when I get back," he said, and when he got back, the first call I got was from the Aviation Officer. We never had trouble getting aircraft after that.

## BERETS

Jane and I were in our quarters at Nellingen, and there was a rap at the door. It was Sgt Joiner. He says, "Hate to bother you, but we had a meeting. We'd like to have a beret." I replied, "Well Joiner, I'll tell you something. I was with the Special Forces when they first got the beret, and it was a real pain. It was 'take them off, put them on, take them off, put 'em on,'" but I said, "OK if you want berets, we'll get the berets." So he says, "What color?" My wife says, "The British Commandos have maroon," so I said, "maroon." And that's how we got the beret. I gave him my Special Forces beret and told him to get a copy made. I don't know where the hell Joiner got them made, somewhere locally, though.

I don't know if they ever were authorized, honestly, but we just wore them. One day I got a call from the IG at Corps. He was wondering what my authority was for the berets. I said "CO Maltese." He said, "What do you mean?" I said, "Look, you send me your authority for wearing those DeGaulle hats, and I'll show you the authority for these berets." There wasn't any authority for those damned silly hard-sided hats, and I knew it. Then I got a call from the CG, General Oaks, who said the IG said I wouldn't give him an answer. "Why don't you just tell him I authorized it?" he said. I said, "No, I'm not going to get you in trouble. After all, what can they do to me? I'm not going to make the Army my career!" I never heard much about it after that.

A man from V Corps got killed on a parachute jump, and I was appointed the investigating officer. So I was up there, and they said that the Corps Commander, General Michaelis, wanted to see me. The general said, "What happened?" and I told him, "His parachute didn't open. I don't know why it didn't open, the doggoned parachute just didn't open." I said, "It's unusual, but that's the way it is. It wasn't due to anybody's negligence." He says, "OK, but that's not why I got you in here. How come VII Corps LRRP CO wears berets?" "Because I said they could," I answered. "Well, if a doggoned major can authorize them, I can authorize them, I'm a three star general." That's exactly what he said, and that's how they got their berets.

Colonel Edward V. Maltese retired in 1972, after a distinguished career that included Officer Basic in 1942, jump school and World War II airborne action with the 505 PIR of the 82nd. He also served and jumped with the 187th in

Korea, was in the OSS with Colonel Aaron Bank (who started the SF), and went to Vietnam for 18 months as Director of Target Acquisition. He activated at least five companies as their first commander, from Special Forces to Armor, "but it was the LRRPs that I really enjoyed. It was the NCOs, they were all outstanding. They never caused me any major problems I couldn't resolve. I'm proud that I never had to reduce any one of them. Not that we didn't have problems, but we handled them." He formed the company with the best people he could find or steal, and trained them to be even better. "The VII Corps got most of the recognition," he says. "Maybe it was because I was so obnoxious, but we got pretty much what we wanted."

# THE BEGINNING

*By Colonel Ellis D. Bingham, US Army (Ret)*

The VII Corps Long Range Reconnaissance Patrol Company (Airborne), was authorized June 9, 1961, under TOE 7-157. Major Edward Maltese was appointed Company Commander with the tremendous task of recruiting and training an organization to be the eyes and ears for the VII Corps and Seventh Army. Executive Officer was Captain Ed Hunt, a highly decorated WWII Airborne soldier. Operations Officer was Captain Frank Garbers and Signal Officer Captain Ellis Bingham, and 1st Sergeant Patty Flynn was the first NCO assigned to the organization. Lieutenant General Charles Bonesteel was Commanding General, VII Corps, and knew that it was essential that the unit be well trained to carry out its mission and to communicate information accurately and timely.

The primary mission of the Long Range Reconnaissance Patrol Company (Airborne) was to enter patrols into specified areas within enemy held territory to observe and report enemy dispositions, installations, and activities. Lost over the years was the patrols' primary mission, which was atomic target acquisition. LRRP operations, if employed properly, allow commanders to exercise economy of force for both atomic targeting and ground-force activities. The atomic targeting mission was the reason the unit was a double volunteer organization. To minimize the threat to the patrols the location of all known caves was maintained in Corps G-2 and LRRP Operations.

Upon releasing the call for volunteers, airborne soldiers and airborne rangers in true American fighting-man fashion ran to the sound of the bugle. As the company's ranks began to fill it soon became apparent that the lack of qualified CW communications personnel was going to be a major problem. To be fully operational and effective the company required 76 CW operators. Twenty-eight CW operators needed to be experts in their field for operation of the three base stations and communications platoon headquarters. Forty-eight CW operators were required to fully man the 24 patrols. To alleviate this problem Staff Sergeant "Granny" Granstrom, Communications Platoon NCOIC (Non-Commissioned Officer in Charge), made arrangements with the 3rd Division communications NCOIC to use their CW training facility for 30 days. One hundred and twenty two airborne soldiers were sent for CW training. Because of the rigorous schedule, rapid attrition was encountered and out of the original 122 men, as I recall, 82 became qualified as low speed operators. Because of the fragile aspect of CW operations, low power to high

## HISTORY OF THE RANGER DEPARTMENT/RANGER TRAINING BRIGADE
From *The Ranger Handbook*

The Ranger Course was conceived during the Korean War and was originally known as the Ranger Training Command. On 10 October 1951, the Ranger Training Command was inactivated and became the Ranger Department, a branch of the Infantry School headquartered at Fort Benning, Georgia. Its purpose was, and still is, to develop combat skills of selected officers and enlisted men by requiring them to perform effectively as small unit leaders in a realistic tactical environment, under mental and physical stress levels approaching that experienced in actual combat. Emphasis is placed on the development of individual combat skills and abilities through the application of the principles of leadership. Military skills are cultivated through the planning and execution of dismounted infantry, airborne, airmobile, and amphibious independent squad and platoon-size operations. Graduates return to their units where it is expected they will pass on these skills. From 1954 to the early 1970s, the Army's goal, although seldom achieved, was to have one Ranger-qualified NCO per infantry platoon and one officer per company. In an effort to better achieve this goal, in 1954 the Army required all combat arms officers to become Ranger/Airborne qualified. The Ranger course has undergone little change since its inception. Until recently, it was an eight-week course divided into three phases. The course is now 61 days in duration and divided into three phases, as follows:

• BENNING PHASE (4th Ranger Training Battalion) – Designed to develop the military skills, physical and mental endurance, stamina, and confidence a small unit combat leader must have in order to successfully accomplish a mission. It also teaches the Ranger student to properly maintain himself, his subordinates, and his equipment under difficult field conditions.

• MOUNTAIN PHASE (5th Ranger Training Battalion) – The Ranger student gains proficiency in the fundamentals, principles and techniques of employing small combat units in a mountainous environment. He develops his ability to lead squad-sized units and to exercise control through the planning, preparation, and execution phases of all types of combat operations, including ambushes and raids, plus environmental and survival techniques.

• FLORIDA PHASE (6th Ranger Training Battalion) – Emphasis during this phase is placed on the further development of combat leaders, capable of operating effectively under conditions of extreme mental and physical stress. The training further develops the student's ability to plan and lead small units on independent and coordinated airborne, air assault, amphibious, small boat, and dismounted combat operations in a mid-intensity combat environment against a well-trained, sophisticated enemy.

On 2 December 1987, on York Field, Fort Benning, Georgia, the Ranger Department, in accordance with permanent orders number 214-26, became the Ranger Training Brigade with an effective date of 1 November 1987. After 40 years and 23 Directors and Commanders, the Ranger Course is still dedicated to producing the finest trained soldier in the world... the United States Army Ranger!

power, communications training was an ongoing and essential part of the companies everyday operation when in garrison.

When in the field for training, Major Maltese not only proved himself to be an outstanding commander but a hard taskmaster. If employed patrols failed to make contact with any of the base stations they were not re-supplied with equipment or rations. This concept proved to be an outstanding motivator for the patrol NCOIC and the two radio operators. However, it was Major Ed Hunt, Executive Officer, who had an acute appreciation for the Base Station's operation, whose personnel had to get used to receiving weak signals 24 hours a day when the patrol teams were deployed. During the first field operations, the three base stations were located with the Corps CPs at the assistance of the Corps Signal Officer, which proved to be difficult for the base stations to receive all of the transmissions from their patrols because of skip distances. Upon Major Hunt assuming command in June 1962, this problem was brought to his attention and he agreed with his signal officer. Upon expressing our view, an altercation between the Corps Signal Officer and the LRRP Signal Officer occurred regarding the location of the three LRRP Base Stations. The Corps Signal Officer wanted the base stations to remain co-located with the Corps Forward, Main and Rear Command Posts. As we all know, sky-wave communications is not an exact science because of atmospheric conditions, distances involved, frequency selection and skip distances. Captain Bingham's recommendation, with the concurrence of Major Hunt, was to locate Base Station No.1 near the Corps CP, closest to the FEBA, to serve as the LRRP Net Control Station and to pass all information to the Corps G-2. Base Station No. 2 was to be located approximately 100 miles to the rear of BS No. 1 and Base Station No. 3 approximately 150 to 200 miles behind the FEBA. This controversy came to the attention of General Bonesteel and he requested a briefing on the different concepts by the Corps Signal Officer and the LRRP Signal Officer at his next Commanders Conference. At the conclusion of the briefings, General Bonesteel stated that he preferred the LRRP communications concept. The Corps Signal Officer raised an objection, but before he could go any further General Bonesteel raised his hand for silence and stated, "If I am not mistaken, I am the commander of this Corps." Then he proceeded to inform the Corps Signal Officer that the communications concept proposed by the LRRP Company was the same system he used in WWII when he was in the OSS. Within a short time the patrols and base stations became highly proficient in their operation. During the next VII Corps exercise, the employed LRRPs were pitted against the Army's new airborne Side Looking Radar (SLR) system. The outcome: reconnaissance patrols averaged a return of information to the VII Corps' TOC (Tactical Operations Center) 20 minutes to one hour before the SLR information was received. This record made a believer out of the Corps G-2 Section and General Bonesteel, who was already an avid supporter of the LRRP concept.

It was during the break-up of General Bonesteel's Commanders Conference, when he supported the LRRP's communications concept, that the Corps G-1 locked my heels together because I had forgotten and had worn our maroon beret to the meeting. During his lecture on the fallacy of wearing unauthorized headgear, General Bonesteel happened to come out of the conference room at that time and tapped me on the right shoulder and stated, "Captain Bingham, I like your headgear." Needless to say, that ended the G-1's conversation and from that time on we wore our berets. It was some time later that the US Army finally approved the maroon berets for airborne soldiers.

Upon General Bonesteel's departure from VII Corps, to assume command of the Seventh US Army in Europe, he still maintained his association and support of LRRP activities. Upon my departure from the LRRP Company in October 1962, the Corps G-2 Section threw a farewell party for me at the Officer's Club and, much to their surprise, the Seventh Army Commander, General Bonesteel, showed up for the occasion. This was a distinct honor for my wife and me as he spent some time talking with us. Serving with airborne soldiers in the VII Corps LRRP Company (Airborne) and serving with the Airborne Brigade, 1st Cavalry Division in Vietnam in 1966 and 1967 have been the highlight of my 25 years of military service. AIRBORNE!

It should be pointed out that Colonel Bingham did it the hard way – up through the enlisted ranks of the Marine Corps! He came to the company as a leg signal officer, with the understanding that he would go to jump school as many of us did, in Wiesbaden. Colonel Bingham jumped at the LRRP reunion in 2003 at Fort Campbell, Kentucky.

# THE VIETNAM WAR

The following section is provided courtesy of the 75th Ranger Regiment Public Affairs Office:

With the growing United States involvement in the Vietnam War during the 1960s, Rangers were again required. The 75th Infantry was reorganized once more on January 1, 1969, as a parent regiment under the Combat Arms Regimental System. Fifteen separate Ranger companies were formed from this reorganization. Thirteen served in Vietnam until inactivation on August 15, 1972.

Ranger companies, consisting of highly motivated volunteers, served with distinction in Vietnam from the Mekong Delta to the Demilitarized Zone. Assigned to independent brigade, division, and field force units, they conducted long-range reconnaissance and exploitation operations into enemy-held and denied areas, providing valuable combat intelligence. The companies assumed the assets of the Long Range Patrol (LRP) units, some of which had been in existence in Vietnam since 1967. They served until the withdrawal of American troops. An Indiana National Guard Unit, Company D, 151st Infantry (Ranger), also experienced combat in Vietnam.

At the end of the war in Vietnam, Ranger companies were deactivated, and their members were dispersed among the various units of the Army. Many men went to the 82nd Airborne Division at Fort Bragg, North Carolina. However, two Long Range Reconnaissance Patrol (LRRP) units were retained in the force structure. Transferred to the Army National Guard (D/151st, Indiana and G/143rd, Texas), they were designated as Infantry Airborne Ranger Companies.

This history deals with the activities, personnel, and accomplishments of the 75th Infantry (Ranger) Regiment companies during the period February 1, 1969, to October 15, 1974, and makes reference to the units who preceded the designation of the 75th Infantry (Ranger).

Throughout history, the need for a small, highly trained, far-ranging unit to perform reconnaissance surveillance, target acquisition, and special-type combat missions has been readily apparent. In Vietnam this need was met by instituting a Long Range Patrol program to provide each major combat unit with this special capability. Rather than create an entirely new unit designation for such an elite force, the Department of the Army looked to its rich and varied heritage and on February 1, 1969 designated the 75th Infantry Regiment; the present successor to the famous 5307th Composite Unit (Merrill's Marauders), as the parent organization for LRP units, and the parenthetical designation (Ranger) in lieu of (LRP) for these units. As a result, the Long Range Patrol Companies and Detachments (LRP): formally the Long Range Reconnaissance Patrol (LRRP) (Provisional) assigned to the major Army commands in the Republic of Vietnam, became the 75th Infantry (Ranger) Regiment.

Soon after arriving in Vietnam the commanders of the divisions and separate brigades realized the need for an elite reconnaissance element to provide the combat intelligence needed to accomplish the mission of finding a very elusive enemy that fought a sustained battle when and where it chose.

The Department of the Army had authorized a company-sized reconnaissance element at corps level throughout the US Army but the personnel and equipment had never been assigned to the corps-level command. In fact the only corps-level reconnaissance elements that existed were the V Corps' and VII Corps' Long Range Reconnaissance companies that were stationed in Germany. These units had the primary mission of a stay-behind force that would provide the corps-level command with the intelligence needed after the allied forces had withdrawn from West Germany. The reconnaissance teams would report on enemy troop movements and tactical deployment of the enemy forces.

With the escalation of the Vietnam War, each division and separate brigade stationed in the Republic of Vietnam (RVN) formed a LRRP unit. Many variations of organizational make-up characterized this ad hoc form of unit. Each brigade commander organized the LRRP to suit the needs of his command and the Tactical Area Of Operational Responsibility (TAOR). Command and Control was decentralized and given to the brigade commanders who asked for volunteers from the infantry units assigned to the brigade.

These units lacked peacetime schooling and had no Department of the Army approved Table of Organization and Equipment (TO&E). The leaders were the officers and NCOs who previously had attended the Ranger Course or the Reconnaissance Commando (Recondo) schools of the 101st Airborne Division and 82nd Airborne Division or the Jungle Operations Center in Panama. These units were functional for the period of May 1965 to December 1967. In December 1967 the Department of the Army authorized the formation of the

Long Range Patrol (LRP) companies and detachments who absorbed the personnel of the previously unauthorized Long Range Reconnaissance Patrol (Provisional) units.

The Vietnam-era South Vietnamese Rangers, Biet Dong-Quan (BDQ), Long Range Reconnaissance Patrol, Long Range Patrol, and Ranger Units were led by US Army Ranger Advisors: Military Assistance Advisory Group (MAAG) 1960–62 and Military Assistance Command Vietnam (MAC V) 1962–73.

## UNIT MAJOR COMMAND

Co. D, 17th Infantry (LRP) V Corps Federal Republic of Germany
Co. C, 58th Infantry (LRP) VII Corps Federal Republic of Germany
Co. E, 20th Infantry (LRP) I Field Force Vietnam
Co. F, 51st Infantry (LRP) II Field Force Vietnam
Co. D, 151st Infantry (LRP) II Field Force Vietnam
Co. E, 50th Infantry (LRP) 9th Infantry Division
Co. F, 50th Infantry (LRP) 25th Infantry Division
Co. E, 51st Infantry (LRP) 23rd Infantry Division

### DEFINITIONS OF LRRP/LRP/RANGER AND BDQ UNITS

**South Vietnamese Ranger Units Biet Dong-Quan (BDQ):**
A counter-guerrilla force of light companies trained and led by US Army Ranger advisors whose unit mission was primarily to conduct patrols, raids, and ambushes. They were also used as reaction forces for regular Vietnamese units.

**Long Range Reconnaissance Patrol (LRRP)/Long Range Patrol (LRP):**
A company or detachment assigned or attached to a major army command that specialized in reconnaissance and was tasked by the commander to conduct specialized patrols, raids, ambushes, and prisoner-snatch missions within or behind enemy lines up to 50km from the nearest friendly forces. The Long Range Reconnaissance Patrol (LRRP) and Long Range Patrol (LRP) teams operated in four- to 12-man teams with a typical team consisting of six men.

**Ranger Company:**
A company assigned or attached to a major Army command that specialized in reconnaissance and was tasked by the commander to conduct specialized patrols, raids, ambushes, and prisoner-snatch missions within or behind enemy lines up to 50km from the nearest friendly forces. The Ranger team operated in four- to 12-man teams with a typical team consisting of six men.

**ABOVE**
A painting commemorating the exploits of the Long Range Reconnaissance Patrol. (USASOC)

Co. E, 52nd Infantry (LRP) 1st Cavalry Division
Co. F, 52nd Infantry (LRP) 1st Infantry Division
Co. E, 58th Infantry (LRP) 4th Infantry Division
Co. F, 58th Infantry (LRP) 101st Airborne Division
71st Infantry Detachment (LRP) 199th Infantry Brigade
74th Infantry Detachment (LRP) 173rd Airborne Brigade
78th Infantry Detachment (LRP) 3rd Brigade, 82nd Airborne Division
79th Infantry Detachment (LRP) 1st Brigade, 5th Mechanized Division

These units continued to operate throughout the four Military Regions of the RVN, providing the major commands with the intelligence needed to find the enemy and disrupt his lines of communication and supply. The mission designator of "Reconnaissance" was dropped as these units performed not only reconnaissance-type missions but also combat missions such as ambush, prisoner snatches, and raids.

Each individual unit conducted its own training and indoctrination classes. On February 1, 1969, the above units became 75th Infantry (Ranger) companies except for D Company, 151st Infantry (LRP) of the Indiana National Guard, which not only dropped the (LRP) designation but added the (Ranger) designation. The Department of the Army ordered that the above shown units would now be designated as shown below.

## UNIT MAJOR COMMAND PERIOD OF SERVICE

Co. A (Ranger), 75th Infantry Ft Benning / Ft Hood Feb 1, 1969–Oct 15, 1974
Co. B (Ranger), 75th Infantry Ft Carson / Ft Lewis Feb 1, 1969–Oct 15, 1974
Co. C (Ranger), 75th Infantry I Field Force Vietnam Feb 1, 1969–Oct 25, 1971
Co. D (Ranger), 151st Infantry II Field Force Vietnam Feb 1, 1969–Nov 20, 1969

### 75TH INFANTRY (RANGER) REGIMENT, VIETNAM ENTITLEMENTS

*Campaign Streamers, Vietnam*
 Counteroffensive Phase VI
 Tet 69 Counteroffensive
 Summer–Fall 1969
 Winter–Spring 1969
 Sanctuary Counteroffensive
 Counteroffensive Phase VII
 Consolidation I
 Consolidation II
 Cease Fire
*Decorations, Vietnam*
 RVN Gallantry Cross w/Palm – 23 Awards
 RVN Civil Actions Honor Medal – 10 Awards
 US Valorous Unit Award – 6 Awards
 US Meritorious Unit Commendation – 2 Awards

Co. D (Ranger), 75th Infantry II Field Force Vietnam Nov 20, 1969–Apr 10, 1970
Co. E (Ranger), 75th Infantry 9th Infantry Division Feb 1, 1969–Oct 12, 1970
Co. F (Ranger), 75th Infantry 25th Infantry Division Feb 1, 1969–Mar 15, 1971
Co. G (Ranger), 75th Infantry 23rd Infantry Division Feb 1, 1969–Oct 1, 1971
Co. H (Ranger), 75th Infantry 1st Cavalry Division Feb 1, 1969–Aug 15, 1972
Co. I (Ranger), 75th Infantry 1st Infantry Division Feb 1, 1969–Apr 7, 1970
Co. K (Ranger), 75th Infantry 4th Infantry Division Feb 1, 1969–Dec 10, 1970
Co. L (Ranger), 75th Infantry 101st Airmobile Division Feb 1, 1969–Dec 25, 1971
Co. M (Ranger), 75th Infantry 199th Infantry Brigade Feb 1, 1969–Oct 12, 1970
Co. N (Ranger), 75th Infantry 173rd Airborne Brigade Feb 1, 1969–Aug 25, 1971
Co. O (Ranger), 75th Infantry 3rd Brigade 82nd Abn. Feb 1, 1969–Division
Nov 20, 1969
Co. P (Ranger), 75th Infantry 1st Brigade, 5th Mech. Feb 1, 1969–Division
Aug 31, 1971

The above Ranger companies of the 75th Infantry conducted combat Ranger missions and operations for three years and seven months, every day of the year while in Vietnam, and companies A, B, and O performed Ranger missions stateside for five years and eight months. Like the original unit from whence their lineage as neo-Marauders was drawn, 75th Rangers came from the Infantry, Artillery, Engineers, Signal Medical Military Police, Food Service, Parachute Riggers, and other Army units. They were joined by former adversaries, the Vietcong and North Vietnamese Army soldiers who became "Kit Carson Scouts" and fought alongside the Rangers against their former units and comrades.

Unlike Rangers of other eras in the 20th century who trained in the United States or in friendly nations overseas, Rangers in Vietnam were activated, trained, and fought in the same geographical areas, a high-speed approach to training. Training was a combat mission for volunteers. Volunteers were assigned and not accepted in the various Ranger companies until after a series of patrols in which the volunteer passed the acid test of a Ranger, combat. Only then was he accepted by his peers. Following peer acceptance, the volunteer was allowed to wear the black beret and red, white, and black scroll shoulder sleeve insignia bearing his Ranger company identity. All Ranger companies were authorized for parachute pay.

*Modus operandi* for patrol insertion varied; however, the helicopter was the primary means for insertion and exfiltration of enemy rear areas. Other methods included foot, wheeled or tracked vehicles, airboats, Navy swift boats, and stay-behind missions where the Rangers stayed in place as a larger tactical unit withdrew. False insertions by helicopter were a means of security from ever-present enemy trail watchers. General missions consisted of locating the enemy bases and lines of communication. Special missions included wiretap, prisoner snatch, platoon and company-sized raid missions and Bomb Damage Assessments (BDAs) following B-52 Arc Light missions, as well as the ambush mission that was common after the Ranger team had performed its primary mission.

Staffed principally by graduates of the US Army Ranger School Paratroopers and Special Forces trained men, the bulk of the Ranger volunteers came from the soldiers who had no chance to attend the school, but who carried the fight to the enemy. Rangers in the grade of E-4 to E-6 controlled fire from the USS *New Jersey*'s 16in. guns in addition to that from helicopter gunships and piston-engine and high-performance aircraft. They frequently operated far beyond conventional artillery and infiltrated enemy base camps, capturing prisoners or conducting other covert operations. The six-man Ranger team was standard and a 12-man unit was used for combat patrols in most instances. However some units operated occasionally in two-man teams in order to accomplish the mission.

# COMPANY N (RANGER), 75TH INFANTRY

The following history of this unit and the mission performed by Team Delta under Staff Sergeant Patrick Tadina is provided by Roy Boatman, N/75.

This history deals with the activities, personnel, and accomplishments of Company N (Ranger), 75th Infantry, during the period February 1, 1969, through August 25, 1971, and makes reference to the units who preceded the designation of Company N (Ranger), 75th Infantry.

Following the creation of the 75th Infantry Regiment, the 74th Infantry Detachment (LRP), formerly the 173rd Airborne Brigade Separate (LRRP) (Provisional) assigned to the 173rd Airborne Brigade (Separate), became Company N (Ranger), 75th Infantry.

The 173rd Airborne Brigade (Separate) deployed to the Republic of Vietnam on May 5, 1965, on Temporary Duty [TDY] status, and was the first army "combat" maneuver element to arrive in Vietnam. On 5 August 1965 the TDY status was changed to Permanent Change of Station [PCS]. It quickly became apparent to Brigadier General Ellis W. Williamson that a reconnaissance element was needed to supplement Troop E, 17th

Company N (Ranger), 75th Infantry. (Pat Tadina)

Cavalry, who were mounted troops and had the mission of providing road security and were ill equipped or poorly trained to perform dismounted reconnaissance missions. General Williamson tasked the 1st and 2nd Battalions of the 503rd Infantry to ask for "Volunteers" to form the Long Range Reconnaissance Patrol (LRRP) detachment.

The volunteers would not be permanently assigned to the LRRP detachment as there was no Table of Organization and Equipment [TOE]. The LRRP (Provisional) was formed from volunteers from the infantry battalions and placed on Special Duty [SD] status. Team makeup consisted of one lieutenant (team leader), one staff sergeant (assistant team leader), and two enlisted personnel (scouts). Training was given to the LRRPs by the 1st Royal Australian Regiment who were familiar with jungle operations and were veterans of combat operations in Malaysia. The LRRP detachment could not be maintained at full strength (four teams/16 personnel) due to combat losses of the infantry battalions who requested that their SD personnel be returned. The first Long Range Patrol operation was in support of Operation *New Life* in the La Nga River valley north of Vo Dat on November 21, 1965. The teams had to twice swim rivers to get in to their Area of Operations [AO]. Many of the operational techniques learned during actual combat patrols became standard operating procedure [SOP] for the personnel who became replacements for those troops returning to stateside assignments after their one year tour of duty. Lieutenants were no longer assigned as team members and the patrol leaders were the experienced non-commissioned officers of the LRRP detachment.

The LRRP detachment became a permanent part of Troop E, 17th Cavalry, in June 1966. Many of the original members of the LRRP platoon

A typical Ranger team, probably in 1968. Pat Tadina is on the far left, and top right was identified as Medal of Honor recipient Laszlo Rabel. (Pat Tadina)

were trained at the 101st Airborne Division RECONDO school at Ft. Campbell, KY. Additional training of the volunteers was On the Job Training [OJT] and at the RECONDO school at Nha Trang. Many of these volunteers never had the chance to attend any formal training as the 173rd Airborne Brigade was constantly on operations throughout the III Corps and II Corps areas of the RVN. However, infiltration and extraction techniques were refined and were SOPs for the duration of the LRRP's operations in Vietnam.

The misnomer that was in the mission statement for LRRPs was the word "Reconnaissance." Many of the missions given to the LRRPs were of a combat nature. The major unit commander had a highly trained and motivated force on the ground which had located an enemy force of various sizes and had the opportunity to inflict casualties upon a elusive enemy. The commander frequently utilized this option. Teams were typically briefed that when their mission of surveillance was completed they would ambush or capture a prisoner on the last day of their mission. Occasionally the LRRPs would receive an ambush or snatch mission as their primary mission.

The Department of the Army officially authorized the formation of the 74th Infantry Detachment (LRP) on December 20, 1967, and all personnel of the LRRP platoon were absorbed into this unit. The 173rd Airborne Brigade had moved to Dak To in the II Corps area of Vietnam. The 74th Infantry Detachment (LRP) was awarded the Presidential Unit Citation for its actions during the Dak To battles in November 1967; however, this was in error as the 74th Infantry Detachment (LRP) did not exist at the time. The award should have been presented to the 173rd

Airborne Brigade (LRRP) (Provisional). The 74th Infantry (LRP) continued to perform missions as directed by the 173rd commander through out the II Corp region of Vietnam and eventually established a base camp at An Khe.

Team leaders and potential team leaders were now able to attend the RECONDO school conducted by the Special Forces at Nha Trang on a rotating basis while continuing to be the "Eyes and Ears of the Commander." Staff Sergeant Laszlo Rabel, 74th Infantry Detachment (LRP) was awarded the Medal of Honor for his actions on November 12, 1968. He was the only LRP member to be awarded the medal during the Vietnam War. Much credit needs to be given to the personnel of the LRRP platoon and the 74th Infantry Detachment (LRP) for establishing the doctrine that would become SOP for Company N (Ranger), 75th Infantry, which absorbed the personnel of the 74th Infantry Detachment (LRP) on February 1, 1969. Company N

## COMPANY N (RANGER), 75TH INFANTRY IS ENTITLED TO THE FOLLOWING:

Campaign Streamers:
*Vietnam*
> Counteroffensive Phase VI
> Tet 69 Counteroffensive
> Summer–Fall 1969
> Winter–Spring 1969
> Sanctuary Counteroffensive
> Counteroffensive Phase VII
> Consolidation I
> Consolidation II
> Cease Fire

Decorations:
*Vietnam*:
> RVN Gallantry Cross w/Palm
> RVN Civil Actions Honor Medal

Traditional Designation: November Rangers
Motto: *Sua Sponte* ("Of their own accord")
Distinctive Insignia: The shield of the coat of arms

Symbolism of the coat of arms: The colors: blue, white, red, and green represent four of the original six combat teams of the 5307th Composite Unit (Provisional), which were identified by a color code word. The unit's close cooperation with the Chinese forces in the China-Burma-India Theater is represented by the sun symbol from the Chinese Nationalist Flag. The white star represents the Star of Burma. The lightening bolt is symbolic of the strike characteristics of the behind-the-line activities.

(Ranger), 75th Infantry established a base camp at Landing Zone [LZ] English, Bong Son, RVN, from which to launch their deep-penetration missions behind or within enemy-controlled areas.

The 173rd Airborne Brigade had assumed the mission of "pacification" of the Bong Son plains – Company N (Ranger), 75th Infantry, would become a Ranger screen while the brigade was on pacification. The TO&E specified that the "November Rangers" would consist of three officers and 72 enlisted personnel. The assigned officers served as the commander, executive officer, and operations officer. There were 12 operational teams of six men, each composed entirely of enlisted personnel. The remaining enlisted personnel had the duties of platoon sergeant, and as Tactical Operations Center [TOC], supply, and administratio personnel. Missions for the Ranger company were typically three to five days with a two-day break in between for debriefing, rest, and preparation for the next mission. The Rangers were operating in the mountainous terrain of the An Lao, An Do, Suoi Ca, Crows Foot valleys, the Highland Fishhook, and Nui Ba and Tiger mountains of northern Binh Dinh province, which bordered the I Corps area. This area of responsibility was to remain the domain of Company N for the remainder of the war. The brigade Tet 69 campaign lasted from February 9 to March 26, 1969, and marked the first independent employment of a Ranger company in screening operations of the Vietnam War.

During this period which was typical of ranger operations, Company N conducted over 100 Long Range Patrols that resulted in 134 sightings of enemy personnel and 63 enemy killed by direct action, plus five prisoners and a much larger number of enemy killed by ranger-sponsored indirect fire and reaction elements. The Rangers' casualties for this period were one KIA, 20 WIA, and none captured or missing. In November 1969 the brigade permanently increased the size of the company to full company strength of 128 Rangers. Acceptance into the Rangers was based upon factors of a GT score of 100 or higher, no physical or mental impairments and voluntary request for the Ranger company. All prospective personnel were interviewed prior to acceptance and full acceptance was not granted until the volunteer had completed a period of individual training conducted by the company and had participated in a few patrols to prove his abilities. Training was a combat mission for volunteers.

Company N, (Ranger), 75th Infantry, received numerous experimental systems to maximize performance. Numbers of 9mm pistols with silencers were sent to the company from civilian firms in the United States; these were used to take out the North Vietnamese Army/Viet Cong [NVA/VC] sentries that guarded base camps and way stations. An experimental system for firing electronically detonated Claymores that were daisy chained (Widow Makers) became a staple of Ranger ambushes. Company N personnel were called upon to conduct special contingency missions such as the Bright Light mission of prisoner rescue and the destruction of the VC infrastructure throughout Binh Dinh province. During April 1971, the brigade commander finally put the unofficial black beret on a Ranger's head during a ceremony that honored the men of the Ranger company for an earlier action. The beret had been denied the Rangers primarily because of senior officer opposition to further distinctions between unit paratroopers. On August 25, 1971, Company N (Ranger), 75th Infantry was solemnly deactivated. The Rangers of Company N performed with exceptional courage and valor throughout their existence and service in Vietnam, a period totalling two years and six months. Today, the modern Rangers of the 75th Ranger Regiment continue the traditions of being the premier fighting element of the active army.

# ONE MISSION BY THE QUIET PROFESSIONALS

Below are the details of one 1969 mission undertaken by the Rangers in Vietnam.

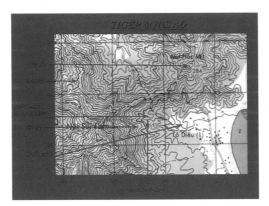

**Team Delta**
Team Leader SSG Tadina
Assistant TL SSG Fowler
RTO SP/4 Stankowitz
Scout SGT Campbell
Scout SP/4 Nisby
Scout Kit Carson Thon

Company N (Ranger)
75th Infantry
173rd ABN BDE (SEP)

### Sequence of Events
Warning Order given 17 September 1969 and visual recon (UHID) in the afternoon.
Situation: Enemy has been using coastline along Lo Dieu villages to conduct ambushes along QL1 and has politically assassinated village chiefs and other civilians.
Mission: Recon, search and ambush VC/NVA moving from Lo Dieu villages (I, II, III)
Execution: Infil a Ranger team for four days on 18 September 1969.

### Actions before Insertion (Team SOP)
Company Commander and Operations Officer brief the Team Leader on the mission. Team Leader gives warning order to the team and the ATL is in charge of weapons and equipment.
ATL draws any special equipment needed for mission from the supply sergeant. Team Leader and ATL and Operations NCO/Platoon Sergeant go to helipad for visual reconnaissance flight of AO.
Team Leader and Insertion NCO fly border/perimeter of AO. TL is looking for a good insertion LZ and likely route of march and extraction LZ. TL tells pilot where the LZ is and requests a specific approach to LZ for the insertion the next day. Pilot returns to helipad and coordinates the time of insertion.

TL goes to artillery Liaison at Brigade TOC and pre-plots any defensive targets (DT) and checks to see if artillery coverage is possible.

TL returns to company area and draws overlay of AO (3 copies), showing insertion LZ, possible route of march, preplanned artillery fires on call, E&E rally point and extraction LZ. Distribution: 1-Company TOC, 2-BDE TOC, 3-Artillery Liaison.

Team moves to firing range to practice Immediate Action Drill and test-fire weapons.

Team Leader and Assistant Team Leader inspect each team member's gear.

**Team Equipment**
PRC 25 Radio – RTO
Extra hand-set – TL
Long antenna – RTO
URC 10 – TL
Signal mirror – TL & ATL
Field glasses – TL
Batteries PRC 25 (2)
Maps – TL & ATL
KAC code – TL & RTO
Freqs – TL & RTO
Strobe light – TL

**Weapons**
1 AK-47 (150 rounds) – TL
3 M16 (300 rounds) – ATL & 2 scouts
1 .22 caliber Pistol (silenced) 20 rounds – TL
1 CAR 15 (300 rounds) – RTO
1 AK-47 & M79 – Scout
5 Frags per man (minimum)
2 Smoke per man (minimum)
2 CS tear gas (TL & ATL)
2 white phosphorus – TL & ATL
2 pen flares – TL & ATL
6 claymores

**Individual equipment**
Ground cloth & poncho liner
Normal LBE
Rucksack
Two-Quart canteens (2)
One-Quart canteen (1)
Swiss seat with snap link (1)
Morphine surest (2)
Albunum blood expander (1)
Camouflage stick (1)
Air panel, orange (1)

Indigenous or LRP rations
Knife (K-bar or survival)
Pill kit (Darvon, Dex, anti-diarrhea, malaria, anti-stomach cramp)

### Conduct of Mission (TL's notes)

1. Infil at 171700 HRS, 17 September 1969: made pass to confirm PLZ. PLZ (BR 963945)

2. Moved to the OP using primary route. Trail along hill top 400 SE to NW is being used by enemy. Trail junction grid (BR 947954) is booby trapped with 2 (two) 105 mm rounds on North side of trail. Reset booby traps to detonate at approximately 181200 HRS if enemy does not trip before then.

3. Establish OP at 2030 HRS (BR 954951). Observed area until 2200 HRS noticed lights moving from (BR 961955) to Lo Dieu (1). Can't ID (too dark), lights about 75 meters apart, might be point and drag lights. Will not engage with artillery, will give enemy freedom of movement for later ambush. 0330 HRS movement from Lo Dieu (1) back to (BR 961955). Might be same group, lights same as before. Enemy did not move over pass (BR 955963). Can observe at that coordinates, might be base camp or way station between Lo Dieu (1) and pass, possible base camp at (BR 957957). Will check at daylight. 180830 HRS observed two VC/NVA moving on trail at (BR 955963). Wpns (2 AKs), Black PJs, no rucks. 1000HRS. did not resight VC/NVA, they had enough time to get to Lo Dieu (1). 1030 HRS, contacted TOC, moving to possible base camp.

4. 1130 HRS, found base camp water point at (BR 957956) as I came into view of water point, I knew camp was near. The trail leading away from the water point was well used all indicators point to a sizeable camp. We could hear them talking. I prepared team for assault, Campbell and Nisby on my right, Thon and Fowler on my left and Stankowitz to the rear, as we move to the top of the knoll, I could see a bunker on the left side of the trail. Two VC/NVA were sitting on the top of the bunker with their backs towards me. Hand signaled to team not to fire, I would take out sentries with silenced .22 cal pistol. Eliminated both sentries with headshots. (2 weapons; 1 RPD and 1 AK-47). Moved to hootch on top of knoll, 4 VC/NVA in hootch (classroom), intended to capture (weapons stacked outside), captured all four, now POWs. Three VC/NVA came from the east and Campbell killed all three with M79 and M16. Could now see main base camp (4 hootches and approx. 10–15 VC/NVA were in camp and we were now receiving fire. TL used captured RPD to suppress enemy fire and enemy broke contact and fled north on trail. Had no commo with TOC so did not search the dead, moved along trail with POWs to LZ at (BR 964954), used recon by fire on move to extraction LZ. Came under fire from ridgeline to the north. Enemy was moving back towards my position. Rigged a daisy chained claymore at 150 meters from PZ and moved back to PZ, saw 10–12 VC/NVA at claymore site and engaged with claymores and RPD with unknown results, no more enemy fire. Still no commo. At 1330 HRS, RTO made contact with the CC aircraft and gunships. Gunships

Patrick Tadina served for 60 consecutive months in Vietnam, never losing a single man in action. He represents the epitome of the professional NCO. (Pat Tadina)

worked the base camp area. 13245 HRS, slick came in for extraction, sent ATL, 2 scouts and 4 POWs out on the slick. At 1415 HRS, slick on short final and base camp on fire. Extracted at 1415 HRS. TL's note: During the contact the preset booby traps fired around 1200 HRS.

Debriefed at Brigade TOC: Results: 4 POWs, 5KIAs, 1RPD CIA, 8AKs CIA. No other KIAs could be confirmed due to the enemy presence in the base camp.

# RANGER HALL OF FAME NOMINATION

Below is one of many letters nominating Rangers active during the Vietnam War for induction to the Ranger Hall of Fame.

RANGER RICHARD EHRLER is nominated for selection to the Ranger Hall of Fame by the 75th Ranger Regiment Association Inc. for his valorous service to his country during the VietNam War and for his long time service and dedication to the Ranger community. I think you will find Ranger Ehrler is a well qualified candidate and most deserving of this honor.

Ranger Richard (Rick) Ehrler was drafted into the military service at the age of 19 from Ft. Lauderdale Florida on October 19, 1967. Ranger Ehrler arrived in the Republic of VietNam trained as a light weapons infantryman and promptly volunteered for E. Company, 50th Infantry, (Airborne) (Long Range Patrol), 9th Inf. Div. Upon his acceptance into the Company in April of 1968 he quickly advanced from scout to assistant team leader to team leader. E Company, 50th Infantry, which would later become E/75th Rangers was assigned one of the most difficult areas for small unit operations in the IV Corp area of Vietnam known as the Delta. This unit was the only Army unit to work with the Navy Seals and received support from elements of the Brown Water Navy.

Ranger Ehrler's actions of the night of 27 January, 1969, reflected great credit upon himself, E. Company and the Ranger Community. His actions were demonstrative of the Ranger Creed well before it was written. As a Team Leader of Team Savage Assault 17 Ranger Ehrler and the other 5 members of his team found themselves surrounded by a vastly superior force of over 60 Viet Cong and North Vietnamese Regulars.

In the initial seconds of a battle that was forever to change his life Sergeant Ehrler saw two of his men killed, effectively reducing the team a full one-third.

"Never shall I fail my comrades."

Sergeant Ehrler, in an effort to put effective fire on the enemy, exposed himself to murderous fire and in that maneuver was wounded by a rocket propelled grenade that detonated 3 feet in front of him. The blast throwing him across the hooch and blinding him in the process. He crawled and found his radio to keep contact with the gunships flying out to support the team and with the Artillery battery on stand by. At this point another explosion occurred and another team member was thrown across the hooch. Ranger Ehrler attended to this mortally wounded team member as he worked to keep his team in communication with the gunships that were on the way. After about 15 minutes of heavy fighting the team was low on ammo.

"Surrender is not a Ranger word."

Ranger Ehrler handed out what ammunition was left and kept one grenade just in case they were overrun. Ranger Ehrler made the decision that they would never surrender. Sgt. Ehrler called once again for the gunships and advised those listening that in a few more minutes they would only need to send graves registration as a reaction force.

"I will never leave a fallen comrade to fall into the hands of the enemy..."

Shortly after the gunships arrived and Sgt. Ehrler marked his position with a strobe light he then advised the remaining two team members that they came in as a team and would leave as a team. At this point an extraction Huey came in and with Sgt Ehrler carrying the mortally wounded team member and holding on to the web gear of a team member who was carrying the body of another member they made their way to the extraction ship. The firing of the enemy was so suppressed that he made the decision to secure the team equipment also. All members of the team and equipment were extracted thanks to the courage demonstrated by Ranger Ehrler.

For his actions that night Ranger Ehrler was awarded the Silver Star, his second Purple Heart and the Vietnamese Cross of Gallantry.

Richard's demonstrations of determination and courage did not stop that night in RVN. After his retirement for medical reasons Richard went to college and obtained a degree in Computer Programming. Richard lived in Florida, California, Nevada and finally settled in Boise, Idaho in 1980.

In Boise Richard met and married Linda Sanderson in 1981. Linda was the light of his life and in 1985 she was diagnosed with a rare disease that slowly destroyed her heart and lungs. Linda passed away in 1987.

Others, of lesser character, would have been totally destroyed but the Ranger Spirit in Richard would not let that happen. He and his brother in law got together in 1990 to raise money for the American Lung Association by riding a tandem bike through the Sawtooth Mountains of Idaho. This trek is an annual fund raising event and Richard has been the top money raiser since 1990. In 1992 Richard and his brother in law, Steven Sanderson, were named as shining "Point(s) of light" by President Bush.

In 1993 Richard was instrumental in finding many of the members of E/50th and E/75th and holding their first reunion after 25 years. Richard again led the way by chairing the second reunion held in 1995 and finding even more members. This company has held bi-annual reunions thanks to Richard Ehrler.

In 1994 Richard was elected Vice-President of the 75th Ranger Regiment Association Inc. and promptly selected to account for all the members of the Long Range Reconnaissance Patrol Companies, Long Range Patrol Companies, Ranger Companies and Ranger Advisors who were killed in action in Vietnam. In less than one year Richard had accounted for over 95% of the names we now have. In 1996 Richard was elected to the position of President of the 75th Ranger Regiment Association Inc. During Richard's tenure bricks for the Ranger Memorial have been purchased and instaled for all the KIAs. This is over 380 bricks.

Richard has not let his disability stop him. This Ranger has traveled to numerous countries including Australia, Germany, Switzerland, Russia and VietNam. He enjoys bike riding, skiing and has made a tandem freefall. Richard has demonstrated that Rangers Lead the Way!

# MEDAL OF HONOR – THE FIRST AND ONLY ONES

Ranger Recipients of the Medal of Honor (*Posthumously Awarded)
  Robert D. Law*
  Gary L. Littrell
  Robert J. Pruden*
  Laszlo Rabel*
The Medal of Honor is the highest military medal awarded by the United States. The individuals presented here as recipients served in a unit contributing to the lineage of the 75th Ranger Regiment.

Rangers awarded the Medal of Honor for their actions in Vietnam. (Duke DuShane)

RANGER
Vietnam
Medal of Honor Recipients

Specialist Four Robert D. Law      22 Feb. 1969    Staff Sergeant Laszlo Rabel      13 Nov. 1968   Staff Sergeant Robert J. Pruden      29 Nov. 1969
Company I. (RANGER) 75th Infantry                  74th Infantry Detachment. Long Range Patrol     Company G. (RANGER) 75th Infantry
1st Infantry Division                              173rd Airborne Brigade                          23rd Infantry Division (AMERICAL)

## Law, Robert D.

Rank and organization: Specialist Fourth Class, US Army, Company I (Ranger), 75th Infantry, 1st Infantry Division
Place and date: Tinh Phuoc Thanh province, Republic of Vietnam, 22 February 1969
Entered service at: Dallas, Texas
Born: 15 September 1944, Fort Worth, Texas
Citation: For conspicuous gallantry and intrepidity in action at the risk of his life above and beyond the call of duty. Sp4c Law distinguished himself while serving with Company I. While on a long-range reconnaissance patrol in Tinh Phuoc Thanh province, Sp4c Law and 5 comrades made contact with a small enemy patrol. As the opposing elements exchanged intense fire, he maneuvered to a perilously exposed position flanking his comrades and began placing suppressive fire on the hostile troops. Although his team was hindered by a low supply of ammunition and suffered from an unidentified irritating gas in the air, Sp4c Law's spirited defense and challenging counterassault rallied his fellow soldiers against the well-equipped hostile troops. When an enemy grenade landed in his team's position, Sp4c Law, instead of diving into the safety of a stream behind him, threw himself on the grenade to save the lives of his comrades. Sp4c Law's extraordinary courage and profound concern for his fellow soldiers were in keeping with the highest traditions of the military service and reflect great credit on himself, his unit, and the US Army.

## Littrell, Gary Lee

Rank and organization: Sergeant First Class, US Army, Advisory Team 21, II Corps Advisory Group
Place and date: Kontum province, Republic of Vietnam, 4–8 April 1970
Entered service at: Los Angeles, California

Born: 26 October 1944, Henderson, Kentucky

Citation: For conspicuous gallantry and intrepidity in action at the risk of his life above and beyond the call of duty. Sfc Littrell, U.S. Military Assistance Command, Vietnam, Advisory Team 21, distinguished himself while serving as a Light Weapons Infantry Advisor with the 23d Battalion, 2d Ranger Group, Republic of Vietnam Army, near Dak Seang. After establishing a defensive perimeter on a hill on April 4, the battalion was subjected to an intense enemy mortar attack which killed the Vietnamese commander, 1 advisor, and seriously wounded all the advisors except Sfc Littrell. During the ensuing 4 days, Sfc Littrell exhibited near superhuman endurance as he single-handedly bolstered the besieged battalion. Repeatedly abandoning positions of relative safety, he directed artillery and air support by day and marked the unit's location by night, despite the heavy, concentrated enemy fire. His dauntless will instilled in the men of the 23d Battalion a deep desire to resist. Assault after assault was repulsed as the battalion responded to the extraordinary leadership and personal example exhibited by Sfc Littrell as he continuously moved to those points most seriously threatened by the enemy, redistributed ammunition, strengthened faltering defenses, cared for the wounded and shouted encouragement to the Vietnamese in their own language. When the beleaguered battalion was finally ordered to withdraw, numerous ambushes were encountered. Sfc Littrell repeatedly prevented widespread disorder by directing air strikes to within 50 meters of their position. Through his indomitable courage and complete disregard for his safety, he averted excessive loss of life and injury to the members of the battalion. The sustained extraordinary courage and selflessness displayed by Sfc Littrell over an extended period of time were in keeping with the highest traditions of the military service and reflect great credit on him and the U.S. Army.

## Pruden, Robert J.

Rank and organization: Staff Sergeant, U.S. Army, 75th Infantry, Americal Division
Place and date: Quang Ngai province, Republic of Vietnam, 29 November 1969
Entered service at: Minneapolis, Minnesota
Born: 9 September 1949, St. Paul, Minnesota

Citation: For conspicuous gallantry and intrepidity in action at the risk of his life above and beyond the call of duty. S/Sgt Pruden, Company G, distinguished himself while serving as a reconnaissance team leader during an ambush mission. The 6-man team was inserted by helicopter into enemy controlled territory to establish an ambush position and to obtain information concerning enemy movements. As the team moved into the preplanned area, S/Sgt Pruden deployed his men into 2 groups on the opposite sides of a well used trail. As the groups were establishing their defensive positions, 1 member of the team was trapped in the open by the heavy fire from an enemy squad. Realizing that the ambush position had been compromised, S/Sgt Pruden directed his team to open fire on the enemy force. Immediately, the team came under heavy fire from a second enemy element. S/Sgt Pruden, with full knowledge of the extreme danger involved, left his concealed position and, firing as he ran, advanced toward the enemy to draw the hostile fire. He was seriously wounded twice but continued his attack until he fell for a third time, in front of the enemy positions. S/Sgt

Pruden's actions resulted in several enemy casualties and withdrawal of the remaining enemy force. Although grievously wounded, he directed his men into defensive positions and called for evacuation helicopters, which safely withdrew the members of the team. S/Sgt Pruden's outstanding courage, selfless concern for the welfare of his men, and intrepidity in action at the cost of his life were in keeping with the highest traditions of the military service and reflect great credit upon himself, his unit, and the U.S. Army.

## Rabel, Laszlo

Rank and organization: Staff Sergeant, U.S. Army, 74th Infantry Detachment (Long Range Patrol), 173d Airborne Brigade
Place and date: Binh Dinh province, Republic of Vietnam, 13 November 1968
Entered service at: Minneapolis, Minnesota
Born: 21 September 1939, Budapest, Hungary
Citation: For conspicuous gallantry and intrepidity in action at the risk of his life above and beyond the call of duty. S/Sgt Rabel distinguished himself while serving as leader of Team Delta, 74th Infantry Detachment. At 1000 hours on this date, Team Delta was in a defensive perimeter conducting reconnaissance of enemy trail networks when a member of the team detected enemy movement to the front. As S/Sgt Rabel and a comrade prepared to clear the area, he heard an incoming grenade as it landed in the midst of the team's perimeter. With complete disregard for his life, S/Sgt Rabel threw himself on the grenade and, covering it with his body, received the complete impact of the immediate explosion. Through his indomitable courage, complete disregard for his safety and profound concern for his fellow soldiers, S/Sgt Rabel averted the loss of life and injury to the other members of Team Delta. By his gallantry at the cost of his life in the highest traditions of the military service, S/Sgt Rabel has reflected great credit upon himself, his unit, and the U.S. Army.

The established criteria follow:

a. The Medal of Honor [Army], section 3741, title 10, United States Code (10 USC 3741), was established by Joint Resolution of Congress, 12 July 1862 (amended by acts 9 July 1918 and 25 July 1963).

b. The Medal of Honor is awarded by the President in the name of Congress to a person who, while a member of the Army, distinguishes himself or herself conspicuously by gallantry and intrepidity at the risk of his life or her life above and beyond the call of duty while engaged in an action against an enemy of the United States; while engaged in military operations involving conflict with an opposing foreign force; or while serving with friendly foreign forces engaged in an armed conflict against an opposing armed force in which the United States is not a belligerent party. The deed performed must have been one of personal bravery or self-sacrifice so conspicuous as to clearly distinguish the individual above his comrades and must have involved risk of life. Incontestable proof of the performance of the service will be exacted and each recommendation for the award of this decoration will be considered on the standard of extraordinary merit.

From chapters 3–6, Army Regulation 600-8-22 (Military Awards) dated February 25, 1995.

# PART II

# AMERICA'S SMALL WARS

# The Modern Rangers

## America at war

The Ranger companies were mostly deactivated after the Vietnam War. Still reeling from its defeat, with manpower dwindling and its image and reputation tarnished, the US Army was in very bad shape. Drugs and racial problems plagued the military just as they did society as a whole. Atrocities committed during the conflict, including some by high-profile Special Forces-attached personnel, had come to light, and the nation was divided on the necessity of having waged war in the first place. The Cold War was in its third decade, and the 1973 Arab-Israeli War was a reminder to military leadership of the need for a high-quality force capable of deploying to any worldwide hot spot on a moment's notice. It is against this backdrop that the Army created two new units – the 1st and 2nd Battalions, 75th Infantry (Ranger). The 1st Battalion Commander was Lieutenant Colonel Kenneth Leuer; the 2nd Battalion, formed a few months later, began under the command of Lieutenant Colonel A. J. Baker. Leuer was tasked with creating a unit that would be the beginning of the Army's transformation from its badly mauled state, inundated with low morale, to a body capable of executing foreign policy missions on a global scale. The US military needed a bright shining light at the end of the tunnel – *Fiat Lux* [Let there be light].

Kenneth Leuer also wanted to convert the Ranger Department (Ranger Training Brigade – the 4th, 5th, and 6th Battalions) into a second regiment of the 75th Infantry. Fortunately, this did not happen. The new battalions would be staffed by Ranger School qualified NCOs and officers. Like any selection process, it required some time. Other qualified soldiers were sent to Ranger School after having spent some time with the battalions.

**ABOVE**
Little birds carrying members of the 3rd Battalion, 75th Ranger Regiment during training exercises at Fort Benning, Georgia. Note the red clay. (Author's collection)

Most of 1st Battalion's cadre were assembled at Fort Benning, Georgia – the home of the Airborne and Ranger departments. The 1st Battalion, 75th Infantry (Ranger) jumped into Fort Stewart on July 1, 1974, with approximately 180 men. The battalion was allowed an personnel overage of 10 percent to cover for losses, training leaves, and so forth. By August 1, 1974, the battalion was at full strength. Its Table of Organization and Equipment (TO&E) was as follows: one headquarters contingent of 51 personnel, three companies each staffed by seven officers and 172 enlisted men. The battalion would comprise 35 commissioned officers, one warrant officer, and 552 enlisted personnel. They would be equipped with 60mm mortars, and 90mm recoilless rifles, and transportation was limited to two jeeps.[37] It was as light an infantry unit as it could be.

Lieutenant Colonel Leuer and his staff were responsible for a number of Ranger traditions, histories, and lineage, such as Banner Day, an all-day sporting event that pitted every company against each other in sometimes brutish sporting events. "Once a month we would pull in, clean everything up, have a day of athletics," recounts author Ross Hall. "We had a banner that was made up of the six colors of Merrill's six combat teams. Whoever won Banner Day got to carry that on their guidon for a month. It was a big thing."[38]

The 1st Battalion Commander enjoyed free rein on anything and everything and much research was done on Ranger history and lineage. Sergeant Major Neil Gentry was placed in charge of everything related to heraldry and history. He also became the author of the famous Ranger Creed.

The Ranger lineage needed to be sorted out. The LRRP units had been reorganized into Ranger Companies. The United States Army, "believing that it would never again activate Ranger units, had already designated 1st Special Forces as the regimental bearer of the Ranger unit history and honors from World War II and Korea. As an alternate parent unit, the keepers of the Army's organizational history considered the 75th Infantry, which traced its lineage to Merrill's Marauders of World War II fame. The Marauders were a different type of unit from the LRRPs, but they did have a unique character, a distinguished history, and not least, an active veterans' organization. In the end, the Army decided to bestow the Ranger title on the LRRPs and adopt the 75th Infantry as

**BELOW**
Activation of 3rd Ranger Battalion and Regimental HQ. (US Army)

**BELOW RIGHT**
Business cards. locally manufactured, advertising goods for sale. (US Army)

Call on us anytime, anywhere in the world
1st Battalion (RANGER) 75th Inf

# RANGER

We perform the following:

| | | |
|---|---|---|
| RAIDS | SCUBA | HOSTAGES RESCUED |
| RECONS | DEMOLITIONS | POW'S FREED |
| AMBUSHES | PARACHUTE ASSAULTS | EMBASSIES GUARDED |
| SF RESCUED | AIRMOBILES | NUCLEAR OPNS |
| HALO | AIRLANDS | RIVER OPNS |

*YOU'VE SEEN THE REST: HERE'S THE BEST*
Highly Disciplined          Satisfaction Guaranteed          Professional

parent regiment for the new Ranger companies. General Westmoreland signed off on the authorization on December 2, 1968 and the orders went into effect in February 1969."[39] The Merrill's Marauders Colors were held in custody by the Ranger Department after the Special Forces handed them back and now belonged to the Vietnam-era 75th Ranger Companies. In 1973, the Merrill's Marauders presented their colors for the activation of the 1st Battalion, 75th Infantry (Ranger).

The newly minted Rangers adopted a black beret as their official headgear, as it was worn unofficially by Airborne Rangers of the Korean conflict as well as the Ranger Department – all unauthorized (see page 167). The official unit patch would be modeled after that of Darby's Rangers, originally designed by Ranger Rada and the flash, worn on the beret, was based on the six colors used by Merrill's Marauders' combat teams – green, red, khaki, orange, white, and blue. Their uniform was modeled after that worn by the Long Ranger Patrollers – the cammies, camouflaged with slanted pockets.

Ross Hall's interview with now-retired General Leuer reveals some of the finer points of those early days:

> There is no such thing as a written Abrams' Charter. Now, there was no tape recorder, there was nobody taking notes, I've got a little 3x5 card, but I'm listening, I'm not writing. Everything that exists that you see as the Abrams' Charter came out of that room in my head. People have added to it, taken from it, whatever. The things I remember; it'll be the Gold Medal Infantry of the world; they'll be able to do more with their hands and weapons than any other infantry unit in the world. Wherever they go they'll

An excellent photo showing the old khaki uniforms. (Alex Mordine)

## THE RANGER CREED

**R**ecognizing that I volunteered as a Ranger, fully knowing the hazards of my chosen profession, I will always endeavor to uphold the prestige, honor and high esprit de corps of my Ranger Regiment.

**A**cknowledging the fact that a Ranger is a more elite soldier who arrives at the cutting edge of battle by land, sea or air, I accept the fact that as a Ranger my country expects me to move further, faster and fight harder than any other Soldier.

**N**ever shall I fail my comrades. I will always keep myself mentally alert, physically strong and morally straight; I will shoulder more than my share of the task whatever it may be, one hundred percent and then some.

**G**allantly will I show the world that I am a specially selected and well-trained Soldier. My courtesy to superior officers, neatness of dress and care of equipment shall set the example for others to follow.

**E**nergetically will I meet the enemies of my country. I shall defeat them on the field of battle for I am better trained and will fight with all my might. Surrender is not a Ranger word. I will never leave a fallen comrade to fall into the hands of the enemy, and under no circumstances will I ever embarrass my country.

**R**eadily will I display the intestinal fortitude required to fight on to the Ranger objective and complete the mission, though I be the lone survivor.

be recognized for their superior excellence. There will be no hooligans or bums in that organization. If there are it will be disbanded immediately. If, in any way, you disgrace the United States Army or the US as a nation, the commander alone will bear the consequences. There will be a Creed that they will develop, that they will live by, train by, and fight by. In the beginning everybody had to know everything about Ranger history. We were more concerned because we drew our lineage from Merrill's Marauders that we know mostly that. We knew about the WWII Battalions, the Korean War Companies, the Vietnam Companies, but our history was the Marauders – Galahad.

The Coat of Arms (75th Infantry, Ranger) you didn't describe as blue and green. The 75th crest was described as a shield, quartered, vert and azure, with the sun of China in the left hand quadrant, upper, and the star of Burma in the lower right. The star represented the working relationship in that theater of operations (Merrill). The star of China has 13 points, which represents the 13 colonies of China. The lightning bolt, which goes from upper right to lower left, represents the quick-strike characteristics of the Rangers.

[Ross Hall notes that the lightning bolt is also used to signify a bastard unit – one with no parent unit. Subsequent discussions with Phil Piazza, President of the Merrill's Marauders, reveals that the lightning bolt represents the Marauders' long-range penetration between India and China and that they were originally known as Commandos during their training period in India.][40]

You had to know that on January 30, 1974, that General Order, I believe it was 131, was the order that started the Ranger Battalion. You had to know that General Creighton Abrams was the father of the original Ranger Battalion. These are things you had to learn in the first area [era].

According to a 75th Ranger Regiment PAO document, "On January 25, 1974, Headquarters, United States Army Forces Command, published General Orders 127, directing the activation of the 1st Battalion (Ranger), 75th Infantry, with an effective date of January 31, 1974. In February, the worldwide selection had begun and personnel assembled at Fort Benning, Georgia, to undergo the cadre training from March through June 1974. The 2nd Battalion (Ranger), 75th Infantry soon followed with activation on October 1, 1974. These elite units eventually established headquarters at Hunter Army Airfield, Georgia, and Fort Lewis, Washington, respectively."[41]

**BELOW LEFT**
Copy of an early recruiting brochure. (Tim Abell)

**BELOW**
Back of the brochure. (Tim Abell)

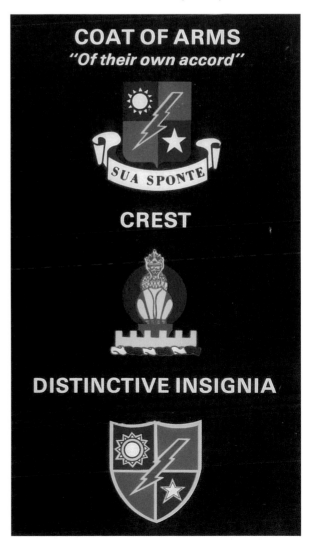

Rangers were hard; the pool of men included all economic demographics, but what set them apart from the regular Army was their individual toughness, their desire to be the best, just like the first Rangers who hunted and patrolled colonial America. They were rugged individuals who wanted to succeed and yet work within a team environment – for the good of all. This type of individual still makes up the rank and file of the 75th Ranger Regiment. The handful of original Rangers would set the standard for all future Rangers.

Ranger Tim Abell, who joined the Rangers within a few years of the creation of this new elite light infantry unit, recalls his early days as a Ranger in the 2nd Battalion. He also chronicles the differences between them and the regular Army in Europe whose purpose was to counter any Warsaw Pact threat. His story is important in that it demonstrates everything that is to follow in the history of the modern Rangers. Hard training, discipline, the desire to excel, and a fierce competitive edge – trademarks that few soldiers possessed, in an army whose standards had fallen below acceptable levels. The creation of the modern Airborne Rangers at this time was far more important than it would have been during any other time in America's history – it was meant to re-instill a fighting spirit, a discipline, and a pride in the maligned uniform of the United States soldier post-Vietnam.

My new squad gave me the lowdown on the Battalion life, RIP, Pre-Ranger, Ranger School and what was expected of me for the most part; aside from massive beer consumption of course.

Always have your Ranger coin handy, or suffer the consequences, which means, even when you're in the shower, you better have your coin tucked neatly in your ass crack just in case. Penalties ranged from buying beer for all those in your AO to a swift punch and pummel to 50 push-ups. Wear your uniform and especially your beret with extreme pride wherever you go. Starched Vietnam-era slant pocket cammies, with your starched cammie pant-legs wrapper around your ankle and your spit-shined jungle boots pulled over your pant leg to create a sharp, tight Ranger peg-leg blouse. No f*****g blousing rubbers here! A good Ranger haircut, beret liner removed and wet-formed to your own individual head. This was SOP for going anywhere on post. But the field was another matter indeed. Patrol caps were worn with a cool Ranger crush, which accentuated your jump wings, and if you had it, your "coveted" Ranger tab, with a single fleshette dart slipped neatly between the N and the G, of RANGER, stitching. Well-worn cammies bleached from sun, rain, water, mud, from crawling, climbing, countless grueling road marches, cross-country runs, PLFs and countless washings. They were stitched together in the crotch, the ass and the knees. Jungle boots worn down to their natural leather color. And LCE, worn open and with all metal buckles wrapped in black or green 100-mile-an-hour tape. In addition, we carried our over-burdened rucksack. Which was always good for the rucksack flop. [Resting against it whenever you could.]

Once being assigned to our respective Companies, all the new guys were to go through a fairly new program called the Ranger Indoctrination

Program. RIP for short. RIP was fairly new at this time and did not have a concrete structure. The Training NCOs were for the most part short timers who were given RIP Training instead of going out into field for training. From what I remember, all the NCOs looked like action heroes. Very strict, intense, individuals, who were tasked with weeding out all those weak spirited, physically challenged, wannabe Rangers who were not meant to be here.

We were a small group of newbies, perhaps 10–12, who all thought we had what it took to be Rangers. Over half a dozen dropped out during the first week. We were to soon find out during our two-week Ranger Indoctrination Program if we did indeed, have the intestinal fortitude to complete RIP.

Training consisted of learning the Ranger Creed, Ranger standards, and Ranger history, current and past. From Rogers' Rangers and his Standing Orders to Mosby, the Gray Ghost of the Confederate Army, to Darby's Rangers, to Ranger units in Korea and Vietnam, all the way to the 1974 reactivation of the 2nd/75th Rangers. We learned about the Ranger shield, the sun, the lightning bolt, the star, the green and blue background, night or day, land, air, or sea we will strike with lightning swiftness. Learning all this made me feel very proud of the unit I was hoping to join. And it fueled my desire not to fail.

We had to take a swim test. We had to be able to complete the combat survival swim test, which consisted of swimming 15 meters in full combat gear, including a rubber M-16, and stepping off the dive board into the deep end, dropping your LCE and weapon, and then diving back down to don and retrieve all gear.

We performed the Ranger version of the Army Physical Fitness Test many times. Sit-ups, sit-ups on the back of another Ranger, push-ups, incline push-ups, pull-ups – palms forward, palms reversed – legs in L shape, flutter kicks, run dodge and jump, rope climbing, lunges, jumping jacks, wind mills and obstacle courses. I got bitched out by one of the action figure RIP NCOs for not cranking out more sit-ups than he felt I could perform. I was having trouble knocking out 100 sit-ups in two f*****g minutes. Bam! I got socked with remedial training. I can run 2 miles in 12 minutes.

We did some map reading; land navigation, both night and day, where I learned that a Ranger is NEVER lost, only mis-oriented, and knot tying. All of which I loved, due to growing up hunting in the woods of Maryland and Virginia; I also excelled at weapons-training due to growing up with them as a young man. I loved the smell of the cleaning solvents, the oil, and the smell of the powder after discharging a round. My weapon was an extension of my arm, something I understood, respected, and valued as a tool of my new trade.

Physical training also included running, a lot of running, 6-minute miles kind of running, running up Noble Hill, running down range road, running cross country, and running back up Noble Hill, and running in place and on and on and on. I loved to run, so this was for me not too bad. I'd been running hard during the last six months and felt well conditioned. Others were lacking and suffered remedial running, name calling from the RIP

NCOs, extra training and in some cases, some men voluntarily dropped from the program. They weren't meant to be here.

What I hated with a passion were the forced marches with full packs and weapons. Especially with my brand new jungle boots that were merciless on my feet. Blisters on top of blisters, bleeding calluses ripped loose. We had to complete at least two of three road marches they had in store for us. The forced marches increased in length and intensity culminating in a ball busting, soul searching, blister bleeding 18-kilometer road march. There was a deuce and a half [truck] following carrying all those who had already dropped out, which included everyone but me and another Ranger. The truck had cold drinks, donuts, and chips... the RIP NCOs were encouraging us to quit but we were determined to continue this insane pace to the end. F\*\*k those other guys, f\*\*k the NCOs, I was going to finish this road march, bleeding feet or not. We finished together and it felt pretty f\*\*\*\*\*g good to have sucked it up and driven on to complete the Ranger objective.[42]

This particular soldier went to the Pre-Ranger Course within seven months at battalion and returned with his Ranger tab thereafter. How did the standards that Lieutenant Colonel Leuer and Sergeant Major Gentry set for their Rangers translate into reality? Ranger Abell presents an excellent account of certain peculiar traditions and his first overseas deployment as a Ranger:

Captain Jackson took over from Captain Wagner as Charlie company commander. What Jackson loved were contact sports and games like King of the Pit and American Ball. All games were very violent, which was always encouraged. With King of the Pit and American Ball, a combination

Portrait of an Airborne Ranger in the 1970s. (Tim Abell)

of football, rugby, soccer – basically kill the ball carrier, there were always sprains, broken noses, various broken bones, concussions, bloody lips, teeth knocked loose... CPT Jackson himself suffered a compound fracture to one of his legs playing American Ball. Very violent, but very fun! You could always count on paybacks during this game. King of the Pit, pitted Alpha, Bravo, Charlie, and Headquarters companies against each other in the Hand-to-Hand pit. In the center of the pit was an instructor's mound, 4 foot high, and approximately 8' x 8'. On this mound, LTC Wayne Downing would assign one of the company commanders and his officer staff and then surround him with his company with the mission of protecting their company commander and keeping him on top of the center mound. LTC Downing would then position the other companies on all sides, with the mission of gaining control of the center mound, placing their own company commander in the center, while kicking off the other companies and their commanders. And then hold that ground until Downing blew the whistle... 10 minutes, 20 minutes, up to 30 minutes. The rules were, that there were no rules. This was the original fight club. It was a bloody business. But by God it was fun! It built teamwork, camaraderie, and warrior spirit that separated the men from the boys and the Rangers from the wannabes.

All of this building of the warrior spirit was an important part of being a ranger. It made us feel like Spartans readying ourselves for the ultimate test. It fueled our motivations. Inspired our actions. Filled us with a sense of pride that oozed out of our pores. It showed in the way we walked, talked, how we wore our uniforms and our black berets or patrol caps. We were young men who were proud of who we were, what we were doing, proud to be called Rangers. Hooah!

All this testosterone, pride, and esprit de corps, which we were filled with, played a major part during one of our REFORGER (Return of forces to Germany) exercises. We had proven ourselves within the battalion. The wannabes had been weeded out. We knew we were something special and not just because LTC Wayne A. Downing told us so. We trained hard daily – some of us loved running so much, we ran during our off time with rucks filled with bags of lead shot, or with rocks or bricks in our hands.

Our days were filled with, weapons training (both NATO and threat weapons), demolitions, mines and booby traps, leadership traits and principles, SERE [Survival, Escape, Resistance, Evasion] training, survival, first aid, fire support, communications, waterborne operations, mountaineering, helo rappelling, stream and water crossings [just like Rogers' Rangers], anti-armor training with LAWS, Dragons, and TOWs, land navigation, map reading, combat patrols, patrol orders, actions at the objective and last but certainly not least, the all important field exercises where we put all this physical training and knowledge to the test. We were physically fit, highly motivated, lean mean fighting machines! We were not like those slugs down the street. Those rag-tag, fat, marijuana-smoking, prideless slugs of the regular Army! We knew our shit in the field. We were highly trained professionals who felt that we were the epitome of military competence and efficiency. We wanted to be tested and we were about to get that chance in Germany.

We flew from McCord AFB to Ramstein AFB in Germany in a passenger configured C-5A. Then we were bussed down to a small German reserve base called Dahn, which is in southwest Germany not far from the French and Swiss borders. Open bays, military cots, open latrines with a row of shitters and showers. Privacy was not abundant, but this only proved to strengthen our camaraderie. This tends to happen when you shower with, take your morning shit with, your buds on your left and right, and at night the cacophony of odd sounds echoing through the open bays ranged from; snoring, farting, dream-mumbling, whispers, giggles, to one of the NCOs shouting, "Shut the fuck up and go to sleep!"

We were tasked with being the "aggressors" which meant that we were the bad guys, the Warsaw Pact nations. We had trained hard to understand our enemies. We studied their light weapons, their aircraft, their armored vehicles, their artillery, their tactics and training. We watched training videos that depicted our enemy as heavy drinkers (ahh, a common link), unhappy, divorced (another commonality), unmotivated due to a repressive heavy-handed government, but, who were well-trained and would fight viciously against their country's enemies due to that same oppressive government and what the ramifications would be if they didn't fight; the gulags, the secret police, doors being kicked down in the middle of the night, interrogations by the KGB, all these things kept the Warsaw Pact soldiers in line. For us, we just liked to fight.

LTC Downing asked his Rangers for two things: Conduct yourselves in the exemplary manner that is expected of a US Airborne-Ranger on and off the field, and to kick some f*****g ass in the field to show the regular

Army where their weaknesses were in Europe. Ranger Downing loved his Rangers and was always the first to stand up for and praise our dedication and abilities as a fighting unit. But, he had no tolerance or sympathy for any Ranger who disgraced or embarrassed his ranger unit. These things included; public drunkenness, DUIs, bounced checks, starting bar fights (but not finishing one you didn't start, especially if it pertained to some derogatory statement about the Rangers), drugs, stealing (especially from other Rangers), lost weapons and equipment in the field, and insubordination. LTC Downing was a very fair man who led from the front and because of this he was well respected by his rangers.

We learned the rudimentary German phrases that were essential, such as: *Ein Bier bitte!*

Our mission as a battalion was to attempt to infiltrate the imaginary front lines and kill or capture various elements of the US Army of Europe. CPT Jackson's Charlie company rangers were to parachute in to a designated DZ (Drop Zone), and move to and subdue an aviation unit that was providing air support, med evac, supplies and troop movements in support of the other units being hit by Alpha and Bravo Rangers.

The day of our movement I cut the hell out of my right index finger with my super-sharp Buck folding knife that I always carried on my LCE, and I had to have Doc fix me up with five beautiful little stitches and a couple of Motrin painkillers. I thought for sure my SSG was going to pat my shoulder gently and say: "Ranger Abell, I'm sorry but you can't go out in the field with that finger in that condition. Go get some rack time." Instead he laughed and said: "Get the fuck in that truck Ranger. We got work to do." So, with my throbbing f*****d finger wrapped neatly in a white bandage, camouflaged with my cammie stick, my fully packed rucksack, my M-203, my personal Colt .45 ACP Light Weight Commander

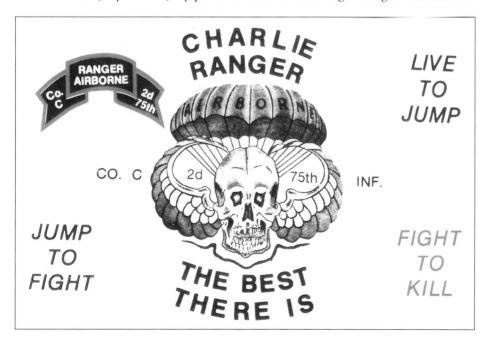

Death Card! The tradition of leaving a "calling card" on the body of an enemy fighter killed in combat probably started in Vietnam. (Tim Abell)

(which I purchased at the age of 14) and my f*****g Dragon, off we went to board our aircraft and make our jump into the dark cold German night.

It was a bumpy f*****g ride in our C-130 that night. I always enjoyed the ride because it rocked me to sleep like a baby. I could sleep anywhere. But others weren't so lucky. They suffered. Which meant those around them suffered as well, due to the projectile vomiting splashing out of their steel pots or vomit bags – the putrid smell of recently eaten C-rations. The turbulence got worse and it looked as if the jump was going to be called off. Our pilots were going to circle once more and at that time our jumpmasters would make a decision. We were first in the sortie of 12 C-130s, and we were quite sure the jump was going to be canceled and that we would have to land back at the air base and be trucked in. Which meant that we could catch some more ZZZZs before hitting it hard. But, as the rear doors opened, and CPT Jackson talked with the jumpmasters and the pilots, it became very clear that Jackson was determined to jump that night.

We got the command to stand. We checked each other's gear. We got the command to hook up. I was somewhere in the middle of my stick and could hear the chatter coming from the front of the stick about how strong the winds were and how this wasn't a good idea. But, no one protested by unhooking. You just go along with it like cattle in a chute. As you see the red jump light turn green, and you hear the words "GO! GO! GO!" you just shuffle along pressed into your buddy's parachute pack, following along until you reach the door, and get the command to "STAND IN THE DOOR," and then, a sharp slap on the back when you hear "GO!" I used to get so uncomfortable standing there with all my gear hanging off me, weighing me down, by the time I got to the door I just wanted to jump out into the night to get the weight off. It didn't matter if I thought it was a good idea or not. If I thought I was going to die or not. I knew I was going out that door regardless of what thoughts were in my head. It always felt like diving into dark water for those few moments before your static line ripped your chute out of its casing. And then a violent jerk. Thank God my chute opened!

This night, it became quite clear, was not a good night to be jumping, at all. As I was descending at a near horizontal attitude at about 17mph, I was struggling to toggle my T-10 chute into the wind which would mean that I'd be traveling backwards at about 10mph. I was looking for the horizon so I'd know when to pull my quick releases for my ruck, my weapons container, and my "albatross" the Dragon. I couldn't see the horizon, all I could see was blackness, and so I decided to start popping my quick releases just in case. As I was flying backwards, and reaching down to my quick releases, I realized I was in the f*****g trees already! Trees to my left, trees to my right, and at that moment I was hoping that there wasn't a tree in my flight path. As I pulled my quick releases for my ruck, which was at my knees, I slammed ass first, followed by the back of my head into the soft grassy soil of a small clearing belonging to some German farmer.

As I lay there for a moment processing where I was and that I was indeed still alive, I realized my chute was pulling me across this small field surrounded by trees, towards an old tractor that sat next to an old wood

Some Rangers attended HALO School and jumped in their spare time at the local parachute clubs. (Tim Abell)

fence. I managed to get to my feet, with my Dragon still attached as well as my weapons container, ran around and collapsed my chute. After I got my weapon out, bagged my chute, and replaced my steel pot with my trusty patrol cap, I slipped my ruck on my back with my Dragon strapped to it – I knew I needed to find Charlie Company's rally point. But being that we were not on the proposed DZ, I started to look for my fellow Rangers with whom I'd just shared my ride. As I looked around, I didn't see that many men moving on the ground or falling from the sky. The first man I came to had slammed into the old tractor by the old wood fence and wasn't able to stand. I stayed with him until my squad leader showed up and pointed me towards 3rd Squad, 1st Platoon in the tree line.

What was quickly disseminated was that only the first three C-130s were allowed to jump. All the others were returning to the airbase and would be trucked in later. Much Later. Next, we learned that we had nearly 50 percent casualties of the three planes to jump. We had men in the trees, men on barbed-wire fencing, men slamming into farm equipment. There were Rangers with lacerations, broken bones, and concussions. But by God we were going to see it through! Jackson issued a frag order and made some adjustments, arranged for those hurt and not able to carry on to be medevaced out via truck and on we went into the night – with my bloodied throbbing freshly stitched finger.

I ended up carrying the PRC77 [radio] in addition to my other equipment and had the pleasure of being right behind CPT Jackson throughout the operation. At least I knew what the f**k was going on, being privy to all radio communications. We moved across the German countryside in silence through the pitch-black forests following the glowing Ranger eyes sewn onto the back of all Ranger patrol caps (which had a slightly hypnotic effect on me, taking me back home for a few moments at a time wondering what my girl was doing or who she was doing), across large streams (which we all hated when we were nice and dry), up steep hills, over huge dead falls, all through the night, the night, the night, until we were within striking distance of our objective.

Once the ORP was secured and security was in place our SFC and a small team of Charlie Rangers were sent to reconnoiter the objective, the nearby terrain, and to determine troop strength [a leader's recon]. While awaiting the leader's recon return, CPT Jackson, the platoon leaders, and the platoon sergeants lay under a poncho with a red filtered flashlight and a map to go over, once again the plan of attack, actions at the objective, actions on enemy contact, command and signal, rally points, contingencies, fire support, security, and extraction. Once the recon team returned with their drawings of the objective and other pertinent information concerning troop strength, enemy security, and activity, a frag order was issued and appropriate adjustments were made to our op orders and we prepared to attack just before dawn... "Dawn's when the French and Indians attack."

By now I've been relieved of my radio duties and reunited with my buds in 3rd Squad, 1st Platoon. We left our rucks, our dragons, and any other extra equipment behind in our ORP with rear security. We were to carry our LCE with maximum blank ammo and grenade/artillery simulators so that we could move fast through the sleeping enemy's base camp. Not one sentry awake, not a single sign of any security whatsoever, not one trip flare rigged to warn them of their impending doom. They were about to have a very bad morning.

We positioned ourselves in the tree-lined hill awaiting the other platoons' signal that they were in place and ready to assault. CPT Jackson would initiate the attack once we had crept on our bellies to within a few meters of the medevac helicopters that were on the outer edge of the Aviation unit's other helicopters. Once the signal was given and the parachute flares were popped, we opened up within our fields of fire. M-60s blazing, 90mm recoilless rifles blasting away, M-16s, CAR-15s, my M-203 popping 40mm grenade simulators right into the middle of their tent city, illuminating the killing ground. After this initial wake up call, we charged directly into the tent city on line, screaming like wild men, filled with testosterone and blood lust! And at this moment I lost all sensation of my bloodied, throbbing finger as I yelled at the top of my lungs screaming like Crazy Horse at the Little Big Horn.

We ripped open tent flaps and fired on full auto at those cold and timid souls who were still lying zipped up in their warm Army sleeping bags. We tossed grenade simulators in still-closed tents. We blew some of these tents completely apart, not to mention the poor bastards' eardrums. They were completely taken by surprise. Some were coming out of their tents in their skivvies and were promptly body-slammed and told not to move because "you're fucking dead." A few female soldiers were crying, one young Specialist was begging for his green-faced Ranger tormentor not to hurt him. My one friend who was a 60 gunner, was to my left, ripping tents apart, with his M-60 machine gun, this was due to having lost his blank adapter somewhere along the way. He came to this one tent with an older looking gentleman exiting out of his tent with his sleeping bag still wrapped around him, screaming something unintelligible about being the commander of this unit and how much trouble we were all in, when my friend the M-60 gunner, at point-blank range, let rip with a long blast right into the chest of this gentleman and blew him right back into his warm and comfortable tent with his sleeping bag smoking from the unplugged barrel. I skipped 40mm grenades across the ground towards their vehicles where aviation troops were running to – to escape this nightmare. I popped one 40mm right above the open cab of a jeep that was attempting to escape. The driver promptly stopped.

It was quite a scene with all the different colored smoke hanging in the pre-dawn air. The acrid smell of expended blank ammo and exploded hand-grenade simulators was a smell that I rather enjoyed. The sound of orders being shouted, vehicles being moved, people crying, some yelling, especially the colonel whose slumber had been so abruptly interrupted, were muffled in my ears – partially deafened due to all the weapons being fired on my left and right, the M-60, the flash bangs, my own M-203, plus the wild screams of my Ranger *compadres* as we assaulted the objective.

We completely overwhelmed these bozos without them firing one shot, without them being able to radio their higher command to inform them that the "war" had started and that they were all "dead." We had moved through the entire encampment, secured all vehicles and aircraft, collected all Intel, corralled, contained, and accounted for all "enemy troops." The older gentleman was indeed the aviation unit's commanding officer and boy was he pissed off. Not just because he got blown right out of his slippers from my buddy's M-60, but because his unit got caught with their pants down and got their f*****g asses spanked! He should have been pissed off. Pissed off at his own incompetence, his own lax standards which if this had been the real deal, they'd all have been dead meat, and it was his fault.

CPT Jackson, and his Charlie 2/75 rangers secured the objective, and then withdrew to our ORP to collect our gear and to obtain a status report. We then moved a safe distance towards our link-up site and disseminated all information collected, and to make contact with the rest of our battalion who were given a reprieve on jumping last night and were trucked in to the DZ instead.

We were all feeling rather euphoric after our rout of the aviation unit, and were delighted in sharing our stories. Alpha Company and Bravo Company had similar stories of overwhelming their objectives, treating the opposing forces to a game of "King of the Pit!" There were many complaints levied against 2/75 due to our brutality; heavy-handedness, man handling, wild manner in which we attacked our objectives and our merciless, soulless morality. We actually hurt people. Slapped them, knocked them down, tied them up, shot them at point-blank range, yelled at them, and scared the shit out of them. Boo f*****g hoo! Better scared and hurt than cold and f*****g dead.

Back at Camp Dahn a day later, LTC Downing was going to address the battalion and the scuttlebutt was he'd gotten his ass chewed out good for

how rough his Rangers were with the opposing forces. The supposed "good guys!" We murdered them and the higher ups – the generals in charge of the forces in Europe all had egg on their faces! They were quite upset at being humiliated by LTC Wayne A. Downing's 2/75 Ranger Battalion and chewed his ass out good from what we heard. And now we were all waiting for the shit to roll down hill and smack us squarely in our asses for being too aggressive, for hurting some "enemy," for shooting an aviation company commander while draped in his sleeping bag, for blowing up tents with flash bangs, we were sure to lose some men to Article 15s by the time the day was done.

LTC Downing stared down at us looking left and right with a very stern look on his face. His speech went something like this: "Rangers, I've been taking a lot of heat for your aggressive behavior in the field; for completely overwhelming the US European forces, for making some of them cry, for yelling at them, for shooting them in their tents in their sleeping bags, for tossing flash bangs in their AO; for disrespectful attitudes towards unit commanders of the opposing forces. Well, I just have to say to you all – HOOAH, RANGERS! RANGERS LEAD THE WAY! I am very proud of you all and I will take all the heat they can muster for men who fight the way you do, completing your Ranger objectives in such overwhelming fashion. I am very proud of you all! NOW let's go do it again! HOOAH!" We went f*****g wild at that little pat on the back from "THE WAD!"

I never realized how high our standards were in battalion until we were pitted against the regular Army in Germany. Being in battalion was like being in an entirely different Army. And that was the Army I wanted to be a part of.[43]

# Operations *Eagle Claw* and *Urgent Fury*

Not such sharp talons

## OPERATION *EAGLE CLAW* AND DESERT ONE

Iran was, is, and will be America's most beloved and hated surrogate. Created in the aftermath of World War II, it has withstood the petroleum passion, the CIA, British oil interests, and the orchestration in 1953 by intelligence services to oust Iran's prime minister Mohammed Mossadeq, who was elected in 1951 and who also had been elected to parliament in 1923 and again in 1944. The Pahlavi Dynasty, however short-lived, was placed on the fabulous Peacock Throne thereafter. Some good things did come out of the change – economic growth, and modernization, and, for the United States, a dependable and pro-Israeli partner in the Middle East. Yet oppression reared its head, and over the years an ideology-fuelled rebellion broke out, dethroning the Shah who fled to Egypt and subsequently died in exile. Religious fundamentalists under the Ayatollah Khomeini led the country toward a theocratic republic. During the rebellion Americans were taken hostage at the US Embassy, long suspected and finally confirmed as a haven of intelligence activity.

The first action the newly founded Rangers would participate in was to happen during the period of April 24–25, 1980. Iranian students had stormed the US Embassy and after a long fruitless series of negotiations, President Jimmy Carter authorized a rescue attempt codenamed Desert One. It was primarily a Special Forces operation with Rangers providing additional muscle – a task that would stay with the Rangers permanently.

The newly founded Delta Force (1st Special Forces Operational Detachment – Delta) was the actual unit responsible for the hostage rescue, while Captain David Grange's Charlie Company, 1st Battalion, 75th Infantry (Ranger), was tasked with perimeter security among other missions. One of the security teams detained a bus carrying approximately 45 Iranians, while shortly thereafter they fired on a fuel truck that had failed to stop when challenged.[44] Rangers from C Company were also prepared to secure an airfield for follow-on operations 35 miles south of Tehran.

Unfortunately, an accident during the early part of the operation resulted in eight deaths, five Air Force personnel and three Marines – and the mission was aborted. The bodies of the Americans were left behind during the panic and confusion, as were several intact helicopters, equipments, maps, and other material. It proved to be a valuable lesson for American Special Operations Forces (SOF) – just one of the painful experiences that served as a building block for future operations.

# GRENADA OPERATION *URGENT FURY* – TESTING GROUNDS NEEDED

The United States' invasion of Grenada on October 25, 1983, codenamed Operation *Urgent Fury*, tasked the 1st and 2nd (-) Battalions, 75th Infantry (Ranger) with several missions, not all of them planned. One mission was to locate, seize, and secure the lives of American citizens at the True Blue Medical Campus, restore democracy to the island by evicting any and all Cuban influence, and conduct air-assault follow-on operations to isolate and eliminate pockets of resistance. This primary task of seizing and securing the airfield was conducted without any new intelligence, as the SEAL team which intended to insert clandestinely was repelled. The Rangers nonetheless conducted a combat parachute assault from 500ft.

The 2nd Battalion, alerted on October 23, linked up with its sister unit at 1st Battalion's Hunter Army Airfield in Savannah, Georgia. Unfortunately, and to the detriment of the Rangers, few aircraft were available, and a number of Rangers were left behind. Decisions on who would fly were based on rank (E-4 and above), Ranger School qualification, and considerations of mission critical assignments.

The Rangers anticipated heavy resistance, though not particularly well-trained units – at a minimum, a company-strength force that was dug in and well armed, including but not limited to Soviet small arms, machine guns, mortars, and ZSU 23-4 antiaircraft guns. The men were also informed that they might either air-land or parachute into Point Salinas Airfield. This was the first time the Rangers were told of the mission objective.

Lieutenant Colonel Wesley B. Taylor, upon receiving notification that the first C-130 was taking fire, decided to jump below the aircraft fire at 500ft during the flight. The 2nd Battalion's Lieutenant Colonel Ralph Hagler decided to forgo reserve parachutes.[45] The Rangers rigged as best and fast as they could, and with the jumpmaster leading the way, parachuted onto the Grenadian airfield. Two Rangers became entangled as they tried to exit and were pulled back into the aircraft.[46] The battalions dropped between 0530 and 0700 hours.

Though scattered during landing, the Rangers had assembled within 30 to 60 minutes, a task completed while exchanging fire. The Rangers gathered at either end of the airfield. Some of them had even hot-wired a bulldozer and were using it to clear obstacles strewn on the runway. The two companies attacked the Cuban defenders, who fought back with small arms and machine guns.[47] Later that same afternoon, the Rangers would repel a lightly armored counterattack comprised of three BTR-60 armored personnel carriers. With some of the gun jeeps, the Rangers rushed to the east end of the runway where the 90mm recoilless rifle gunners from both battalions obliterated the relieving force. Gunships from the carrier USS *Independence* suppressed the armored personnel carriers, and the Rangers surrounded and captured about 250 Cubans.[48] At 0900 hours, after consolidating at the objective, some Rangers were tasked with a follow-on mission, where the Rangers, after a firefight, rescued 138 American medical students at the True Blue Campus next to the airfield only to learn that 233 more were still trapped at Grand Anse, a few miles to the north.

One operation was the raid on the Edgmont Training Compound/Calivigny Barracks, supposedly crawling with 400–500 enemy personnel. Three Black Hawk helicopters with Rangers had crashed and littered the objective, but the

Uniform of Wesley B. Taylor, worn during the invasion of Grenada, and now at the Infantry Museum. (Author's collection/Camera 1)

defenders numbered no more then a dozen or so. The Rangers made quick work of the objective, although three Rangers were killed during the mission.[49]

The Rangers engaged in another mission in support of Delta, as they had done three years earlier, with the highly secretive TF-160 (The Army Special Operations Airwing). The mission, a raid on Richmond Hill Prison was repulsed, however, as the SOF incurred casualties.

The following are first hand accounts of two actions during Operations *Urgent Fury*, the Grand Anse rescue and the Calivigny barracks raid.

# GRAND ANSE RESCUE

It was such a blur that I don't remember. We got the mission to air assault onto the beach at Grande Anse to rescue about 200 Americans holed up in one building. Paul Andreasen and I (both Sergeants then) climbed aboard a USMC CH-46 just before the mission. SFC Magana was my PSG and Goss was my Platoon Leader. The bird held about 15 of us, the whole platoon, as I recall (only about 250 from 2nd battalion went). As the rotors spooled up, the two .50 cal Marine door gunners were blessing themselves, and checking their guns, obviously terrified. I was scared shitless myself, about to go into a hot LZ in broad daylight, but found strength in the fact that at least I was not the MOST scared. One Marine turned to us and asked (his eyes showing that he REALLY wanted a good answer) "Have you guys ever done this?!" to which Paul replied, beautifully, "Oh yah, we do this all the time!" (and he's got this shit-eating grin, and we just start laughing out loud; and I'm thinking, what a great line... and this Marine is now convinced that we are maniacs, and blesses himself again...)

The bird takes off, and heads out to sea, along with what seems like dozens of others, both '46's and CH-53's. I sat next to one of those punch-out escape windows. The actual window had been removed even before takeoff because we KNEW we may have to use them, making a nice way to get out. Looking out the windowless opening, I could see nothing but helicopters coming in low over the ocean, making a bee-line for the Grande Anse beach. It was a view right out of "Apocalypse Now." We started taking ground fire, and the birds broke off the attack and did a racetrack. Cobras continued in with guns firing.

Heading in again, as our bird approached the beach (not close to where the rest of the birds were landing), things started to go wrong. Strange sounds. Were they rounds hitting the bird? Don't know. The '46 started shuddering violently. Pilot put it down in the surf, so close to the Palm trees (no beach, just some rocks) that the blades were trashed by the trees. The rear ramp opened a crack and then stopped, as water started filling the floor of the bird. All the Marines on that bird were the first to go. They left us in there like a target. I'm thinking, "this is not good," and with my 100 pound ruck, tried to go out that escape window. The 2 LAWs under the top flap of my ruck held me up. Magana shouts "DROP RUCKS," then manages to get the ramp to drop. We struggle to get out into the water, about 4 feet deep. My ruck, one strap off, and one caught on my M-16 sling tangles and I go right underwater as if I've got an anchor around my neck. Slipped out of the ruck, and made it to the shore. By this time there is close air or some other shooting, hell I was so disoriented at this point, it was hard to say where the fire was coming from, but seemed directed at the trees along the beach. Believe now it was a Navy fast mover with nose cannon firing up the treeline. Things then got quiet, we get up and run up the beach a couple hundred meters to where the rest of 2nd Bat is landing.

I am prone, securing the corridor between the building where the hostages are and the PZ (which is a strip of beach so narrow that the birds have their wheels in the water to avoid having the blades hit the palm trees). At this point, I think it was AC-130 that was putting steel around us. I saw Goss jumping on one foot, barking out instruction and pointing. I was an alternate on the aid and litter team, yelled over to SP4 Morales to help me, then grabbed Goss by the waist with both arms to carry him to the nearby "precious cargo" bird to be evacuated, rotors were whipping, forcing us to yell to be heard. He pushed me away, yelling: "GET BACK TO THE LINE!" I did.

Within minutes, birds were doing the touch and go as Americans were hustled aboard and whisked off. As the perimeter collapsed and we boarded another bird to leave, I sat on the seat across from Goss, and went for his bloody foot. Again, he pushed me (and Andreasen, who was also right there, along with SFC Magana) back. Pain was on his face, but he would not let any of us touch him. The bird lifted, and during that short ride back to Pt. Salinas Airstrip, I watched the puddle of blood under Goss' foot get bigger and bigger. Paul and I met eyes, and without words, agreed that we would grab him when he finally fell over from loss of blood.

Grenada raider wearing his beloved patrol cap the only way – with a Ranger crush. He is displaying captured weapons. (US Army)

Goss collapsed just as we touched down. We drug him off the bird, and started ripping his gear off. My knife was razor sharp and gashed his foot as it went through the boot. Gamma goat from the 82nd pulled up and medics joined in. Someone started an IV. At this point, people were working on him that knew more than Paul and I, so we just backed off.

For a few seconds there, standing on that huge expanse of tarmac, sounds of rotor blades fading, the enemy several clicks away, I felt suddenly exhausted. The adrenaline was gone, for now, and I was gulping air. Paul and I started walking to a spot of ground, south of the airstrip, that C Co had claimed as their own. The Americans that we had rescued were nearby,

## THE 160TH SOAR (A)

The 160th Special Operations Aviation Regiment (Airborne) provides aviation support to Army Special Operations Forces. The regiment consists of MH-6 and AH-6 light helicopters, MH-60 helicopters, and MH-47 heavy-assault helicopters. The capabilities of the 160th SOAR (A) have been evolving since the early 1980s.

Shortly after the failed hostage-rescue mission in Iran, Desert One, the Army formed a special aviation unit. The unit drew on the best aviators in the Army and immediately began an intensive training program in low-level night operations. The unit became a battalion of its own on October 16, 1981. Designated the 160th Aviation Battalion, the unit was popularly known as Task Force 160 because of the constant attachment and detachment of units to prepare for a wide variety of missions. Its focus on night operations resulted in the nickname the "Night Stalkers."

guarded now in a perimeter of 82nd troops. As Paul and I approached, they all stood up, recognizing Rangers as their rescuers (and not the 82nd), and started cheering. There is nothing I can put into words to describe my feelings upon seeing those Americans cheer us after that rescue.

Paul raised his fist, shaking it, and shouted "WE DO EMBASSIES TOO!!" at this point we were laughing hysterically, more than anything, I think, out of relief to still be alive. (As our bird was going down, only 30 minutes earlier, I thought we were dead men). I have tried to compare those intense, complicated emotions to other situations before or since in my 37 years... There are none. I was never more proud to be a Ranger.

*Kurt Sturr*
*C Company, 2nd Battalion, 75th Infantry (Ranger)*

# CALIVIGNY BARRACKS RAID

After a couple days in Grenada we were all pretty much surviving on adrenalin but that was still running extremely high. Our OpOrd [operations order] for the Calivigny Barracks objective pushed the adrenalin into extra-super-duper-overdrive. Spectre and the Navy would prep the objective and lift fire just in time for us to go in. We would be broken into chalks of eight Blackhawks [Chalk denotes a Ranger unit on helicopters] to insert into an open area within the built-up compound. This open area looked awfully small but we knew the pilots were very good and they'd make sure we all fit. We were all rigged up and ready to go in, double-checking everything we already double-checked and then double-checking the guys next to us even though we already double-checked them a few times. The prep started... everything else stopped.

We could hear the burrrping and thunk thunk of Spectre intermixed with a crumphing that must have been the Navy guns. Off in the distance we could see smoke billowing up from beyond the hills. We continued double-checking (our weapons and gear) as we stole glances toward the growing cloud of smoke. Each burrrrp, thunk and carumph brought a tight hint of a smile to our faces – less of them to deal with, more of us to come back.

After an eternity of gunfire we got the signal to move to the aircraft. I was on Chalk Two so I got in position awaiting the return of the first chalk. All heads followed the Blackhawks as they took off with our Ranger buddies and headed toward the large black cloud of smoke. The aircraft were little specks when we noticed the silence. The prep had stopped... the rest was ours. We kept looking off toward the Blackhawks long after they were no longer visible. The silence in the distance was matched with an equal silence amongst ourselves. The only movement was that of hands subconsciously checking equipment... silently.

As one, our heads turned ever so slightly toward the now visible speck of the returning aircraft. The hands stopped moving. The speck grew larger. The speck became two specks, then three... four... five... five – just five. The First Sergeant starts shuffling folks around... silently. Some move back for another chalk... silently. We can make out the dull staccato of the rotors as the Blackhawks grew larger. There was no doubt now, there were only five aircraft returning. What the hell could have been left out there after all that shit that was dumped on them? How was Chalk One fairing?

The Blackhawks took up their positions on the PZ [Pick-up Zone]. We could tell which aircraft positions were empty and strained to recall who was on those birds. We crammed ourselves in tight, muzzles down, trigger guards clear, check the guys next to you. I don't think anyone looked each other in the eyes, I know I didn't, either I didn't want to see the fright in their faces or I didn't want them to see the terror in mine. I just looked at equipment... and then toward the smoke... and then we took off.

The Blackhawks began banking as they started their zig-zag, I thought about how much more comfortable I was when squeezed in tightly as we were, as if the compressed bodies would prevent each other from falling out if the aircraft turned on its side. Shit... there I go again... concentrate... actions at the objective, assembly positions, directions of fire, TRP [target reference points] locations, reaction teams, search teams, how the hell was Chalk One faring?

I could feel the slight descent of the aircraft as they dipped below a tree line and edged closer to the ground. From front to rear elbows nudged and hands went up with index finger extended. One minute out. Actions at the objective... assembly positions... my helmet's on my head, right? directions of fire... TRP locations... it's good to be squeezed in tight... reaction teams... search teams... how the hell was Chalk One faring? That was a pretty darn long minute. The aircraft turned, flared, I saw... carnage.

I couldn't believe five birds could fit into the LZ [Landing Zone]. They landed rotor to rotor. Blown out walls to one side, something that may once have been a shack on another, over there is an aircraft mockup, part of an obstacle course, large piles of debris, a helicopter laying on its side, and another, and another. A small group of Rangers protected the LZ as the rest expanded the perimeter. They checked us out as we landed and quickly turned their attention back to their front. Some didn't move at all.

Before the Blackhawks could touch down we were scrambling out and heading to our positions relieving the security team to catch up with their Ranger buddies. Our mortar teams automatically moved into place and within seconds were prepared to fire supporting missions. All personnel accounted for and all teams in place.

My radio comes to life...

The duck-hunter uniform made to look good by Bravo Company, 2/75. (John Galetzka)

"One One Charlie this is One Three Foxtrot, fire mission, over" ... FIRE MISSION! I signal the gunners and they acknowledge they're ready. "Immediate fire for effect, grid 12345678, over" [fake grids coordinates] I mark the grid on my control board, spin the disk to align the gun marker, read the deflection and range, check the charge book and call the guns... "Three rounds in effect... Deflection 3095... Charge 0... Elevation 1011." The gunners are bowed over their sights, left hand down under the bipod turning the elevation wheel, right hand on the traversing wheel, check level bubbles, recheck sight picture... assistant gunners get the prepared rounds from the ammo bearers and prepare to drop them down the tubes... number one gun sounds off first with "Hang it... FIRE!" They're immediately followed by the Number Two and Three guns... "Hang it, FIRE!" "Hang it, FIRE!" a quick check of the bubbles and sight picture... "Hang it, FIRE!" "Hang it, FIRE!" "Hang it, FIRE!" check again "Hang it, FIRE!" "Hang it, FIRE!" "Hang it, FIRE!" I've called the shot out to the FO [Forward Observer] and follow the second hand on my watch... "Splash over" "Splash out" In the distance I can hear the carumph, carumph, carumph of the rounds striking the ground.

In training, a fire for effect is usually followed by an effect report with buildings burning, hundreds of casualities, widows crying and reporters on the scene. I wasn't sure what I wanted to hear this time. The distant crackling of automatic weapons firing let me know that they weren't just sitting there idle. I never did get an effect report. Just as well.

Time passed... hours... Another fire mission, same as before. The fire missions take a minute or two to complete. It's amazing just how many things are going on simultaneously, how detailed each action is, how exact these gun teams can be in such a short amount of time. Each moment seems to freeze but the next moment comes too quickly, a stroboscopic skipping through time as you automatically jump from one task to the next. In the end it seems like a half-second has gone by but a day's worth of effort was put into it. Then the wait... hours... I check my watch. We've been on the ground 15 minutes.

My radio crackles again, the FO warns me that a fast mover was coming through with something a little bigger than 60mm, danger close, and by the way, "Splash over." I signal the guns to take cover. I don't recall seeing the fast mover but he may have gone by while I was on the radio because I'm just settling down behind my ruck as I hear the shooshing of offset incoming. This shooshing had a bit of a whistle to it... and it was getting much louder than normal, much faster than normal... WHAM!!!! JESSSUUUUSSSS CHHHHRRRIIISSTTTTT!!!! With what was left of my hearing I detected another whistling, getting louder, COVER!!! WHAM!!!! What looked like an inch thick trash can lid lands about twenty feet away. It was quiet after that.

We prepared for the night...

It's getting noticeably darker and it's been quiet for a while now... too quiet... no SitReps over the radio. I really wanted to know what was happening, what's happened, but I knew better than to bother asking, I would get what info I needed as I needed it, let the rest of the Rangers do their jobs, I had to concentrate on mine.

The first chalk had cleared the immediate area of enemy personnel and established the outer perimeter. My mortar section became the inner perimeter and would clear the area in more detail. HQ Elements would be joining us in the morning for gathering intel and casualty handling. SSG P. was the acting Platoon Leader, I was the acting PSG and SGT D. was my right hand man with FDC [Fire Direction Center] and gun team control. SSG P. took over the radio and covered FDC while SGT D. and I checked the area for things that might go bump in the night.

The compound was a training area complete with mock aircraft, climbing tower with windows, and what appeared to be a tunnel system. One end of the tunnel, or culvert, or whatever it was, was near our position and had a hatch covering the entry. We cleared the tunnel and SGT D. rigged the hatch so we'd know if it moved. Right next to us was one of the downed Blackhawks and nearby were the other two, the wounded had already been evacuated, we'd come back to this site later. We moved on to the buildings.

The first building was a small house-like structure. The outside walls were pitted with holes and craters from the initial prep but I was surprised that it was standing at all after all the ordinance that was thrown at it. We checked for wires in the entryway and slowly made our way inside. Sectioned into offices with nice desks and nice stuff on the walls (used to be on the walls) this was apparently the Commander's building. We weren't there for intel collection, just ensuring that there was no threat, so we moved through relatively quickly. The next building had living quarters that were just slightly nicer than the old WWII barracks I was housed in during Airborne School, this was their officers' quarters. Back outside... there were the Blackhawks... later...

The obstacle course area was fairly open. A large wall designed for rappelling, windows cut out for training use, nothing here. Mock aircraft; kinda like a C-130 mockup but laid out differently... nothing here either. Some remnants of huts and sheds, now little more than piles of rubble, nothing here.

*Jim Hicks*
*B Company, 2nd Battalion, 75th Infantry (Ranger)*

The Rangers proved their value during operations on Grenada. Rigorous training and an insistence on high standards aided the individual Ranger in overcoming any obstacle he encountered. The 75th Infantry (Ranger) conducted combat operations with minimal intelligence and proved to be an asset to the overall commander of Operation *Urgent Fury* who employed them in a variety of tasks throughout the short campaign.

The Ranger battalions had excelled, unlike the majority of the other Special Operations or infantry units during Operation *Urgent Fury*. They would pay for it later – with the creation of the 75th Ranger Regiment – increasing the Ranger

B Company, 2/75 1987–88. Black berets and class A uniforms. The officers and senior NCOs are in the front row. (Author's collection)

battalions from two to three in addition to the Regimental Headquarters. Things were going to change. A new culture was ascending in the military – older Vietnam veterans were retiring, and older Battboys, who had become used to doing things a certain way, would flee in the hundreds during the heavy-handed growth of the Regiment.

## RANGER CASUALTIES IN OPERATION *URGENT FURY*

| Soldier | Battalion | Date KIA |
| --- | --- | --- |
| SGT Randy E. Cline | 1-75 | 25-Oct-83 |
| SGT Phillip S. Grenier | 2-75 | 25-Oct-83 |
| SGT Kevin J. Lannon | 2-75 | 25-Oct-83 |
| PFC Markin R. Maynard | 1-75 | 25-Oct-83 |
| SGT Mark A. Rademacher | 1-75 | 25-Oct-83 |
| PFC Russell L. Robinson | 1-75 | 25-Oct-83 |
| SGT Stephen E. Slater | 2-75 | 25-Oct-83 |
| SPC4 Mark O. Yamane | 1-75 | 25-Oct-83 |

# All Hail the Regiment

## A new beginning

"No good deed goes unpunished" is an old saying, and this was to be the case for 1st and 2nd Battalions of the ten-year old 75th Infantry (Ranger). Although back in 1973–74 there had been discussions of a 3rd Ranger Battalion, this

The Colors of the Regiment –
all hail the regiment.
(Author's collection/Camera 1)

Fort Benning. Note the brand new high-speed-looking sign – money is spent on the 75th Ranger Regiment and rightly so. (Author's collection/Camera 1)

desire was never consummated due to the budget cuts affecting the US Armed Forces. However, with the ascendancy of the actor Ronald Reagan in 1980, the Department of Defense's budget was again increased. After the self-perceived successful flexing of her military might with test partner Grenada, and with the Soviet Union bogged down in its own war of hell in Afghanistan, the decision was made to reorganize the Rangers as well as create a unifying Special Operations Command (SOC). On July 1, 1984, the two Ranger battalions had a headquarters component, stationed at Fort Benning, Georgia, placed on their broad backs. By February 3, 1986, the 75th Ranger Regiment was officially birthed, with lineage and honors bestowed upon them from their predecessors; the Regiment was proudly composed of one Regimental Headquarters, a 3rd Ranger Battalion, also at Fort Benning, and the old Ragnars from the right and left coasts who'd been having a glorious time all by themselves. Spirited wild men, meet your jailers! All those fabulous sayings about serving one's battalion were replaced with the heinous word "Regiment."

Although in the existing structure training was awesome and operating procedures were in place, they apparently could not be left alone. With the Regiment's creation arose a new dreaded officer-led ascendancy of the Ranger Standard Operating Procedure (RSOP). Whereas the Airborne Rangers could liberally sprinkle an ammo pouch here or there, and whereas a certain tolerance was granted toward the wearing of the Ranger Crush – only associated with Rangers wearing their beloved patrol caps – and whereas a sense of individuality for the common good was still acceptable, the RSOP sweepingly removed all of that. The manuals that sprang forth and ambushed its unwilling accomplices were so numerous that one could only have drawn the conclusion that dozens of eager beavers were doing nothing but sitting at their desks conceiving new

This poster was created by Rangers of the 3rd Battalion. Who said morale was low during the mid to late 1980s? (Author's collection)

ways of destroying morale. The beloved load-bearing/carrying equipment (LCE) was standardized – one ammo pouch per side with so much space in between, such and such a knot used to tie each item down. Running times are now the Regimental standard of eight minutes per mile and so forth. To be fair, with the expansion of the unit a reasonable amount of standardization was needed. The problem was that it was antagonistic in nature, not inclusive, it went to extremes, to serve not as guidelines, but as rules to be adhered to at all costs. And what were the costs? The old-timers left, and morale plummeted. The Regiment consolidated all of the Ranger Indoctrination Program (RIP) and Pre-Ranger programs to one location, near themselves of course, at Fort Benning – it made sense. The Regiment was also now commanded by a full-bird colonel

# 75TH RANGER REGIMENT INSIGNIA

Shoulder Sleeve Insignia        Distinctive Unit Insignia        Coat of Arms

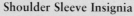

**Shoulder Sleeve Insignia**

**Description:** A black cloth triparted arced scroll with narrow red fimbriations and a ¹⁄₈in. (0.32cm) black border 1²⁹⁄₃₂in. (4.84cm) in height and 3¹¹⁄₁₆in. (9.37cm) in width overall inscribed "75 RANGER RGT" in white letters.

**Background:** The shoulder sleeve insignia was originally approved for the 75th Infantry on July 26, 1984. It was redesignated on February 14, 1986, for the 75th Ranger Regiment. The shoulder sleeve insignia for the 1st, 2nd, and 3rd Ranger Battalions were approved on July 26, 1984.

**Distinctive Unit Insignia**

**Description:** A gold color metal and enamel device 1¹⁄₈in. (2.86cm) in height overall consisting of a shield blazoned as follows: Quarterly Azure (blue) and Vert (green), between in the first and fourth quarters a radiant sun of 12 points and a mullet Argent, a lightning flash couped bendsinisterwise Gules fimbriated Or.

**Symbolism:** The colors blue, white, red, and green represent four of the original six combat teams of the 5307th Composite Unit (Provisional), commonly referred to as Merrill's Marauders, which were identified by color. To avoid confusion, the other two colors, khaki and orange, were not represented in the design. However, khaki was represented by the color of the uniform worn by US forces in the China-Burma-India Theater during World War II. The unit's close cooperation with the Chinese forces in the China-Burma-India Theater is represented by the sun symbol from the Chinese flag. The white star represents the Star of Burma, the country in which the Marauders campaigned during World War II. The lightning bolt is symbolic of the strike characteristics of the Marauders' behind-the-line activities.

**Background:** The distinctive unit insignia was originally approved on March 18, 1969, for the 75th Infantry. It was redesignated for the 75th Ranger Regiment on February 3, 1986.

**Coat of Arms**

**Blazon**

**Shield:** Quarterly Azure and Vert, between in the first and fourth quarters a radiant sun of 12 points and a mullet Argent, a lightning flash couped bendsinisterwise Gules fimbriated Or.

**Crest:** On a wreath of the colors Argent and Azure, issuing in back of an embattlement of a tower with six merlons Or a pedestal Gules supporting a chinthé affronté of the third in front of a torteau within an annulet of the Second.

**Motto:** *Sua Sponte* (Of Their Own Accord).

**Symbolism**

**Shield:** See Distinctive Unit Insignia symbolism.

**Crest:** The organization's service in the China-Burma-India Theater of World War II is represented by the chinthé (a gold Burmese lion). The blue annulet symbolizes the Presidential Unit Citation awarded for service at Myitkyina, Burma, the "gateway to China." The gold embattlement in base refers to the unit's combat service in Vietnam while the six merlons represent six Valorous Unit Awards; the two Meritorious Unit Commendations earned by elements of the Regiment are denoted by the scarlet disc at center.

**Background:** The coat of arms was originally approved for the 75th Infantry Regiment on July 27, 1954. It was amended to add a crest on May 23, 1974. On February 3, 1986, the coat of arms was redesignated for the 75th Ranger Regiment.

Training with the French Foreign Legion in Corsica. (George Kohler)

who, of course, had more power within the overall structure of the SOC, also created in 1986.

Filling the 3rd Ranger Battalion was difficult; most recent graduates of the Ranger Indoctrination Program shuddered at the thought of having to go to the dark side. Groups of Rangers would quit often and repeatedly, and the Regiment was undergoing birthing pains. One Ranger recalled the enormous pressure that was placed on the Ranger Regiment's commander by his superiors from SOC – "you have got to fill those battalions, no matter what..." The battalions were filled, which at times was only accomplished by easing standards. RIP classes that usually would graduate fewer than 50 percent, now passed the majority of the recruits – slots needed to be filled. The Ranger Regimental Reconnaissance Detachment (RRD) was created, and many of its early members were privates who were sent straight to Ranger and HALO schools. Now, of course, RRD is made up of experienced, highly trained professionals. But those were the difficult days of change – the ascendancy of the officer corps, lip service to its professional NCOs, strict enforcement of SOPs (such clever and petty things as not wearing the patrol cap with a Ranger Crush), replacing the black physical training (PT) uniforms with the standard-issue gray Army PT uniforms, switching from the cammies to the jungles to the universally hated battledress uniform of the regular Army, as well as a departure from the most important of all charters of Abrams Charter, that of the commander taking sole responsibility for his men. No longer did Rangers take care of their own... no, indeed minor transactions could land you in leg land, excellent field soldiers who could not adapt to the new ways of vigorous barracks maintenance were forced out or quit. For many Airborne Rangers, the transition to US Army Rangers was painful, the pain delivered by the machinations of officers and senior NCOs at Fort Benning.

As the 1980s were passing, America as a whole was suffering from new ailments with which the Rangers were at times infected: drug abuse, theft, and sycophancy were all present. Morale was low and a certain double standard for officers becoming more and more evident... or so at least it seemed. Still, the Regiment did produce good soldiers and as one Ranger officer commented during that time: "Sure, we're not as good as the old timers, we'd take more casualties, but we'd still accomplish the mission."

Not all the changes of the 1980s were destructive, however. The one thing the regimental officers were painfully aware of was the misuse of Rangers throughout America's wars. Often Rangers were employed as regular infantry units, destroyed in the meat grinder of conventional war. The creation of the Special Operations Command gave the commanders a reason to put forth a doctrine for the proper employment of the Ranger Regiment in support of US Foreign Policy. The subsequent Ranger Doctrinal Statement (see Appendix F) helped clarify the role and capabilities of the Rangers, defining them as a specialist resource rather than as general infantry.

# From *Just Cause* to *Desert Storm*

For emergency use only

The 75th Ranger Regiment was once again called to arms in December of 1989. Nothing much had happened worldwide since the invasion of Grenada six long years before. The US Army Rangers had been rehearsing for combat for almost a year, although few of them knew that they were training for the invasion of Panama. Finally, however, there was to be action. The Regiment was tasked with two principal missions: the seizure of the airfields at Rio Hato and Tocumen-Torrijos, Panama.

Panama's elected leader was Manuel Noriega who slipped easily from ally into the role of dictator and drug-runner for a public-relations savvy US Administration that had previously supported him for a great many years. In 1986 Noriega survived an internal coup attempt and furthered his iron-fisted rule over Panama. The United States decided to remove Manuel Noriega and restore Panama's government, soon to take domain over the highly valuable Panama Canal.

The overall invasion and subjugation would be very easy indeed, as the United States had had bases and military personnel operating out of Panama for decades. As a matter of fact, the US military conducted jungle training out of the excellent Jungle Operations Training Center at Fort Sherman, Panama, from 1953 to 1999. In general terms the invasion would be more akin to an extended live-fire training exercise than the genuine invasion Americans were more accustomed to during World War II.

The Ranger Regiment always conducts real-world missions. Any and all training exercises are based on real-world events and places. So it comes as no surprise that the missions the Regiment were tasked with had been rehearsed for years, although few Rangers knew of the true nature of the training exercises. Twice a year the 75th Ranger Regiment conducts Joint Special Operations

Readiness Training exercises (JRTs). One Ranger officer recalls that all those "missions went into a 'Prayer Book' that basically contained a number of different war plans and contingency missions. The mission templates had been rehearsed and were validated during the JRTs and other special operations training missions."[50] Effectively, the US Special Operations Command (SOC) was capable of pulling out any number of different plans for virtually any place in the world. Especially during the preceding months of the invasion, the Rangers conducted rehearsals based on the Panama template. This was the first time the full Regiment participated in a JRT exercise. All three battalions, including Regimental Headquarters, as well as other sister Special Operations units from the Army, Navy, and Air Force participated.

The rehearsals at Eglin Air Force Base ended on December 14, 1989, and a couple of days later the battalions returned to their home bases; 1st Battalion to Hunter Army Airfield in Georgia, 2nd Battalion to Fort Lewis in Washington, and 3rd Battalion bussed back to Fort Benning, also in Georgia. Seemingly the invasion would take place the following year and some of the Battboys were looking forward to Christmas leave for a two-week period. Much to their displeasure and in typical Ranger Regiment fashion, the entire Regiment was put on alert on Sunday afternoon, December 17, 1989. Two staging areas became the assembly points for the 75th Ranger Regiment. All of 2nd Ranger Battalion and A and B Companies from the 3rd Ranger Battalion would combine at Fort Benning, while C Company, 3/75, would join the 1st Ranger Battalion at Hunter Army Airfield. Operation *Just Cause*, formerly known as Operation *Blue Spoon*, was about to launch.

The Panama invasion force responsible for executing Operation *Just Cause* was the Joint Task Force South (JTFS). The Special Operations component attached to JTFS was the Joint Special Operations Task Force (JSOTF), commanded by Major General Wayne A. Downing, and was organized into smaller task forces: Task Force Red comprised the Army's 75th Ranger Regiment,

Task Force Black was made up by Army Special Forces, and Task Force White constituted elements from the Naval Special Warfare component made up by SEALs and Special Boat Units. Completing the Special Operations Task Force were Psychological Operations and Civil Affairs units, Army Special Operations helicopters, and US Air Force air commando units.[51]

# TASK FORCE RED

Task Force Red was by far the largest element of the JSOTF. The order of battle was as follows: 75th Ranger Regiment, contingents from the 4th Psychological Operations Group (PSYOP), and 96th Civil Affairs (CA) Battalion, as well as Air Force Special Tactics teams and Marine Corps/Naval Gunfire liaison troops (ANGLICO). Close air support aircraft included AH-6 attack helicopters from the 160th Special Operations Aviation Regiment, AC-130H gunships from the 1st Special Operations Wing, and from the conventional forces, AH-64 Apaches and F-117A fighter-bombers. "The JSOTF's principal H-Hour missions were the capture of Noriega and the destruction of the Panamanian Defense Forces' (PDF) ability to fight. As it turned out, the U.S. forces did not know Noriega's location at H-Hour; accordingly, the JSOTF focused on the H-Hour missions against the PDF."[52]

Task Force Red was divided into two sub groups. The first element comprised the 2nd Ranger Battalion with two companies of the 3rd Ranger Battalion (Alpha and Bravo) would conduct a nighttime combat parachute assault at H-Hour (0100 on December 20, 1989) onto the military airfield at Rio Hato while simultaneously the 1st Ranger Battalion plus Charlie Company 3/75 would conduct a nighttime combat parachute assault onto the Omar Torrijos International Airport/Tocumen military airport complex. Conventional follow-on forces would then free up the Rangers for additional missions.

Three Rangers several hours after successfully assaulting Rio Hato. (Rodney LeMay)

# RIO HATO

The following is by a Bravo Company Ranger at Rio Hato:

I enlisted for the college money. RIP [Ranger Indoctrination Program] was very good and I graduated August 28, 1987.

Some odd things still stand out: 2nd Bn had a high dx rate versus Rangers ets'ing, something like 3 Rangers got canned for every one who finished his contract. Training needed to be more realistic, especially with hand grenades. A Ranger from 3rd Platoon injured himself seriously in Rio Hato. But I am getting ahead of myself. Pre-Ranger is possibly the best program I ever attended whereas Ranger School tended to be far too arbitrary and the instructors not always the best, nonetheless, you learn a lot about people and yourself.

Battalion was micro-managed at the time but training picked up around August or so of 1989, possibly in preparation for *Just Cause*. I returned from PLDC (Primary Leadership Development Course) and alert was in effect for one day already. Although LT Andrews, our PL, tried to convince everyone that the unit would deploy to Fort Bliss, we knew better. Air Force personnel were running around with side arms.

At Benning we received our warning order, which was rather brief and very little was said about the political situation in Panama. It was difficult to believe that we were to go to Panama during Christmas.

I felt very comfortable at the platoon and company level. Even if Battalion screwed up I was confident with 1st Platoon and Bravo Company. We were the best company in the Battalion.

## THE MISSION AT RIO HATO

B Co was to take out 2 companies (Infantry, Mechanized). 1st and 3rd Platoons were the assault elements and 2nd Platoon was the aid and litter unit.

C Co's objective was Noriega's beach house.

A Co was tasked with securing the Cadet School at Rio Hato.

1st Platoon, B Co, had about 35 Rangers deployed. Weapons Squad was relatively inexperienced and I think Ranger Kendall (Gun 3) burned in with a partial parachute malfunction.

In general, I found the operations order and other information to be somewhat misleading and not as good as I would liked to have had it. By the way, I was the third Ranger at the assembly area after about 20 minutes from the time of the drop. We had about 60 Rangers (1st and 3rd) who were supposed to take out 2 companies of maybe 300–400 soldiers. Would the Panamanians fight? The super-secret bomb drop via the Stealth plane was bullshit. The crater looked too small for a supposed 2000lb bomb. That's at least what the AF liaison said when we used it for a defensive perimeter. Back to the story.

We jumped at about 0100 hours, red tracers were everywhere. Spectre and little birds were used. I think I saw about 3 APCs on the dropzone, driving and shooting at everything. Oddly enough, lights were flashing on the APCs. My ruck weighed 100 pounds and I landed on the tarmac and hit my elbow pretty hard on the asphalt. I got out my gun, laid behind the ruck which was full of 10 lbs of C-4. 4 grenades, 400 rounds or so of 5.56mm and a claymore. Why am I using this for cover? Am I stupid or what?

## THE FIRST OBJECTIVE

It was pretty easy to find our AA and at about 0230 we moved out, but not at 100% strength. The "Bob Marley" was a great idea for identification purposes. The terrain to our first objective was supposed to be good, a little bit of grass with few trees. But it turned out to be heavy. It was very dark and it took us about 30 minutes to navigate to our objective.

Once we got out of the "jungle" we spotted the two lane road running parallel and just past it we saw the fence. Now this fence had 2–3 feet of concrete at the bottom with an 8 foot chain-link fence on top of it. 10 yards past this fence the compounds started.

1st Platoon took the left side and 3rd the right side of the barracks. There was no real covering fire, no M-60s. They either burned in or did not work. Little birds prepped the back of the compounds. 2nd Squad cleared the first building. Two-storied, day-room or recreation room with bad equipment and cokes.

MOUT training was no good. In training you are supposed to enter from the top. How do you do that? Also the manual was based on European building structures. You are not supposed to use doors but the windows are full of glass. Entering through the door you would take your chances that they may be booby trapped. But the enemy, in this case, may not have had enough time to do that. We used frags or concussion grenades and then 3-round bursts to clear the rooms.

3rd Squad took the next building. Long, with a kitchen, hot food on the table, ice in drinks, no lights, very dark. We entered another building with a long row of double beds, sheets hanging from the bunks for privacy. We lined up our fire team and fired rounds into them. By the way, the concussion grenades looked like smoke grenades but were black. Some failed to go off but the frags worked well.

From the last building, off at a half-right, there was a roofed shed which housed either boats or 75mm recoilless rifles. The distance was about 20 or so yards. A-team covered B-team. We took fire, ricochets chipping granite off blocks. A-team leader, Sergeant B., fired a 203 round HE (high explosive, dual purpose) at the building but it did not arm because of the short distance. I moved forward again with a private and kicked in the door to the shed. The private to the side yelled that something was there. I did not shoot because I knew 3rd Platoon was off to our right. On the left side I heard another shout and that private fired a short burst from his SAW. I joined him and saw a Panamanian with an AK-47, barrel in hand. I yelled at him several times to drop his weapon and finally walked up to him and knocked the weapon out of his hand. We

Rangers applying make-up?
Regimental SOP prescribes a
tiger-stripe pattern alternating
between green and loam.
(US Army)

crawled back. I noticed that the Panamanian was bleeding from the nose
and ears, deaf and in shock. I took him to Lieutenant Andrews at the end
of the compound fence and the EPW ended up with the RIP Detachment
who were guarding prisoners.

## THE SECOND OBJECTIVE

We moved 50 meters or so through the jungle to our second objective. This
was around 0400. It took us one hour or maybe one and a half hours to
clear the first objective. 1st Squad in front. The lead Ranger fell into a
ravine. He told us to move off toward the right to avoid the ravine. We
came out of the jungle into an open area and saw a two-story building on
fire, possibly Spectre or little bird damage. We formed up as we did on the
first objective. 1st Squad left, then 2nd and 3rd on the right. 1st Squad
received fire. 2nd and 3rd cleared the buildings. We stopped and formed a
wagon wheel defensive perimeter. It is here that our Medic, Ranger P., told
us about Sergeant Howard getting shot and that Lear was dead. I could not
believe it. Damn, damn, damn. I passed the word along to Malecha Jr.

Daylight and we moved toward the ocean. A big building with a Red
Cross symbol, roads – nothing. We went to the city of Rio Hato and rounded
up all males between 14 and 80, kicked in doors, flex-cuffed individuals and
took them to Bn HQ or Regimental HQ – they were handling all EPWs.

We set up another perimeter in a crater near the mechanized company area, our second objective. Spectre was on station all night. We did not account for over 300 enemy personnel. I was worried and confused but yet I went to sleep.

Squads patrolled the next day. One set up an ambush between the airfield and our first objective. Sniper fire had been reported. Nothing happened but we did find a parachute in the trees. Nobody knew nothing and no information was passed down the line.

We moved back to our first objective area and spent our third night there. At dusk the intel was that the Panamanians might counterattack. Spent a bad night, worried. We got some reinforcements from privates who had air-landed. Spent another night.

In the morning the 7th ID showed up. We didn't know that we were supposed to be relieved. The soldiers were pointing their weapons everywhere. An E-6 had his weapon off safe and was pointing it in our direction. Finally a Ranger got up and put the weapon on safe.

We moved to the airfield, loaded onto a C-130 and flew to Howard AFB and from there to an elementary school. Lots of rumors were floating around and nobody was allowed to call home for one or two days. Our platoon had an after action review.

Subsequently, we flew in Chinooks to Alcade Diaz, did some road blocking, patrolled streets to be visible, moved elsewhere and did the same all over again. Our platoon set up a CP at a paper factory and we had a two jeep reaction teams ready, just in case.

Whereas our Battalion Commander was driving around in an air conditioned car, barely cracking the window, to jack us up, the Regimental Commander Buck Kernan and Regimental Sergeant-Major Guerrero walked all over the perimeters and talked with us. That was great for morale! Our BC even fired a Platoon Leader for purchasing food and drink for the troops. Procurement was not officially sanctioned, yet, everybody bought food stuffs from the locals. Eventually, I think the PL was reinstated by Kernan – HOOAH!

*Name withheld by request,*
*Bravo Company, 2nd Battalion, 75th Ranger Regiment*

The following is a Ranger perspective of Panama:

We had four missions in Panama:

1) Rio Hato: 2nd Platoon, A/Co, 3/75 was tasked to attack and occupy the PDF Cadet Academy at Rio Hato. The jump was a f*****g madhouse. I am still not sure where I landed. I think it was above the lake. It took me 3 hours to link up with my platoon. They had already taken the objective and were moving the EPWs to a collection point. The cadets pretty much gave up and the cadre split for the woods. The next morning we still had about 10 guys from our Platoon who hadn't linked

up. We got mortared that morning by about two or three rounds about 100 yards behind our position (could have been 203 rounds and not 60mm).

2) Penonome Prison: 2nd Platoon mission was to provide security for a Delta force assault on the prison. My task was to set up a blocking position with an M-60 on a road leading up to the shit hole. This place was a f*****g trip. Big stone walls about 15 feet high and a stone tower 20 feet high in each corner. The PDF were holding some political prisoners here that our government wanted free. AC-130 was to provide air cover. TF 160 flew us in. We were to fast-rope in and move to our position. Each tower had an M-60 GPMG and 3-5 PDF. TF 160 door gunners were supposed to take out the towers. Since I was the only one with a real weapon I was going down the f*****g rope first. The bird was going to hover between two towers with M-60s about 100 yards apart and I'm supposed to slide down that stupid rope with two guns shooting at me? I was more scared thinking about that than the Rio Hato jump. And the icing on the cake – the SOUTHCOM Commander actually called the PDF prison commander and told him "my BOYS are coming to kick your ass if you don't surrender in one hour." Can you believe that stupid mother f****r? My platoon sergeant told us this as we were loading our birds – greatly increasing the pucker factor. About one minute from the target we learned they had surrendered and we were air-landing. I move to my blocking position, set up for about 30 minutes then reconsolidated. We got to spend the night lying on the floor of a cell in the prison. f*****g wonderful. [See opposite for details]

3) David: Company sized airfield seizure. 2nd Platoon was to secure the fire station and set up blocking positions near airfield gate. The mission also called to locate and possibly capture Del Cid, the second man in Noriega's government. Inserted by TF 160 Chinooks to a crowd of cheering Panamanians, about 2,000 m********s (I wonder if the SOUTHCOM CDR placed another call?). I set up our post and hung out. Two local chicks started bullshitting with 1st Squad to whom I was attached. We also had a local Civil Affairs interpreter with us. The highlight of our glorious mission was when a moped cruised by us real slow with two hard-asses aboard, checking us out. The chicks started yelling UESAT, UESAT (the PDF version of Delta force). They put the gas down and hauled, never did catch them. 7th SFGA was seriously wired into this town. They had done a lot of snooping and asset building. Another stroll in the park for the mighty 3/75. Boring.

4) Isla de Coiba: The fantasy island mission. This was another PDF prison. Our objective was to secure the prison and free about 30 politicos who had participated in the recent coup against Noriega. TF 160 Chinooks and AF MH-53 (they must have been bored) inserted us. No action. The Shark Platoon all swam away. Another snoozer.

## Penonome Prison raid in detail

Our squad, Weapons Squad, 2nd Platoon, A Co., 3/75 Ranger Regiment, stood in a loose semi-circle, hanging on every word that our acting Squad Leader Specialist J. M. said. Had a new mission, our first after the jump into Rio Hato. M. took over the squad when our regular squad leader was seriously injured on the jump in. As he went over the mission and I took notes, two things stood out. One, that the op order called for us to do a fast-rope insertion under fire and two, if anything happened to the SL, I would be the man on the hot seat – responsible for 10 other Rangers since I was the next senior E-4 M-60 gunner.

The mission was simple. It seems like they always say that when things are about to go to shit. Elements of A Co, 3/75th and Delta were to assault the Penonome Prison, secure selected political prisoners and exfil. A Co would set up blocking positions and secure the perimeter, while the D-Boys kicked in doors, blew shit up, exfilled first and covered themselves in glory, while we laid in some Panamanian farmer's shit-filled goat pen covering their asses.

Penonome Prison had high stone walls in a square configuration with large guard towers at each corner. Picture a French Foreign Legion fort in the middle of the desert and that's Penonome. According to Intel the prison contained 35–50 guards with small arms, pistols, M-16s, AK-47s. Each tower mounted an M-60 GPM and two guards. This was particularly worrisome since our Black Hawk was going to insert us roughly 200 meters from the prison walls between two of the guard towers. I wondered if the chain of command knew what the word cross-fire meant. Oh, that's right, they wouldn't be riding on my bird. The plan said that TF 160 gunners on the Black Hawks would use their Mini-guns to neutralize the towers. We also would have Spectre to support us. My specific mission was to take my gun-team, myself and my AG PFC S.M., down a road running up to the prison and set up the gun.

Let's get back to this fast-roping thing again. Have you ever watched Discovery Channel's weekly SEAL Team documentary when they fast rope? It's about a 60-footer. There is one guy at a time on the rope and each one lands daintily on his feet and jogs off before the next man slides down. At 3rd Batt things were done a bit differently. A 60-foot fast-rope usually had 5 or 6 guys on the rope at a time and 5 or 6 guys in a dogpile at the bottom of the rope. At this time I had done probably 10 fast-ropes and I don't recall ever landing on my feet and running off. Crawling more like it.

About an hour prior to our loadtime word was passed down that the SOUTHCOM Commander had called the prison Commandant and told him that his BOYS were going to kick his ass tonight if he didn't release the political prisoners. These were guys who were the heart and soul of a future democratic government of Panama. What a load of crap – more likely they were stupid and wanted more of Noriega's piece of the pie and got busted. To this day I don't know if that call was actually made or was rumor control in action?

Loadtime. Oh shit, this is the real deal. Here comes that strange mix of fear, adrenaline and sick excitement that sits in the pit of your stomach. I can't remember if I volunteered to go down the rope first or if I was told to. We had about a 45-minute flight. I sat with my M-60 and feet hanging out of the bird. Hauling ass at low-level with my knees in the breeze was probably my favorite thing to do in the Army. Tonight it wasn't. We flew over the town of Penonome. "Two minutes" came the shouted warning. I looked over to M., got a thumbs-up, checked the gun one last time, and slid my ass a few more inches out of the bird. I tried to look forward to see if any fireworks were appearing at the prison. Couldn't see crap. Suddenly everyone is shouting, "Cold LZ, air-land, air-land, the prison's empty."

The bird landed, we bailed out and did a quick huddle with the Boss. He pointed down the road and off we went. We approached a bend in the road and decided to set up the gun. I looked around and realized that we were probably about 30 meters out in front of the rest of the platoon. Oh shit, maybe we should pull back? So we backed up, set the gun up in a nice little 3 inch ditch next to the road. Cut a hole in some poor farmer's goat corral fence, so if trouble came down the road we could boogie off into the jungle.

After around 30 minutes we picked up and headed inside the prison. A beautiful third-world prison shit-hole. We hung out in the courtyard for a while, awaiting the exfil aircraft. Finally the birds arrived. We loaded and flew off into the sunrise.

Today as I write this it's been 10 years since this mission happened. Parts of it remain quite vivid to this day, other parts have faded to gray. Maybe it's my selective memory, I don't know. I remember back at Benning sitting around bull-shitting with the Boys – everyone talked about wishing that Penonome was a hot target. A combat fast-rope under fire, you could talk some serious shit after that. But I know secretly everyone was glad Penonome was a dry hole. I know I was.

*Name Withheld*
*A Company, 3rd Battalion, 75th Ranger Regiment*

# TORRIJOS/TOCUMEN AIRFIELD

A battalion surgeon's perspective:

My recollection of Operation *Just Cause* begins during a Christmas party for the medics of 1/75. They were all at my house when our beepers went off. We broke up the party and headed into headquarters where I left all of the treats from our party. I don't know if this was the best-planned mission ever, but it certainly had the best-fed planners ever as my wife is an excellent cook. Only the details had to be worked out. The mission was planned months in advance.

The planning phase went by uneventfully but I remember doing PLFs in several inches of icy water during sustained airborne training. Hard to

The true face of battle. Enemy dead of the Panamanian Defense Force defending Rio Hato. (Author's collection)

believe how cold and icy it was in the U.S. compared to how relatively warm it was in Panama.

During the flight over, the commander on my aircraft relayed messages he received from a satcom operator. The PDF (Panamanian Defense Force) somehow knew we were coming as evidence by their passing out live ammo and posturing at all of their defense points. This information did not really concern me at the time, as ignorance is a great shield from fear. We trained so often doing just what we were doing now that it felt just like another training mission. I guess the first point at which I noticed that this was real was when we collected our base load before we left. I was impressed with how much ammunition a Battalion Surgeon was issued. They had claymores, all kinds of pyrotechnics and tons of 9 or 5.56mm. I only took what I thought I might need. When we were uploading the aircraft, I noticed that there were cameramen recording the mission. That was something new also. During the flight over, the commander relayed the information that some MIGs were trailing us. I didn't worry about that much either because what could I do about it anyway?

I was the 7th man on the left door in the 3rd aircraft. I knew we would only make one pass so I tried to get to the door as quickly as possible. Kind of hard to do when you are carrying enough stuff to open a small hospital between your legs. Seems like every time I thought I was packed, I would think of one more thing I needed. "Just one more liter of IV fluid might mean the difference between survival or not for some young Ranger" kept going through my mind. Sort of a variation of mission creep kept occurring. The huahs probably have a set load established but I think many did the same. It would take a Mack truck or a Ranger to carry some of the rucks I saw.

It all seemed real for me for the first time right about the second that I stepped out the door of the aircraft. It was real dark, almost black except for where Spectre was shifting fire. I could see a trace of red light in my left peripheral vision where the AC-130 was smoking one last bunker. Looked kind of like a god throwing down a lightning bolt. Glad they were on our side!

As I was floating down I tried to figure out where I was. I could see and hear small arms fire in a lot of places but most seemed to be in a corridor that lay straight in front of me. I later realized that the field I was looking at was one which led from the airfield to an adjacent neighborhood. It was a good egress rout for the PDF that decided to run at the last moment. Noriega himself hung out in that neighborhood for days. He was visiting the airfield to dedicate a new medical clinic the next day. We woke him up and he just barely slipped away with rounds from one of our blocking positions following him.

I distinctly remember thinking, "come on ground," as I wanted to get down as fast as possible. Even starting at 450ft, it seemed to take a long time to get down. When I did land, I managed to find just about the only tree on the whole airfield. It was a short bushy tree only about 30ft tall. I didn't really do a PLF but just managed to get through the branches to the ground. There I found myself sitting on cut grass with a trace of white light illuminating me from a window of what I later found out was the fire station. I was looking at the elephant grass wall about 20 meters away that was the beginning of the field leading away from the airfield to where Noriega was.

The elephant grass must have been about 5 or 6 feet tall because I could just make out the outline of two shadows approaching me. I knew they weren't Rangers because they couldn't have gotten out of their chutes before me. Now I was scared. My rifle was in its container keeping it from being damaged on the jump. If I could see these guys, they could see me better. Sometime about then I had one of those experiences where time moves slowly. I remembered my whole past present and future in about 3 milliseconds. The only thought that remained was something like: "Oh shit, I have been studying for my whole life to be a doctor and now some bastard is going to kill me before I even get a chance to use those skills that took me my whole adult life to acquire." The whole time I am thinking this, I am grabbing my nine mil from its holster. The only thing that saved the guy on the left was lack of tritium sights. I shot him a little too high but square in the head and tried to hit the second one but he dove for the taller elephant grass. Now I couldn't see either one but I knew one or both were still alive. I wanted to shoot and move but I couldn't find the quick release to unhook my lowering line. I previously released my canopy when I first hit the ground. I tried to shoot the lowering line with my pistol. It would have worked on TV but it didn't in real life. When I realized I couldn't get the harness free on the ruck and chute, like all good doctors or Rangers, I quickly executed plan B. I took off the harness, pulled my CAR15 out of the container and tossed a frag in the direction opposite of where I was headed. Once again, it would have worked on TV but real life is not always so kind. My grenade hit branches from the tree mentioned earlier and made it close to the two guys behind me but too close to me also. When my internal clock counted to 5, I dove for the ground. I felt a burning in my left triceps and hip. I jumped up and ran around the building and took a knee behind what I thought was a pallet. I just tried to let my eyes adjust to the dark and my ears adjust to the sounds around me.

I was just getting my wits about me when the building erupted with the sounds of gunfire. I could hear a few hundred rounds being expended. I wasn't sure whether our side or theirs was being represented until two troopers emerged and threw a chemlight over the door. That was the signal that the building had been cleared. Interestingly, later one very scared military fireman emerged from the fire station somehow unscathed.

I had my radio and weapon and now knew I was roughly where I needed to be. We planned on setting up the Battalion Aid Station at the fire station in case we wanted to use white light inside. Not having seen a casualty yet I figured that would soon change. The next Ranger that came near offered to cover me while I ran across the open to pick up my ruck. I did a 360 around the building ending up next to the "pallet" that I kneeled next to earlier. Along the way, I saw a SOCOM interpreter with a badly broken ankle. I gave him a couple of Tylenol three and told him not to worry. The pallet turned out to be a bunker with a 30 caliber heavy machine gun mounted on a tripod. Along side it were RPGs [rocket-propelled grenades], AK-47s and bunches of ammo. Turns out my glide path led me right across this position on my way to the tree. I later found out that the bunker was manned at the time of our jump.

One of our young lieutenants broke his jaw playing combat football on organization day during Thanksgiving. He rode on the AC-130 flying over our objective as a Ranger liaison. He told me that he could see that the bunker in front of the fire station was manned when we jumped but the PDF soldier ran when the time was right. I imagine seeing roughly 700 Rangers coming at you in earnest would give me pause too. Leaving while they are still under canopy sounds like a pretty good idea. As an aside, that lieutenant joined up with us the next day. I lent him my CAR15 and he stayed for around a week. He had a battery-operated blender, which he used to crush MREs with so he could stuff food past his teeth, which were wired shut. A few days after his batteries died he was looking pretty pale from not eating so I had to request that he be sent home.

We established the Bn Aid Station near the fire station and were saddened to hear that one of our medics was killed. James Markwell, who I had only recently come to know well, was shot in the chest. He was trying to stop a vehicle driving on the airfield. Many of the PDF changed into civilian clothes and tried to drive vehicles by and shoot at us. That way, they could drive off if things weren't going well. Most found that not to be a very good idea. Amazingly, the AC-130 can hit moving targets. There is a sign in front of the PDF barracks that has three 105 rounds through it. Looks like a giant above the earth was shooting a rifle down at them. In a manner of speaking, he was.

Most of our casualties were picked up on their part of the drop zone by a medivac instead of bringing them to the Bn Aid Station. We had a

SOCOM satcom operator coordinating these medivac runs. That worked well except when the 82nd kept tying up our air space. We called in that the airfield was secure, but they kept dropping jumpers well into the next day during daylight. A day later, we were having a staff meeting on the tarmac and an 82nd trooper walks up looking just like Tom Selleck on Magnum PI. He was wearing flip-flops, jeans, and a Hawaiian shirt. He asked us where his Bn of the 82nd was. Tom had apparently landed in the neighborhood adjacent to the airfield and decided to ditch his gear and go native for a day. Now that the coast was clear, he was trying to find his unit.

I have other recollections like delivering babies for the locals who heard that American doctors were at the airfield. Ultimately, I think we were pretty lucky that the PDF did not more vigorously defend the airfield. There is not much cover out there. I expect we would have prevailed but the cost would have been much higher. As I recall, they had roughly 20–30 KIA versus our one. Lest you think that a small price to pay though, imagine that one was you or someone very important to you. Our commander made some comments on that subject. I think for me that this experience was a very humbling one. I realize that Rangers in the past and in the future have been or will be called upon to accomplish some mission that will require a much more dear payment.

One of my medics was heart broken that he got left behind because he was in a school and missed the mission. Other classmates risked going AWOL and returned to the Bn just on the chance that there might be a mission. I remember a line of Rangers some sporting casts outside the aid station prior to the mission. Every one of them wanted to be put back on duty, casts and all. I don't think my friend who missed the jump is any less Ranger for having missed that operation. I have no doubt that he would have done whatever the mission required.

Being a Ranger means being a part of something bigger than you are. Those young soldiers exemplify what is good about being an American. They are intelligent, well trained, motivated, and selfless in their devotion to duty. I am proud to have once been a member of their ranks. To all the Rangers of the past, present, and future, Sua Sponte, Rangers Lead The Way!

*LTC T. Scott McGee, MD*
*Headquarters, 1st Battalion, 75th Ranger Regiment*

| RANGER CASUALTIES IN OPERATION *JUST CAUSE* | | |
|---|---|---|
| Soldier | Battalion | Date KIA |
| SSG Larry Barnard | 3-75 | 20-Dec-89 |
| PFC Roy Brown, Jr. | 3-75 | 20-Dec-89 |
| SPC Philip Lear | 2-75 | 20-Dec-89 |
| PFC James W. Markwell | 1-75 | 20-Dec-89 |
| PFC John Mark Price | 2-75 | 20-Dec-89 |

As well as a test of classic soldiering, the invasion of Panama was also a testing ground for hi-tech weapons. When a Stealth bomber dropped a 2000lb smart bomb near its intended target in Rio Hato, then Secretary of Defense Dick Cheney announced the news victoriously in a press briefing, eager to demonstrate its value to American warfighting – forgetting, of course, that technology only aids the conduct of war, and does not dictate it.

# DESERT STORM – AN EXERCISE IN FRUSTRATION

Saddam Hussein was a US ally against the Iranians during the Iran-Iraq War (1980–88). He waged a brutal war, reminiscent of the slaughterhouses of the Great War (1914–18), and afterwards was insisting on reducing his debt to his Arab allies. Unable to do so for a variety of reasons, and never having acknowledged Kuwait as an independent nation-state, he decided to settle the affair with an invasion. After a meeting with a US representative, where Saddam believed he was given tacit approval, Iraqi forces quickly overcame what pitiful resistance Kuwait could muster. Hussein in the past had created an image of being a modern-day Saladin, capable of unifying the Arab world, while defying the United States and Israel. Never mind that the war between Iran and Iraq had produced a million deaths and had seen the use of poison gas. Also, never mind that the US administration had aided Iraq directly with intelligence, weapons, and direct actions from 1982 on. In 1988 the USS *Vincennes* shot down an Iranian commercial airliner, killing nearly 300 civilians in the process, and seemingly engaged some small Iranian vessels as well. Yet, ironically, President Reagan's administration was also selling weapons to Iran and using the proceeds to fund the Contra rebels in Nicaragua, who ultimately overthrew a

Rangers during *Desert Storm* – none too pleased. (D. Sirois)

pro-communist government.[53] It was against the backdrop of Irangate that Saddam Hussein's army invaded America's neo-colony Kuwait on August 2, 1990.

Rangers would play virtually no role during the Gulf War as the commanding general, Norman Schwarzkopf Jr, was not too fond of Special Operations Forces in general. Though it is a hard pill to swallow, the general is correct in his assertion that SOF units do not win wars and this clearly was a conventional war. Nonetheless, the Ranger Regiment did find a mission here or there.

The history released by the Regiment attempts to paint a better picture:

> Elements of Company B and 1st Platoon Company A, 1st Battalion, 75th Ranger Regiment deployed to Saudi Arabia from February 12, 1991 to April 15, 1991, in support of OPERATION DESERT STORM. The Rangers conducted raids and provided a quick reaction force in cooperation with Allied forces; there were no Ranger casualties. The performance of these Rangers significantly contributed to the overall success of the operation, and upheld the proud traditions of the past.

Additionally, Regimental Headquarters and the 1st Battalion, 75th Ranger Regiment participated in a glorious forced road march after a parachute jump onto the Ali Salem airfield in Kuwait as part of Operation *Iris Gold* whereupon they fired their weapons in a show of frustration, during a live-fire exercise of course.[54]

Actions on the Objective – raid

Critical Tasks
Secure and occupy ORP
Leader's recon of OBJ:
 Pinpoint OBJ
 Determine positions
 Establish surveillance
Confirm plan
Emplace security element
Emplace support element
Emplace assault element
PL initiates raid
Support lifts/Shifts fire
Assault element assaults
 through OBJ
Establish LOA/security
Consolidate/reorganize
 Reposition as necessary
 Search OBJ
 Treat wounded
Assault withdraws
Support withdraws
Security withdraws
Patrol consolidates in ORP
(from US Army Ranger
Handbook)

# Somalia Operation *Gothic Serpent*

## A dark place indeed

Somalia was formed in 1960 by the union of British Somaliland and Italian Somaliland. At civil war since 1977, Somalia has approximately 14 major factions participating in internecine warfare. The majority of Somalis are Sunni Moslems. In 1991 the Somali government collapsed after decades of civil war in which killings and beheadings became common occurrences. The already-weakened infrastructure, coupled with a drought, led to the death of hundreds of thousands of Somalis from starvation. Food relief missions, initiated by private organizations, were seized by various clans who in turn used these assets to procure additional weapons and pay their followers.

The violent nature of the Somali clans hampered further relief efforts to such a point that the United Nations approved Resolution 751 in April 1992 to provide humanitarian aid to Somalia (UNOSOM I). Unable to accomplish the mission properly, due to the lack of proper resources, the United States initiated Operation *Provide Relief*. Although temporarily successful and welcomed by many Somalis, additional security measures were needed, and a few months later Operation *Restore Hope* sought to provide military as well as humanitarian support.

In March 1993, Operation *Restore Hope* was turned over to UN Peacekeeping Forces and UNOSOM II was created, making it the first ever UN-directed peacekeeping mission. The mandate called for three distinct phases: disarm Somali clans, rebuild the political infrastructure, and create a more secure environment. Twenty-one nations contributed personnel to UNOSOM II. Turkish General Bir and retired Admiral Jonathan Howe, acting as special representative to the UN Secretary-General, were in command.

# EFFECTS OF UNOSOM II

UN nation-building efforts in Somalia threatened certain clans, most notably the Somali National Alliance (SNA) under the leadership of Mohammed Aidid, the former chief of staff. Headquartered in Mogadishu, Aidid trained in guerrilla war and quickly initiated a campaign of resistance against the UN which ultimately led to a series of ambushes killing 24 Pakistani peacekeepers. These soldiers were physically torn apart and dismembered by the drugged-up clansmen.

The UN was forced to demonstrate its willingness to protect its peacekeepers and the next day the UN and the White House, under the leadership of UN Secretary-General Boutros-Ghali and Madeline Albright, passed Resolution 837, authorizing action against those held responsible, namely Aidid. Strained relations between the Clinton administration and the military led to the exclusion of any input from the Pentagon regarding Resolution 837.

The humanitarian mission evolved into a military one. Gunships arrived, and with the additional firepower, numerous Aidid assets were destroyed or seized. Boutros-Ghali had been a longtime enemy of Aidid, and was unable quickly to resolve the escalating military situation in Mogadishu. Howe placed a $25,000 bounty on Aidid. The battles became personal. Bir and Howe became frustrated enough to request proper troops for the manhunt – SFOD-Delta and US Army Rangers.

# TASK FORCE RANGER

Task Force Ranger (TFR) was placed under the command of General William Garrison. Although numerous raids took place, Aidid was not caught. Additional firepower in the form of mechanized vehicles and armor was denied by the Secretary of Defense Les Aspin after an American helicopter was shot down.[55]

Mogadishu and its devastation.
(75th RR)

Frustrated and under pressure from the White House, which had secretly opened negotiations with Aidid, TFR undertook an unnecessary but daring daylight raid, resulting in the battles of October 3–4, 1993, where 18 American servicemen died and Somali casualties ranged from 350–700 killed and thousands wounded. The White House withdrew US troops shortly thereafter.

The 75th Rangers Public Affairs Office sums up the Rangers' action as follows: "From August 26, 1993, to October 21, 1993, Company B, a Platoon from A Company and a command and control element of 3rd Battalion, 75th Ranger Regiment, deployed to Somalia to assist United Nations forces in bringing order to a desperately chaotic and starving nation. Their mission was to capture key leaders in order to end clan fighting in and around the city of Mogadishu. On October 3, 1993, the Rangers conducted a daring daylight raid with 1st SFOD in which several special operations helicopters were shot down. For nearly 18 hours, the Rangers delivered devastating firepower, killing an estimated 600 Somalis in what many have called the fiercest ground combat since Vietnam. Six Rangers paid the supreme sacrifice in accomplishing their mission. Their courage and selfless service epitomized the values espoused in the Ranger Creed, and are indicative of the Ranger spirit of yesterday, today, and tomorrow."[56] (For a detailed timeline of events, see page 152.)

One of the conclusions produced by the Mogadishu battle was that the intelligence and military communities' dependence on high technology in a zero-

B Company, 3/75, the day of Black Hawk Down. (Anton Berendsen)

tech environment clearly demonstrated a command failure. Human intelligence gathering was non-existent and not properly supported throughout. Some analysts believe that Aidid set up TFR with faulty intelligence. There is no direct evidence supporting that statement. It has been asserted that intelligence collaboration with other UN forces would have been appropriate. Given the "neutrality" stance of certain countries this would have led to a disaster. The Italians have been accused of alerting the clans whenever US troops (TFR) departed for missions.[57]

The so-called failure in Somalia led to the Clinton Administration's refusal to intervene in the Rwandan civil war that saw the massacre of at least 800,000 people.[58]

# A NEW PARADIGM – DELTA AND RANGERS ARE NOT INVINCIBLE

As a member of the US Army's 3rd Battalion, 75th Ranger Regiment, Specialist John M. Collett was sent with his platoon to Somalia to assist UN forces in the city of Mogadishu. His group had completed approximately six missions prior to the Sunday described on the following pages. This account of the mission that began on Sunday, October 3, 1993 was written by John immediately upon his return from his 18-hour ordeal. John received the Purple Heart for wounds received in action and was awarded the Bronze Star Medal with a "V" device for heroism.

> For those of us who lived, we will always remember
> For those who died, they will never be forgotten
> For those who weren't there, they will not fully understand.

It started out as every Sunday had the four weeks since we arrived in the Mog (Mogadishu, Somalia, Africa). We woke up when we wanted. There was no first call on Sundays. Everyone was playing volleyball and tanning as usual. Tile beach runs had stopped because we weren't allowed in the water; a shark had eaten a Russian a few days earlier.

All in all we hadn't hit the ground on a mission for about two weeks. We hadn't been mortared for several days. (The chain of command had told us over and over not to become complacent.)

Then word came we were getting orders to go on a mission. However, there were several things that had to go right before we could launch. Shortly we were given the order to prepare and launch.

It was October 3, 1993. It didn't occur to anyone until later that the 3rd Ranger Battalion had been formed nine years earlier on this same day.

As usual people would come running out of the command center with photos of the objective areas, TGT (target) buildings and where we were going to infiltrate. SGT Watson was the chalk leader, CW3 (Chief Warrant Officer) Wood was our pilot, SGT Norton was our crew chief and door gunner.

We got our equipment on as usual. Putting on our bullet-proof vests, LCE (load carrying equipment), and K-pot, I carried an M149 SAW (squad automatic weapon). This was a day mission so no night vision devices were taken. I had 950 rounds of 5.56 mm ammunition and one frag. We moved to the aircraft, which was already spun up. SFC Watson passed around the map again so everyone would see the target building. Mr Wood came from the JOC (Joint Operations Center) where he received all the last minute night instructions. He put on his flight suit and we were ready to go. As usual the little birds (helicopters) took off first. The Hardy Boys (Delta Force) gave us the thumbs up as they usually did when they flew by. When the bird takes off is when the adrenaline starts pumping. The Black Hawk took off and we took our standard position in the flight formation. We were Chalk 3, our bird was Super 66. Shortly after the helicopters formed up SFC Watson gave us the thumbs up. The mission was a go. SGT Norton began passing the countdown, 6 min, 3 min, 1 min as we neared the objective. We had two brown outs where we could see nothing, but Mr Wood held tight and got us right on target. Tin was blowing off the roofs of buildings, people were getting blown around below us. We got the signal to ready the fast rope. I looked at SGT Ramaglia and we were both making the Catholic cross at the same time. This was our 7th mission and the first time I made the sign of the cross.

It felt different this time. As we hovered over the Somalis, waiting to fast rope down, they were waving to us to come down and play, so we did. We were given the signal to throw the ropes. SGT Hulst was first out the door, followed by SGT Ramaglia, then me. I hit the ground, got up against a building and started pulling security up the street. There was sporadic gunfire all around us. We ID'd (identified) our target building, then RPGs (rocket propelled grenades) started going off. I saw one of the birds smoking, so I knew it had been hit. I looked back and saw SGT Watson yelling at SGT Hulst to move down another alley in an effort to link up with Chalk 1. We moved across the street and into another alley and linked up with Chalk 1. We were receiving gunfire from another alley and cross-fire from the alley we were in. SSG (Staff Sergeant) Elliott and a few others were facing the alley laying down suppressive fire. I was set in next to a gate that was an entrance to the objective building. SPC Errico and SPC DeJesus were engaging targets down the alley, also saying there were people in the trees and building windows shooting at us. At this time I had no really good field of fire. I was watching under the gate to make sure that no enemy would try to hit us from the side.

The Humvees pulled up about then and SGT Strucker got out and started talking to SFC Watson. The .50 cal on top of the Humvee started hosing (killing) people that were shooting at us. It's funny that at that time I thought to myself "shit another mission I won't get to fire my SAW." I could have never been more wrong. The shit hadn't hit the fan yet, hell they hadn't even turned on the fan. We got word that in fact a bird (helicopter) had gone down about two blocks away and that we were going to have to secure it, while they tried to get the casualties out. The Humvees moved out. I watched as our means of exfill drove on by, but we had a more important mission, that was to secure the crash site. Chalk 1 picked up, CP Black Assault Force came out of objective building, and Chalk 3 started moving towards the crash site. We had someone laying suppressive fire on the alleys as we executed the "scrolls of the road," modified to a MOUT environment. We ran up the street and made a left, as we were moving the fire from the enemy increased. Branches were falling from the trees as gun fire hit them. Bullets have a very distinctive sound when they are being shot at you, and not away from you. We made a left and stopped. As we were proceeding up the previous alley, SFC Watson was on the left side of the street and I was on the right. Bullets were hitting above our heads as we were moving out at a trot. He looked over at me, as casual as can be and said, "this sucks."

Back to the alley where we had stopped. PFC Young, our forward observer took up a position on the corner, facing the direction we had come from. Doc Strouse was next to him, Errico was to my left. We were almost shoulder to shoulder firing at the corner of a building. We were taking fire from the building by people sticking AK-47s and oilier weapons around the corner and spraying them in our general direction, PFC Young kept suppressive fire in the direction we had come from. We were taking a hell of a cross fire down that alley. We now also started taking fire from our left. PFC Neatherly was also on the corner with his M60 firing. I yelled at SGT Ramaglia to put a 40mm round in the alley. He fired a round and it was short, blowing up about 10m in front of our position. I told him it was short. He tried a second round and it hit square into the building blowing it up. We didn't receive near as much effective fire from that corner after that. I remember SGT Ramaglia could not get his 203 off safe. He pulled a round out of his jacket and started hitting the safety. I have never seen such determination on anyone's face before.

The only on-the-ground photo taken during the fire-fight and released. (75th RR)

SFC Watson knew we were taking a hell of a crossfire, so he pulled Neatherly back and put him in the middle of the road behind a rock, a position I would soon occupy for many hours. As I said we were starting to take effective fire from the alley on our left. PFC Young repositioned himself so he would have effective fire down this alley, Doc Strouse positioned himself to fire to the right. They threw a frag at us. I looked up and saw it coming through the trees. I saw the spoon hit the ground. It landed about 15m in front of our position and exploded. PFC Errico yelled "frag." We hit the ground as it exploded. Doc caught some shrapnel in the leg. Errico caught some in the ankle. SFC Watson told us to start pulling back so we could defend until night. Doc pulled back and started bandaging himself.

SFC Watson yelled for him to get behind cover, Errico pulled back, then me. Neatherly moved to tile other side of the alley. He was laying down suppressive fire and shot some "Sammy" (Somali) in the face. A few seconds later he got shot in the right arm and yelled, "I'm hit." I was in the prone position at that time in the middle of the road behind some rocks and a mound of dirt. In this position it was hard for the "sammys" to effectively engage me. I had a great field of fire. I laid down some fire so Doc, Errico and Kurth could run over to me. Just before that though, a few seconds before I set in, I looked back to watch Chalk 1 and Delta move up the street we were on, Just as I looked back at them one of the D-boys got shot in the head. It rocked his head back and blood went everywhere. The man behind him grabbed him and started pulling him back to cover. He got shot in the neck. When he got shot he put his hands to his face and screamed. I thought, "shit." I knew the shit had hit the fan. A few seconds later Neatherly got shot as I stated before. Right after Neatherly got shot I threw my frag towards the building where the fire had come from. It blew up and silenced them for a little while. Doc and

Peacetime picture of little birds in action. (Anton Berendsen)

One of the 5-ton trucks carrying captured Somalis and Rangers. (Anton Berendsen)

Kurth started providing aid. SGT Tomas got on the M60. Meanwhile I was laying suppressive fire down an alley where there was random shots coming at us. SGT Tomas asked SFC Watson for some frags. SFC Watson in his irritated voice said, "S. Tomas use the law on your back." SGT Tomas looked back puzzled, "the law, motherfucker." [LAW anti-tank rocket.] SGT Tomas smiled and pulled the law off his back, extended it and fired. SGT Tomas then started providing aid to Neatherly along with Doc Strouse. Errico pulled out of the little alley he was covering. A few minutes later he got shot in the same arm. After shooting a few sammys,

SGT Hulst low crawled to my position carrying with him an aid bag. SGT Torres then picked up the aid bag and carried it to the casualties. A few minutes later a "sammy" walked in front of our position all chilled out, like nothing was going on. He looked at me and our other positions. I guess he was a recon man, well he didn't get to tell much. Someone behind him yelled something, as the sammy turned I saw an AK-47 under his shirt. The recon was over, I laid a good burst on him and at the same instant PFC Floyd opened up. The sammy staggered and fell behind a building.

The intensity of the battle began to slow a bit. I don't know if they were running out of ammo and had to get more or what. A few minutes later though a grenade landed about 2 meters in front of me. I thought, "oh shit" and put my head behind a K-pot size rock in from of me. I remember thinking, "this is it." The grenade blew up and knocked me around a bit. I looked up and Kurth was yelling at me. I couldn't understand what he was saying. I looked over and gave SFC Watson the thumbs up. I was happy that I was still alive. A few minutes later a Sammy came out of a corridor with an RPG and Floyd and I lit him up. He was gone with a puff of smoke, I guess an RPG exploded when we shot him.

Ammo conservation was a big thing. SFC Watson kept reminding us to keep controlled bursts, which we did. We stayed in this position until dark. SGT Tomas had already moved the casualties, Errico and Neatherly, to our CP (command post) which was about two buildings behind me. When it got dark we started withdrawing to the buildings behind me where we would set up our defenses for the night. Everyone went past me. I picked up last. As we started for the building the firing picked up again. SGT Tomas and SGT Ramaglia were outside and heard a few explosions from hand grenades and 203 rounds being fired. When they came in we marked our position with an IR strobe placing it on the roof of the building we were in. This was done so the little birds (helicopters) could start doing their gun runs. I've never felt so much relief when they started lighting up the buildings around us with 7.62 mini guns and $2\frac{1}{2}$in. rockets. Both FOs (forward observers) were wounded so the CO called them in. The decision was made that we would stay here until the reaction forces could get us out. I was oriented facing out of the building with my SAW.

Several hours later it was decided that we needed to move to the next building. Before making the move a Black Hawk came in and made an IV and ammo resupply. The helicopter hovered overhead blazing away with the mini guns. They were taking all kinds of fire. Any time a bird came into the area the enemy fire would pick up.

We were told that the reaction forces were on the way. SFC Watson, SGT Tomas, SPC DeJesus, PFC Floyd, myself and some Hardy Boys picked up, went outside and moved to an alleyway. We moved down the alley and linked up with some D-boys. I was oriented towards the street. The D-Boys were in the building next door. We pulled back down the alley and went through a window into a courtyard. This is where I spent several hours listening to the reaction forces trying to get to us.

Casualties of war. Special
operations soldiers killed in
action during the Battle of
the Black Sea – Mogadishu.
(Anton Berendsen)

Casualties of war. Special operations soldiers killed in action during the Battle of the Black Sea – Mogadishu. (Anton Berendsen)

DeJesus and Surankig were put on a barrel in a concrete building facing down the road. The little birds continued to do gun runs and fire rockets. They kept our spirits up. Floyd and I were pulling guard on the window that we climbed through to enter the courtyard. An RPG was shot at us. The location where the RPG came from was marked with a tracer and blown up with a rocket. After that, RPG fire tapered off. We went out the window, but that was okay with me. I kept looking at my watch wondering where the reaction force was. I was praying a lot for all of us. The firing from the enemy lulled a little bit. We found a spigot and we started doing a water resupply by putting canteens on a stick and passing them through the window next door where the casualties were. This particular water resupply wasn't taught in Ranger School, that's for damn sure.

At about 4:00 a.m. the reaction forces finally linked up with us. We gave the Ranger running password. They secured the surrounding area and we moved back to the building that we previously had been in. SFC Watson got a head count and the casualties were put on APCs (armored personnel carriers). I kept looking at my watch and daylight was coming nearer. We couldn't leave yet because they were still getting the pilot out of the downed helicopter. They were having to cut him out, piece by piece because the damage was so bad.

At about 5:45 a.m. they had finally recovered the bodies at the crash site. We were told that there wasn't enough room in the APCs for us. Therefore we would be exfilling by foot. I thought, "oh shit," that's when the Mogadishu 500 began. It was a mad dash for our lives. The sun was up and thus began a new day in the Mog. Chalk 2 led, followed by Chalk 1, the D-boys, then us, Chalk 3, picking up the rear. We started to move with the APCs next to us trying to provide cover. As we ran across roads we were moving over the same roads we had infilled on.

Fire was coming from everywhere. It seemed as if the sammys had gotten a good night's rest and were ready to fight. The APCs took off and left us, that sucked. Here we were running down the streets "scroll of-the road" in a manner I've never seen before. Everyone was watching everyone else's back. We stopped at a corner. SGT Ramaglia and I were pulling security down an alley when bullets started hitting all around us. I remember I felt something hit my arm and knock me back. I looked over and there was a gash in my BDU, knocking the American flag off my arm. The same bullet that grazed me hit SGT Ramaglia in the side taking out a good chunk of meat. I told him he was hit and for him not to worry about it. We crossed the street and continued the Mog 500. Gunfire was coming from everywhere. We passed a 5 ton truck that had been blown up. There was blood all over the streets. We kept pushing on. We turned a corner and there were two tanks sitting in the road, what a sight. We all got under cover near the tanks. Nearby was a tan Humvee that had "security police" written on the side. A guy was in the turret. The guy got shot in the neck. One of the tanks fired a round at the building where the gun fire came from. The entire building was leveled. I thought "holy shit." We started moving again and saw APCs leaving. I thought "here we go again." We yelled at the APCs but they wouldn't stop. Some of the guys had gotten on the APCs but there were about 25 of us who could not. We were running alongside of the APCs. We ran about another 2 blocks before the APCs stopped. We piled on them and got the hell out of there. We drove to the Paki Stadium. We got out at the stadium and shook everyone's hands. By the way the PAC and MAL were the ones in the APCs that got us out. The casualties were evacuated to the hospitals. We then found out who had been killed during the mission, 6 Rangers, 4 D-Boys and 4 airmen.

The mood was somber. We ate some food and were flown back to our hanger. It had been 18 hours since we had left. Everyone soaked up what had happened.

There was a memorial the next day. Many tears were shed and many more will be for the ones that we lost. I know this event has forever changed my life.

## RANGER CASUALTIES IN OPERATION *GOTHIC SERPENT*

| Soldier | Battalion | Date KIA |
|---|---|---|
| CPL James M. Cavaco | 3-75 | 03-Oct-93 |
| SGT James C. Joyce | 3-75 | 03-Oct-93 |
| SPC Richard W. Kowalewski | 3-75 | 03-Oct-93 |
| SGT Dominick M. Pilla | 3-75 | 03-Oct-93 |
| SGT Lorenzo M. Ruiz | 3-75 | 03-Oct-93 |
| CPL James E. Smith | 3-75 | 03-Oct-93 |

# 75th Ranger Regiment Timeline of Events, Mogadishu, October 3–4, 1993

| TIME | EVENT |
| --- | --- |
| 1350 | BLANK reports possible Salad/Qeydid mtg at house near VIC Olympic Hotel (grg sheet 24,12.8/M.8; UTM NH36122665). |
| 1403 | Recce launch (2 x H-530 & 1 x OH-58D): Reef point previously on station. |
| 1410 | Coords passed to Capt Donahue (UNOSOM LNO). Confirmed no NGO in vicinity of target. MG Montgomery notified. |
| 1415 | BLANK reports source/signal may have occurred prior to arrival of Recce. |
| 1424 | Recce reports white Toyota land cruiser parked in front of hotel – fits description given by source. |
| 1427 | Source vehicle (silver with red stripes on the doors) stopped in front of target house and raised hood IAW prearranged instructions to let us know he was at target. |
| 1434 | BLANK will remain on meeting house location; BLANK will track white Toyota vehicle. |
| 1447 | Source may not have given prearranged signal in front of target house (gave signal only to let us know he was in the vicinity); Recce possibly on wrong target; J2 attempting to reconfirm/pinpoint actual target location. |
| 1450 | Source will drive around block again and give signal to reconfirm target location (approx location 1 block northeast Olympic Hotel; GR sheet 24, 12.9/M.5. |
| 1459 | Source confirmed on target. Recce manuevering to provide video of both sides of building. Recce advises this area has reported numerous small arms fire in recent past. Aircrews/ground forces brief mission. |
| 1505 | Confirmed airspace deconfliction with QRF helos. |
| 1509 | Recce provides obstacle/hazzard info on planned helos. |
| 1519 | BLANK reports 1+00 fuel on-station remaining BLANK = 1+10. |
| 1523 | (AH-6) Flight repos to FARP. |
| 1527 | Assault force route passed to Recce; BLANK flight will have rockets – no preplanned fires at this time. Convoy route (K4 – National – Olympic) 9 x HMMWV & 3 x 5 tons: will depart when helo force departs airfield. |
| 1529 | Assault force pax loaded and ready for launch. |
| 1530 | Recce reports 2 x roadblocks (burning tires) VIC intxn 21 Oct Rd and National. Route checked against possible land mine locations. |
| 1532 | Helo assault force launches. |
| 1535 | Ground reaction force convoy departs TF Ranger compound. |
| 1537 | Initiate assault codeword passed to all elements. |
| 1540 | Recce passes convoy route is clear of all obstructions. |
| 1542 | Helo assault commences on target/exact target building unknown/city block will be cleared. |
| 1543 | Super 61 reports ground force hitting the ground; Recce is providing flight following instructions to ground force. |

| | |
|---|---|
| 1545 | Ground reaction force at preplanned hold point. |
| 1546 | AK-47s sighted/reported in compound; BLANK reports forces too close to hotel to fire rockets. |
| 1547 | Large crowd coming up National toward target. Ground forces report sporadic ground fire contact – No KIA/WIA. |
| 1550 | Super 61 reports friendlies on roof of target building. |
| 1551 | Recce reports 8–9 enemy (militia) approx one block over and en route to target. |
| 1553 | RPG/small arms fires reported 1 block east next to green water tank; ground reaction force moves to effect link up with assault force. |
| 1555 | Super 62 will engage green water tank; man with RPG ran down street and is in small shack – barber will engage. Women/children in area; star ELE to RTB for FARP. |
| 1558 | RPG reported hit 5-ton – one WIA (gunshot to leg) and vehicle disabled. |
| 1600 | Recce reports troops with AK-47s moving toward target. |
| 1602 | LTC McKnight reports 9 x PC with possible principal captured. |
| 1604 | All forces to begin collapsing to building #1 for link up and ground exfil of all forces and PC. Will use bldg #1 roof pz if required. |
| 1610 | Super 61 reports RPG burst over target; location of fires passed to barber. |
| 1613 | McKnight reports one critical WIA will evacuate by ground asap; helos will provide guns as required. GRF #1 at building #1 for exfil. |
| 1620 | Super 61 shot down by RPG – Somalis approaching crash site. GRG sheet 24, 16.2/0.7, UTM NH 36142685. Ground reaction force BLANK moving to secure crash site. Survivors climbing out of wreckage – ACFT is not on fire. Assault force personnel (approx 7) securing the position. Report: area secure for MH-6 ELE to effect exfil of casualties (2 x KIA, 2 x WIA). |
| 1622 | Report: Large crowd of Somalis approaching crash site. |
| 1624 | MH-6 has landed at crash site – Super 62 providing cover – RPG gunner reported in target area – barber inbound. |
| 1626 | GRF #1 will move to crash site with ASLT force and PC; move to crash site #1 approximately 1635. PC enroute back to TF Ranger compound via 5 ton with HMMWV security. QRF assistance requested; QRF to report to TF Ranger compound to link-up. |
| 1628 | Super 68 (SAR) infils SST at crash – Super 68 hit by RPG – require RTB asap. |
| 1630 | Super 68 lands TF Ranger compound. Crew transloads to spare aircraft. |
| 1631 | MH-6 exfil 2 x WIA from crash. |
| 1634 | Report: RPG fire 200 meters east of crash site. |
| 1641 | Super 64 is down – RPG; Grid 36402625, Super 62 fastropes 2 x snipers on site. BLANK directs assault force assist asap. Reports: large crowd moving toward second crash site. |
| 1644 | RPGs being launched from numerous locations. |
| 1654 | GRF #1 reports numerous casualties (Numbers/type unknown). |
| 1655 | Unable to leave crash site #1 – cannot recover 1 x KIA in aircraft. |
| 1656 | GRF #1 reports heavy sniper fires. |
| 1701 | Super 62 taking regular/close RPG fire; most from west side of 2nd crash site. |

| 1703 | Second Ranger ground (GRF #2) ELE reconstituted as recovery force for 2nd crash site. (27 pax on 7 HMMWVs). |
|---|---|
| 1710 | QRF arrives compound. |
| 1713 | PC w/security and WIAs en route to TF Ranger compound. GRF #1 continuing to crash site #1 under heavy fire. |
| 1715 | BLANK ELE RTB to FARP. |
| 1720 | GRF #2 approaching 2nd crash site; road has been blocked with tire fires; GRF #2 receiving heavy fire. |
| 1723 | BLANK RTB to FARP; BLANK req GRF #1 return to crash site #1 to reconstitute. U64 has numerous casualties – cannot return to crash site. |
| 1726 | ASLT Force elements move overland to crash site #1 and secured. |
| 1727 | Super 62 hit – going down at new port – req medevac asap – numerous casualties. |
| 1730 | Super 68 (spare) en route to new port to evacuate casualties. |
| 1734 | BLANK 2 x urgent casualties at northern crash site – need GRF assist asap; also live casualties at southern site still in ACFT – need GRF to secure that site also. |
| 1735 | QRF dpt for crash site #2. |
| 1740 | GRF #2 link-up w/GRF #1 (-) at K-4 circle. GRF #2 attempting different routes; receiving heavy fire wherever he goes; chance link-up BLANK (-) returning to compound transload PC and WIA from disabled vehicles – entire force RTB. |
| 1743 | Super 68 will pick up remaining pax at Super 62 (New Port). |
| 1744 | AH-6 continues taking RPG fires (approx 50M north of 2nd crash site); BLANK reports aircraft has taken numerous rounds – can still fly. |
| 1745 | QRF in fire fight vic K-4 circle; will proceed to crash sites asap. |
| 1746 | Somali road block being built at 2nd crash site – Barber will engage to dissipate crowds. |
| 1751 | Req EOD to disarm poss active grenade at TF Ranger compound on remains – 10th Mtn notified (TF Ranger EOD w/assault force). |
| 1755 | ASLT force reports running short of ammo and med supplies. |
| 1758 | AH-6 right gun jammed – will RTB and get it replaced. |
| 1801 | AH-6 rockets only capable – at crash site #1. |
| 1808 | AH-6 taking fires – no damage. |
| 1810 | QRF (van Arsdale w/BN C2) pinned down at K-4 circle. |
| 1820 | ASLT Force ammo getting critical. |
| 1830 | Super 68 will RTB & P/U ammo and IV bags/QRF reconstitutes force after breaks in contact caused by ambush; RTB TF Ranger compound. |
| 1836 | Numerous RPG launches in VIC N-crash site; still have one body trapped in ACTF – unable to get due to numerous small arms. |
| 1854 | AH-6 break from K-4 and RTB north crash site. |
| 1855 | AH-6 taking RPG fires. |
| 1856 | North crash site still working recovery of body from ACFT – will not leave the body. |
| 1900 | Plan approved for QRF to move to crash site w/2 x Malaysian mech companies & 1 x Pakistani armor lt. |

| | |
|---|---|
| 1908 | Super 66 will drop resupply items BLANK at crash site #1; PZ marked by IR strobe; BLANK (AH-6?) supporting with guns. Assume friendlies at the strobes. Taking fires from 9-o'clock; resupply successful. At least 20 enemy with AKs in VIC. |
| 1926 | ASLT requests QRF get to crash site #1 asap!! Need to look at driving to Paki stadium then get air exfil to afld. BLANK reports 21 Oct hwy is clear/quiet. |
| 1947 | Report from ASLT. Pilot still pinned in crash, will need jaws to retrieve him, requests evac (again) for 2 x critically wounded pax asap. |
| 2025 | ASLT advises that "If QRF does not get there (North crash) soon, there will be more KIAs from previously received WIA; Get the one star to get his people moving!" |
| 2027 | ASLT force advises 1 x critical WIA at crash site #1 is now KIA. |
| 2032 | BLANK Will sparkle RPG site which just fired on AH-6 ELE, AH6 will service. |
| 2035 | There is a lot of frustration over QRF/QRC not moving to assist. MG Garrison, BLANK, and LTC McKnight discussing QRF plan of attack with BG Gile and QRF staff. |
| 2100 | Sitrep crash sites. Crash site #1: 99 total pax (13 x WIA/3 x KIA). Crash site #2: No report, situation – unknown. |
| 2108 | BG Gile reports to CG – QRF will probably not be able to move until approx 2200. |
| 2130 | QRF enroute to linkup with Malaysians at new port. |
| 2200 | QRF arr New Port/link-up w/Pakis & Malaysians/finalizes plan: establish holding area between crash sites; move 1 company to each crash site, reconstituted Ranger Force (& 8 x HMMWV, 56 pax) to secure area/act as reserve. |
| 2224 | BLANK called. Covered oprep 3 report with him. |
| 2228 | MG Montgomery requests QRF convoy route for possible "improvement" planning prior to departing. No estimate on when convoy will proceed to crash sites for TF Ranger relief. |
| 2230 | Final PC status: 24 detainees; 1 x WIA, 3 x KIA = 24 total; enemy KIA are currently in 507th mortuary support ELE (at Afld) |
| 2300 | Telecom between BLANK requests stop jamming – BLANK said no – not until all TF Ranger forces recovered; BLANK request BLANK put up cash reward for anyone who aids Americans or helps recover remains; Also, try to get "sources" in VIC of crash sites to inform on what's going on. |
| 2305 | BLANK called BLANK and requests plus-up LONG BLANK. |
| 2323 | QRF departing New Port. |
| 2345 | QRF receiving fire en route to holding area. |
| 2350 | QRF arrive holding area/A Co dispatched to crash site #1. |
| 2353 | AH-6 will break for fuel. |
| 2357 | QRF convoy and crash sites taking heavy small arms fire. Friendlies believed south of southern crash site based on pls codes being picked up in that VIC (old Saudi embassy). |
| 0002 | QRF believes location approx 200M from TFR crash site #1 under heavy contact. Lead ELE of QRF (TF Ranger LNO ELE) has quickie saw to cut remaining body from aircraft. |

| | |
|---|---|
| 0026 | Pakistani tanks refuse to move on/APCs very reluctant to move, but eventually do. Roadblock removed by hand, by dismounted QRF troops. |
| 0036 | BLANK relays QRF troops dismounted way too soon. Approximately 3–4 blocks from TFR forces. |
| 0120 | BLANK reports QFR approx 300M from TFR location. |
| 0122 | Friendlies believed in abandoned building approx 100M south of old Saudi embassy (crash site #2). |
| 0148 | Enemy forces approx 150M east of crash site #1. |
| 0155 | Link up between TFR and lead QRF element; ensure good accountability personnel prior to movement & cut KIA out of ACFT. |
| 0210 | QRF en route to crash site (#2). |
| 0227 | Crash site #2 secure – no sign of aircrew. |
| 0230 | CG receives approval to bring replacement aircraft into theater. C5 will bring 5 x MH-60 and 2 x AH-6 with supplemental crews. |
| 0239 | BLANK reports 4 x barrel gun firing (possibly Paki) have them check fire. Enemy illum at site #2. |
| 0248 | QRF (TF Ranger LNO) advises several hours required to cut free/recover KIA in ACFT at site #1. |
| 0249 | No bodies found at crash site #2 (Super 64) & no one answers to aircrew's names in VIC. (4 x aircrew plus 2 x BLANK snipers should have been there). |
| 0300 | Thermite grenades set on crash site #2 (south) – no confirmation they have been lit. |
| 0336 | AH-6 returns to airfield with inoperative fuel gauge and "Fuel low" light. |
| 0348 | Pakis request to fire mortars into Villa Somalia. (Mortar position). |
| 0350 | Reef point very briefly picked up 2 x pls in VIC crash site #2. |
| 0400 | AH-6 service RPG launch location VIC crash site #1. |
| 0409 | Pakistanis cleared road from Paki stadium to CP207, no mines reported. |
| 0415 | AH-6 RTB for main rotor blade replacement, estimated 30 min downtime. |
| 0420 | Phonecon from BLANK report 2 x Malaysian APCs reported hit by RPGs vicinity grid NH363265. Requesting assistance from TF Ranger gun helos. Passed to TF Green. |
| 0424 | Pakistanis rpt they have not cleared road fm stadium to CP207. Pakis have a guide to RDVZ W/ BLANK at CP on National. |
| 0438 | BLANK querying avail of additional transport to pick up dismounted troops. |
| 0453 | ASLT rpts he has 200 dismounted, (QRF/assault force/Rgr blocking force) will link w/trans on National once body recovered. |
| 0500 | ASLT query about possible resupply of 5.56/40MM/and water to BLANK advises redistribute fm vehicles, high helo threat. Still at least 20 minutes to cut body from wreckage. |
| 0515 | ASLT rpts attempting to cut out majority of body from wreckage. |
| 0523 | LNO reports no control over Malaysian vehicles, APCs abandoned Dragon 6 position, Malays appear returning to Paki stadium. |
| 0530 | Body recovered. Destructive charges set on helo. BLANK providing cover fire for withdrawal from crash site #1. |
| 0542 | ASLT moving all elements out of tgt site. AH-6 ELE continues fire support. |
| 0550 | Terminator & Kilo elems linking up with Dragon ELE. |
| 0605 | Not enough transport, 50 pax still dismounted. ASLT requesting more APCs. |

| 0610 | 30 pax of kilo mounting APCs. |
|------|------|
| 0620 | All pax loaded, convoy moving out. |
| 0627 | Cobras making tow shot on abandoned APCs. |
| 0630 | Convoy pulling into Paki stadium. |
| 0715 | Confirming names of 20 pax RTB to New Port so BLANK can check his headcount. |
| 0720 | BLANK RTB. |
| 0734 | AH-6 ELE all on standby at FARP. |
| 0745 | AH-6 or ASLT? feels that 2 snipers inserted to crash site #2 are possibly responsible for taking bodies and equip fm site. Might be in hiding near site. |
| 0810 | Begin shuttle of Rangers, fm stadium RTB. Net monitoring weak intermittent transmissions fm VIC of crash site #2. |
| 0815 | BLANK possible beacon transmission, freq being investigated. |
| 0827 | BLANK being launched. AH-6 being stood down. |
| 0845 | Voice came in over beacon saying "my arm is broken." Attempting to DF source. |
| 0915 | Continued attempts to establish comms with Beacon station unsuccessful. Beacon being turned on or off. |
| 0916 | Ground commanders report all pers accounted for except for the 4 crewmembers and 2 snipers inserted into crash site #2. |

# OPERATION *UPHOLD DEMOCRACY* – NO NEWS IS GOOD NEWS

September 10, 1994, saw Special Operations Forces on standby for the possible invasion of Haiti. "As the deadline for the invasion neared, SOF moved their equipment and supplies to their air and sea ports for possible embarkation. Ranger moved to their waiting planes, prepared for an airborne assault."[59] However, a last-minute deal struck on September 18 saw US forces abort their missions.

# PART III

# THE GLOBAL WAR ON TERRORISM

## IN THE BEGINNING

September 11, 2001, started like any other day in the world. In the United States corporate suits were going about their daily routines of drinking coffee, reading their papers, or checking on their e-mails at work, all in the pursuit of gathering wealth. Throughout the underdeveloped world people were struggling to eek out a living barely sufficient to be considered humane. No matter one's race, religion, or status in life, however, all would soon become familiar with one individual – Osama bin Laden.

Somewhere on September 11, a young Army recruit, with a look of a deer caught in the headlights, was being yelled at by a drill sergeant of dubious quality while a Ranger Indoctrination Program (RIP) student was getting his mettle tested by a RIP Instructor at Fort Benning, Georgia. And, quite possibly, Battboys on the east coast were finishing their breakfasts at their dining facility, while Rangers from the 2nd Battalion were starting their physical training in the early morning hours in the fabulously crisp air of Washington State. Soon the world would be glued to their television sets to witness a spectacle almost impossible to believe, yet warned about repeatedly, most recently just the prior month.

Between 0845 and 1010 hours four American commercial airliners hit or missed their intended targets. Two crashed into the World Trade Center, one hit the Pentagon and the last one crashed in Pennsylvania. Nearly 3,000 civilians, including 125 military personnel at the Pentagon, were killed in less than two hours. (Nearly 2,400 were killed by the Japanese attack on Pearl Harbor on December 7, 1941.) One of the most brilliantly conceived and executed operations against mainland America was carried out by 19 fundamentalists who gave their lives to strike at the heart of the United States

**ABOVE**
Rangers conducting rehearsals in support of Operation *Enduring Freedom*, Afghanistan.

New York City after the
September 11 attack. (NOAA)

and the heart of their perceived evil enemy. The world at large was stunned and generous with sympathy toward the United States – a sympathy that would ultimately be rejected by the actions of the US government – never to be rekindled again.

Conspiracy theories abounded in the aftermath: why did the buildings blow up? Was the plane in Pennsylvania shot down by the US military? Why were numerous Israeli art students arrested before and after the attacks? Why did the President of the United States continue to read to children at a photo opportunity immediately after receiving the news of the attacks? Was the government involved? Others, scholars and historians, attempted to place the attack in historical context, such as Chalmers Johnson in his eye-opening book, *Blowback: The Costs and Consequences of American Empire*, where he argues that "blowback" – the unintended consequences of American foreign policies – have come back to haunt us presently.[60] Question after question, theory after theory circulated the world through the Internet. One fact, however, could not be refuted or challenged – the world had changed. The New World Order had begun.

# THE WORLD PRIOR TO SEPTEMBER 11, 2001

Back in December 2000, Republican candidate George W. Bush had won a contentious presidential election against Democrat Al Gore. Although the Bush and bin Laden families have long-standing social, political, and economic ties, it can safely be assumed that no genuine relationship existed between Osama and George until September 11, 2001. Although the new President was briefed on many occasions by the Director of the Central Intelligence Agency (CIA) during 2001 about bin Laden's organization al-Qaeda ("The Base" or "The Foundation"), and one presidential brief dated August 2001 reported specifically on the likelihood of an attack by this organization against the US mainland, no appropriate actions were taken by the Bush administration, which dismissed the reports during subsequent hearings as mere historical documents.[61]

The grievances and insults allegedly suffered or perceived by al-Qaeda and its supporters are long-standing and numerous. The most important one, however, is that they strongly believe Muslim societies and Islam to be under attack by Israel, the United States, and corrupt Arab regimes. Notions that al-Qaeda and similar networks were to form a caliphate to rule the world are absurd and no such evidence exists. One important fact about al-Qaeda is the absence of a genuine international network. It resembles more or less a number of loosely associated cells with clearly independent command and control elements. And there can be little doubt that various intelligence services have known and monitored Osama bin Laden for years.

The list of grievances against al-Qaeda and its associates is as long if not as old. They include, but are not limited to, the twin bombings of US embassies in August 1998 in Nairobi, Kenya, and Dar es Salaam, Tanzania, killing approximately 300 people and wounding thousands. Additionally, al-Qaeda is thought to have executed the attack on October 12, 2000, against the USS *Cole*, killing 17 sailors. The US launched a few Tomahawk missiles toward an al-Qaeda training site at Zhawar Kili in Afghanistan in 1998 in response to the embassy bombings.[62]

The following Congressional testimony on al-Qaeda, dated December 18, 2001, by J. T. Caruso, Acting Assistant Director, Counter-Terrorism Division, FBI, before the Subcommittee on International Operations and Terrorism, Committee on Foreign Relations, United States Senate, presents a detailed knowledge of bin Laden and his organization:

## AL-QAEDA INTERNATIONAL

"Al-Qaeda" ("The Base") was developed by Usama Bin Laden and others in the early 1980s to support the war effort in Afghanistan against the Soviets. The resulting "victory" in Afghanistan gave rise to the overall "Jihad" (Holy War) movement. [One estimate stipulates that between 175,000 and 250,000 Mujahideen fought in Afghanistan annually. Almost half of them were Saudis.][63] Trained Mujahedin fighters from Afghanistan began returning to such countries as Egypt, Algeria, and Saudi Arabia,

The Pentagon after the
September 11 attack. (NOAA)

with extensive "jihad" experience and the desire to continue the "jihad."
This antagonism began to be refocused against the U.S. and its allies.

Sometime in 1989, Al-Qaeda dedicated itself to further opposing non-
Islamic governments in this region with force and violence. The group grew
out of the "mekhtab al khidemat" (the Services Office) organization,
which maintained offices in various parts of the world, including
Afghanistan, Pakistan and the United States. Al-Qaeda began to provide
training camps and guesthouses in various areas for the use of Al-Qaeda
and its affiliated groups. They attempted to recruit U.S. citizens to travel
throughout the Western world to deliver messages and engage in financial
transactions for the benefit of Al-Qaeda and its affiliated groups and to
help carry out operations. By 1990 Al-Qaeda was providing military and
intelligence training in various areas including Afghanistan, Pakistan, and
the Sudan, for the use of Al-Qaeda and its affiliated groups, including the
Al-Jihad (Islamic Jihad) organization.

One of the principal goals of Al-Qaeda was to drive the United States
armed forces out of Saudi Arabia (and elsewhere on the Saudi Arabian
peninsula) and Somalia by violence. Members of Al-Qaeda issued
fatwahs (rulings on Islamic law) indicating that such attacks were both
proper and necessary.

Al-Qaeda opposed the United States for several reasons. First, the
United States was regarded as an "infidel" because it was not governed in
a manner consistent with the group's extremist interpretation of Islam.
Second, the United States was viewed as providing essential support for
other "infidel" governments and institutions, particularly the governments
of Saudi Arabia and Egypt, the nation of Israel and the United Nations
organization, which were regarded as enemies of the group. Third, Al-
Qaeda opposed the involvement of the United States armed forces in the

## PRESIDENTIAL DAILY BRIEFING

For the President Only
August 6, 2001 [Declassified and Approved for Release, April 10, 2004]
*Bin Laden Determined to Strike in U.S.*

*Clandestine, foreign government, and media reports indicate bin Laden since 1997 has wanted to conduct terrorist attacks in the U.S.* Bin Laden implied in U.S. television interviews in 1997 and 1998 that his followers would follow the example of World Trade Center bomber Ramzi Yousef and "bring the fighting to America."

After U.S. missile strikes on his base in Afghanistan in 1998, bin Laden told followers he wanted to retaliate in Washington, according to a _____ service. An Egyptian Islamic Jihad (EIJ) operative told an _____ service at the same time that bin Laden was planning to exploit the operative's access to the U.S. to mount a terrorist strike.

*The millennium plotting in Canada in 1999 may have been part of bin Laden's first serious attempt to implement a terrorist strike in the U.S.* Convicted plotter Ahmed Ressam has told the FBI that he conceived the idea to attack Los Angeles International Airport himself, but that in _____, Laden lieutenant Abu Zubaydah encouraged him and helped facilitate the operation. Ressam also said that in 1998 Abu Zubaydah was planning his own U.S. attack.

Ressam says bin Laden was aware of the Los Angeles operation.

*Although Bin Laden has not succeeded, his attacks against the U.S. Embassies in Kenya and Tanzania in 1998 demonstrate that he prepares operations years in advance and is not deterred by setbacks.* Bin Laden associates surveyed our Embassies in Nairobi and Dar es Salaam as early as 1993, and some members of the Nairobi cell planning the bombings were arrested and deported in 1997.

*Al-Qaeda members – including some who are U.S. citizens – have resided in or traveled to the U.S. for years, and the group apparently maintains a support structure that could aid attacks.* Two al-Qaeda members found guilty in the conspiracy to bomb our Embassies in East Africa were U.S. citizens, and a senior EIJ member lived in California in the mid-1990s.

A clandestine source said in 1998 that a Bin Laden cell in New York was recruiting Muslim-American youth for attacks.

We have not been able to corroborate some of the more sensational threat reporting, such as that from a _____ service in 1998 saying that Bin Laden wanted to hijack a U.S. aircraft to gain the release of "Blind Sheikh" 'Umar 'Abd al-Rahman and other U.S.-held extremists.
Nevertheless, FBI information since that time indicates patterns of suspicious activity in this country consistent with preparations for hijackings or other types of attacks, including recent surveillance of federal buildings in New York.

The FBI is conducting approximately 70 full-field investigations throughout the U.S. that it considers bin Laden-related. CIA and the FBI are investigating a call to our embassy in the UAE in May saying that a group of bin Laden supporters was in the U.S. planning attacks with explosives.

Gulf War in 1991 and in Operation *Restore Hope* in Somalia in 1992 and 1993, which were viewed by Al-Qaeda as pretextual preparations for an American occupation of Islamic countries. In particular, Al-Qaeda opposed the continued presence of American military forces in Saudi Arabia (and elsewhere on the Saudi Arabian peninsula) following the Gulf War. Fourth, Al-Qaeda opposed the United States Government because of the arrest, conviction, and imprisonment of persons belonging to Al-Qaeda or its affiliated terrorist groups or with whom it worked, including Sheik Omar Abdel Rahman ['Umar 'Abd al-Rahman], who was convicted in the first World Trade Center bombing.

From its inception until approximately 1991, the group was head-quartered in Afghanistan and Peshawar, Pakistan. Then in 1991, the group relocated to the Sudan where it was headquartered until approximately 1996, when Bin Laden, Mohammed Atef and other members of Al-Qaeda returned to Afghanistan. During the years Al-Qaeda was headquartered in Sudan the network continued to maintain offices in various parts of the world and established businesses which were operated to provide income and cover to Al-Qaeda operatives.

## Al-Qaeda Ties to other Terrorist Organizations
Although Al-Qaeda functions independently of other terrorist organizations, it also functions through some of the terrorist organizations that operate under its umbrella or with its support, including: the Al-Jihad, the Al-Gamma

This Osama bin Laden propaganda poster was found in an al-Qaeda classroom during operations in Afghanistan in 2002. (USN)

Al-Islamiyya (Islamic Group – led by Sheik Omar Abdel Rahman and later by Ahmed Refai Taha, also known as "Abu Yasser al Masri"), Egyptian Islamic Jihad, and a number of jihad groups in other countries, including the Sudan, Egypt, Saudi Arabia, Yemen, Somalia, Eritrea, Djibouti, Afghanistan, Pakistan, Bosnia, Croatia, Albania, Algeria, Tunisia, Lebanon, the Philippines, Tajikistan, Azerbaijan, the Kashmiri region of India, and the Chechen region of Russia. Al-Qaeda also maintained cells and personnel in a number of countries to facilitate its activities, including in Kenya, Tanzania, the United Kingdom, Canada, and the United States. By banding together, Al-Qaeda proposed to work together against the perceived common enemies in the West – particularly the United States which Al-Qaeda regards as an "infidel" state which provides essential support for other "infidel" governments. Al-Qaeda responded to the presence of United States armed forces in the Gulf and the arrest, conviction, and imprisonment in the United States of persons belonging to Al-Qaeda by issuing fatwahs indicating that attacks against U.S. interests, domestic and foreign, civilian and military, were both proper and necessary. Those fatwahs resulted in attacks against U.S. nationals in locations around the world including Somalia, Kenya, Tanzania, Yemen, and now in the United States. Since 1993, thousands of people have died in those attacks.

## The Fatwahs of Al-Qaeda

The Fatwah Against American Troops in Somalia

At various times from about 1992 until about 1993, Usama Bin Laden, working together with members of the fatwah committee of Al-Qaeda, disseminated fatwahs to other members and associates of Al-Qaeda which directed that the United States forces stationed in the Horn of Africa, including Somalia, should be attacked. Indeed, Bin Laden has claimed responsibility for the deaths of 18 U.S. servicemen killed in Operation *Restore Hope* in Somalia in 1994.

February, 1998 Fatwah

On February 22, 1998, Bin Laden issued a fatwah stating that it is the duty of all Muslims to kill Americans. This fatwah read, in part, that "in compliance with God's order, we issue the following fatwah to all Muslims: the ruling to kill the Americans and their allies, including civilians and military, is an individual duty for every Muslim who can do it in any country in which it is possible to do it." This fatwah appears to have provided the religious justification for, and marked the start of logistical planning for, the U.S. Embassy bombings in Kenya and Tanzania.

In February 1998, Usama Bin Laden and one of his top lieutenants and leader of the Al-Jihad organization in Egypt, Ayman Al Zawahiri, endorsed a fatwah under the banner of the "International Islamic Front for Jihad on the Jews and Crusaders." This fatwah, published in the publication Al-Quds al-Arabi on February 23, 1998, stated that Muslims should kill Americans – including civilians – anywhere in the world where they can be found. In or about April 1998, one of the defendants in the East Africa trial, Mohamed Sadeek Odeh, discussed the fatwahs issued by Bin Laden and Al-Qaeda against America with another defendant, Mustafa Mohamed Fadhil. This discussion took place in Kenya.

In short, [there is] little doubt that the East Africa embassy bombings were carried out as a joint operation of Al-Qaeda and EIJ. The testimony in the trial confirmed that:

- Al-Qaeda has access to the money, training, and equipment it needs to carry out successful terrorist attacks.
- They plan their operations well in advance and have the patience to wait to conduct the attack at the right time.
- Prior to carrying out the operation, Al-Qaeda conducts surveillance of the target, sometimes on multiple occasions, often using nationals of the target they are surveilling to enter the location without suspicion. The results of the surveillance are forwarded to Al-Qaeda HQ as elaborate "ops plans" or "targeting packages" prepared using photographs, CADCAM (computer assisted design/computer assisted mapping) software, and the operative's notes.

# RANGERS IN TRAINING

For Rangers not much had changed since a handful of their comrades had fought in Somalia in 1993. Many Rangers quit or moved on to civilian life, while others reenlisted. New recruits filled the Ranger ranks as they continued to uphold the traditions of the 75th Ranger Regiment. Training in foreign countries, endless field exercises and immediate action drills continued to be the staple of Ranger training. However, more and more missions were turning the Regiment into personal bodyguards for Delta Force. Certainly, the founders of the battalions in 1974 did not envision that their selectively trained Rangers would become the muscle in case of emergencies for other Special Operations units. Nonetheless, the Regiment had successfully survived the creation and integration of the 3rd Ranger Battalion and its Regimental Headquarters in the late 1980s without sacrificing too many of its high standards. Serving the frequently talked about but less publicized Delta Force would be another task among many. Certainly it did not hurt that Delta had large numbers of former Rangers in its ranks.

As the Rangers continued their training at the dawn of the 21st century, the US Army was reevaluating its performances in the small wars it had participated in around the globe, most notably those in Kosovo and Somalia. Hard lessons learned and weaknesses acknowledged, Chief of Staff General Eric Shinseki sought to remold the image and performance of the Army. A lighter and more flexible strike force, slimmed down from its older, more Cold War era styled heavier divisions, and more reliant on superior technology, was part of his bold vision. One of the stated goals was the ability to be able to deploy a brigade worldwide within four days, a division within five days, and five divisions within 30 days. This strategy, the objective force, states that "heavy forces must be more strategically deployable and more agile, with a smaller logistical footprint, and light forces must be more lethal, survivable, and tactically mobile. Achieving this paradigm will require innovative thinking about structure, modernization efforts, and spending." Shinseki expected the Army to become "an all-wheeled, non-tracked, force by 2010, a prediction that raised howls of protests from Army traditionalists who believe that armored invincibility on the battlefield should never be traded for speed of deployment."[64] Retired Marine Corps General Paul Van Riper called Shinseki's plan "imaginary and far-reaching." It bears to note that the 1st and 2nd Ranger Battalions had been founded in 1974 to meet some of these rapid-deployment needs as smaller wars were emerging on the world stage post-Vietnam – maybe the Ranger Battalions were lacking some of the tactical mobility requirements but certainly the Rangers could deploy worldwide on a moment's notice and indeed were lethal. The objective force was nothing groundbreaking in and by itself. The most important point was the fact that General Shinseki realized the need to overhaul a military that had become stagnant, and remold the fighting edge of the US Army.

General Shinseki's vision of transforming the US Army also required the immediate lifting of morale of its soldiers and the shining symbol of greatness was the 75th Ranger Regiment. Tough, rugged, and near-legendary within the general armed forces, their black beret designated them as the most formidable infantry unit in the US military. The beret has historically only been awarded to airborne units in the modern Army, although some berets had crept unofficially into other units, notably tankers. Only three units were authorized to wear the beret: Airborne troops wore maroon, Special Forces (including Delta) were commonly known as the "Green Berets," and the 75th Rangers sported the black beret, the color of night operations. In one fell swoop General Shinseki declared that the entire US Army would adopt the black beret for garrison wear; a move he deemed would immediately restore pride to the regular Army while the transformation was progressing. He stated: "As another step towards achieving the capabilities of the objective force, effective June 14, 2001, the first Army birthday of the new millennium, the Army will don its new headgear. Special operations and airborne units will retain their distinctive berets, but starting next June, the black beret will be symbolic of our commitment to transform this magnificent Army into a new force." Sergeant Major of the Army Tilley stipulated that Ranger units "will be given the option to go to another color, that something would be worked out to do what's right for the Rangers."[65]

The outrage within the Ranger community was enormous. Leading former Rangers condemned the move, other Rangers saw an opportunity to make money by selling t-shirts, and some simply could not have cared less. Instead of embracing Shinseki's vision to make the US Army better, some Rangers finally had a *cause célèbre* to rally around. The Rangers felt they would surely persuade recently elected President Bush to rescind the order. They were wrong.

# THE BLACK BERET – A BRIEF HISTORY

The beret is European in origin, not American. The word "beret" is defined in the New American Heritage Dictionary as "a round, visorless cloth cap, worn originally by male Basques." [French *béret*, from Old Gascon *barret*, cap, from Late Latin *birrus* (of obscure version), hooded cape.][66] The word can be traced back to the early 19th century and this particular type of headgear has its roots in the northern mountainous regions of Spain and southern France, the Pyrennes, in a cap called *boina*. The *boina* (Basque for beret) is a small, round woolen cap with a flattened top, and still typifies Basque peasant dress.[67] The beret was introduced to Spain during the First Carlist War, 1833–39, and a red beret identified the wearer as a Carlist (*txapelgorri* in Basque, that took the meaning of "Carlist soldier") while *Isabellines* wore white berets. Today the Basque police force, the *Ertzaintza*, wears red berets.[68]

Some of the early settlers on the American continent were of Scottish and Irish descent. These men brought along bonnets as headgear. Made of cloth and wide-brimmed, these caps were usually blue, although some merchants sold them in various other colors as well.[69] Their origin stems from as far back as the 17th century and there is evidence that bonnets were of several types – cut and sewn, knitted, and woven.

One noted Ranger historian embroiled in the black beret controversy and interested in preserving his era's contribution to the beret history writes: "American Rangers did not wear Berets in colonial times. The French were the enemy."[70] He further stipulates that although no headdress was standardized, Rangers who could acquire them preferred to wear the Balmoral Bonnets – a bonnet with a round ball on top, the ball usually red. This is of

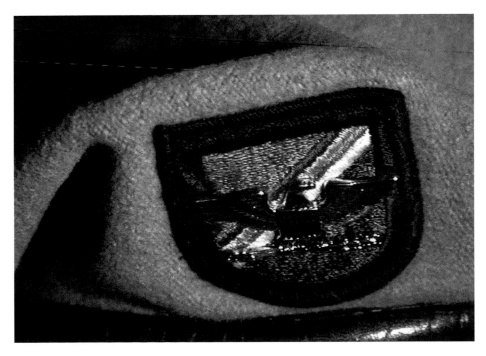

The Tan Beret.
(Author's collection)

## RANGER TAN BERET STATEMENT

Fellow Rangers,

The purpose in writing this note is to inform you that the 75th Ranger Regiment will exchange our traditional Black Beret for a Tan Beret. The Army's donning of the Black Beret, as its standard headgear is a symbol of the "Army's on-going Transformation" and a "symbol of excellence." The 75th Ranger Regiment fully supports our Army's initiative to don the Black Beret.

The Tan color of the new Ranger Beret reinvigorates the historical and spiritual linkage throughout the history of the American Ranger. It is the color of the buckskin uniforms and animal skin hats of Rogers' Rangers, the first significant Ranger unit to fight on the American continent, and the genesis of the American Ranger lineage. Tan is the one universal and unifying color that transcends all Ranger Operations. It reflects the Butternut uniforms of Mosby's Rangers during the American Civil War. It is reminiscent of the numerous beach assaults in the European Theater and the jungle fighting in the Pacific Theaters of World War II, where Rangers and Marauders spearheaded victory. It represents the khaki uniform worn by our Korean and Vietnam War era Rangers and the color of the sand of Grenada, Panama, Iraq, and Mogadishu, where modern day Rangers lead the way as they fought and, at times, valiantly died accomplishing the Ranger mission. Tan rekindles the legacy of Rangers from all eras and exemplifies the unique skills and special capabilities required of past, present, and future Rangers.

The Ranger Tan Beret will distinguish Rangers in the 21st Century as the Black Beret recognized them as a cut above in the past. With the donning of this new Beret, rest assured that the 75th Ranger Regiment will continue to Lead the Way with its high standards.

I made this decision because I feel it is best for the Ranger Regiment and our Army, today and in the future.

Following the announcement that on 14 June 2001 the Army would adopt the Black Beret as its standard headgear I asked the Regimental Command Sergeant Major to put together a uniform committee to examine some possible uniform options for the Regiment. These options included maintaining the current Black Beret, adding distinctive insignia to the Black Beret, and adopting a different color beret (ultimately six different colors were examined). The committee I established met three times over two months to consider input from Rangers of all ranks in the Regiment. The members of this group included the Honorary Colonel of the Regiment, DCO [Deputy Commanding Officer], RSM [Regimental Sergeant-Major], CSMs [Command Sergeant-Major] of each Battalion, and 1SGs of RHHC [Regimental Headquarters and Headquarters Company] and RTD [Ranger Training Detachment].

From the initial options, the committee narrowed consideration to maintaining the current Black Beret, augmenting the Black Beret with a WWII Ranger "diamond" patch attached next to the flash, and an option of replacing the Black Beret with a Tan colored beret. The committee explored each option historically giving equal consideration to its appearance when donned with each of our uniforms. After receiving input from the units, the Tan Beret was selected.

Shortly after 1st Ranger Battalion was reactivated in 1974, the Army formally authorized the Black Beret for Rangers. By so doing, I do not believe it was saying the Rangers were different from the rest of the Army, but that they were distinctive within the Army, that more was expected of them, and that they would set the standards for the rest of the Army. They would be asked to "Lead the Way" as Rangers had done since WWII.

As today's Rangers follow in the footsteps of those who preceded them, they continue to uphold the high standards of the Regiment as they prepare for tomorrow's battles. Changing from the Black Beret to the Tan Beret is not about being different from the rest of the Army, but about a critical aspect that unifies our Army and makes it the best Army in the world – High Standards.

One of the Rangers' most visible distinctive "physical features" is the beret. In the past, the beret distinguished the Rangers and acknowledged that they are expected to maintain higher standards, move further, faster, and fight harder than any other soldiers. I believe Rangers today and in the years to come deserve that same distinction.

Rangers have never been measured by what they have worn in peace or combat, but by commitment, dedication, physical and mental toughness, and willingness to Lead the Way – Anywhere, Anytime. The Beret has become one of our most visible symbols, it will remain so.

Unity within our Army is absolutely critical to combat readiness and Rangers have always prided themselves in being part of that unity. Unity among Rangers, past and present, is essential to moving forward and ensuring we honor those who have put the combat streamers on our colors and acknowledge the sacrifices and dedication of the Rangers and their families who serve our nation today.

I hope that when our Army dons the Black Beret and our Rangers put on the Tan Beret we will move forward and focus on what is ultimately the most important task in front of us – ensuring the continued high state of Readiness of the Ranger Regiment. We can do that by training hard and taking care of our Rangers and their families. The continued support of all Rangers to our Army is important to sustaining that Readiness.

Thanks to our Army, the 75th Ranger Regiment today is fully resourced and combat ready. Our focus in the future is maintaining that high state of readiness.

Again, thanks to each of you for everything you have done for our nation and our Rangers.

Rangers Lead the Way!

*P. K. Keen*
*Colonel, Infantry*
*11th Colonel of the Regiment*

course absurd. What woodsman would wear a brightly colored bonnet or beret? It seems highly unlikely that Rangers would probably choose to wear colors that would alert the enemy. Noted colonial Ranger scholar Gary S. Zaboly describes in his masterful book *The Annotated and Illustrated Journals of Major Robert Rogers* that: "I recall a battle reenactment between Rangers and French forces. The Rangers came slinking down a tree-clad hill to surprise the enemy in the flank. Even though the trees were in full foliage, I could still make out the red poms and the light-to-middle blue bonnets plunging down the slope, and then I realized that the Rangers of the 1750s, in the field at least, would never have worn bonnets this particular shade of blue, and especially not with red poms on them."[71] During the colonial period Zaboly concludes Rangers wore a multitude of different headgear – from animal skins to jockey caps and bonnets in various colors and other felt hats usually cut down to brims about 2in. wide.[72]

In 1891 the French mountain troops, *Les Chasseurs Alpins*, adopted an extremely large version of the beret. The color chosen or easily found at the local merchant or supplier was dark blue. At an earlier time French Marines had worn a normal-sized dark blue beret.

With the advent of industrialization and the wholesale slaughter of infantry during the Great War, soldiers returned to the early traditions of wearing steel helmets. However, berets were also introduced "into the main-stream of Western military uniforms. Nearly all sources identify the tank as the causal agent. Its cramped and obstructive confines compelled the British Royal Tank Corps, for one, to adopt a more functional headgear than their cumbersome and easily stained khaki cap. Officially adopted in 1924, the new British black Beret was a compromise between the 'skimpy' beret of the Basque peasant and the 'sloppy' beret of the French Chasseurs Alpins."[73] European armies adopted the beret universally as well as permanently.

During World War II, the US Army's 1st Ranger Battalion, commonly known as Darby's Rangers, formed in Northern Ireland in 1942 and began its long association with the world-renowned British Commandos. Completion of training at the Commando Depot afforded those Rangers the right to wear the British Commando green beret and the tartan of the Clan Cameron of Lochiel.[74] The US Army did not authorize it and Darby's Rangers never donned their berets. Instead, in an effort to Americanize these specialty troops, the Army permitted each Ranger to wear the Ranger Scroll on his left shoulder, identifying him as a member of the: "1st RANGER Bn."

The maroon beret also had British military ancestry. In 1942, British paratroopers began wearing the beret. "The maroon beret was first seen by German troops in North Africa, and within months they had christened the ferocious Paras "*Rote Teufel*" – Red Devils. This distinctive headdress, since adopted by parachute troops all over the world, was officially introduced at the direction of General Browning, and the Pegasus symbol – Bellerophon astride winged Pegasus – became the emblem of British Airborne Forces."[75] In 1943, General Browning granted a battalion of the US Army's 509th Parachute Infantry Regiment honorary membership in the British Parachute Regiment and authorized them to wear British maroon berets.

In 1951 and again in 1976, the US Marine Corps flirted with the idea of wearing berets, blue and green in color, but decided not to adopt them. In 1951, the 10th Airborne Ranger Company put their men in black berets, but they were only locally authorized and only worn briefly until their deployment to Korea to join the 45th Infantry Division.[76]

In the US Army, Headquarters, Department of the Army (HQDA) policy from 1973 through 1979 permitted local commanders to encourage morale-enhancing distinctions, and Armor and Armored Cavalry personnel wore black berets as distinctive headgear until Chief of Staff of the Army (CSA) Bernard W. Rogers banned all such unofficial headgear in 1979. Other units that had worn the black beret included: F Company (LRP), 52nd Infantry, 1st Infantry Division, in 1967 in the Republic of Vietnam; H Company (Ranger), 75th Infantry, 1st Cavalry Division, in 1970 in the Republic of Vietnam; and N Company (Ranger), 75th Infantry, 173rd Airborne Brigade, in 1971 in the Republic of Vietnam. A brown or olive beret was worn in Alaska by the 172nd Infantry Brigade as well as members of the brigade's 1/60 Infantry who wore their brown berets with light-blue flash insignias. E Troop/17th Cavalry wore a tan-colored beret from 1965 to 1967.[77]

Black berets again were authorized in the 1970s for US Army personnel assigned to Ranger units and for all female soldiers. The newly minted Rangers of the 1st and 2nd Battalion, 75th Infantry (Airborne) received authorization to wear their black berets officially via AR 670-5, Uniform and Insignia, the date: January 30, 1975. The Rangers switched to tan on June 14, 2001.

# THE MILITARY AND THE NEW POLITICS

The Global War on Terrorism (GWOT) took place against the backdrop of some renewed antagonism between the US government and the US military. With President Bush's ascendancy to the White House, on January 20, 2001 he appointed veteran businessman and diplomat Donald Rumsfeld as Secretary of Defense and Paul Wolfowitz to the position of Deputy Secretary of Defense. As Vice-President Cheney, Rumsfeld, and Wolfowitz promoted their allies and fortified their positions in 2001, senior military and state department personnel ran afoul of them as expressed by General Tommy Franks, former commander of CENTCOM, and Secretary of State Colin Powell.[78] The beginnings of this power struggle started in the Pentagon with Donald Rumsfeld. The media, more or less ignorant or uncaring of the ongoing power struggle between the civilians and the military, played along, condemning General Shinseki.[79] Rumsfeld during the early part of his tenure was considered a brilliant publicist. Shinseki, less capable in the public light, though by no means a knight in shining armor, and struggling with traditionalist thinking amongst some of his peers and having to wage a media campaign against offended former Rangers, stood no real chance of completely implementing his transformation plans. Shinseki's steadfast refusal to fully support Rumsfeld and his hawks in a war against Iraq was the final straw. The Secretary of Defense announced a new Chief of Staff to replace Shinseki when his first term would end. The *New Yorker* magazine went so far as to call Rumsfeld's move of announcing a new Chief of Staff well over a year in advance "cunning" and "brilliant."[80] Such a move had been unheard of in the past. Usually an announcement would be

## THE NEW FLASH FOR THE 75TH RANGER REGIMENT

(US Army May 18, 2001)

Regimental Flash
A shield-shaped embroidered device with semi-circular base, 2¼in. (5.72cm) in height and 1⅞in. (4.76cm) in width overall, edged with a ⅛in. (0.32cm) black border; an inner black border notched scarlet at the horizontal center line, four diagonal lines, upper scarlet, khaki, orange and lower white from upper right to lower left dividing the shield approximately in half. The upper left being green and the lower right being ultramarine blue.

1st Battalion: A shield-shaped embroidered device with semi-circular base, 2¼in. (5.72cm) in height and 1⅞in. (4.76cm) in width overall, edged with a ⅛in. (0.32cm) black border; an inner black border notched scarlet at the horizontal center line, four diagonal lines, upper scarlet, khaki, orange and lower white from upper right to lower left dividing the shield approximately in half. The upper left being green and the lower right being ultramarine blue.

2nd Battalion: A shield-shaped embroidered device with semi-circular base, 2¼in. (5.72cm) in height and 1⅞in. (4.76cm) in width overall, edged with a ⅛in. (0.32cm) black border; an inner black border double notched scarlet at the horizontal center line, four diagonal lines, upper scarlet, khaki, orange and lower white from upper right to lower left dividing the shield approximately in half. The upper left being green and the lower right being ultramarine blue.

3rd Battalion: A shield-shaped embroidered device with semi-circular base, 2¼in. (5.72cm) in height and 1⅞in. (4.76cm) in width overall, edged with a ⅛in. (0.32cm) black border; an inner black border triple notched scarlet at the horizontal center line, four diagonal lines, upper scarlet, khaki, orange and lower white from upper right to lower left dividing the shield approximately in half. The upper left being green and the lower right being ultramarine blue.

made toward the last months of one's service. This is what really rubbed the professional core of the military the wrong way. Ultimately, Shinseki's bold vision and reluctance to follow blindly did not match Secretary of Defense Donald Rumsfeld's transformation theories. Retired Marine Corps General Paul Van Riper calls Rumsfeld's theories "professionally unschooled" and his treatment of the Chief of Staff Shinseki as "a slap in the face" that has left "a bitter feeling in the retired military community."[81] But none of this would yet be important. Suffice it to say that Donald Rumsfeld's vision, though similar to a degree to Eric Shinseki's, required fewer troops on the ground and a complete dependence on technology. Budget cuts affected the Army but benefited the Air Force tremendously. Rumsfeld's hawks, also derisively known as chickenhawks, had no military training or background, but would forge ahead, solidifying their grasp on military and foreign policies without any military philosophical schooling.[82]

Rangers, having taken umbrage at the alleged insult regarding their black berets, should have viewed it as a compliment instead and realized the importance of the ongoing struggle within the Pentagon. The Regimental Commander at the time did include this statement regarding the Regiment's decision to adopt a new colored beret:

> Unity within our Army is absolutely critical to combat readiness and Rangers have always prided themselves in being part of that unity. Unity among Rangers, past and present, is essential to moving forward and ensuring we honor those who have put the combat streamers on our colors

**BELOW**
Paul Wolfowitz, one of the principal architects of the modern war against terrorism. (DoD)

**BELOW RIGHT**
Paul Van Riper, outspoken critic of Donald Rumsfeld and Paul Wolfowitz. (USMC)

and acknowledge the sacrifices and dedication of the Rangers and their families who serve our nation today.

One is left to ponder this prescient paragraph. Plenty of other Rangers had been promoted and progressed in their careers and surely must have been aware of the dangers when presenting themselves at the Pentagon... but maybe even they failed to realize the enormity of the impending doom that would divide the country in the coming years because of it. Certainly the negative press of the black beret issue and the media's love affair with Rumsfeld helped create a chasm that would plunge the nation into a war with Iraq unwanted by the military and improperly planned for by the architects of the new world order. But that would be a few years in the future. The architects of this relatively new vision of Pax Americana would first have to contend with Afghanistan.

## THE TALIBAN

Ahmed Rashid's *Taliban: Militant Islam, Oil & Fundamentalism in Central Asia* remains the best source on the founding of the brotherhood of Islamic students – the talib.

> There is now an entire factory of myths and stories to explain how [Mullah Mohammed] Omar mobilized a small group of Taliban against the rapacious Kandahar warlords. The most credible story, told repeatedly, is that in the spring of 1994 Singesar neighbours came to tell him that a commander had abducted two teenage girls, their heads had been shaved and they had been taken to a military camp and repeatedly raped. Omar enlisted some 30 Talibs who had only 16 rifles between them and attacked the base, freeing the girls and hanging the commander from the barrel of a tank. They captured quantities of arms and ammunition. "We were fighting against Muslims who had gone wrong. How could we remain quiet when we could see crimes being committed against women and the poor?" Omar said later.
>
> A few months later two commanders confronted each other in Kandahar, in a dispute over a young boy whom both men wanted to sodomise. In the fight that followed civilians were killed. Omar's group freed the boy and public appeals started coming in for the Taliban to help out in other local disputes. Omar had emerged as a Robin Hood figure, helping the poor against the rapacious commanders. His prestige grew because he asked for no reward or credit from those he helped, only demanding that they follow him to set up a just Islamic system.
>
> The stated goals of the Taliban are: restore peace, disarm the population, enforce Sharia law [traditional Islamic law] and defend the integrity and Islamic character of Afghanistan.[83]

# THE EXECUTORS OF THE NEW WORLD ORDER

Although shortly after September 11 various US cells and teams infiltrated Afghanistan to join forces with anti-Taliban units, the American public had yet to see any overt signs of retaliation or blood of the enemy. Nevertheless, savvy public relations campaigns by the Department of Defense and the US news media fueled the public's rage against the Taliban who themselves had very little to do with the attacks against American soil. Using this line of reasoning, Germany or South Korea could be held responsible for worldwide US attacks as they both host American military bases. In yet another ironic twist, the very same Taliban now held responsible for not only consorting with the enemy but also ruling Afghanistan with an iron fist, had earlier traveled to the United States to negotiate oil treaties. Therefore any subsequent arguments that the Taliban were not a legitimate representative of the country, or that the federal government was unaware of their human rights violations, were devoid of logic.

On October 7, 2001, President Bush declared: "On my orders, the United States military has begun strikes against al Qaeda terrorist training camps and military installations of the Taliban regime in Afghanistan. These carefully targeted actions are designed to disrupt the use of Afghanistan as a terrorist base of operations, and to attack the military capability of the Taliban regime... We did not ask for this mission, but we will fulfill it. The name of today's military operation is *Enduring Freedom*... Peace and freedom will prevail... May God continue to bless America."[84]

# Operation *Enduring Freedom I*

Rangers lead the way!

The 75th Ranger Regiment, newly attired in their tan berets, would soon form a crucial role in the ever-expanding public relations campaign waged by the Department of Defense. The Rangers would participate in two highly publicized combat operations: the combat parachute assault on Objective Rhino on October 19, 2001, and the actions involving a small Ranger Quick Reaction Force at Takur Ghar on March 3–4, 2002. But these were not the only missions conducted by the Regiment. Indeed, long-range combat patrols in Desert Mobility Vehicles would remind the general reader of missions

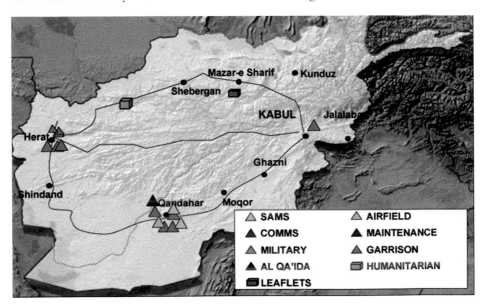

Afghanistan during the opening stages of *Enduring Freedom*. (DoD)

conducted by the British Special Air Service (SAS) and the Long Range Desert Group (LRDG) during World War II in North Africa. The LRDG conducted over 200 operations behind enemy lines and usually operated in small groups, sometimes with as few as two vehicles.

Additional Ranger tasks would include using long-range patrols and aerial resupply reminiscent of Merrill's Marauders' incredible World War II campaigns in order to blockade TAQ (Taliban and al-Qaeda) fighters (see box below) from protected areas. Another task involved combining joint force assets deep in Afghanistan, enabling attack helicopters to launch from within the country using the refueling and rearming stations set up by Ranger Special Operations Forces (SOF), who created moving airfields and gas stations. These Shadow Warriors would disappear silently into the night after each operation.

The Ranger battalions, as we have learned, are generally assigned tasks with missions specifically tailored to a shorter duration. The deployment schedules can be just a few days or as long as several months, but the one-year overseas duty as experienced by regular forces is unheard of for the Ranger Regiment. Such was to be the case in Afghanistan. Ranger battalions rotated their overseas duties, then returned to refit and recover from their combat operations. Battalions that remained stateside continued their training cycles. Rangers were thus able to satisfy the needs of their Special Operations Command (SOC) planners throughout the changing campaign against the Taliban and al-Qaeda fighters. Their operational histories would be labeled Operation *Enduring Freedom I, II, III* and so forth.

Although certain cells of the Department of Defense and other intelligence-gathering units had begun working in covert operations in Afghanistan a short time after the attacks on September 11, the self-appointed "War President," George Bush, and his cabinet needed to demonstrate to the zealously patriotic general populace that indeed America was waging a war against evil – presently in Afghanistan and embodied by al-Qaeda and the Taliban. A month had passed since the attacks on American soil, and clearly a point had to be made to the world that the United States could reach out and touch someone or something whenever and wherever it wanted to on the planet. This task was handed to the best Special Operations infantry unit in the world – the 75th Ranger Regiment. The first mission was a Ranger classic: an enemy-held airfield seizure – Objective Rhino, Helmand Desert area, Kandahar. Unlike previous Ranger low-level combat parachute assaults, such as those executed in Grenada and Panama, no

## TAQ FIGHTERS

A combination of Taliban and al-Qaeda, "TAQ" represents all like-minded fighters from a diverse ethnic pool. TAQ fighters can include, but are not limited to, Afghans, Pakistanis, Saudis, Uzbeks, Chechens, Egyptians, Iranians, and even citizens of Western countries, including Britains and Americans.

follow-on forces would relieve them; instead they would conduct a daring but short nighttime raid.

The Global War on Terrorism (GWOT) proper had begun. Special Forces teams infiltrated northern Afghanistan to join their anti-Taliban allies, the so-called Northern Alliance, while 200 or so Rangers conducted a low-level night combat parachute assault in the south. Ongoing airstrikes had already crippled much of the TAQ militias' fighting abilities. Antiquated tanks and facilities as well as antiaircraft locations were decimated with great ease. The launch of Objective Rhino on October 19, 2001 marked the US's willingness to respond overtly, demonstrating her power. The American media proved to be a willing and unquestioning mouthpiece, spoonfed by the Pentagon's elaborate propaganda machine.[85]

The official history commissioned by US Army Special Operations Command (USASOC), *Weapon of Choice: US Army Special Operations Forces in Afghanistan*, describes the media campaign as such:

> Army photographers with night-vision cameras videotaped the parachute assault and the extraction of the Ranger force by MC-130 aircraft. Within hours of the successful night combat operation, a combat camera team had done a first edit of the raw footage of the raid and electronically delivered the reduced footage to a product development team of the 3rd Psychological Operations Battalion (POB) at Fort Bragg. This team edited and transmitted a finished video clip to the Pentagon in time for Secretary of Defense Donald Rumsfeld to show it the following day during his noon press conference and in time for it to be integrated into the American news cycle.[86]

Elements of the 3rd Ranger Battalion conducted the assault moments after Objective Rhino was blasted by the Air Force's AC-130 gunships. As those Rangers parachuted into their first combat action since 1993, another night parachute assault took place north of Rhino with the same objective: to seize an enemy airfield. Unfortunately, two Rangers were killed in that supporting operation, originally launched from Pakistan, when their helicopter crashed. The two Rangers were the first American casualties since operations against al-Qaeda and their Taliban hosts began and within a week CIA officer Mike Spann would be killed at a prison riot at Mazar-e-Sharif.

# OBJECTIVE RHINO, OCTOBER 19, 2001

The 3rd Battalion (-) of the 75th Ranger Regiment was tasked with carrying out the mission against Objective Rhino. Task Force 3/75 Ranger consisted of 199 soldiers, which included a command and control element from the Regimental Headquarters and was supported by four MC-130 Combat Talons. Their missions were as follows:

1. Conduct a night combat parachute assault to seize a remote desert landing strip (DLS).
2. Destroy Taliban forces.
3. Gather intelligence.

4. Provide a casualty trans load site for other simultaneous combat operations.
5. Establish a forward arming and refueling point (FARP) for rotary-wing aircraft.
6. Assess the capabilities of the airstrip for future operations.

On 19 October, the Ranger task force prepared for the parachute assault operation that night. Just before donning their parachutes, the Ranger commanders and sergeants major gave last-minute words of encouragement, and the 75th Ranger Regimental Chaplain invoked a blessing on the force.[87]

The Department of Defense-released video footage shows Rangers in desert camouflage uniforms putting on their equipment in a large hangar, with jumpmasters going through the well-rehearsed movements to ensure that the chutes, main and reserve, and weapons carriers were strapped on correctly. Attention to that kind of detail saves lives and is constantly drilled into all members of the airborne elite. These Rangers had been rehearsing airborne operations for a long time and could successfully execute them while blindfolded. Certainly the excitement level must have been high among the men. They would be the first sizable force conducting combat operations on the ground in Afghanistan, the haven of al-Qaeda terrorists. No doubt many Rangers were pumped and ready to exact some vengeance, while others were plagued with the traditional worries that men about to go into combat, and in this case parachuting into the unknown, often contemplate during the lonely hours prior to the mission. Rehearsals had been conducted much earlier, first at a walking pace and ultimately at full speed. Officers and enlisted men alike

## THE ORDER OF BATTLE FOR THE 75TH RANGER REGIMENT – OBJECTIVE RHINO

| | | |
|---|---|---|
| Detachment, Headquarters and Headquarters Company, 75th Ranger Regiment | 1845Z 19 October 2001 to 0014Z 20 October 2001 | Helmand Desert, Afghanistan |
| Detachment, Headquarters and Headquarters Company, 3rd Battalion, 75th Ranger Regiment | 1845Z 19 October 2001 to 0014Z 20 October 2001 | Helmand Desert, Afghanistan |
| Detachment, A Company, 3rd Battalion, 75th Ranger Regiment | 1845Z 19 October 2001 to 0014Z 20 October 2001 | Helmand Desert, Afghanistan |
| Detachment, C Company, 3rd Battalion, 75th Ranger Regiment | 1845Z 19 October 2001 to 0014Z 20 October 2001 | Helmand Desert, Afghanistan |

Video capture of Rangers waddling to their aircraft just prior to their parachute assault. (DoD)

were fairly well acquainted with the overall mission concepts and the operation orders had covered even minute details, and had been disseminated to the lowest levels. Each Ranger would make sure he was ready – a lackadaisical attitude in training could spell disaster even in non-combat operations. Rangers pride themselves on professional planning, rehearsal, and execution of missions. No doubt 3rd Battalion was ready and willing. The combat scroll and mustard stain were a welcome addition to any Ranger's uniform. Finally rigged and checked, the Airborne Rangers waddled from the hangar to the aircraft, a backbreaking task. Rucks, loaded for bear and strapped upside down to the parachute harness, with their weight forced between the paratroopers' knees, can cause excruciating pain in the back as the paratroopers take tiny steps toward the aircraft just a few hundred yards away – though seemingly miles.

Once loaded in a manner like sardines in a tin can, the MC-130 Combat Talons plus Ranger package had a four-hour flight ahead of them which proved uneventful except for a few "occasional flares punctuating the darkness outside the paratroop doors."[88] About to experience their first combat action, undoubtedly some Rangers fell asleep, while others thought about loved ones at home or quite possibly came to terms with the undeniable possibility of being killed or wounded. Ranger briefings are traditionally detailed and carefully planned – every contingency thought of and addressed. Still, some men must have worried about the impending assault and whether or not the Taliban and al-Qaeda fighters would put up resistance. What did the briefings stipulate? The estimated number of enemy forces, their morale, and anticipated Ranger casualties? Unfortunately, the operations orders remain classified. Undoubtedly, no stiff resistance was expected or otherwise the highly anticipated Pentagon news briefing might not have come to fruition. Nonetheless, the Rangers were prepared for the worst-case scenario.

It could be argued that this global war is the best time to be in a Ranger battalion. Decades of Ranger sweat in training and blood in smaller skirmishes had developed the Ranger standard operating procedures into those used in Afghanistan. Endless years of uninspired toil and rehearsals had fine-tuned the core of the Ranger Regiment; no time was better to be a Ranger than during wartime, the conflict offering a chance to put all that Ranger training into action.

The Task Force delivered their Ranger package at 1845Z (Zulu), October 19, 2001. Although the Rangers were to be the first American force to set foot on Afghan soil, surely Special Operations pathfinders must have parachuted or infiltrated in just prior to the Ranger assault to guide in the planes and provide valuable on-ground intelligence. This was the Rangers' first combat parachute assault since the entire Regiment, all three battalions totaling approximately 2,000 men, jumped onto the Panamanian airfields at Rio Hato and Tocumen-Torrijos in December 1989 and conducted the parachute assault from less than

500ft. In Afghanistan, the Combat Talons flew so low that dust blew inside as the jump doors were opened at about 800ft with zero illumination conditions.[89] The Rangers hoped to jump into the nest of a sleeping enemy. The Department of Defense video intercuts dramatic footage of one aircraft's interior, a Ranger stick shuffling out of the door, and footage showing a master of the low flying aircraft with the blossoming 'chutes as they spill out into the night sky atop their intended target. Rangers led the way, and just as in Panama the Ranger Creed was recited prior to the jump. It provided encouragement to some, while others treated it with the cynicism usually found alive and well within the Ranger rank and file.

Rhino, southwest of Kandahar, had four distinct objectives: Tin, Iron, Copper, and Cobalt. In any event, the Air Force's B-2 Stealth bombers had dropped several 2,000lb, global positioning system (GPS) guided, bombs onto Objective Tin before AC-130 Spectre gun-ships peppered it with their heavy weapons systems. The official history states: "Initial reports were that 11 enemy had been killed and nine were seen running away."[90] The crew of one AC-130 reported that Objective Iron was devoid of enemy personnel and targets, while Objective Copper was not identified positively and thus not engaged. Objective Cobalt on the other hand was sprayed by a gunship that had targeted several buildings and guard towers on the compound's walls.

Elements of Task Force 3/75 had the mission to seize and secure objectives Tin and Iron, and subsequent to that, to prevent the enemy from troubling Objective Cobalt and the desert landing strip that was part of the overall operation. This mission fell onto an under-strength company, Company A (-), 3rd Ranger Battalion. As snipers are a useful combat multiplier, especially in desert environments, one sniper team was also attached.

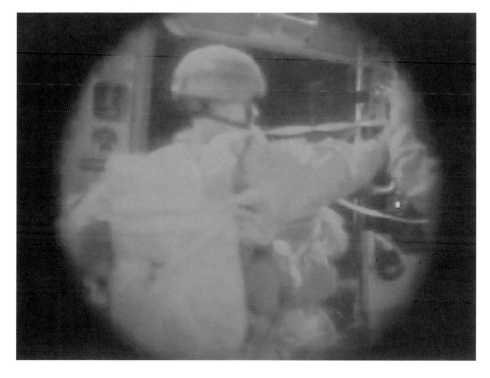

Video capture of Rangers jumping into the darkness. (DoD)

The nighttime parachute assault onto Rhino was prepped by smart bombs and gunships. The Rangers, while descending beneath their deployed canopies, strained to look around the objective, using the fires on Objective Tin to get their bearings. Traditionally when a Ranger hits the ground, he releases his parachute, secures his weapon from the M1956 weapons container, and proceeds to his assembly area. In this case, as follow-on forces would be fixed-wing and rotary aircraft, the Rangers had to retrieve their parachutes, stuff them into parachute kit bags, and finally stack them away from the desert landing strip to keep the runway clear of the potential hazard for the aircraft.

After successfully linking up, Rangers from C Company encountered one lone man and killed him immediately. Rangers assembled with relative ease and cleared Objective Iron, then established pre-planned blocking positions to prevent any possible enemy counterattack, although there can be little doubt that a gunship would have made mincemeat out of any such relieving force. C Company cleared the walled compound at Rhino – Objective Cobalt. Surprisingly the Rangers discovered that the gunship's earlier bombardment had little effect on the compound: "Damage was minimal. The thick concrete walls and building roofs (later discovered to be reinforced with rebar) had either absorbed the blasts or the cannon shells had punched through the roofs and ceilings leaving only holes. The guard towers were in the same condition."[91] Psyops teams broadcast surrender tapes in multiple languages to an empty area. Although the Rangers were well-rehearsed in clearing rooms and buildings, several rooms required an extra effort to open steel doors – either multiple gunshots or explosives. This part of the mission took longer then anticipated, despite the fact that no resistance was encountered.

Although no useful Ranger narrative of the combat jump is available, one member of the Psyops team supporting the mission recalls his experiences:

> It was completely black outside... I could see one of the secondary objectives burning furiously from a bomb hit... I heard sporadic fire coming from Rhino... As I was descending, the last of the aircraft flew overhead, dropping its load of Rangers. Just as it passed over, flares started popping out of it, illuminating the night sky and the airfield below just in time to orient myself on the horizon and prepare to land. I hit the ground like a rock and promptly found myself entangled in parachute suspension lines and 1/4-inch cotton webbing. I cut myself free, chambered a round in my weapon, activated my NVG [night-vision goggles], and scanned the immediate area for the enemy. Convinced that I was in no immediate danger, I gathered my chute and stuffed it into my kit bag, found a Ranger buddy, and moved to the assembly area. As we waited in the assembly area, my element leader spotted an unidentified person coming toward us from the vicinity of the compound. Several of us quickly acquired him and lased him with our PEQ-2s. Fire control was incredible as we watched and waited with lasers dancing all over the target until one found the glint tape arm band identifying him as a friendly Ranger. Once assembled, we moved toward our primary objective. [Tactical Psyop Team]

While moving toward the objective [with the Psyops team], gunfire erupted to our right rear flank. Our immediate response was to get down. Since we did not have a clear field of fire, we just stayed put. A lone Taliban had stumbled into a squad of Rangers guarding our right flank.

It was decided that another airstrike on the compound was necessary to ensure that no other enemy would walk into our formation by chance. Word was passed that an airstrike was imminent, so we lay flat on the ground, pulled security, and waited. The AC-130 Spectre gunship strike can only be described as impressive. I was awestruck because 500 meters from my location high-explosive shells were impacting on the compound. Once the strike was over, we moved to our initial broadcast position.

As the lead Ranger element moved toward the objective, we set up our loudspeaker and began to broadcast our first message. It told anyone in the area that U.S. forces were present and that they needed to exit the buildings, stay away from the airfield, drop any weapons, and get down on the ground if they wanted to survive. We played the message for about 5 minutes. The broadcast resounded across the valley floor into the compound. There was no doubt that anyone in the area had fair warning. This done, we bounded forward to join the rest of the Ranger element at building #1, secured a room, and awaited orders.

We were told to assist in searching the building for any intelligence and weapons, and to be watchful for booby traps. We found a Soviet RPK machine gun with a belt of ammo in the feed tray, expended shell casings, belt links on the ground, a RPG [rocket-propelled grenade] launcher with 10 to 12 rounds nearby, and two AK-47 assault rifles. The rooms had articles of clothing strewn about, mattresses and bedding, and other personal effects. After collecting the weapons, we distributed about 400 leaflets in and around the building. As we lifted off from the airfield to return to base, I proudly showed the machine gun on my back to those around me. We were all elated to have participated in and survived America's first ground strike against terrorism at Objective Rhino. I then got comfortable on the floor and went to sleep.[92]

The overall planning was successful. The planners had created an excellent sequence of events on the objective. Within 14 minutes of the start of C Company's clearing the walled compound on Objective Rhino, the first Combat Talon airlanded a medical team to treat the anticipated injured and wounded (two Rangers were injured during the jump). Six minutes thereafter several helicopters supporting another assault landed and were able to refuel and rearm and continue on their mission. During these ongoing operations "Air Force special tactics squadron (STS) airmen were surveying the DLS to determine its capability to handle larger aircraft. As these activities were conducted, orbiting AC-130 Spectre gunships destroyed several enemy vehicles moving toward the airstrip and a group of people approaching on foot."[93] It is left to wonder who this group of people actually was – whether local guards or reinforcements is left to speculation.

The Rangers collapsed their perimeter bit by bit, maintaining security all the time, and boarded the MC-130s that had provided the supplies for the fueling and rearming of the other helicopters. Once the infrared airstrip markers were picked up, Task Force 3/75 departed Objective Rhino five hours and 24 minutes after its combat drop onto the area.[94]

# OBJECTIVE HONDA, OCTOBER 19, 2001

At the same time as Rangers were parachuting at Objective Rhino, a much smaller element of 26 Rangers from B Company, 3/75, and two Air Force STS members, parachuted or airlanded on another airstrip in support of the Rhino assault. This operation, launched from Pakistan, was designated as a contingency operation with the intended purpose of establishing a site that could support Objective Rhino if needed. Unfortunately, their mission changed instantly from one of support for the larger operation to one of rescue for their comrades. As the second Black Hawk, an MH-60K helicopter, approached to land, it caused a brownout, obscuring the vision of the pilots of the landing area. The brownout seemed to be created by the helicopter flaring, meaning it had come in so hard and fast and at an angle that caused it to kick up the loose dirt, that it tilted over on its side. Some of the soldiers on board were pinned by the helicopter. Rangers Jonn Edmunds and Kristofor Stonesifer were killed in the accident.

*New Yorker* magazine's investigative journalist Seymour Hersh writes in the November 12, 2001 article, "Escape and Evasion: What happened when the Special Forces landed in Afghanistan?" that a different simultaneous assault by Rangers and Delta on leading Taliban leader Mullah Omar's complex ended in a desperate firefight with a dozen Delta force soldiers left wounded after the raid, having been ambushed by TAQ forces. This is possible, as the mission for TF 3/75 included the establishment of DLSs for other operations – yet no information has been unearthed to support the assertion.[95] If indeed this did occur, it would only prove to be another learning experience for America's Special Operations Forces (SOF). No doubt the actions at Objective Honda must have been confusing and could have led to some panic due to the helicopter crashing. Maybe some individuals thought initially that the helicopter was shot down and the communications to higher-up were probably hectic. This could well have been the catalyst for the Delta force rumor.

The Department of Defense was elated with the success of the missions. The Rangers had shown "that American military forces could strike swiftly, silently, and with deadly force day or night. They had shown the Taliban and al-Qaeda that there were no safe havens and that America could project its military power at will. CENTCOM commander General Franks said that the mission was an "unequivocal success."[96] In his ever-growing media presence, General Myers described the actions of October 19, 2001:

> Yesterday U.S. military forces conducted ground operations in addition to our air operations in support of Operation Enduring Freedom. Under the

Colonel Votel's uniform
at the Infantry Museum.
(Author's collection/Camera 1)

direction of the president and the Secretary of Defense and under the command of U.S. Central Command, General Tom Franks, Special Operations Forces, including U.S. Army Rangers, deployed to Afghanistan. They attacked and destroyed targets associated with terrorist activity and Taliban command and control. U.S. forces were able to deploy, maneuver and operate inside Afghanistan without significant interference from Taliban forces. They are now refitting and repositioning for potential future operations against terrorist targets in other areas known to harbor terrorists.

I have several video clips of yesterday's action to show you. This video will be available on DefenseLINK and through the pool after this briefing.[97]

Some Rangers, including the much-admired Regimental Commander Colonel Votel, who participated in the combat parachute assaults, were made available by the Pentagon to CNN and interviewed by Larry King.

# DESERT LANDING STRIP BASTOGNE

| THE ORDER OF BATTLE OF THE 75TH RANGER REGIMENT – DESERT LANDING STRIP BASTOGNE | | |
|---|---|---|
| Detachment, B Company, 3rd Battalion, 75th Ranger Regiment | 1800Z–2334Z 13 November 2001 | in the vicinity of Alimarden Kan-E-Bagat, Afghanistan |

October 19, 2001, saw the 3rd Ranger Battalion as the tip of the spear for America's war on terrorism when, with the media spotlight burning on them ever so brightly, they successfully assaulted Objective Rhino. On November 13, 2001, Battboys from B Company, 3/75, would once again add to the outstanding tradition of the 75th Ranger Regiment. The mission this time called for securing another desert landing strip, establishing and supporting a forward arming and refueling point (FARP) southwest of Kandahar that in turn would enable US attack helicopters to target Taliban and al-Qaeda objectives. The DLS was dubbed Bastogne after the famous battle during World War II where paratroopers from the "Screaming Eagles," the 101st Airborne Division, battled against a determined German foe who had gambled on the Ardennes offensive in late 1944 being the one final push to drive the Allies back. The Germans were audacious and successful, only to have their backs broken when the skies cleared and the Allied fighters were able to penetrate the winter clouds and hit the exposed Germans who were not able to match the American air superiority. It was during the early stages of this battle that the American commander Brigadier General Tony McAuliffe refused to surrender to the Germans by simply saying "nuts." Certainly this was the stuff of legend. In comparison, the seizure of DLS Bastogne would hardly have been a blip on the radar during World War II. During GWOT however, any tangible success with minimal American casualties would be considered fantastic.

Thirty-two Rangers from B Company (-), 3rd Battalion, 75th Ranger Regiment, made the second combat parachute assault during Operation *Enduring Freedom* at 1800Z, November 13, 2001. Their mission was hastily put together, within a 24-hour time frame, and was supported by an MC-130 Combat Talon along with eight Air Force Special Tactics Squadron (AFSTS) airmen. As the night belongs to the Rangers, the jump was conducted in darkness at 800ft and without any pathfinder support, i.e. no markings, and in the desert, thus not even presenting any distinguishable landmark for orientation. The Rangers, always on the leading edge of technology, would of course have a tool at their disposal to eliminate potential problems such as dispersal and simply being lost in the wide-open desert – GPS.

Once the Rangers successfully parachuted into the area without casualties, they again collected their parachutes, bagged them and placed them away from the DLS. The official history mentions that night combat jumps during World War II were characterized by paratroopers being scattered across the landscape, and historically the assembling of units, and sometimes just groups, of paratroopers was extremely slow. "Technology, though, has progressed far beyond the 'cricket' tin noisemakers the 82nd and 101st Airborne Division soldiers used on D-Day at Normandy. Using hand-held GPS devices (about one per fire team of four to five soldiers), Rangers punched in the coordinates of the assembly area, and that single technological advancement enabled the troops to assemble, with parachutes, in about 45 minutes."[98]

This is an interesting point that deserves some attention. Battalion-sized parachute assaults have taken, in training and in combat, anywhere from 30 minutes to three hours to assemble. Combat effectiveness, in essence, is being able to assemble enough men to begin the mission, which usually takes 30–45 minutes for those elements conducting the actual assaults. Consider a 40-men stick exiting an aircraft within a few seconds in the desert – something most Rangers, particularly Rangers from the 2nd Battalion, are very familiar with, as they have the Yakima Desert in Washington State. Forty-five minutes sounds like a long time for so few men, although ultimately fire teams with one GPS would have to account for their teammates prior to moving out, and all it takes is one lost Ranger to cause a delay. Combat parachute assaults at night in hostile territories can be disastrous and must be executed with caution. Assembling platoon-sized elements can take up to one hour and however great a GPS is, it is just another tool and in general terms does not make for a faster assembly time. The parachute assaults in Panama were more akin to the massive airborne drops executed during World War II and, without a doubt, a modern battalion-sized jump is still very similar to a World War II jump – some things cannot be rushed. Parachutists will be scattered and will take time to assemble – these are the very things that make up the friction of war.

In any event, as the Rangers conducted their mission at the objective, Air Force personnel determined the landing strip to be suitable for C-130 planes. The C-130 is truly a remarkable plane, requiring very little runway and being hardy enough to land on dirt. Most paratroopers can remember the exhilaration of standing in the door of a C-130 with the wind slamming into the face and body – lights dancing in the distance – waiting for the jump master to give the "go" signal. Today's planes are fitted with door devices allowing the paratrooper to simply step out of the plane – pushing into obsolescence the age-old paratrooper ritual of standing in the door.

The STS unit deployed infra-red landing lights up and down the strip and by 1915Z, one hour and 15 minutes after the parachute drop, an MC-130 landed with its content of two helicopters and a FARP. By 1930Z another one landed with the same content. Four helicopters and two FARPs were assembled and ready to go within less than 15 minutes – the helicopters en route to their objectives. The speed and efficiency of the mission were truly a remarkable achievement.

DLS Bastogne became the hub for an aerial raid. While the helicopters were flying toward their objectives, the two MC-130s departed for aerial refueling. By 2100Z the helicopters had returned, refueled, and rearmed to go on yet another raid against Taliban and al-Qaeda targets. One hour and 22 minutes later, the Combat Talons had returned, packed up and reloaded the two FARPs. The entire Bastogne package, including the four helicopters, was assembled, loaded, and airborne by 2334Z.[99]

This operation, in its simple sophistication, is testimony to the resourcefulness of the planners and soldiers of the Army Special Operations Forces. The Rangers had proven yet again their prowess in nighttime combat parachute assaults and their ability to comfortably work in a joint force structure.

# Operation *Relentless Strike*
## World War II remembered

As with earlier operations, in Operation *Relentless Strike* Rangers would parachute into a suitable area, set it up as a refueling station to support the attack helicopters in conducting their missions, and keep the area secure for the duration of those missions. As previously stated and seen throughout the history of the American Rangers, versatility and adaptability are key factors to their continued success. Instead of parachuting into the unknown of the dark night, however, Rangers would this time insert with their desert mobility vehicles in order to establish forward arming and refueling points (FARPs) throughout denied areas. Rangers from A Company, 3/75, would become modern-day long-range desert groups akin to the fabled British LRDG units during their World War II campaigns in North Africa. This ability added another dimension to the strike at the Taliban and al-Qaeda forces from virtually anywhere. The purpose of the operation was to find suitable desert landing strips that could carry the weight of fully loaded MC-130s, establish a FARP to support further operations, and all the while provide complete security for the members of the task force.

Ranger operations are usually conducted at night and this was to be the case for the insertion of a team at DLS Anzio, which was deemed suitable for the operation. "Anzio" referred to the location of the Allied invasion of western Italy in January 1944 – ironically it was during this campaign that two Ranger battalions were surrounded and captured by battle-hardened Germans. On November 16 and 17, six desert mobility vehicles (DMVs) were inserted by Combat Talons, the Air Force's special operations workhorses, with a package consisting of 48 Rangers and AFSTS airmen. There were eight men per vehicle. In typical Ranger tradition, the area for the subsequent operation was carefully reconnoitered. Rangers conducted their vehicular movements in similar fashion as they would have when on foot patrols. "Employing standard Ranger procedures, such as listening halts, bounding overwatch with the DMVs and leader recons, the Rangers confirmed the second DLS."[100] Once the Rangers established that no enemy forces were in the area, they traveled to a suitable predetermined location. This was DLS Bulge, a name yet again derived from a World War II battle – the Battle of the Bulge, also known as the Ardennes Offensive, ran from December 1944 to January 1945. It was one of the largest battles fought on mainland Europe, and resulted in the death of approximately 19,000 GIs, not to mention other Allied and Axis casualties.

At Bulge, Rangers provided security as the STS "assessed the area, verifying the dimensions; noting potential hazards and obstacles; and taking core samples of the runway area and determined that it was also suitable for MC-130 landings."[101] Then the small task force hunkered down in a hidesite, having removed the physical tracks left behind by their vehicles. Here the Rangers camouflaged their vehicles and once in the laager, they conducted and reviewed all necessary tasks at hand – communication checks, security arrangements, escape and evasion plans, immediate action drills, and a myriad of other tasks including cleaning their weapons and catching up on sleep for those not on security detail.

On November 18 the Ranger task force was notified to secure DLS Bulge. Rangers provided the muscle and their expertise while the AF personnel set about marking the strip for the incoming flights. "At 1600Z, the MC-130s landed with their cargo of helicopters, the FARP, and a resupply bundle for the Rangers."[102] Although the actions around the DLS were routine, they were hardly common – this type of mission was Special Operations in nature and required excellent communications and planning. Interestingly, the official history notes a peculiar event during this mission: "When the attack helicopters returned, they, like the Rangers, reported seeing heavy rocket fire in the distance. The next day both groups were informed that they had witnessed a meteor shower."[103]

Following two separate strikes by the helicopters, DLS Bulge was swept clean by the Rangers, who removed all trace of their presence. The same type of

Rangers preparing to hunker down for the evening. Later on they will seize and hold an objective for FARP ops. (USASOC)

mission was conducted the following night and it proved to be the last one, successfully concluding Operation *Relentless Strike*. On November 19 the entire task force was airlifted out of the area.

The insertion of small Ranger elements to establish and secure FARP sites added a new dimension to the operational capabilities of the USASOC. Inserted via parachute, air-landed with or without ground mobility vehicles, Rangers could operate with impunity. The area of operations in Afghanistan was too large to present a valid target to the TAQ fighters. Of course what applies to American forces also applies to TAQ militias. Just as it was tough to locate the Coalition forces conducting pinpoint raids through FARP sites, hunting down and smoking out the bad guys would prove to be equally difficult. Nevertheless, those difficulties would be encountered in subsequent missions, most notably in the actions around Tora Bora.

The Rumsfeldian theory of war relies heavily on technology – airpower with smart bombs – and few boots on the ground. In November and December 2001, the aerial bombardment and haphazard handling of ground troops by the Secretary of Defense allowed Osama bin Laden to escape unharmed from the mountainous region of Tora Bora.[104] Most of his several hundred bodyguards escaped into the night as well.[105] This failure, coupled with the preparations since September 11, 2001, for an invasion of Iraq, would spell disaster for the Rangers and other SOF within a few short months.

During the December 2001 questioning by the US Senate on how the current military actions might affect al-Qaeda, the FBI's Acting Assistant Director of its CounterTerrorism Division, J. T. Caruso, the following was spoken: "It is too early to tell, from a law enforcement perspective, how the current military campaign in Afghanistan will affect al Qaeda and its ability to operate in the future. Determination and vigilance will remain the keys to any success. It is one thing to disrupt an organization such as al Qaeda, it is another to totally dismantle and destroy it. This must truly remain an international effort, with international cooperation on all levels, in order to be successful. All agencies within the US government must remain vigilant, and must continue to cooperate and work together, in order to truly eradicate this scourge to all mankind everywhere known as al Qaeda."

Carl Conetta, in *Strange Victory: A critical appraisal of Operation Enduring Freedom and the Afghanistan war*, published in January 2002, appraised the situation as follows:

> A reasonable estimate is that 3,000 to 4,000 Taliban coalition troops are dead, including those killed in battle, captivity, and by strategic bombardment.
>
> Among these dead may be 600–800 "Afghan Arabs" affiliated with Al Qaeda (out of an original total of 2,000–3,000). Notably, only a fraction of Al Qaeda fighters – perhaps 25 percent – are pledged members of the organization; the remainder are foreign volunteers brought to Afghanistan to fight in the civil war under Al Qaeda auspices.
>
> Approximately 7,000 Taliban and foreign troops were prisoners as of 15 January; fewer than 500 of these had been transferred to US custody.
>
> A disproportionate number of the prisoners held by the Northern

Alliance militias were foreign fighters, especially Uzbek and Pakistani.

Most of the top Taliban leadership has survived the war and eluded capture; many are in Pakistan and seeking to re-integrate into Afghanistan. Of more than three dozen Taliban leaders on the Pentagon's "wanted list," more than 12 have been killed, injured or have defected.

At least eight of the 20 top Al Qaeda leaders and aides pursued by the Pentagon in Afghanistan are believed dead. However, only two had been reported captured as of 15 January.

Eleven training camps affiliated with Al Qaeda, and many other Al Qaeda facilities in Afghanistan, have been destroyed or overrun.
Translating these achievements into qualitative terms:

The Taliban have been driven from power in Afghanistan, fragmented as a political force, and widely discredited as an ideological movement. Nonetheless, many members and veterans are likely to re-assume a role in the Afghan polity – some as provincial insurgents, others as members or even leaders of other formations.

Al Qaeda infrastructure and operations in Afghanistan have been destroyed, a substantial proportion of their core cadre have been attrited, and their capacity to act globally has been disrupted significantly – although perhaps only temporarily.

But most of the US military effort and most of the troops killed or captured in the operation were only indirectly related to Al Qaeda's global terrorist activities. The Taliban regime, which absorbed most of our attention, bore only a contingent relationship to Al Qaeda's activities outside the region. In fact, most of the Al Qaeda facilities and most of the foreign troops under their control in Afghanistan had to do with the civil war there. Most of the organization's capabilities to conduct far reaching terrorist acts resided and resides outside of Afghanistan, and thus fell beyond the scope of Operation Enduring Freedom. The essential importance of Afghanistan to the extra-regional goals and activities of Al Qaeda was not that it provided a sanctuary and training site for terrorists. Instead, Afghanistan served the organization's global activities principally as a recruiting ground for future cadre. The capacity of Al Qaeda to repair its lost capabilities for global terrorism rests on the fact that terrorist attacks like the 11 September crashes do not depend on the possession of massive, openair training facilities. Warehouses and small ad hoc sites will do. Moreover, large terrorist organizations have proved themselves able to operate for very long periods without state sanctuaries – as long as sympathetic communities exist. The Irish Republican Army is an example. Thus, Al Qaeda may be able to recoup its lost capacity by adopting a more thoroughly clandestine and "state-less" approach to its operations, including recruitment and training.[106]

By early 2002 Coalition forces had the former students of Islam, the Taliban, and the hard-core al-Qaeda fighters on the run. It was just a matter of smoking out a handful of dedicated fighters in the mountainous eastern regions of Afghanistan, with minimal resources of course, as the invasion of Iraq and the destruction of the ever-shifting evil was paramount.

# Operation *Anaconda* and Takur Ghar

## All glory to the Regiment

## AWARDS CEREMONY

### Hunter Army Airfield – 1st Battalion, 75th Ranger Regiment – January 16, 2003

A huge American flag, similar to the one seen in the movie *Patton*, decorated the interior of the building. The Truscott Facility was abuzz with hushed voices and eager anticipation. It was to be a great day in the combat annals of the 75th Ranger Regiment. Civilians and military, retired and active duty alike, were preparing for the arrival of Army Chief of Staff General Eric Shinseki and Air Force Chief of Staff General John Jumper. A number of Rangers in Class As (dress uniform) were present, their tan-colored berets setting off their green uniforms nicely. Thirty-six members of the 1st Ranger Battalion were about to receive military honors for their combat service in the previous year during Operation *Enduring Freedom*.

Finally the ceremony began; the awardees and other Rangers marched in and stood in their respective formations. Lieutenant Colonel Michael Kershaw, Commander, 1st Battalion, 75th Ranger Regiment, who spent most of his career with the Regiment, began his speech to commemorate the event – placing the ceremony in its proper historical context:

> I think it's appropriate today that we hold this ceremony here at the Truscott facility – a name certainly most associated with the glory of the 3d Infantry Division but also an officer who was instrumental in the formation of the fighting men you see assembled before you today.

As a young Lieutenant Colonel, [Lucian] Truscott was tasked by the CSA to examine the lessons of the British Commandos early during World War II, to look at forming an American force of similar design, to help get Americans into the fighting as soon as possible.

You see, General Marshall knew, that although the war would last a long time and would require a massive mobilization and creation of an Army the size no one but him could probably imagine, that the formation of such units was absolutely critical to the absolute success of the American war effort.

Truscott understood the benefit of consolidating a small group of men to harness their collective skills – a unit whose exclusive purpose would be to execute exceptionally dangerous missions under precarious circumstances when success was absolutely critical. He chose a young artillery officer, believe it or not, Major William Orlando Darby, to form the 1st Ranger Battalion...[107]

Colonel Kershaw, 1st Battalion commander and General Eric Shinseki during an awards ceremony. (US Army)

Nearly a year earlier, the world did not appear as straightforward as it did during this particular ceremony. Looking down from their Special Operations helicopters, members of the Ranger Quick Reaction Force (QRF) saw the mountaintop of Takur Ghar melting away into the night – much like a bad dream. The seven dead comrades below, however, were very real. Sixteen hours earlier they had been alerted for a mission to extract a missing commando. They had known little else.

The Truscott Facility did not have the best acoustics, and barring any real interest from the rank and file, one or two Rangers allowed themselves to doze off, lost in their thoughts, but still careful not to lock back their knees, which as they had learned in early training would restrict the blood flow, and possibly ultimately cause them to faint – and no Ranger could survive that humiliation. Some of the Ranger veterans being honored were probably counting their lucky stars, hoping never to return to Afghanistan. Just as one Ranger was dreaming of civilian life, another was hoping the night's formalities would pass quickly, while secretly cursing his commander and the brass. Other Rangers were paying strict attention to their battalion commander's speech:

> Welcome Service Chiefs, SOCOM Comrades, Friends here at HAAF/3ID, Friends from Savannah, Friends and Families and distinguished alumni of 1st Ranger Battalion.
>
> Why are we here? To honor the men of 1st Ranger Battalion who participated in OEF I, and, in particular, those who distinguished themselves above and beyond the call of duty. What they will tell you: That they were just doing their job, just doing what they were trained to do, doing it for their friends and buddies... to not let them down...
>
> ... Battle Streamers on our Battalion Colors have names: El Guettar, Myitkyina, Chipyong-Ni and Grenada... places that before this battalion, and members of this Regiment, fought there, were unknown to most Americans.

Truscott Facility, HAAF, Georgia.
(Author's collection)

My Dad once told me that a man makes three important choices in his life: the woman he'll spend the rest of his life with, if he'll father children, and what will be his calling in life.

These men made choices before that fateful day – they volunteered to serve in our great Army, airborne school, to serve in a Ranger Battalion. They made choices to get on a helicopter, to fly into a dangerous situation, without perfect knowledge, without everything they needed. They did it because they were ordered to, because they were expected to and because there was a comrade in distress...

They did it because they believed in the words of a creed we follow – that they are not just words to be said but, rather, words to be lived and... if necessary followed to the death... Words that say we never leave a fallen comrade to fall into the hands of the enemy. They chose to do something when many others today will choose to do nothing, or worse.

People often ask me what kind of country I think we have today. I haven't spent much time in it lately, so often I reply that I don't know. [But as Ralph Waldo Emerson notes] "the true test of civilization is not the census, nor the size of the cities, nor the crops – no, but the kind of man the country turns out."

Takur Ghar (and Robert's Ridge) have joined Chipyong-Ni and the other places that are carried on our battle streamers.

We stand here today not only to honor their courage and service but also to reaffirm our own commitment to defend freedom wherever the call may take us. So that the great ideas of liberty, freedom and justice that have so blessed our country can be shared with all who truly yearn for freedom.

Because from now on, as long as there is a United States Army and Air Force, a 1st Battalion, 75th Ranger Regiment and a country such as this – these men before you, their names, their deeds and exploits, will be forever associated – like our battle streamers – with this great Battalion. And many days long after we are all gone, when old Rangers gather to pass on the deeds of those who have before us, your names will be entered into that pantheon of heroes that have given so much to our country.

Rangers Lead the Way![108]

# OPERATION *ANACONDA*

The events leading up to this particular operation had begun much earlier. In the previous months American forces were struggling to root- and smoke-out Taliban and al-Qaeda (TAQ) fighters. Osama bin Laden and his group of dedicated fighters had escaped the previous year at Tora Bora and US surveillance, human and technical, continued to scour the mountain ranges of eastern Afghanistan. In January and February much TAQ activity was found in the Shah-I-Khot valley located southeast of Gardez. Small reconnaissance teams made up of American and Coalition Special Operations Forces (SOF) pinpointed these forces, providing some intelligence for Task Force Mountain, the headquarters of US ground forces. Estimates of enemy fighters ranged from 150–250, not including their accompanying families.[109] Ultimately the number of fighters was said to have been between 1,000 and 2,000.[110] The targeted area was named Objective Remington.

Commanded by Major General Franklin L. Hagenbeck, Task Force (TF) Mountain devised an operation, based upon an earlier Special Operations plan, to trap the TAQ fighters concentrated in the western part of the valley. US-led Afghan forces would push in from the west, driving the dispirited enemy militia before them, straight into the blocking positions located in the east, the "cauldron of death," consisting of American troops of the 101st Airborne and 10th Mountain Divisions. This hammer-and-anvil operation would crush the fleeing TAQ forces and eliminate enough of them to extinguish any future threat. All of this would be played out in a 60–70 square mile area of operations. Any captured personnel might also provide valuable intelligence in the unrelenting pursuit of Osama bin Laden.[111] The key element originally conceived by Special Operations planners, and adhered to and executed by Hagenbeck and his staff, was the push of the hammer element, TF Hammer, comprised of SOF troopers and their mostly untried allied Afghan forces. They reasoned that the indigenous Afghans would be able to determine friend from foe as the group pushed forward through the valley and the villages, driving the Taliban and al-Qaeda forces before them – so at least it was planned.

Providing the eyes and ears of this Coalition onslaught, dubbed Operation *Anaconda* (March 2–19, 2002), would be the highly effective small SOF teams placed strategically along ridges of the objective area. These observation posts could pinpoint enemy movements, call in air strikes to kill enemy personnel and destroy vehicles, as well as provide realistic and real-time intelligence vital to the combat operations.[112]

Despite all of this, Hagenbeck and company were often deprived of other intelligence sources due to the micro-management and confused chain of command

## COMPOSITION OF TASK FORCE MOUNTAIN

Commander: Major General Franklin L. "Buster" Hagenbeck, 10th Mountain Division.

Commander of TF Rakkasan: Colonel Frank Wiercinski, 3rd Brigade "Rakkasans," 101st Airborne Division (Air Assault).

1,500 men from 1st and 2nd Battalions, 187th Infantry, 10th Mountain Division, and 1st Battalion, 87th Infantry, 10th Mountain Division [60mm, 81mm and 120mm mortars]. Approximately 200 Coalition soldiers from Australia, England, Canada, Denmark, Germany, and Norway were to be used for reconnaissance missions (TF K-BAR), as well as 900 Afghans shepherded by 40 Special Forces personnel.[113] Twenty-four Army cargo, utility and attack helicopters; and Air Force, Marine and Navy aviation assets.[114]

created and orchestrated by the Secretary of Defense and his CENTCOM Commander, General Franks, both of whom erroneously believed that operations could be conducted via video feeds, Powerpoint presentations, and with directives heavily reliant on wishful military doctrine.[115] This they attempted while simultaneously directing a media campaign – the product being Rumsfeldian netcentric warfare at its worst. To top it off, Rumsfeld vehemently opposed conventional troops on the ground, as these were needed for the invasion of Iraq.[116] TF Mountain was tasked with sweeping up the crumbs of the TAQ fighters with a miniscule amount of troops and support. General Hagenbeck and his subordinates would have to make do with inadequate numbers of Apaches, Chinooks, fixed-wing aircraft, and artillery.[117] TF Mountain was de-clawed from the start – after all, the Taliban had collapsed in but a few short weeks.

The one thing American planners did not properly take into account was the morale of the enemy. Although the TAQ militia was easily crushed in the early parts of Operation *Enduring Freedom*, its spirit was not broken. It is easy to see how Coalition planners were highly confident. TAQ militias were nothing more than ill-trained light infantrymen without the support most industrialized armies could draw upon, and their resistance had crumbled within a few short days after the Coalition attack. An enemy on the run could be viewed as defeated, but in Afghanistan, with her long history of resistance to invading armies, running could also mean returning at a more convenient time to continue the struggle. Just prior to the launch of Operation *Anaconda*, a CIA intelligence brief assessed that Objective Remington was crawling with 700+ fighters. This crucial information was not relayed to the intelligence section of TF Mountain.[118] The impression there was that but a couple of hundred third-rate gangsters were occupying the intended target. Additionally,

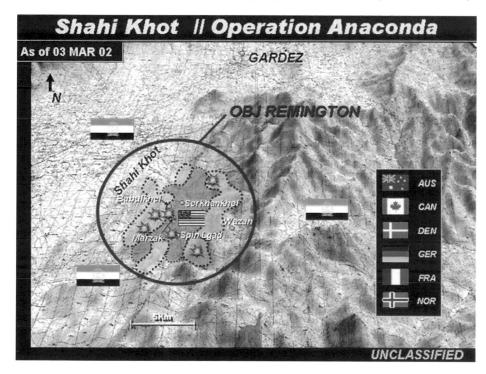

Map detailing the activities of Coalition forces during Operation *Anaconda*. (DoD)

the amassing of US troops certainly did not go unnoticed, thereby removing any possibility of a surprise attack.[119] The CIA brief also offered a glimpse of the TAQ fighters' organization. They reported that three rings formed the defensive perimeter; the outermost, providing security more or less, were the light-armed Taliban, the second security ring comprised Chechens and probably Uzbeks armed with machine guns, while the innermost ring was made up of hardcore al-Qaeda soldiers, equipped with mortars, sniper rifles, and Stinger antiaircraft missiles. This model may be questionable, as one SEAL recon team ambushed a machine-gun position during the opening phases of *Anaconda* where they encountered several different ethnicities – all of them fighting and dying together.[120]

Though traditionally belittled by the highest civilian and military leaders as mere cowards and terrorists, a Pentagon-released document called the al-Qaeda fighters "disciplined and well-trained."[121] These fighters stood and fought against the advancing Coalition forces. Indeed US reports indicate, as might be expected by anyone familiar with the Mujahideen struggle against the Soviet Union from 1979 to 1989, that reinforcements even rushed to the frontlines in order to send the infidels to their deaths.

American soldiers, during the early stages of Operation *Anaconda*, reported that the TAQ "would poke their heads up and shoot... and [incredulously] a couple of times they were waving at us."[122] TAQ fighters were also far more accustomed to humping up and down 10,000ft mountain ranges than their Western counterparts who suffered miserably from the task. Free from personal body armor and excess ammunition, as weapons and ammunition were regularly stockpiled throughout Afghanistan, TAQ soldiers waged a familiar guerrilla war. Popping up behind a rock and sending a rocket-propelled grenade against the much-despised Americans was a challenge few wanted to miss. American soldiers on the ground grew increasingly frustrated by their inability to deploy all their troops in specified locations and grew even more frustrated by their inability to close with the enemy. Operation *Anaconda* was falling apart.

The enemy line of resistance ran along a series of draws and trails at the southern end of the valley near Marzak and stalled the US/Afghan push east toward the so-called "Whale" – a prominent terrain feature south-east of Gardez. The Afghan forces withdrew to Gardez; the push had petered out, and the American troops that did manage to be heloed into their blocking positions were too few in number to overcome the well-coordinated mortar and small-arms fire of the TAQ militia. "They [the Taliban] had their act together," a US soldier said,

> We were hitting them too, but not in the kind of numbers we wanted... All day, enemy fighters would rush into caves or other hiding spots if they heard a U.S. jet or helicopter approach. Then after the bombing stopped, they just popped back up and started firing again.[123]

A senior military official from the Pentagon subsequently acknowledged that flawed intelligence and analysis put the soldiers in this vulnerable spot:

They were supposed to be the blocking force, and all of a sudden, they found themselves at the bottom of a valley with fire raining down on them from these guys in entrenched positions on a mountainside. They basically had them pinned down for 18 hours. We would hope to have had a better sense of the force size.

The official added: "There was also a sense that if confronted with a ground force, that these guys would choose to bail, that if they had good escape routes staked out, they would break and run. But it didn't work out. So we had to regroup and rethink." Defense Secretary Rumsfeld defended the intelligence gathering that went into the operation, for which US forces had been preparing for weeks.[124] What else could he have said? He was in absolute command, even going so far as to personally approve or disapprove every item related to any mission. Milan N. Vego notes in "Operational Command and Control in the Information Age" (*Joint Force Quarterly*, Issue 35) that "over-centralized command and control undermines morale and encourages an unwillingness to act independently." As we shall later see during the firefight at Takur Ghar, one aircraft did not take actions because no guidance had been given to them from headquarters.

Operation *Anaconda* had launched on March 2, 2002, and immediately had run into trouble. Precisely what went wrong? The Special Forces-led Afghan militias, driving large unwieldy Ginga trucks carrying 30–40 men each, melted away after one of the SOF troopers and two Afghans were killed when an Air Force AC-130 gunship mistook the convoy for enemy forces.[125] The blocking elements, only partially occupied by American soldiers of the 101st Air Assault Division and 10th Mountain Division, were pinned down and suffered 20–30 wounded within a short time; the flight of Taliban and al-Qaeda fighters, highly anticipated by American analysts, turned out to be an absolute myth. Some of the lead elements of the anvil were cornered, and might have been overrun were it not for the superior technological edge of the US soldiers, which included Kevlar body armor and helmets as well as complete air superiority. Proving their worth, the SOF teams that dotted the ridgelines provided much relief by directing pinpoint accurate air strikes and at times acting directly in support of the conventional troops, who were in dire need of reinforcements. The action was particularly dicey in the south at helicopter landing zone (HLZ) Ginger, east of Marzak.[126] In one instance, a Spectre supposedly killed 200 attacking TAQ fighters,[127] but not all SOF teams had their close air support (CAS) calls answered – resources were stretched.

The hammer-and-anvil maneuver now seemed to be completely collapsing, with mounting casualties including one Killed in Action (KIA) – the Special Forces soldier killed by the US gunship – and three dozen or so wounded out of 1,200 troops deployed, and with careers on the line. Hagenbeck managed to realign his forces in an attempt to advance from the northern end of the Shah-I-Khot valley and dislodge the enemy fighters. One Defense Department report noted, "as the battle became more fluid, eyes were needed on the southern tip of the valley to provide surveillance and call in more air strikes against the numerous concentrations of enemy forces."[128] Underestimating the will of the

hunted TAQ fighters by US planners was egregious, arrogant, and the principal cause for the near-collapse of Operation *Anaconda*.

Although Operation *Anaconda* is often called a battle, one would be hard-pressed to call it more than a prolonged skirmish involving several thousand soldiers when compared to traditional battles of the past. Though the participants might beg to differ, the statistics bear witness to the less than lethal environment in which the operation was conducted. The *Army Times* article by Sean Naylor dated April 22, 2002, "Life Savers: New armor stemmed casualties in Bagram, but surgical team still had its hands full" explains "that about 2,000 U.S. troops saw action in Anaconda, but only 76 were wounded [one KIA during opening phases, seven KIA during a rescue mission]. Many of those wounds were to their extremities, not to their vital organs and part of that was the fact that the guys have been wearing their Kevlar jackets."

However, at this stage the game was still afoot, and the search for the world's leading terrorist and his entourage was still viable. Hagenbeck and his staff, although considering a withdrawal, were made aware that the SOF teams were doing a good job of making life extremely dangerous for the TAQ militias maneuvering in the mountains and valleys.[129] More teams were needed in order to salvage the frail operation. Additional eyes on the valley were needed and the commander of all special operations, Air Force General Gregory L. Trebon, wanted SEALs (TF Blue) involved, and hence they replaced the Delta recon teams and their commander right in the middle of an ongoing operation.[130] Hagenbeck was not in the decision-making loop – and he was the overall commander of the operation.

One of the best locations for Coalition SOF observation posts (OPs) was a mountaintop peaking at approximately 10,500ft called Takur Ghar. This mountain dominated the southern approaches to the valley and provided an excellent view of Marzak, about 1 mile to the west. The view also extended to

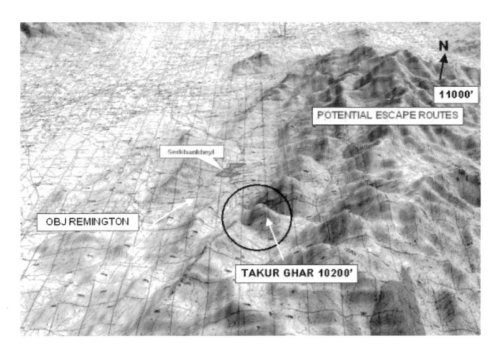

Map detailing Takur Ghar in relation to Objective Remington. (DoD)

the other side of the valley, the Whale. Takur Ghar was indeed a perfect observation point, providing visibility of over 15 miles of the valley. However, the mountain was covered in snow up to 3ft high in places causing some difficulty for overhead reconnaissance flights as snow can provide excellent camouflage. Takur Ghar provided just one suitable location for a helicopter landing zone (HLZ), thereby making it relatively easy to defend. Ultimately, reconnaissance failed to spot two snow-covered, concealed bunkers near a large rock that were also camouflaged by the foliage of the trees. Other enemy positions situated within crevices or cracks of the mountain, one concealed by a simple green canvas tent, also avoided detection. The western and eastern sides of Takur Ghar were sheer drop-offs, and one side was mostly snow-free as it was facing the sun. Looking at the Predator (an unmanned aerial vehicle – UAV) footage of Takur Ghar, however, one can make out numerous trails dotting the mountaintop. Hi-tech surveillance met its match in low-tech natural camouflage; intelligence briefs stipulating an enemy presence were dismissed by the SEALs.[131] The fog of war was descending on a handful of men who were about to make history.

# TAKUR GHAR – SEALS OUT OF WATER

Directives from the Pentagon interfered with the proper planning and execution of the largest engagement in Afghanistan – Operation *Anaconda* in the Shah-I-Khot Valley. Handicapped by the inability to deploy fully all assets required for this type of operation and further crippled by several non-integrated chains of command, the men executing the mission had their hands full not only with the TAQ fighters, but also with absurd higher-level decisions that would ultimately lead to the deaths of American soldiers.

SOF planning, specifically directed by General Trebon who was nowhere near the area of operations, called for the insertion of two additional teams the following night, March 3.[132] Two MH-47E helicopters from TF Brown, in this case the 2nd Battalion, 160th Special Operations Aviation Regiment (Airborne), commonly known as Nightstalkers, would insert two teams made up of US Navy SEALs (Sea-Air-Land) from DevGroup (formerly known as SEAL Team 6) plus Air Force combat controller (CCT) personnel. One MH-47E, Razor 04, would deploy a team near Objective Ginger (TF Rakkasan location) while the other MH-47E, Razor 03, would simultaneously drop off the other recon element near Takur Ghar to establish an observation post (OP). Standard operating procedures called for two aircraft to travel together in case of emergencies. Once the insertions were complete both helicopters would return to Bagram Air Base.

The original SOF recon teams never inserted via helicopters – this was considered too dangerous as the TAQ militias, who could still mount good antiaircraft defenses, were becoming familiar with helicopter flight paths.[133] Trekking across the mountain ranges was considered the best and safest manner of reaching their intended observation posts. According to Sean Naylor's excellent book on Operation *Anaconda*, *Not a Good Day to Die*, the SEALs wanted to avoid climbing and seemingly were always looking for an easier way to conduct their missions.[134] Undoubtedly some of the SEALs were as good as their Army counterparts, yet one cannot help but wonder how many waterborne operations have been carried out by Delta and how many non-maritime operations at all had been conducted by the frogmen? Nonetheless, the only easy day was yesterday... and inserting directly onto Takur Ghar would be their undoing. The previous recon teams, who had spent months perfecting their knowledge of the area, and their commanders, were taken out of the communication chain by General Trebon and the SEALs in the midst of an ongoing operation.[135]

Around 0300 hours one of the helicopters, Razor 03, was approaching its HLZ at Takur Ghar. Pentagon after-action reports note that the original plan had called for an earlier insertion at a different helicopter landing zone (HLZ), an offset site, but maintenance issues as well as an air strike by a B-52 in the vicinity prevented the proper execution of the mission.[136] The B-52 strike also prevented NAIL 21, an AC-130 Spectre, from putting eyes on the objective, although intelligence had confirmed the sites were "relatively" secure.[137] Supporting Operation *Anaconda* was vital at the time, as some desperate US units had been whisked away to safety, others inserted, and the Coalition assault was close to turning into a catastrophe. Considering the dire situation on the ground and the delay of the mission, the SEAL team leader Mako 20 made a decision to land the SEAL reconnaissance team directly onto the mountaintop of Takur Ghar at a staggering 10,200ft. One is left to wonder that had SEALs been inserted at an offset location, how would they have managed to reach the top with gear in excess of 100lb on their backs? Surely they would not have been able to reach the top during darkness? Prior recon teams had steadfastly inserted in vehicles, and trekked along the mountains to their objectives – a process that took hours if not days. Helicopter insertions were fast, but deemed too dangerous. The new Navy SEAL commander just placed in charge disagreed –

it was a risk worth taking. The anticipated insertion would still allow the team an hour's worth of darkness. NAIL 21 was replaced by NAIL 22 and cleared the LZ/OP. However, six minutes prior to the insertion it was tasked with another mission, and Takur Ghar was left unobserved.

One thing must be pointed out; the SEALs in 03 and 04 had been near their targets prior to the B-52 strikes a respective six and nine minutes when the AC-130 had to clear the airspace for the strike. It was the lack of Spectre protection that made the pilots decide to return to Bagram, only 15 minutes away. There they encountered mechanical problems, had to swap aircraft, and then wait for TF Rakkasan to conduct an air assault.[138]

Although various intelligence sources had reported far greater numbers of enemy fighters and that Takur Ghar was "highly likely" to be occupied by TAQ fighters,[139] by 0230 hours local time, Razor 03 and 04 departed Bagram with an anticipated insertion time of 0245. This would leave them one hour of complete darkness in which to move into position and establish a hidesite – insufficient time to land at their location and climb to the top. Insertion on Takur Ghar was the decision, an option chosen over delaying the mission.

Razor 03 descended onto the saddle top as pilots and others spotted fresh tracks in the snow.[140] More precisely, as the Chinook was hovering, one of the helicopter crew spotted an unmanned heavy machine gun (a DShK) approximately 50 yards off the nose of the Chinook at the 1 o'clock position. This was not uncommon in Afghanistan, where one could find numerous such weapons dotting the mountains. However, this one was in excellent condition. Other military hardware was spotted across the HLZ. A donkey was observed at the 3 o'clock position, tied to a tree. The SEAL team leader Mako 20 was notified of this as another crewmember informed them that he spotted a man ducking behind a berm at the 9 o'clock position. Mako 20 decided to take the hill.[141] The team should have been experienced enough to abort the mission. The much-desired close air support (CAS) was not available, as it was engaged in supporting another mission for Operation *Anaconda*. The lack of CAS proved fatal.

During these short moments, the team was at the rear ramp ready to exit the craft and, following standard operating procedure, with one of the crewmembers holding the SEALs back with his arm. Upon being told that the team would insert, he lowered his arm to release them. Just as the SEALs moved forward, one enemy fighter stood up and initiated an ambush on the 52ft-long medium-sized helicopter, knocking out the electrical system and rendering much of the equipment inoperable, including the intercom that connected the crew with one another. An RPG missile and 7.62mm rounds fired by the TAQ fighters ripped through the fuselage, shredding everything in their path, injuring a crewmember, and snapping the pilots into evasive action. One small-arms round hit a crewmember in the helmet, a fact which he barely noticed.[142]

Mako 20 shouted: "Get us out of here!" as more rounds punctured hydraulic and oil lines, causing a small fire and smoke to fill the interior of the aircraft. "Fire in the cabin! Rear ready!" the rear crewmember yelled into the only functioning intercom. "Pick it up, pick it up, pick it up! Go, go, go!" As the gunner engaged a target, one of the Navy SEALs, Petty Officer Neil Roberts,

# MH-47 CHINOOK HELICOPTER

SOC Fact Sheet

The MH-47 conducts overt and covert infiltrations, exfiltrations, air assault, resupply, and sling operations over a wide range of environmental conditions. The aircraft can perform a variety of other missions including shipboard operations, platform operations, urban operations, water operations, parachute operations, forward aerial refueling point (FARP) operations, mass casualty, and combat search and rescue operations. With the use of special mission equipment and night vision devices, the air crew can operate in hostile mission environments over all types of terrain at low altitudes during periods of low visibility and low ambient lighting conditions with pinpoint navigation accuracy.

The 160th Special Operations Aviation Regiment (Airborne) currently operates two variants of the Chinook Helicopter.

The MH-47E is a heavy assault helicopter based on the CH-47 airframe, specifically designed and built for the special operations aviation mission. It has a totally integrated avionics subsystem. This avionics package combines a redundant avionics architecture with dual mission processors, remote terminal units, multifunction displays and display generators to improve combat survivability and mission reliability. The "Echo" model also has an aerial refueling (A/R) probe for in-flight refueling; external rescue hoist; and two L714 turbine engines with Full Authority Digital Electronic Control which provides more power during hot/high environmental conditions.

The MH-47D Adverse Weather Cockpit (AWC) Chinook is a twin engine, tandem rotor, heavy-assault helicopter that has been specifically modified for long range flights. It is equipped with weather avoidance/search radar; aerial refueling (A/R) probe for in-flight refueling; Personnel Locator System (PLS) for finding downed aircrews; Forward Looking Infrared (FLIR); secure voice communications; Fast Rope Insertion Extraction System (FRIES) for insertion of personnel/equipment and extraction of personnel; defensive armament system consisting of two M-134 machine-guns and one M-60D machine-gun; and internal rescue hoist with a 600lb capacity.

**MII-47D and MH 47E Performance Characteristics**

Normal cruise airspeed: 120 knots
Maximum dash airspeed: 170 knots
Normal fuel burn rate: 2,750lb per hour
Maximum altitude: 20,000ft

slipped on the slick floor and "tumbled" toward the ramp which had remained down due to the hydraulic leak. The rear gunner managed to grab the SEAL as another member of the crew rushed over and grabbed onto both. However, the evasive actions of the pilots sent a shudder through the Chinook, breaking the men's hold of the naval commando. Two men spilled over the ramp as the helicopter hovered between 5 and 6ft above ground – the SEAL fell onto the snow-filled mountain top, and the crew member was left dangling from his

Razor 03, which was carrying TF Blue, at the crash site. (USASOC)

Damage to Razor 03. The pilot would have been able to feel those rounds hitting his Chinook. (USASOC)

safety harness... as bullets searched for the lumbering helicopter, he remained tethered to the fuselage, to be pulled in shortly thereafter.[143]

A report released several months after the action described the events in more detail:

> The pilot struggled to get the Chinook off the landing zone and away from the enemy fire. [SEAL] Neil Roberts stood closest to the ramp, poised to exit onto the landing zone. Roberts and an aircrew member were knocked off balance by the explosions and the sudden burst of power applied by the pilot. As Neil and the crewman reached to steady each other, both slipped on the oil-soaked ramp and fell out of the helicopter. As the pilots fought to regain control of the helicopter, other crewmembers pulled the tethered crewmember back into the aircraft. Un-tethered, Neil fell approximately 5–10 feet onto the snowy mountaintop below. The crew managed to keep the aircraft aloft until it became apparent it could fly no more. The pilots executed a controlled crash landing some seven kilometers north of where

Petty Officer Roberts fell from the helicopter. He was now alone and in the midst of an enemy force.[144]

How feasible is it to think that Roberts heard the "go, go, go" but not the "get us out of here" part? With engines screeching, machine gunners firing, people shouting, and vision blurred... it is not impossible to conceive.

# FLASHBACK

A Ranger chalk was being inserted onto an objective during a training exercise involving Libya in 1988. The helicopter was a Chinook. All Rangers were snap-linked to the floor wearing a Swiss rope harness with a safety release to rapidly undo the rope and "unass" the bird. This was not an unusual method of insertion, and standard operating procedures called for the men to release the rope once the wheels had touched down, wait for the signal of the crewman, and once given, to exfiltrate the helicopter in a pre-determined manner, thus avoiding the rotor blades that might be angled toward the ground if the Chinook was hovering at an angle. The signal for the exfiltration was the airman yelling: "go, go, go" and lowering his arms, which he had placed in front of the first man. Of course, the platoon leader (PL) had said earlier: "When the wheels hit you go." Upon approach, the rear gunner opened up on the objective, wheels touched down, snap links unfastened, and seemingly the "go" command was given as the bird shuddered during landing. One Ranger, an M-60 gunner, burst out of the ramp, taking a sharp left turn, hustled to a berm whereupon he emplaced his machine gun and engaged his target. Moments later the rest of the squad appeared with an irate Pacific Islander squad leader (SL). He queried as to what the Ranger had done, exiting the helicopter when the airman had yelled "No, No, No" as the Chinook had not properly settled yet. If the Ranger had not taken the sharp turn upon exiting, his head would have been taken clean off. That was in training. Lessons learned by all. The PL, the gunners, the SL and the crewman who momentarily had lost his balance thereby dropping his arm... and yelling "no" while trying to balance himself.

No doubt, Roberts was cocked and locked, ready to roll... Many members of the Special Operations community were frustrated by a lack of action. This mission in particular had been delayed several times and the men were probably eager to get on with it. But no matter what... a SEAL had fallen out... the shit had hit the fan.

Razor 03's pilot and crew were desperately fighting for control of the Chinook – all in an effort to return to the mountaintop and retrieve their comrade... the impossible had happened, the Chinook had crashed 4½ miles from the mountain, leaving one SEAL alone on Takur Ghar and the rest of his team and crew helplessly stranded in hostile territory. People who could have helped immediately were unaware that the recon team had decided to insert atop the mountain, and assumed them to be elsewhere, ready to hump up the ridgelines. A close-by American infantry unit who would subsequently be misidentified as an enemy force, and who later would thank their gods that a Spectre gunship was not given permission to fire on them, might have been able to help stage a rescue effort.[145]

# HERO WORSHIP

There is a tendency to ascribe great deeds onto those who have died, particularly men who have died in combat. Roberts was no exception and one wonders about the human need to glorify someone's death. It seems that in this case a desire to be part of something important or meaningful was a motivating factor, and quite possibly the "Quiet Professionals" wanted to ensure that the general public was made aware of the sacrifices of the men in Special Operations. It should be remembered that in the years prior to September 11, 2001, the US military was not held in particularly high regard by the American population. No matter, Roberts had died, and the Internet was abuzz with proclamations of Olympian demi-god valor. One, of course, should not belittle anyone's accomplishment yet in this case the obverse is true. This does a disservice to historical fact and probably causes some anguish as well for the surviving family members who may end up doubting previous assessments... especially when the accompanying medals are not in the highest order. Thus it is in the best interest of all to let the facts speak for themselves.

US Navy SEAL Neil Roberts, 32, who died surrounded by TAQ fighters after being stranded on top of Takur Ghar on March 4, 2002. (USN)

In any event, a few accounts claimed actions worthy of the Medal of Honor for Neil Roberts – single-handedly fighting off the TAQ terrorists, charging a machine-gun nest, being wounded several times, and, after having expended all his primary and secondary ammunition including grenades and down to his empty pistol, succumbing to his wounds. Andrew Exum recalls in *This Man's Army* how "the bigwigs at Bagram told them they had watched Roberts try to escape but got captured, tortured and when special operators landed and joined the fight, then Roberts was killed with a 9mm round to the head.[146] One email claims: "The Predator video footage shows Neil point shooting with his pistol at very close ranges to the enemy."[147] Sean Naylor believes the events surrounding Neil Roberts' death to have transpired in this manner:

> Roberts had landed in the middle of an enemy command post. The SEALs' decision to proceed with their infil without AC-130 coverage deprived him of the protective fires from the sky he would otherwise have enjoyed in the first minutes after his fall. He was armed only with a SAW and a pistol. He also had an MBITR radio, but it wasn't powerful enough to communicate with his teammates. Grim 32, flying toward him, did not have his frequency. TF Green (Delta Force) and the AFO [prior recon teams] recce teams always loaded the line-of-sight frequency to the AWACS, for just such emergencies, in case they needed the command-and-control aircraft to arrange immediate close air support. It was the sort of step the SEALs might have taken had they had the time in Gardez to fully integrate themselves into the operation.

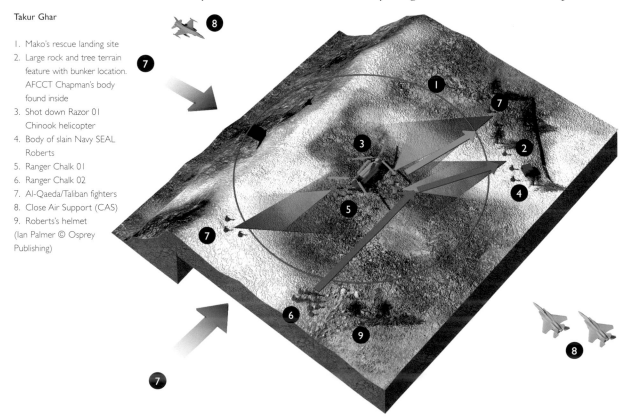

Takur Ghar

1. Mako's rescue landing site
2. Large rock and tree terrain feature with bunker location. AFCCT Chapman's body found inside
3. Shot down Razor 01 Chinook helicopter
4. Body of slain Navy SEAL Roberts
5. Ranger Chalk 01
6. Ranger Chalk 02
7. Al-Qaeda/Taliban fighters
8. Close Air Support (CAS)
9. Roberts's helmet
(Ian Palmer © Osprey Publishing)

But in the haste to push the teams into the Shahikot, it was apparently overlooked. Roberts's radio was therefore useless. He activated his infrared strobe, but the enemy had seen him. Within minutes they were firing at him. He fought back fiercely, returning fire with his SAW, trying desperately to buy himself some time. But while his would-be saviors were being held back by the confusion that paralyzed the TF 11 [Trebon's headquarters] command setup, an enemy bullet to his right upper thigh struck him down. Bleeding in the snow, he continued firing, his blood dripping onto the bullets as they were fed into the weapon until it jammed. Within about thirty-five minutes of falling out of the helicopter, his wound had weakened him to the point where he was probably too weak to fire the heavy SAW anyway. Al Qaida fighters walked over to him, dragged him to his feet, and moved him up the slope to a tree and bunker complex. No one knows exactly what transpired between the American warrior and his captors, but at 4:27 a.m., the enemy fighters clearly decided Roberts was of no more use to them. One of them raised a gun to Roberts's head and fired a single round, killing him instantly. An Al Qaida fighter straddled his body for a couple of minutes, probably stripping it of any useful gear, and then walked to a nearby bunker. About an hour and a half after falling from Razor 03, Neil Roberts was dead.

One of the reasons Naylor believes Roberts to have been executed rests on the fact that his helmet, with a bullet hole, was found at a different location.

However, official records stipulate that:

Nobody knows exactly what transpired over the next few minutes on that mountaintop. There were no surveillance aircraft over the mountaintop at the time Roberts fell from the helicopter. Based on forensic evidence subsequently gathered from the scene, we believe Roberts survived the short fall from the helicopter, likely activated his signaling device, and engaged the enemy with his squad automatic weapon (SAW). He was mortally injured by gunfire as they closed in on him.[148]

Another DoD News Briefing conducted by a senior military official who had led a research team to investigate the action at Takur Ghar said:

My best understanding, because we have no exact knowledge of what transpired in the ensuing hours after he fell off, we have been able through our analysis to determine that he did engage the enemy, based on what we found with his weapon. And we were able to tell that he did engage the enemy, but his wounds were such that he possibly lost consciousness due to blood loss, or was engaging the enemy and the enemy killed him at close range.[149]

Naylor quotes in an email a passage from a War College paper by Andrew Milani, the Army investigator, now commander of Special Operations Aviation Regiment (SOAR):

Roberts was discovered at the location where his IR strobe-light was illuminated and when [where] GRIM 32 saw eight–ten enemy personnel. This is the same location that, upon careful viewing of the Predator tape, one sees an individual knocked to the ground at 0427, where he lies motionless. Someone else appears to straddle this body for about two minutes, and then departs towards a nearby bunker at 0430 (0000Z). The body remains in this position throughout the ensuing events, progressively cooling (as seen with the thermal image). Ultimately, the Rangers discover Roberts in this exact location.

Certainly, another possible reconstruction of events, based on forensic evidence of Roberts' blood identified inside his SAW (indicating he was holding and firing his weapon while blood seeped into the chamber), is that Roberts was shot during those short moments after his fall and at close range in the head. His helmet was probably not made of Kevlar, as those can withstand hits from close proximity. One Ranger during Operation *Just Cause* in Panama was shot execution-style by a member of the Panamanian Defense Force, the muzzle inches away from his helmet. Although the bullet did penetrate, the expended bullet swirled inside the helmet leaving only a scar! Getting shot in the helmet is what happened to other troops during Operation *Anaconda* and also during the firefight at Takur Ghar with the Ranger QRF. One also needs to remember that one of the airmen from Razor 03 was hit in his helmet as well and survived. No evidence exists that he was captured, tortured, and executed. The most probable scenario is that he was killed in action. Only the pathology reports of the US Armed Forces could clear up the possibility of torture, but repeated Freedom of Information Act Requests have been denied. The US Navy would have presented the Medal of Honor if enough evidence were available to merit it.

The facts of Neil Roberts' death:

He fell onto the snow-covered mountaintop.

He was engaged in a firefight.

He was wounded badly enough to warrant the possibility of bleeding to death.

His strobe light was engaged for about 30 seconds.

Several people were seen near him (although the very same AC-130 crew that reported this also misidentified Special Forces Warrant Officer Harriman with TF Hammer and killed him and two of his Afghan allies).

His body was recovered at the big rock and tree location.

His helmet was recovered elsewhere.

His gear and equipment had been looted.

He is dead, killed in action, either succumbing to wounds or shot in the head at close range.

No Predator or other craft were in the area at the time.

There can be little doubt that most soldiers' greatest fear is to be abandoned and left behind enemy lines. One other thing is for certain as well, however, no person joins Special Operations units in pursuit of a safe life. Without a doubt, Neil Roberts was a well-trained commando in one of the best units of the US

Navy. The respect of his peers is the best tribute a man can attain. His death, albeit tragic, is a stark reminder that accidents can and will happen at all the wrong times and places; the fog of war, the friction of war and, ultimately, war in its true inherent nature, is uncontrollable. "Proper planning prevents piss poor performance" is an old axiom – decisions by senior military and civilian leaders, politically astute but tactically ignorant or too far removed from the area of operations (AO), however, can have a profound impact on the lives of soldiers in the field.

# HOOYAH! TASK FORCE BLUE

Having successfully inserted its recon package at 0300 hours, Razor 04 was rerouted to the crash site of Razor 03. Razor 04 arrived 30 minutes after the crash of Razor 03. Here, in a bit of panic, they loaded the stranded members onto their craft and returned to Gardez. The Chinook would be too heavy to return to Takur Ghar and leaving 03's crew behind unprotected was out of the question. If only they had been informed of friendly forces in the area from the 101st, who might have been able to establish a defensive perimeter and thus allow the SEALs to rescue their fallen comrade, but faulty chains of command and a variety of communication issues created the false notion that the friendly forces were TAQ fighters instead. Lucky for the 101st, higher command was in such a shambles that requested authorization to fire on their personnel was denied.

Once at the base, the SEALs and pilots of Razor 04 drew up a hasty plan to go back and rescue Roberts. Valuable time had been lost in returning to Gardez, and undoubtedly the men were anxious to return as soon as possible. During this phase an AC-130, now on station at Takur Ghar, reported what they believed they were seeing; a handful of TAQ fighters surrounding Roberts. The pressure was mounting and ultimately all members of the Coalition SOF wanted to be the Quick Reaction Force (QRF). Some of them were loading and unloading again when ST-6 decided to go back by themselves. No doubt this left a bitter taste in some people's mouths.[150]

Racing against all hope, Razor 04, five SEALs, and Air Force Technical Sergeant Chapman departed Gardez and headed back to Roberts' last known location on Takur Ghar. Some things were known: Operation *Anaconda* was not going well, resources were stretched, their last attempt at insertion was greeted by devastating small-arms fire, and Neil Roberts had been on his own for a long time. Was he alive or captured? For the moment, concerns of where they would land and what they would do once there occupied them enough to push back unpleasant thoughts. One thing was for certain, time was of the essence and the team could ill-afford to land below the mountaintop, as the difficult climb would add even more time to their operation. In and out near the site where they had been engaged before was the answer. With daylight fast approaching, Razor 04 was approaching the hot HLZ.

Nobody really cared about the confusing mess back at the tactical operations center (TOC). Nobody cared about obstacles or concerns or issues or... it was the reports from Grim 32 of a handful of people on Takur Ghar that occupied their minds.

Nobody really knew what was going on or what had happened – everything was an absolute mess. Moreover, the enemy was not asleep. NAIL 22 had not cleared the area because they were unable to positively identify Roberts.[151] As Razor 04 was inbound at 0455, one of the crew spotted a TAQ fighter manning the DShK heavy machine gun. Muzzle flashes were dancing to the front of the Chinook. The left side mini-gunner alerted the pilot that they were taking incoming fire from the 11 o'clock position of the helicopter. Querying whether or not it was effective, and receiving an affirmative answer, the pilot said "Then return fire!"[152] The TAQ fighters directed small-arms fire into the hulking mass of the helicopter as it flared and created a mini blizzard which obscured the scene and masked the surrounding incoming fire. Mako 20, the SEAL team, and their AFCCT inserted uninjured around 0500 hours local time. The left door gunner got off a short burst before his mini-gun jammed while the right rear window gunner managed to release a long burst from his M-60.[153] The MH-47E, Razor 04, damaged, lumbered back to base after it had remained on holding pattern as long as its fuel supply had allowed.

Having accounted for all six men, and wearing night-vision devices, the team headed for the high ground, hoping to locate their teammate Roberts. Three two-man teams advanced toward the hill, the most prominent features on Takur Ghar being a big rock and a tall tree on the northern part of the hilltop. They had landed near Roberts' last known location but several hours had passed. The Taliban and al-Qaeda fighters had engaged the approaching helicopter from their dug-in positions. As the rescue team approached the tree, AFCCT Chapman and Mako 20, Britt Slabinski, spotted two fighters in a fortified position, engaged and killed them almost immediately. The fight was on. TAQ fighters opened fire from a nearby bunker approximately 20 yards to their front. Chapman was hit by a burst and badly wounded. The SEALs resolutely conducted immediate action drills; small-arms fire and hand grenades hit the enemy bunker. The small teams were taking fire from the north and south. From just behind the tree and rock area a machine gun opened up on them from a small bunker. Grim 32 reported that tracers and lasers were all over the place.[154] Chapman was hit and went down, seemingly killed as the firefight grew in intensity – hand grenades, M-203 rounds, and automatic weapons fire at extremely close and lethal range. According to the subsequent Air Force Cross award citation: "Chapman engaged and killed two enemy personnel then continued advancing until engaging a dug-in machine gun nest. At this time, the rescue team came under effective enemy fire from three directions. Chapman exchanged fire at close range with the enemy until succumbing to multiple wounds. His engagement and destruction of the first enemy position and advancement on the second enemy position enabled his team to move to cover and break enemy contact. The team leader credited Chapman's aggressive and selfless actions with saving the lives of the entire team."[155]

Conditions had rendered Spectre useless as friend and foe were indistinguishable, and the team's radio was with the striken AFCCT. Two SEALs exposed themselves to enemy fire and one of them was wounded. TAQ fighters engaged the ST from numerous locations and wounded one more commando. Several fighters had been killed. One of the two-man teams, engaged to the rear, saw Mako and the others breaking contact. In a frenzied bounding maneuver, while covering each other, the mauled team jumped over the mountain's cliff and "glissaded 800 meters down the south side of the mountain."[156] Sustaining 50 percent casualties within a few short moments, the Americans were hanging on for dear life. Another DoD report states that "finding themselves in a deadly crossfire with two of their teammates seriously wounded and one killed and clearly outnumbered, the SEALs had to disengage. They shot two more al Qaeda

## NAVY CROSS CITATION

*The President of the United States Takes Pleasure in Presenting The Navy Cross To:* Britt Slabinski, United States Navy

*For Services as Set Forth in the Following Citation:*
    For extraordinary heroism as Sniper Element Leader for a joint special operations unit conducting combat operations against enemy forces during Operation Anaconda, Sahi-Kot Valley, Afghanistan on 3 and 4 March 2002, in support of Operation Enduring Freedom. On the evening of 3 March, Senior Chief Petty Officer Slabinski led his seven-man reconnaissance team onto the snow-covered, 10,000 foot mountaintop known as Takur Ghar, to establish a combat overwatch position in support of U.S. Army forces advancing against the enemy on the valley floor. As their helicopter hovered over the mountain it was met by unrelenting rocket propelled grenade (RPG) and small arms fire by entrenched enemy forces. As a result of several RPG hits, a member of Senior Chief Petty Officer Slabinski's team was ejected from the helicopter into the midst of the fortified enemy positions. The badly damaged helicopter conducted a controlled crash, at which time Senior Chief Petty Officer Slabinski immediately took charge and established security on the crash location until the crew and his team were recovered to a support base. At this point, Senior Chief Slabinski, fully aware of the overwhelming, fixed, enemy forces over the mountain, but also knowing the desperate situation of his missing teammate, now reportedly fighting for his life, without hesitation made the selfless decision to lead his team on an immediate, bold rescue mission. He heroically led the remainder of his SEAL element back onto the snow-covered, remote mountaintop into the midst of the numerically superior enemy forces in a daring and valiant attempt to rescue one of their own. After a treacherous helicopter insertion onto the mountaintop, Senior Chief Petty Officer Slabinski led his close quarter firefight. He skillfully maneuvered his team and bravely engaged multiple enemy positions, personally clearing one bunker and killing several enemy within. His unit became caught in a withering crossfire from other bunkers and the closing enemy forces. Despite mounting casualties, Senior Chief Petty Officer Slabinski maintained his composure and continued to engage the enemy until his position became untenable. Faced with no choice but a tactical withdrawal, he coolly directed fire from airborne assets to cover his team. He then led an arduous movement through the mountainous terrain, constantly under fire, covering over one kilometer in waist-deep snow, while carrying a seriously wounded teammate. Arriving at a defensible position, he organized his team's security posture and stabilized his casualties. For over fourteen hours, Senior Chief Petty Officer Slabinski directed the defense of his position through countless engagements, personally engaging the enemy and directing close air support onto the enemy positions until the enemy was ultimately defeated. During this entire sustained engagement, Senior Chief Petty Officer Slabinski exhibited classic grace under fire in steadfastly leading the intrepid rescue operation, saving the lives of his wounded men and setting the conditions for the ultimate vanquishing of the enemy and the seizing of Takur Ghar. By his heroic display of decisive and tenacious leadership, unyielding courage in the face of constant enemy fire, and utmost devotion to duty, Senior Chief Petty Officer Slabinski reflected great credit upon himself and upheld the highest traditions of the United States Naval Service.[157]

as they moved off the mountain peak to the Northeast – with one of the wounded SEALs taking point." No doubt the SEALs had no choice but to retreat. Staying would have been suicidal as the initiative lay now with the TAQ fighters.

With their AFCCT dead, one of the SEALs took over communications and proceeded to contact the AC-130 on stand-by, Grim 32. Retreating down the side of the mountain, Grim 32 provided lifesaving fire with their 105mm howitzers. This fire support enabled the five men to withdraw; however, they were still in danger of being overrun.[158] The SOF tally at this point included one destroyed helicopter, another one damaged, two seriously wounded SEALs and most importantly, two dead men. Certainly Takur Ghar had proven to be a more deadly engagement than any other part of Operation *Anaconda* thus far.

One disturbing fact remains to this day. As subsequent Predator footage reveals, at the same time as the SEALs break contact by popping a smoke grenade, someone is firing from the bunker. Several fighters engage the bunker near the location where AFCCT Chapman had been hit. Shortly thereafter they clear the bunker where subsequently Chapman's body is discovered. According to *Army Times* correspondent Sean Naylor, Chapman had wounds to the upper and lower part of his body. He argues that probably Slabinski confused Chapman with the dead body of Roberts and as Chapman was hit but advanced the firefight became so intense that the Strike Team Leader (STLDR) did not have the opportunity physically to check the fallen comrade. Although the officially released reports did not present this scenario, other soldiers familiar with the footage and events surrounding the firefight are sure that indeed Chapman had continued the assault but was killed during the retreat of Mako.[159] Certainly the headquarters personnel hundreds and thousands of miles away had no clue of the severity of the firefight the naval commandos had encountered. Transformation policies, micro-management and reliance on talentless but politically astute commanders failed their men yet again. Worse was to follow...

# TASK FORCE RED – RANGERS BLEED THE WAY

Operation *Anaconda* was in full swing. Special Operations missions conducted by TF Blue had encountered the enemy, resulting in one man missing (Roberts), one man killed (Chapman), several wounded, one Chinook destroyed, and another inoperable due to hostile fire. The SEAL rescue team had become trapped, and as the situation worsened they requested a Quick Reaction Force (QRF) – the purview of Task Force Red. Comprised of Rangers from the 75th Ranger Regiment, TF Red was put on alert. One of its most challenging recent roles had been acting as armed security guards for TF Blue and Green.[160] Being glorified armed guards is not a Ranger mission and was a morale-killer for an elite unit whose principal tasks are direct action in nature and whose men consider themselves superior in the planning and executing of Special Operations missions. As a QRF, where speed of action in emergencies was paramount, little information was available to them. QRFs thus require flexibility, adaptability, firepower, and a strong sense of independent leadership.

The Rangers, who had been in country for two months, were from A Company, 1st Battalion, 75th Ranger Regiment, and had yet to see any combat. Like most of their peers, they prayed for action. Captain Nathan Self, the Platoon Leader (PL) of 1st Platoon, had been recently promoted (Ranger platoon leaders are first lieutenants) and had been the PL during his tour at 1st Battalion – he knew his men and his job well. Self had been told that a helicopter had crashed somewhere in the Shah-I-Khot valley – but nothing else. Armed with this spartan information he prepped for the mission, reviewing satellite images, maps, and anything else he could think of or get his hands on.

The absolute flurry and chaos emanating from the TOCs throughout the world must have been spectacular. The ongoing faltering operation, now further complicated by the actions around Takur Ghar, caused all sorts of information, some grievously false, to travel throughout the chains of command.[161] Various SOF were competing for aircraft to the QRF for the anticipated rescue effort. Ultimately, Self convinced the pilots that indeed TF Red was the proper QRF for the operation and that he would need two Ranger teams with fewer Air Force Combat Search and Rescue (CSAR) members on board, as he had to consider weight and personnel needed. Initially Captain Self was told that only one chalk plus four CSAR, from a different unit than the one the Rangers had been training with, was to be the QRF. He needed more men and contacted the 1st Ranger Battalion's operation officer. All was clarified later when the senior Special Operations commander at Bagram noticed the "gyrations at the flight line" and ordered two Ranger teams (chalks) with a slightly reduced CSAR package, from four to three men.[162] Self, as part of his duties, went through the tactics and procedures with the AF personnel from the 23rd Special Tactics Squadron.

Just as TF Red made frustrated attempts to make sense of everything, TF Brown's pilots needed to dig deep for patience, having been told for the third time that their request for aircraft for the mission had been bumped. The biggest problem for TF Brown was a lack of MH-47Es – with only 21 available, they were stretched thin to support ongoing operations.[163] At long last, the QRF was ordered to proceed from Bagram to Gardez and to remain on standby there, as Gardez was but a 15-minute flight to Takur Ghar. The official ARSOF history accounts for the following: Razor 01 carried nine Rangers, one AF Enlisted Tactical Air Controller, and three Combat Search and Rescue personnel along with the flight crew, and Razor 02 was packed with 13 more hard-charging killermen from 1st Battalion. The Chinooks departed Bagram just past 0500 hours, local time, for their 40-minute flight to Gardez. Headquarters was finally able to piece enough information together, realizing that Razor 04's SEAL rescue package had indeed inserted around Takur Ghar.

One of the first after-action reports released notes that "the 23-man QRF loaded on two waiting MH-47Es, Razor 01 and Razor 02. Razor 01 carried 10 Rangers, an enlisted tactical air controller (ETAC), a combat controller (CCT) and a Pararescueman (PJ). Razor 02 carried 10 Rangers."[164] AF Enlisted Tactical Air Controller (ETAC) Kevin Vance, attached to the QRF, recollects that his Chalk 01 consisted of ten people (Rangers), three AF special tactics squadron

## TROOP LEADING PROCEDURES[165]

• Troop leading is the process a leader goes through to prepare his unit to accomplish a tactical mission.

• Begins when he is alerted for a mission or receives a change or a new mission.

• The troop-leading procedures comprise the steps listed below. Steps 3 through 8 may not follow a rigid sequence. Many of the steps may be accomplished concurrently.

**Step 1.** Receive the mission.

**Step 2.** Issue a warning order. Detailed example:

The leader provides initial instructions in a warning order. The warning order contains enough information to begin preparation as soon as possible.

• The warning order mirrors the five-paragraph OPORD format.

• The following information may be included in a warning order.

  • The mission or nature of the operation. (mission statement)

  • Time and place for issuance of the operation. (coordinating instructions)

  • Who is participating in the operation? (coordinating instructions)

  • Time of the operation. (timeline)

Example:

WARNING ORDER. Warning orders give subordinates advance notice of operations that are to come. This gives them time to prepare. The order should be brief, but complete. A WARNING ORDER DOES NOT AUTHORIZE EXECUTION UNLESS SPECIFICALLY STATED. A sample annotated WARNORD format follows:

WARNING ORDER _____ (Number)

References: Refer to higher headquarters' OPORD, and identify map sheet for operation.

Time Zone Used throughout the Order: (Optional)

Task Organization: (Optional) (See paragraph 1c.)

1. SITUATION

a. Enemy forces. Include significant changes in enemy composition dispositions and courses of action. Information not available for inclusion in the initial WARNO can be included in subsequent warning orders.

b. Friendly forces. (Optional) Only address if essential to the WARNO.

(1) Higher commander's mission.

(2) Higher commander's intent.

c. Attachments and detachments. Initial task organization, only address major unit changes.

2. MISSION. Concise statement of the task and purpose (who,

what, when, where, and why). If not all information is known, state which parts of the mission statement are tentative.

3. EXECUTION Intent:

a. Concept of operation. Provide as much information as available. The concept should describe the employment of maneuver elements.

b. Tasks to maneuver units. Provide information on tasks to subordinate units for execution, movement to initiate, reconnaissance to initiate, or security to emplace. Identify special teams within squad and platoon.

c. Tasks to combat support units. See paragraph 3b.

d. Coordinating instructions. Include any information available at the time of the issuance of the WARNO. Include the following:

- Uniform and Equipment Common to All (changes in SOP e.g., drop rucks, drop or pick up helmets).
- Time line.
- CCIR.
- Risk guidance.
- Deception guidance.
- Specific priorities, in order of completion.
- Guidance on orders and rehearsals.
- Orders group meeting (attendees, location, and time).
- Earliest movement time and degree of notice.

4. SERVICE SUPPORT (Optional) Include any known logistics preparation for the operation.

a. Special equipment. Identifying requirements, and coordinating transfer to using units.

b. Transportation. Identifying requirements, and coordinating for pre-position of assets.

5. COMMAND AND SIGNAL (Optional)

a. Command. State the chain of command if different from unit SOP.

b. Signal. Identify current SOI edition, and pre-position signal assets to support operation.


**Step 3.** Make a tentative plan
**Step 4.** Initiate movement
**Step 5.** Reconnoiter
**Step 6.** Complete the plan
**Step 7.** Issue the complete order
**Step 8.** Supervise

members composed of an ETAC, a combat controller and a Pararescue man, plus the eight Army crewmembers of the MH-47E – a total of 21 personnel.[166]

While the QRF was en route, the heavily embattled SEAL team had retreated down Takur Ghar and requested their immediate support. The SEALs' situation

## SPECIAL TACTICS

*USAF Fact Sheet*

Special Tactics is the U.S. Air Force's Special Operations ground combat force that executes a myriad of Special Operations missions to enhance air operations deep in enemy territory.

Special Tactics operators integrate with other air activities supporting the overall military campaign. Special Tactics can conduct personnel recovery missions, collect intelligence and provide terminal guidance for attacks against valuable enemy targets. Their work frees other military assets to strike other priority targets. Special Tactics operators can strike enemy targets that are beyond the capabilities of precision munitions.

Operating with Navy SEALs, Army Special Forces and Rangers, Special Tactics personnel are specially trained to seize enemy airfields and recover distressed personnel in hostile territory.

Special Tactics operators were instrumental in the rescue of two Air Force pilots shot down during Operation *Allied Force* in Kosovo and most recently in securing airfields and calling air strikes in Afghanistan.

Special Tactics consists of airmen from three different career fields: combat control, pararescue and combat weather.

Combat controllers are certified air traffic controllers who can set up navigational aid equipment anywhere in the world to guide aircraft for landing on makeshift runways without the benefit of a tower or large communications system. They are the first to deploy into restricted environments by air, land or sea tactics to establish assault zones (landing, drop and extraction), control air attacks against enemy targets, provide vital command and control, gather intelligence, survey assault zones and use demolition to clear obstructions and hazards from potential runways and landing zones.

Pararescuemen are the only Department of Defense specialty specifically trained and equipped to conduct conventional or unconventional rescue operations. They are the ideal force for assisted survivor recovery. A pararescueman's primary function is as a personnel recovery specialist. Their emergency medical capabilities are often used in humanitarian and combat environments.

Combat weathermen are weather forecasters with forward ground combat capabilities. They gather and interpret weather data and provide intelligence from deployed locations while working primarily with Army Special Operations Forces. The Air Force provides all the meteorological capabilities for U.S. Army and Army Special Forces.[167]

was dire. Although able to communicate with Grim 32, they could not establish a line of sight between their communications gear and another communications platform, a vital component in coordinating the rescue operation. Communications had to be relayed whenever possible. A military official stipulated "anytime with over-the-horizon communications you are running the risk of them being less than perfect at critical times. And that's exactly what happened here in some instances."[168] Headquarters approved the SEALs' urgent request and ordered the Ranger QRF to proceed immediately to the area and insert their team at an "offset" HLZ – not the same landing zone where Razors 03 and 04 had taken fire previously. One official Pentagon report claims that the Rangers never received any communication directing them to an offset HLZ. Yet in another it is suggested that the Ranger chalks misunderstood the communications relayed to them through other platforms.[169] "Due to intermittently functioning aircraft communications equipment, the Rangers and helicopter crews never received the 'offset' instructions which also hampered attempts to provide tactical situational awareness to the QRF commander aboard Razor 01. Communications problems too plagued headquarters' attempts to determine the true condition of the SEAL team and their exact location."[170]

Another potential problem in conducting operations, conventional or special operations, is the overwhelming amount of communication, reflecting a micro-managerial style of command. The communication element of modern combat operations can be best summed up by the military official tasked with the investigation of the fight at Takur Ghar:

> You're talking to a lot of people... having spent a lot of hours commanding and controlling in one of these 47-Echo helicopters, there are literally five radios all trying to talk and competing at the same time, and it is very difficult to discern one – which radio is talking to you; but the more experience you get, you can tell by the tone which radio it is. But at any given time, these helicopters have about four different radios. Some of them, you know, are line-of-sight. Some of them are over-the-horizon. And they're intermittent at times. They break up at times. It's very difficult to amass

## LIST OF ACCOUNTED QRF PERSONNEL

(160th personnel using pseudonyms as per SOCOM):

*Razor 01 and Chalk 01*
CWO Gaines (former Ranger)
CWO Talbert
CWO Corbin (Pilot)
SFC Lafayette (160th Senior Medic)
SSG Deese (Left door mini-gunner)
SGT Phil Svitak (KIA) (Right gunner and engineer)
SGT Larken (Right rear M-60 gunner)
SGT Walters (Tail gunner)
AFPJ Senior Airman Jason Cunningham (KIA)
AFPJ SSG Miller
AFCCT SSG Gabe Brown
AFETAC SSG Kevin Vance (attached to 75th)
Ranger CPT Self
Ranger SPC Marc Anderson (KIA)
Ranger PFC David Gilliam
Ranger SSG Depouli

Ranger SGT Walker
Ranger SGT Bradley Crose (KIA)
Ranger SPC Anthony Miceli
Ranger SPC Totten-Lancaster
Ranger PFC Matthew Commons (KIA)

*Razor 02 and Chalk 02*
CWO Oliver
CPT Dickerson (AMC) Air mission Commander
Ranger SSG Canon
Ranger SGT Stebner
Ranger SPC Pazder
Ranger SPC Vela
Ranger SGT George
Ranger SPC Polson
Ranger SPC Escano
Ranger SSG Wilmoth
Ranger SGT LaFrenz (Medic)
Ranger SPC Cunningham

all of the information that's coming through your headset on this. So it's difficult to sometimes catch everything that's said and to keep the situational awareness. The commanders in this case grasp situational awareness at different times of this fight. And all didn't have exact information at the times that that information was being made on the ground. I think Clausewitz summed it up when he said that fog and friction of battle rules the day in a lot of cases. And that was certainly the case within the first hour of Petty Officer Roberts falling off that helicopter.[171]

The consequences of a strategy of war with a heavy reliance on technology, coupled with a lack of conventional assets and warfighting capabilities, were starting to show.

Due to the communications issues, Task Force Red's QRF headed straight back to the mountaintop of Takur Ghar, into the awaiting muzzles of the TAQ fighters who by this time may have been reinforced by a few more fighters. Certainly al-Qaeda's disciplined communications network, high- and low-tech, would have had an opportunity to spread the news of the great victory – American devils beware...

# TODAY I FEEL LIKE A RANGER

Nearly two hours and 45 minutes after Navy SEAL Roberts had fallen out of the open ramp of a medium-sized helicopter and his teammates had made an aborted rescue attempt, the Ranger QRF was making a northward approach to Takur Ghar's lone helicopter landing zone. By 0545 hours the eastern horizon was lightening with daybreak as Razor 01, unaware of the danger, hovered above the HLZ. Grim 32, the only unit with a true picture of the situation on Takur Ghar, had been ordered off-station as its AC-130 gunship would offer an excellent target for the Taliban and al-Qaeda RPG launchers, heavy machine guns, and the Stinger missiles sold to Mujahideen warriors during their jihad against the godless Soviets two decades earlier.

Razor 01 and 02 flew over the crashed 03 helicopter, 4½ miles from Takur Gahr, and Razor 01 confirmed their destination with a Navy P-3 Orion infrared surveillance craft as the QRF lacked a complete picture of the situation. The Razor flight received confirmation of the actual HLZ to use as well as possible locations of antiaircraft artillery (AAA). Razor 01, the lead Chinook, surmised from the various radio chatter that they were to land on Takur and join or extract the earlier rescue team. They were completely unaware that the SEALs had taken casualties, fled the mountain and left behind another American casualty.[172] Seemingly no information was made available to the QRF about possible enemy forces.

AFETAC Vance believed that Razor 01 circled the landing zone at least twice before the final approach. His team, he recalled, was only aware that a man was missing and another team was attempting to locate him.[173] Razor 02 was in holding pattern, ultimately receiving a garbled transmission from Razor 01 to return to Gardez as the lead pilot felt that it would be too crowded and Razor 02 could return quickly in case they were needed later. The TF Brown crew felt

"the hairs standing up on the backs of their necks" and one large target was better than two.[174]

What transpired next was certainly reminiscent of the events in Mogadishu, in October 1993, where a much larger number of SOF were pinned down for 18 hours. However here the situation was different. It was a rescue mission for a SEAL team in danger of being overrun with one missing member somewhere on the mountaintop. No city warfare, no hostile civilian population in the vicinity to deal with. Nonetheless, that sinking feeling, experienced by combat soldiers when a mission has been compromised and lightly armed men are left fighting for their lives, is not unfamiliar to Rangers in battle. Rogers' Rangers, Marauders, or Vietnam-era LRRP/LRP/Rangers were all cruelly exposed to overwhelming forces. These 21st-century Rangers were about to continue that hard-won tradition.

By 0600 hours Razor 01 approached the HLZ, the morning light prompting the removal of their night-vision goggles. The naked eye could make out footprints, bombed areas, and quite possibly muzzle flashes from an area around a large rock and tree.[175] The P-3 again confirmed the correct location. As the aircrew spotted a bunker, Ranger Anderson leaned to his assistant gunner Gilliam and expressed the mood of the men who had been fed up with canceled missions and guard duties for a bunch of squids: "Today, I feel like a Ranger!"[176]

Soldiers of Chalk 01: (left to right) DePouli, Gilliam, Totten-Lancaster. (US Army)

**LEFT**
Predator drone footage of Razor 01 being shot at by a TAQ fighter's RPG. (DoD)

**MIDDLE**
Predator drone footage of TAQ fighters on top of Takur Ghar. (DoD)

**RIGHT**
Predator drone footage of Rangers establishing a perimeter. (DoD)

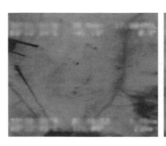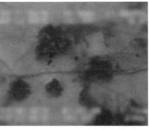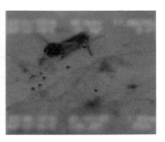

The snow-covered mountaintop at Takur Ghar exceeded 10,000ft in altitude. A squad-sized enemy element, well-entrenched and camouflaged, had killed SEAL Neil Roberts, then engaged a SEAL team sent to locate Roberts, killing CCT Chapman and seriously wounding two commandos. Two helicopters had been damaged, and now a third was en route, erroneously sent to the very same lethal spot.

As the hulking bulk of the transport helicopter descended onto the HLZ, 40ft below, it was slammed by small-arms fire. Two gunners managed to return fire. An RPG smashed into the right side of the craft, now barely 20ft above the HLZ. The small-arms fire ripped into the fuselage, chewing deadly paths of steel through flesh and metal alike. A Predator drone captured the action on tape – grainy, eerie black and white images without sound: in what could almost be mistaken for a flare, the RPG hit sends sparks and debris off the helicopter. On the inside of the Chinook, an AF Special Tactics member described the craft starting to shake violently.[177] Another occupant, combat controller Staff Sergeant Gabe Brown recalled "that the padding that lines the inside of the helicopter was flying around like confetti. All I could think was, here we go."[178] The deadly crossfire disabled the craft, forcing a hard crash from approximately 10–15ft, landing as though the helicopter just fell out of the sky.[179] The crashed Chinook, carrying the QRF and crewmembers, was ironically pointing up the very same hill where Technical Sergeant Chapman had been killed – near the main bunker by a large rock and beneath a large tree – a mere 50 yards away.

During this time, the right side mini-gunner, Sergeant Phil Svitak, returned fire with his mini-gun before he was mortally wounded and fell into the cabin. Corbin was hit in his vest. Gaines was struck in his left leg, another round into his helmet. Left minigunner Deese was wounded in the left leg. Larken was down on impact, his knee wrenched. The two pilots were seriously injured during the crash as well.[180] Rangers – go, go, go – into a maelstrom of steel.

It is clearly visible on the tape that at least one Ranger if not both are killed on the ramp at 01:44:30 Zulu time. The tape also shows the pilot dropping out of his window to seek safety on the ground at 01:44:53, and then proceeding to secure his area.[181]

Incoming tracer rounds started a fire within the Chinook, which was quickly extinguished by Lafayette, who had taken three rounds to his helmet and had the blood vessels in his eye ruptured.[182] The rest of Razor 01 was dealing with the situation as best they could; Gaines with his M-4 and a shattered femur dropped out of the emergency door 2ft into the snow; Corbin fired his M-4 out

Razor 01 during the firefight.
(US Army)

the window; Talbert with weapon moved toward the ramp to set up a defensive position with Walters and Miller.[183]

Ranger Specialist Anderson lay in the mid cabin area – dying. Pararescue Jumper Cunningham tried his best to save the man's life.

The hard landing slammed everyone on board onto the hard steel floor. Both pilots were injured, one door gunner was already dead, and the QRF was piling out of the helicopter. Engaged at close range from three sides, the rear gunner and Ranger DePouli killed a TAQ fighter near the ramp. The small-arms fire exacted a heavy toll immediately – Ranger Anderson died inside the aircraft while Rangers Crose and Commons were killed as they exited the Chinook – all within seconds of crashing.

Air Force Staff Sergeant Vance could not make an immediate exit of the helicopter as he had been pushed during the exit of a fellow Special Tactics Squadron member and his snap link was pulled too taut to release. Some 15 seconds later he managed to exfil from the MH-47E's ramp.[184] He captures a vivid picture of his scramble out of the helicopter:

> By the time I was able to get off of the aircraft, three of our team members were already dead. One team member was on the ramp with a hole in his head. There was no mistaking that he was dead. The second team member was at the end of the ramp face down in the snow. His position was such that if there had been life left in him, he would have moved his head out of the snow. I later found out that he had been shot under the arm through his chest and out above his right nipple. The last deceased team member was lying on his back at the end of the ramp not moving. I knew we had three killed in action [KIA], which left seven of our team, three of which were injured. I had shrapnel in the arm, but did not notice it until later. My platoon leader had shrapnel in his leg, it was a pretty good chunk, and another team member had shrapnel in his lower left calf and was moving slow. Our team knew how to fight and how to operate on the ground. The aircrew did not have the same training.[185]

The ARSOF history describes the furious Ranger action:

Ranger Miceli's position and perspective. (US Army)

SSG Raymond DePouli was the first Ranger off the ramp. Exiting, he was hammered in the back and spun around. The bullet hit his armor plate 1/8inch above his exposed area. He quickly located the enemy fighter wreaking havoc from the 8 o'clock position and emptied a full magazine from his M-4 into him. SGT Joshua J. Walker exited the right side, immediately took several hits on his Kevlar helmet, but managed to empty his M-4 toward the bunker on the right. SPC Aaron Lancaster-Totten, an M-249 squad automatic weapon (SAW) gunner followed Walker into the knee-deep snow. PFC David B. Gilliam grabbed the fallen Anderson's M-240B heavy machine gun and high crawled out the ramp to the right. Air Force SSGT Kevin Vance, the ETAC, slipped off his rucksack carrying the radio and dropped it off the ramp. Thrown backward on landing, CPT Self scrambled over several downed men to reach the ramp. He discovered PFC Matthew A. Commons dead and saw SGT Bradley S. Crose, one of his team leaders, lying motionless, facedown in the snow. Both had been killed while exiting. Self rolled off the ramp and processed the surreal scene. SPC Anthony R. Miceli, a SAW gunner, had had his M-249 shot out of his hands but was uninjured. [The weapon was in four or five pieces.][186] He had picked up PFC Commons' M203 grenade-launcher rifle and was positioned on the left side for security.

In less than three hours, six soldiers had been killed; while Operation *Anaconda* had one fratricide during a two-week skirmish.

The TAQ fighters visible on the video are roughly 50 yards away, moving from one location to another to engage the Americans. Most of them were positioned uphill, shooting down at the crashed helicopter and its crew. Another group engaged the helicopter from about the 2 o'clock position. It seems that at least one RPG was fired toward the helicopter from that location. In any event, as the hail of bullets continued to torment the small commando team now out of the aircraft, Ranger medic LaFrenz and Pararescueman Jason Cunningham attended to the wounded in the fuselage. Corbin bled heavily from his wrist.

Outside of the downed MH-47E, Rangers Totten-Lancaster and Walker bounded to a small rock outcropping to the right while other Rangers provided covering fire. Their forward movement was hampered by the snow, which measured 3ft deep in certain places. On the left, Hooah Nightstalker Gaines covered his area with his side arms – his leg a mess. Self and Vance joined Totten-Lancaster and Walker at the rock cropping. To their right, DePouli and Gilliam moved to another rocky area, after Ranger DePouli had killed an RPG gunner at the 4 o'clock position with a headshot. Here they discovered a bullet-ridden body of a TAQ fighter.[187] Ranger Miceli kept cover over the left side of the helicopter. The Predator footage shows the commandos maneuvering while engaging the enemy. Several RPG trails and at least one mortar explosion about 20 yards shy of the Chinook are easily identifiable. Some of the crew served as ammunition bearers for the depleted Rangers.

Five Rangers and one ETAC were more or less facing the threat to their right side – from the large rock with tall tree that had already seen some action during the SEALs' previous insertions. It was a mere 50 yards away, and the TAQ fighters were lobbing grenades at the cluster of American commandos, injuring Totten-Lancaster in the calf, Self in the thigh, and Vance in the shoulder.[188]

The situation that had developed was as follows. The handful of the remaining QRF established a perimeter, returned fire and evaluated their situation – four dead and nearly everybody else either injured or wounded. An unknown number of enemy fighters were darting around the mountaintop, peppering the area with RPG rounds, at least two of which are visible on the video, and small-arms fire. The AF commandos either directed their efforts toward establishing communications for CAS – Gabe Brown was about 20 yards below Self's position – or joined the depleted Rangers on the perimeter. The Rangers, throwing uphill, were unable to return the favor. Having killed another two TAQ fighters, one of whom was an RPG gunner, and having identified some of the threat areas, the QRF moved into better positions, using rock outcroppings as cover while engaging the TAQ.[189]

Ranger Platoon Leader Nathan Self hastily gathered an assault against the threat area. Staff Sergeant Vance, in a seemingly ebullient mood, describes the tumultuous minutes of the opening firefight:

> I exited the aircraft and threw my rucksack off but kept it within 20m. I figured out which way we were being engaged from and sought cover

## COMBAT CONTROLLER

*USAF Fact Sheet*
## MISSION

Combat controllers are certified air traffic controllers who are an integral part of the Air Force's ground combat team that specializes in unconventional missions.

They can set up navigational aid equipment anywhere in the world to guide aircraft for landing on makeshift runways without the benefit of a tower or large communications system.

Their motto "First There" indicates the CCT commitment to be the first deployed into restricted environments by air, land or sea tactics to establish assault zones. The assault zone is a drop zone for parachute operations, a landing zone for fixed wing or helicopter operations, or an extraction zone for low altitude re-supply.

Combat controllers can also control air attacks for fixed-wing and rotary-wing operations to include aircraft from all military services. In addition, combat controllers provide vital command and control, intelligence gathering, surveying capabilities, limited weather observations and are qualified in demolition to clear obstructions and hazards from potential runways and landing zones.

With CCT support, Air Force operating locations are limitless and global reach capabilities are enhanced.

## COMBAT CONTROLLERS COMMANDOS

Assigned to Air Force Special Operations Command, combat controllers join forces with pararescuemen and combat weathermen to form highly trained Special Tactics teams.

Special Tactics teams frequently operate with Navy SEALs, Army Rangers and Special Forces in "direct action," airfield seizure and personnel recovery missions in hostile territory.

Operating in all climates, day or night, combat controllers maintain the highest standards of physical fitness and proficiency in the use of light weapons. They endure some of the toughest training offered in the U.S. military. Their training, as well as their unique mission, earns them the right to wear the scarlet beret.

Combat Controllers are assigned under the 720th Special Tactics Group, an AFSOC unit with headquarters at Hurlburt Field, Fla. Within the 720th STG they are assigned to four active-duty Special Tactics Squadrons and one Air National Guard squadron in the United States: the 21st and 24th STS at Pope Air Force Base, N.C.; the 22nd STS at McChord AFB, Wash.; the 23rd STS at Hurlburt Field.; and the 123rd STS at the Kentucky Air National Guard in Louisville.

CCT are also assigned to overseas units: the 320th STS at Kadena Air Base, Japan; and the 321st STS at RAF Mildenhall, England.

## TRAINING

Combat controllers complete the same technical training as all air traffic controllers. Plus the following physical and specialized training:

• Air Traffic Control School, Keesler Air Force Base, Miss. – This is the same 15 and a half-week course that all other air traffic controllers attend. This is the core skill of a combat controller's job.

• U.S. Army Airborne School, Fort Benning, Ga. – Trainees learn the basic parachuting skills required to infiltrate an objective area by static line airdrop in a three-week course.

• U.S. Air Force Basic Survival School, Fairchild AFB, Wash. – This two and a half-week course teaches basic survival techniques for remote areas. Instruction includes principles, procedures, equipment and techniques, which enable individuals to survive, regardless of climatic conditions or unfriendly environments and return home.

• Combat Control School, Pope AFB, N.C. – This 12-week course provides final combat controller qualifications. Training includes land navigation, communications, assault zones, demolitions, small unit tactics, parachute operations, water operations and field tactics.

• Air Force Special Operations Command Advanced Skills Training – Advanced Skills Training employs a "warrior training warrior" philosophy, teaching the skills necessary for successful service in the Special Tactics community during this year-long course. Training includes preparation for the Army Combat Divers and the Military Freefall Parachutist Schools. Also included is training in advanced communications and navigational aids, employment techniques, weapons training and small unit tactics.

• U.S. Army Combat Diver Qualification Course, Key West, Fla. – Trainees become combat divers, learning to use scuba to infiltrate areas undetected in this four-week course. The school provides training to depths of 130 feet, developing maximum underwater mobility under various operating conditions.

• U.S. Navy Underwater Egress Training, Pensacola Naval Air Station, Fla. – This one-day course teaches how to safely escape from an aircraft that has ditched in the water. Instruction includes principles, procedures and techniques necessary to get out of a sinking aircraft.

• U.S. Army Military Free Fall Parachutist School, Fort Bragg, N.C., and Yuma Proving Grounds, Ariz. – This five-week course instructs free fall parachuting (high altitude, low opening or HALO) using the high performance ram air canopy. The course provides wind tunnel training, in-air instruction focusing on student stability, aerial maneuvers, air sense, and parachute opening procedures. Each student receives a minimum of 30 free fall jumps including two day and night jumps with supplemental oxygen, rucksack and load bearing equipment.[190]

behind a cutout in the rock-face. It was just big enough for four team members to kneel behind. Two other [Rangers] were back to my right and three to my left. I was closest to the enemy. There were two enemies about 50m north of us near a tree. There was one enemy behind me and to the right – already dead. There were some more enemies to the south. I was shooting an M4. At first, my priority was to keep engaging the enemy to hold them back and then to seek assistance for close air support on the radio. My radio, a PRC 117F, was still in my rucksack. There was a combat controller with us named Gabe Brown who was behind me a bit. I turned around and yelled at him to work on getting communications running, he already was working on it.

First, we shot M203 rounds at the bunker [that it was a bunker was revealed later]. As the squad leader and team leader shot M203s, I stood up and provided covering fire. When he would stand up to fire a grenade at the bunker, I would stand up and shoot at the bunker to cover him. I did the same when the crewmembers would run for more ammo. We tried throwing fragment grenades at the enemy but they were too far away and the bunker was on the backside of the hill. The enemy threw fragment grenades at us but they landed 5–10ft in front of me, buried in the snow and blew up.

There was no power to the aircraft without which we could not operate the mini-guns. One of the team members yelled at a member of the crew to get the power working so we could use those guns. The mini-guns shoot 7.62 ammo and so does our M240. The crew was taking ammo and giving it to our M240 gunner. When the crewmembers would run back to the aircraft for more ammo, I would stand up and shoot at the bunker to cover them. They were also taking M203 rounds and magazines off of the KIA and bringing it to us. The crew pulled off insulation from the aircraft to wrap the casualties in to keep them warm. [The helicopter never regained any power.]

Then four of us (myself, the platoon leader Captain Self, squad leader Staff Sergeant DePouli, and team leader Sergeant Walker) started to assault the tree area where the enemy was coming from while the M240 gunner suppressed it. Captain Self, the platoon leader, was in charge. Once we realized that it was a bunker, a couple of enemy came out from behind a tree and took shots at us. We were moving slow because the snow was up to our knees and we were going uphill. The platoon leader finally said "let's back up and rethink this." We backed up because we could not afford to lose any more guys.

This assault collapsed. The senior leaders realized that their position was tenuous at best and by now air assets in the form of Air Force F-15s were incoming. If only Grim 32 had not been ordered to base when darkness faded...

The Air Force and Army aircrew tended to their wounded while Sergeant Walker and Gilliam, as Walker's machine-gunner assistant, stayed at their defensive position. Gilliam thought he had found a pair of binoculars but they turned out to be night-vision goggles. Self was confused, believing them to belong to the enemy. Even more confounding, he thought he was at the wrong location.[191] The goggles must have belonged to one of the SEALs. The Ranger PL sent DePouli with Miceli to reconnoiter their far right flank and check on any possibility of being flanked by the enemy. Their reconnaissance discovered the sheer cliff on the side of Takur Ghar, as well as two sections cut into the hill that had been used by the TAQ fighters as single sleeping areas. The two Rangers also made a more startling discovery. "DePouli told Self about the cliff and the positions. He then cleared the two positions, first firing into a blanket covering one. In them, he discovered a rucksack, a multiband inter/intra team radio (MBITR), and a bullet-holed helmet filled with blood. Leaving SPC Maceli to cover the right flank, SSG DePouli returned to his original position."[192]

Brown, one of the highly-trained AFCCTs, coordinated air strikes against the most obvious positions. It took several runs but the CAS presence paid off. It was also during this time that the trapped QRF force found out that the SEALs had retreated down the mountain. "Having discovered an MBITR on the mountain, SSG Brown pulled out his and raised the stranded special operations ground force. They told him where they were and their casualties but not why they were down below."[193]

Captain Self tried to put the pieces of the puzzle together. He certainly had very little information and he incorrectly, as the ARSOF history concludes, assumed he was at the wrong location, not being privy to the Navy P-3's confirmation given prior to landing.[194]

The fighter planes, including F-16s, made several strafing and bombing runs, uncomfortable for both the commandos on the ground and the pilots dropping ordinance.[195] Some of the QRF were showered with debris and shrapnel from those runs. Although the Air Force fighters did numerous strafing runs, the TAQ fighters were still maneuvering and popping off shots toward the beleaguered commandos. Ultimately, the bomb runs provided the respite sought. The bunker area fell silent.

By 0700 hours local time Razor 01's survivors were no longer in danger of being overrun. Following traditional infantry tactics, the Rangers consolidated their position and established a casualty collecting point to the rear of the downed helicopter.[196] They decided to wait for reinforcements – the second half of the QRF package. Occasional TAQ mortars attempted to bracket the pocket of resistance. Reinforcements were needed to seize and control the area. There can be little doubt about the existence of tension among the handful of Americans – their own survival and the survival of their seriously wounded comrades was at stake.

Although bad luck had plagued the mission from the start, the SOF, SEALs, and Rangers were rather lucky. The first rescue attempt, composed of Roberts' teammates, ran smack into the middle of a handful of entrenched TAQ fighters and the group was reduced by 50 percent, including one killed, within a few short moments. Retreating, they were barely able to hang on, desperately calling in airstrikes on their pursuers. The arrival of the Rangers on the HLZ at Takur Ghar brought them much relief, as TAQ fighters maneuvered to attack the new threat. The Ranger QRF on the other hand, despite its initial bad luck in approaching a hot landing zone, was extremely fortunate that the chain of command stayed intact, and that they survived insertion and the subsequent attempt to attack a fortified position. Kevlar armor had saved the lives of at least three other men, thereby enabling QRF to retain the semblance of a valid force capable of defending itself.

As things were settling in at Takur Ghar, Staff Sergeant Canon at Gardez was not so nice – he needed to get his chalk to join the other Rangers reaping glory.

# MOUNTAIN GOATS TO THE RESCUE

Razor 02, the other part of the QRF package of ten Rangers, had been moved to Gardez by 0625 hours where it awaited further instructions. They had lost communications with Razor 01. "The communications problem that had kept the senior special operations commanders from acquiring situational awareness on the Takur Ghar problem continued into the following day. This prevented senior commanders from getting control of rescue efforts being launched from areas in 'gray' communications zones. In the confusion at the tactical level, the senior operator on the ground making the most noise, with an incomplete situational picture as well, dominated decisions in this command and control 'void.' This was the environment awaiting Razor 02 when he landed at the Special Forces camp at Gardez with half of the Ranger QRF."[197]

Ultimately, Razor 02 inserted its team of Rangers and TF Blue's commander at an offset location which had been identified as being just a few hundred yards away from the beleaguered Rangers, but turned out to be 2,000ft below Takur Ghar's mountaintop and approximately 900 yards east. It was at about 0830

Soldiers of Chalk 02: (standing left–right) Wilmoth, Escano, Polson, George, Cunningham. (kneeling left–right) Pazder, Vela. (US Army)

hours local time. So there they were, ten Rangers plus one SEAL staring up at the colossal mountain. A tough climb through 3ft of snow, on rocky terrain and steep slopes, lay ahead of them. There were also the SEALs, decimated and physically beaten, about 1,000ft up.

By 0800 hours Staff Sergeant Canon notified his captain of the situation and relayed the SEAL commander's call for help, which sought Chalk 02's help in assisting Mako 20 down the slope. Self adamantly refused permission to do so, instead urging his Rangers to join them as soon as possible as the situation on Takur Ghar was far more critical, a fact still not known by a number of people, including the SEAL officer. This negative response left the TF Blue commander to hook up with his party, while the Rangers would climb to glory.

Undoubtedly none of the Rangers were thinking of glory as the anticipated 30–45 minute climb turned into a two-hour plus ordeal. Any infantryman can appreciate the grueling nature of mountainous terrain – the weight of live ammunition, weapon, gear, and body armor can easily add up to 70–80lb. Not being accustomed to working at high elevations can put additional stress on the body. Crawling, sliding, and cursing, the Rangers huffed and puffed up the mountain. Captain Self authorized the Rangers to discard their rear Kevlar plates, making the climb less torturous, which some of them chose to do. Tossing some of their snivel gear was an added alleviation – only to be regretted later. Sporadic mortar and small-arms fire did not help make the 45–70 degree slope variations any easier to negotiate. The constantly changing arrival time of the relief force did very little to ease the nerves of either of the chalks. Finally Self joined Brown at his location and, unable to raise Chalk 01, Brown "attempted at 0900 hours to contact the special operations TOC in

Razor 01 on Takur Ghar. (DoD)

Bagram, but the radio operators there did not recognize his call sign and asked him to leave their net."[198]

Eventually, the Rangers managed the ascent. The situation on top of the mountain required the wounded to be moved in order to stay clear of the mortar rounds that had started to bracket the downed Chinook to about 20 yards behind the helicopter. It was during this time that the Rangers attempted to assault the rock and tree area, only to discover it was a bunker complex, forcing them to retreat until CAS was available. The bunker complex was ultimately hit by a strike from an armed CIA Predator drone as the incoming mortar rounds shifted away from the Rangers, indicating the arrival below the mountaintop of Ranger Chalk 02.

At Bagram, amid massive interfering input from the various task forces and headquarters, rescue plans were in full swing. The second half of the Ranger QRF reached their brothers and reinforced the perimeter of Razor 02 by 1030 hours. Utterly smoked and barely getting a chance for a breather, the Rangers drew up a hasty assault plan toward the main enemy bunker 50 yards away. The morale of the trapped men had undoubtedly soared with the arrival of their comrades. Now it was time for business. The Ranger battalions had a poster on their walls of a Ranger with shield and machine gun. It said: "I am not the Killerman, but I'm the Killerman's son. And I'll do the killing till the Killerman comes." It can be safely assumed that none of the Rangers on the mountaintop felt like the Killerman's son, but nonetheless that is what they had to do to – kill the enemy, eliminate the threat if they wanted to survive.

AFETAC Vance's debrief states: "Finally, our reinforcements linked up with us. SGT Walker took a couple of rounds in his helmet. When the reinforcements arrived, SGT Walker came forward and told SSG Wilmoth which direction the enemy was located. SGT Walker's helmet had holes in the top of the head and the side of the head."[199] Certainly, the TAQ fighters were as lethal as ever. This was no time to be careless.

The ugly business was at hand. This situation bore no similarity to the paean of the hoplite warriors echoing through the age-old mountains as they charged their soon-to-be defeated enemy. Although it would have made for a beautiful finale, the reality was different, and yet no less glorious.

Following CAS runs, the commandos assaulted the bunker, with two machine guns providing suppressive fire. Seven Rangers staggered toward their objective in the knee-deep snow. Vance continues: "A 500-pound bomb hit just over the backside of the hilltop. It hit at an angle where it blew everything back over the top of us so it was raining debris and metal pieces down around us. That was the only point where we were really concerned with our safety from the friendly bombs. This was the last time we used the 500-pound bombs. Together we started to take the top of the hill."[200]

The majority of the assault team consisted of members of Chalk 02. Rangers excel at basic infantry skills and tasks. The Department of Defense spends millions on the Ranger Regiment and no Ranger has ever complained about a lack of live-fire training. Training is what took over in these trying circumstances. Undoubtedly some of the men were afraid to face the storm of steel of the remaining TAQ fighters – the unknown is always more terrifying than the known. Weapons at the high ready (rifle butts against shoulders), with suppressive fire from two of the excellent M-240 machine guns, the tired men staggered through the snow toward the main bunker 50 yards away. The Rangers unleashed such an enormous amount of suppressive fire onto the ridgeline that some crewmembers yelled at the Rangers to slow down, although much of the mini-gun ammunition from the Chinook was used for the automatic weapons.[201] Grenades were lobbed as the assault team closed with the enemy. Ranger training translated into a good performance. Usually a Ranger squad has two teams that support one another when attacking an objective, as was the case here.

After issuing the fragmentary order (FRAGO), the assault began when the men were ready. "When ready, go!" were the simple words of instruction to the Rangers. Sergeant Stebner managed to slug his way to the top where he discovered a dead American, face down in the snow, near the large rock boulder. This was Roberts, although Stebner had no idea who it was. Staff Sergeant Wilmoth's team cleared the bunker 15ft away, where two dead TAQ fighters lay next to another dead American – Chapman. Managing to get a hold of ST 6, the Rangers were finally informed that the two dead Americans had been part of the SOF team and at long last the Rangers were able to form a clearer picture of the events that had unfolded. It was Ranger Canon who went to identify the two dead Special Operations soldiers.

The Rangers from 1st Battalion cleared the rest of the mountaintop, discovering several reinforced positions as well as a few more dead enemy fighters. By 1115 hours the hilltop was in Ranger hands.

In his debriefing, Staff Sergeant Vance detailed his perspective:

> Once we took the top of the hill we found two more friendly bodies. They included the member who fell out of the helicopter that we were there to find and a member from the team before us that tried to go in to get him. We were sent in because they were not successful. Both members had been shot and killed. We had thirty-three members on the hill (including two deceased we found), sixteen were fighting, and three of those sixteen were wounded. The other half was working on casualties or were casualties themselves.[202]

The Rangers consolidated their position on the top of the mountain, and the wounded were moved to a safer location. This work was exhausting and required four–six men per wounded man.[203]

# THE ALAMO

The end was nowhere in sight. For hours the Rangers would receive sporadic fire, and AF Pararescue Jumper (PJ) Cunningham was wounded. The DoD report states: "As the soldiers moved the wounded, additional al Qaeda began firing from a small ridgeline some 400 meters to the rear of the downed helicopter's position." One of the pararescuemen, Technical Sergeant Miller, who subsequently would receive the Silver Star,[204] remembers that "all of the sudden everything lit up. An RPG rocket flew so closely over his head that he could have caught it with a baseball glove. The trees were crackling and Pine needles were falling on them."[205]

The wounded at the casualty collection point were completely exposed to the enemy fire. While the Rangers maneuvered to return fire against a handful of TAQ fighters, enemy fire struck the Army medic and Pararescue Jumper at the casualty collection point as they worked on their patients. Rangers and helicopter crewmen alike risked their lives, exposing themselves to enemy fire to pull the wounded to the relative safety of nearby rocks. Once again, the combat controller called in CAS, and well-placed bombs and Ranger machine-gun fire eventually silenced the enemy fire. The stricken PJ, Senior Airman Jason Cunningham, eventually succumbed to his wounds. He was married with two children and had been a pararescue jumper for eight months. Jason Cunningham became the first PJ to die in combat since the Vietnam War.[206] Repeated calls to headquarters for evacuation went unheeded as another daylight rescue might have disastrous results. Cunningham had been kept alive for ten hours, until one-and-a-half hours before the eventual night extraction. No doubt this was an absolutely depressing experience.

The Rangers consolidated their position, moved their dead and wounded to the top of the hill, and waited for a night extraction. The enemy air defense and ground situation in the vicinity of Takur Ghar did not lend themselves to another daylight rescue attempt using helicopters. Throughout the day, observation posts on adjoining hilltops, manned by Australian and American

Ranger Pazder's position during the later stages of the fight. (US Army)

SOF, called in fire on al-Qaeda forces attempting to reinforce the mountaintop. During the ensuing hours, the Americans continued to take sporadic sniper and mortar fire. They controlled the top two peaks but not the third. CAS continued to run missions to support the small force including dropping a 1000lb bomb a mere 150 yards away from their knoll.[207] "At one point the Controller informed the exhausted and demoralized men that an enemy force of 70 TAQ fighters was approaching their AO." They never materialized, but one can hardly underestimate the impact it had on the men. The majority of TAQ reinforcements traveled in small groups of four–five men. Once the firing subsided after dark, the frigid weather conditions became life threatening. Everything that could be stripped from the downed aircraft was used for insulation. Food and water were scarce, but hypothermia could have even further increased the death toll.

At about 2015 hours local time, four helicopters from the 160th SOAR extracted both the Rangers on Takur Ghar and the SEALs down the mountain-side. An AC-130 was on station, sporadically shooting at targets to keep the TAQ fighters low to the ground. The first Chinook landed incorrectly, facing the opposite direction, thereby delaying the exfiltration process. Fifteen minutes later the exhausted Rangers had their wounded and dead loaded onto the helicopters.[208] The first aircraft removed the most seriously wounded, four in all, and the seven dead were airlifted out in the second helicopter.[209] Nearly 16 hours later they left the cold-hearted mountaintop of Takur Ghar. The tally was seven dead comrades, ten dead TAQ fighters on the mountaintop, and another unknown number (estimates 40–50) killed during their attempts to reinforce the positions.

"Two hours later, the survivors and their fallen comrades were back at their base. A team of experienced medical staff of the 274th Forward Surgical Team, operating out of the Bagram airport tower, awaited the eleven wounded personnel."[210]

In Graham Bradley's account in *The Washington Post* on the actions at Takur Ghar he writes on Captain Nathan Self's thoughts: "Everybody did what they were trained to do, everybody performed well above the standard. It's negative because, in getting to play the game, losing is very final, it's very ugly. And until you really see it like we got to see it, it's kind of this mysterious thing. Quite frankly, I think that if guys with our job dealt with it or thought about it quite a bit, there would be a lot fewer of us."[211]

AFETAC Kevin Vance "went through so many different emotions, excited, mad, frustrated, sad, any other emotion you could possibly feel, you feel going through this whole thing. And I felt guilty if I felt anything was funny like Sgt Walker's helmet with the holes in it because we had lost members of our team. Everyone out there just did his job. I just did my job, everything came natural and my training kicked in. There is nothing I could have changed about that day. Nothing we could have done different or better. I could not ask for a better group of guys to work with. I have trained for eight years to do this and now I had the chance to get to do my job – that is reward enough."[212]

Ranger Stebner reflected during the awards ceremony at Hunter Army Airfield: "you're up there and it's not going to do anything but get worse. You do what you can to come out on the good end of it."[213]

Of course credit must also be given to all the SOF teams that helped the Rangers to survive over the 16-hour time period. One recon team, in contact with Gabe Brown, informed the beleaguered Rangers during the battle of several enemy fighters "milling on the backside of the mountain, below and behind the bunker."[214] The highly regarded Australians did a fantastic job in supporting TF Red. The *Sydney Morning Herald* dated September 3, 2002, in an article entitled "High praise for diggers who helped save stricken Americans" by Greg Skehan notes that an Australian patrol, which was involved in surveillance and reconnaissance, had played a key role. Al-Qaeda fighters soon surrounded the survivors of the downed aircraft, and the force continued to resist determined enemy efforts to kill or capture them throughout the day. Australian observers coordinated air strikes to prevent the al-Qaeda forces from overrunning the survivors.

A few days later, a combat patrol from the 10th Mountain Division found night-vision devices, load-bearing vests, infrared lasers and global positioning systems that had been captured by the TAQ fighters at Takur Ghar. The gear belonged to the Rangers and other commandos.[215]

Operation *Anaconda* continued for another two weeks and was hailed an unqualified and absolute success by General Tommy Franks.

Colonel Andrew Milani, the prime investigator of the actions around Takur

---

## RANGER DECORATIONS FOR BRAVERY DURING COMBAT ACTIONS – OPERATION *ANACONDA*

### Silver Star
CPT Nathan E. Self
SSG Raymond DePouli
SSG Harper Wilmoth
SSG Arin K. Canon
SSG Eric W. Stebner
SGT Matthew LaFrenz
SGT Joshua J. Walker
SPC Aaron Totten-Lancaster
Air Force
SSG Kevin Vance

### Bronze Star with valor device
SGT Patrick George
SPC Anthony Ross Miceli
SPC Oscar Escano
SPC Chris M. Cunningham
SPC Randy J. Pazder
SPC Jonas O. Polson
SPC Omar J. Vela
PFC David B. Gilliam

### Bronze Star
LTC Raymond A. Thomas
MAJ Jeffrey Cain
MAJ James Mingus
MAJ Christopher Vanek
CPT Andrew Brosnan
CPT Raymond Dillman
CPT Jason Gonzalez
CPT David Haines
CPT George Murray
CPT Jack L. Rich
CPT Joseph Ryan
CPT Nathan E. Self
1SG Darrin J. Bohn
MSG Robert Arendt
MSG Michael Ferussi
SFC Alan Michaud
SFC Corey Perkins
SFC Charles Pressburg
SFC Ivan Rose

### Purple Heart
CPT Nathan E. Self
Air Force SSG Kevin D. Vance

Ghar, assumed command as the ninth colonel of the 160th Regiment on July 2, 2003, and in a press release discussed the operational aspects of his much beloved Nightstalkers:

> Adverse weather presented a challenge with some of the worst weather conditions on earth. The extreme cold, marked by huge temperature deviations, high winds, severe turbulence and poor-to-zero visibility, all contributed to increasing the degree of difficulty. The rugged terrain also added challenges. The Hindu Kush and outlaying Himalayas are some of the most rugged terrain on earth and served to limit the number of suitable landing zones for even the most experienced and capable pilots.
>
> This constantly demanded flexibility in mission execution. In fact, recently in Afghanistan, due to severe icing conditions above them, an MH-47E on a combat mission found itself deviating through a mountain pass where, confronting an 8,500 foot steep banked cul-de-sac, the pilot had to physically back the aircraft up to turn it around.
>
> The number one threat to Army Aviation, including SOAR, continues to be small arms fire and rocket-propelled grenades.
>
> In Afghanistan, a $50 RPG took down one of our $43 million aircraft. They are cheap, easily attainable and abundant.

# CONTINUING OPERATIONS

Currently, the 75th Ranger Regiment continues to cycle its battalions in and out of Afghanistan in support of Operation *Enduring Freedom*.

| THE LAST PUBLICLY ACKNOWLEDGED PARACHUTE ASSAULT IN AFGHANISTAN | | |
| --- | --- | --- |
| Detachment, Headquarters and Headquarters Company, 2nd Battalion, 75th Ranger Regiment | 1345–1445Z 25 February 2003 | near Chahar Borjak, Nimruz Province, Afghanistan |
| Detachment, Company A, 2nd Battalion, 75th Ranger Regiment | 1345–1445Z 25 February 2003 | near Chahar Borjak, Nimruz Province, Afghanistan |
| Detachment, Company C, 2nd Battalion, 75th Ranger Regiment | 1345–1445Z 25 February 2003 | near Chahar Borjak, Nimruz Province, Afghanistan |

# AN ONGOING WAR

Afghanistan and Operation *Enduring Freedom* were no longer the focus of the Bush Administration by the beginning of 2002, as the strategic imperative had shifted to Iraq and Operation *Iraqi Freedom*. Former 2nd Ranger Battalion

Commander David Barno took over command of all US and Coalition forces in Afghanistan. In a briefing entitled *Afghanistan: The Security Outlook*, given at the Center for Strategic & International Studies on May 14, 2004, Lieutenant General Barno noted a change in tactics of the now ousted TAQ forces and their government:

> We believe that the enemy made a significant decision to change the direction that he was operating in, in part because he was getting battered very heavily. [During] May/June of last year [2003], we would have found commonplace that Taliban would be operating in numbers 100, 150, 200, sometimes even larger numbers in those southern areas of Afghanistan. Throughout a series of engagements with our forces last summer there were very severe casualties inflicted on these large Taliban formations. Then we watched an evolution very clearly where the enemy realized that was devastating to his objectives. He was taking severe casualties. And he began to almost regress into an early stage terrorism campaign and he also began, as we saw in the November timeframe in particular, targeting the United Nations, targeting in some cases NGOs out there, and looking for more vulnerable targets to include the Afghan government. We were able to work very closely with the UN to help mitigate that.[216]

By August 1, 2004 one of the most highly respected humanitarian organizations, Médecins Sans Frontières (MSF), had left Afghanistan due to the

Ranger supporting operations in Afghanistan. (75th RR)

continued violence and the paradigm shift of TAQ strategy. Their press release reads as follows: "It is with a deep feeling of sadness that Médecins Sans Frontières has decided to close all of its medical programmes in Afghanistan. This decision has come nearly two months after the killing of our five colleagues in a deliberate attack on June 2nd. The clearly marked MSF car was ambushed on a road in Badghis province. This targeted killing of five of our colleagues is unprecedented in the history of MSF, although we have been delivering medical humanitarian assistance in some of the most violent conflicts around the world over the last 30 years."[217]

Rangers patrolling in Afghanistan. During one of these patrols Ranger Tillman was killed by his own teammates when they returned fire toward a suspected enemy force. (75th RR)

Since the downfall of the Taliban, Afghanistan has rapidly increased its opium production and export.[218]

| AFGHANISTAN OPIUM POPPY CULTIVATION, 1994–2004 (HECTARES) | | | | | | | | | | |
|---|---|---|---|---|---|---|---|---|---|---|
| 1994 | 1995 | 1996 | 1997 | 1998 | 1999 | 2000 | 2001 | 2002 | 2003 | 2004 |
| 71,000 | 54,000 | 57,000 | 58,000 | 64,000 | 91,000 | 82,000 | 8,000 | 74,000 | 80,000 | 131,000 |

One Special Operations Forces member stipulated recently that the "stuff grows right up to our fence – it's everywhere."[219] How much drug abuse has increased by US and Coalition forces remains largely unreported. The much-despised Taliban did reduce drug growth and export phenomenally – their methods were ruthless but effective in a lawless land.

The 75th Ranger Regiment continues to support US foreign policy objectives in Afghanistan. As the campaign in Afghanistan descends into an occupation with limited returns and an ascendancy of guerrilla warfare, Rangers will traverse the deserts, mountains, and rivers in search of objectives – men will die; some by the enemy, others by accidents, and some by their own forces.

## RANGER CASUALTIES – AFGHANISTAN

| Soldier | Battalion | Date KIA |
| --- | --- | --- |
| SPC John J. Edmunds | 3-75 | 19-Oct-01 |
| SPC Kristofor T. Stonesifer | 3-75 | 19-Oct-01 |
| SPC Marc A. Anderson | 1-75 | 4-Mar-02 |
| CPL Matthew A. Commons | 1-75 | 4-Mar-02 |
| SGT Bradley S. Crose | 1-75 | 4-Mar-02 |
| SGT Jay A. Blessing | 2-75 | 14-Nov-03 |
| SPC Patrick D. Tillman | 2-75 | 22-Apr-04 |
| CPL William M. Amundson Jr. | 3-75 | 19-Oct-04 |
| SGT Michael C. O'Neill | 3-75 | 21-Oct-04 |

# Operation *Iraqi Freedom*

Dogs of war

Iraq was invaded on March 20, 2003. Influential defense analyst Ken Adelman stated boldly on February 13, 2002, in *The Washington Post*: "I believe demolishing Hussein's military power and liberating Iraq would be a cakewalk."

## AMERICA 2002–04

In the immediate aftermath of the September 11 attacks, a handful of powerful politicians led by Cheney, Rumsfeld, Wolfowitz, and Feith pressed for an attack against Iraq. According to Bob Woodward's *Plan of Attack*, Vice-President Dick Cheney and Deputy Secretary of Defense Paul Wolfowitz immediately started to look for a connection between Saddam Hussein and September 11.[220] Former Treasury Secretary Paul O'Neill has said the Bush Administration had been discussing an invasion of Iraq since shortly after the inauguration in early 2001 – well before 9/11.[221] No stone would be left unturned in the pursuit of finding incriminating evidence, so much so in fact that Secretary of State Colin Powell thought Cheney had an unhealthy fixation on it and that "uncertain and ambiguous" intelligence was converted by Feith's office, the Office of Special Plans, into fact.[222] Ultimately, facts were deemed irrelevant and unnecessary as the Bush Administration conducted a masterful orchestration of propaganda.

The Bush administration unrelentingly beat the war drum. The desire to invade a foreign country rested with the realization that the catastrophic events that had just occurred at home would enable the implementation of strategic initiatives designed for well over a decade with very little opposition. Iraq had been a principal target for years. The reasons cited were numerous and included,

ABOVE

Operation *Iraqi Freedom*. Here are the regimental commander and the field grade staff of 1/75, some of the best officers come out of the Regiment. (Michael Kershaw)

These Rangers are conducting rehearsals prior to launching another mission in Iraq. (75th RR)

although they were not limited to, the desire for the worldwide projection of American power, access to Iraq's oil reserves, the destabilization and overthrow of a declared enemy of Israel, as well as the establishment of future bases of operations deemed necessary to overthrow or defang other perceived threats in the region – namely Syria and Iran. In fact, 9/11 provided the catalyst for the implementation of Wolfowitz's and the Project for the New American Century's (PNAC) vision of American world dominance through the projection of American military power.

# THE PRECURSOR TO OPERATION *IRAQI FREEDOM* – OPERATION *MILLENNIUM CHALLENGE 2002*

The Department of Defense conducted an experiment in transformational war-fighting in July and August of 2002, with the aim of testing the joint forces doctrines that had been developed over the preceding years. For nearly a year, various elements within the Bush administration had been pushing for the invasion of Iraq, and for three weeks, the military strategists, with nearly 14,000 soldiers, sailors, airmen, and marines and an estimated budget of $250 million at their disposal, would get to attack a fictional Middle Eastern dictator whose army was determined to fight it out.

The basic idea behind MC02 was that US troops would attack Red Forces under retired Marine Corps Lieutenant General Paul Van Riper. Primarily it pitted the highly touted technology-reliant netcentric warfighting doctrine against a low-technology enemy with equipment more or less modeled on mid to late 20th-century arms, armor, and aircraft. To begin with the Red Team absolutely destroyed the Blue Forces, even going so far as sinking the Blue Force fleet (it would be refloated during the exercise).[223] However Van Riper realized that ultimately the exercise was not employed in earnest – that instead it was meant to validate the new transformational doctrines so eagerly supported and demanded by Secretary of Defense Donald Rumsfeld. As a matter of fact, Van Riper claims that his subordinate eventually did not take his directives, but rather took orders from the exercise director – Air Force Brigadier General Jim Smith.[224] Former 75th Ranger Regimental Commander and then head of Joint Forces Command, General William "Buck" Kernan, insisted that this exercise was the "key to military transformation." He vehemently objected to Van Riper's remarks that the experiment was scripted.[225] Of course the pressure on the military was enormous. Huge amounts of money had been spent on the Air Force, and Rumsfeld was not known for patience or cooperation. One can easily see how this exercise had to work and when it didn't – well it clearly showed the shortcomings of the ill-conceived predominance of technology on US military doctrine.

Technology should be a tool and not the driving force behind the art of war. Van Riper stipulates that "we don't have a leadership that is involved intellectually. They want to will through transformation and want slogans from the Pentagon... there is no content and nothing meaningful is written. Paul Wolfowitz doesn't understand the relationship between policy, strategy, and

Rangers, looking more like mechanized infantry, patrolling during Operation *Iraqi Freedom*. (75th RR)

## MILLENNIUM CHALLENGE 02

Sponsored by U.S. Joint Forces Command [USJFCOM]. Moving forward, leading change, towards transformation. Global security demands one flexible, formidable, fighting joint force, utilizing the best people and assets from each of the services to improve combat effectiveness, and the concepts and capabilities that will fully realize our emerging national military strategy. USJFCOM is the leader of change within our armed forces – ensuring we fight smarter, with fewer resources, and with less risk. MC02 focused on how the U.S. explores the military's ability to conduct Rapid Decisive Operations (RDO) against a determined adversary.

Millennium Challenge 2002 (MC02) brought together both live field exercises and computer simulation July 24–Aug. 15, 2002.

MC02 represented a critical building block of future military transformation.

MC02 will incorporate elements of all military services, most functional/regional commands and many DoD organizations and federal agencies. The Secretary of Defense has directed that participants involve elements representative of their future force concepts such as the Air Force's Expeditionary Aerospace Force, the Army's medium-weight brigades and the Navy's "Forward From the Sea" vision.

MC02 simulated a high-end, small-scale contingency that had the potential to escalate to a major theater war and:

Determined the extent to which a joint force is able to implement the principles outlined in Joint Vision 2020 through:

- Establishing and maintaining information/knowledge superiority
- Setting the conditions for decisive operations
- Assuring access into and through the battle space
- Conducting effects-based operations
- Sustaining itself as it conducts synchronized non-contiguous operations
- Developed improved joint training capabilities through experimentation efforts
- Developed goals and objectives for future USJFCOM transformation events
- Produced recommendations for current doctrine, organization, training, materiel, leadership, personnel, and facilities (DOTMLPF) in order to more effectively use our current major systems by developing and adapting a new set of principles.

Joint experimentation fosters an operational, decision-making culture in the defense of our nation by exploring the threats of tomorrow today. The basic premise is that critical decisions on future military doctrine, organization and technology should be based on solid empirical results. We are exploring the future of national defense in order to provide better information for national security decision makers. National defense transformation begins with aggressively setting the joint context for concept development and robust joint experimentation.[226]

# NETWORK-CENTRIC WARFARE

Writing in 2005, the Office of the Secretary of Defense put out a publication that attempted to create an intellectual basis for transformation and netcentric warfare.

Director, Force Transformation, Office of the Secretary of Defense, 1000 Defense Pentagon, Washington, DC 20301-1000, January 5, 2005.

Network-centric warfare is an emerging theory of war in the Information Age. It is also a concept that, at the highest level, constitutes the military's response to the Information Age. The term network-centric warfare broadly describes the combination of strategies, emerging tactics, techniques, and procedures, and organizations that a fully or even a partially networked force can employ to create a decisive warfighting advantage. The implementation of NCW is first of all about human behavior as opposed to information technology. While "network" is a noun, "to network" is a verb. Thus, when we examine the degree to which a particular military organization, or the Department as a whole, is exploiting the power of NCW, our focus should be on human behavior in the networked environment.

NCW and all of its associated revolutions in military affairs (RMAs) grow out of and draw their power from the fundamental changes in American society. These changes have been dominated by the co-evolution of economics, information technology, and business processes and organizations and they are linked by three themes:

- The shift in focus from the platform to the network;
- The shift from viewing actors as independent to viewing them as part of a continuously adapting ecosystem; and
- The importance of making strategic choices to adapt or even survive in such changing ecosystems.

These ideas have not only changed the nature of American business today – they have changed and will continue to change the way military operations are conducted. The development of the intellectual foundation of NCW within the DoD continued with the Information Age Transformation Series of books published by the Department of Defense Command and Control Research Program (CCRP) under the auspices of the Assistant Secretary of Defense for Networks and Information Integration (ASD [NII]). The first book in this series, *Network Centric Warfare: Developing and Leveraging Information Superiority*, provided the first detailed articulation of the tenets that link a robustly networked force to dramatically increased combat power. It also described how information, coupled with changes in command and control (C2), could transform military organizations. Two additional volumes completed the three-volume set, *Information Age Anthology: Understanding Information Age Warfare* and *Information Age Transformation*. Another important book published by the CCRP, *Effects Based Operations: Applying Network Centric Warfare in Peace, Crisis and War*, explored the link between network-centric organizations and processes and mission outcomes.[227]

## THE TYPICAL 21ST-CENTURY RANGER

Average age: 24

Average height/weight: 5ft 9in/174lb

Time in service/time on station: 4½ years/ 2 years

Military training: Basic Combat Training and Advanced Individual Training, Airborne School (3 weeks), Ranger Indoctrination Program (1 month), Pre-Ranger Course (3 weeks), Ranger School (2 months), Ranger First Responder Medical Training (1 week), Primary Leadership Development Course (4 weeks)

Experience: OEF/OIF deployments x 1–4, Joint

Readiness Training Center rotation x 1, Joint Readiness Exercise x 1, live fire exercises x 25

Rank: About half are specialists (pay grade E-4)

Army Physical Fitness Test Score: 275 out of 300

Awards: Expert Infantryman Badge, Combat Infantryman Badge, Army Commendation Medal, Army Achievement Medal, GWOT Expeditionary and Service medals, Ranger Tab, Parachutist Badge

Other Statistics: Fewer than half are married; average number of children is 1.75; most have some college education; about half are Ranger qualified (earned Ranger Tab)

## RANGER DEPLOYMENTS – *IRAQI FREEDOM*

| | | |
|---|---|---|
| Company C, 3rd Battalion, 75th Ranger Regiment | 1830–2230Z 24 March 2003 | Northwestern desert region of Iraq, in the vicinity of the town of Al Qaim, near the Syrian border |
| Detachment, Headquarters and Headquarters Company, 3rd Battalion, 75th Ranger Regiment | 1830–2230Z 24 March 2003 | Northwestern desert region of Iraq, in the vicinity of the town of Al Qaim, near the Syrian border |
| Company A, 3rd Battalion, 75th Ranger Regiment | 1835Z 28 March 2003 to 1200Z 29 March 2003 | At H1 airfield in western Iraq, west of the Hadithah Dam and the town of Hadithah |
| Detachment, Headquarters and Headquarters Company, 3rd Battalion, 75th Ranger Regiment | 1835Z 28 March 2003 to 1200Z 29 March 2003 | At H1 airfield in western Iraq, west of the Hadithah Dam and the town of Hadithah |

military operations."[228] Statistics, operations research, and business analysis cannot provide a guaranteed outcome of war – they are the antithesis to it – for as Carl von Clausewitz remarked so brilliantly nearly 200 years ago – the fog and friction of war are not quantifiable.

General Shinseki insisted that the troop deployment for Iraq would require hundreds of thousands of troops and not the fewer than 100,000 purported by Donald Rumsfeld and Paul Wolfowitz in their non-empirical theory of war – minimal troops on the ground and a heavy reliance on technology.[229] By the end of 2004, the war in Iraq had claimed the lives of over 1,500 American servicemen and women, and well over 15,000 wounded. Its cost, through 2004, is in excess of $120 billion. Iraqi casualty estimates range from 15,000 to over 100,000 killed, not including any wounded. Troop deployments are well in excess of 150,000, not including allies or friendly Iraqi forces.[230] Many of the troops deployed are National Guardsmen or Reservists – most are not properly trained for combat operations. The easy victory predicted was only achieved in the early phases of the war. Iraq to date has become the Vietnam of our generation.

All Americans ought to visit these prescient words by retired general and former President Dwight D. Eisenhower during his farewell address on January 17, 1961: "In the councils of government, we must guard against the acquisition of unwarranted influence, whether sought or unsought, by the military-industrial complex."

Rangers during a religious ceremony in Iraq. There are many Christians in the battalions. (75th RR)

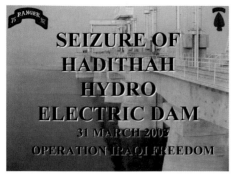

1

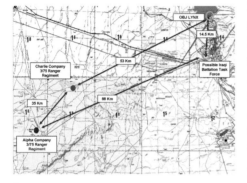

2

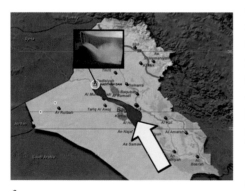

3

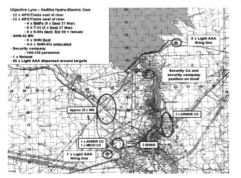

4

# THE BATTLE OF HADITHAH DAM

*Written from the perspective of a platoon sergeant,*
*B Company, 3rd Battalion, 75th Ranger Regiment.*

On the evening of March 31, 2003, B Company, 3rd Ranger Battalion, seized Objective Lynx, Hadithah Dam, on the Euphrates River in west-central Iraq in order to ensure that the dam was not prepared for destruction by enemy forces and to provide a line of communication across the river for follow-on forces (slide 1).

My account of this operation will begin Saturday, March 29, two nights prior at an airstrip in western Iraq that had been seized three days earlier by A Company, 3rd Ranger Battalion. My platoon infiltrated into Iraq with the mission to disrupt enemy activity at key locations. The company planned a 48–72 hour load for the upcoming mission and planned on operating in and out of the airfield. We established an assembly area within A Company's perimeter and began priorities of work until the next cover of darkness. Just before sunset on March 30, B Company departed to link up with a platoon from C Company, 3rd Ranger Battalion, and continued movement to a Rest Over Day (ROD) site (slide 2).

We arrived just as the sun came up in our ROD site. We quickly established security and camouflaged our vehicles. This is when I found out we had just received a FRAGO, a short order to change our mission. Intelligence reported the Iraqi military had begun an IO, or information operations, campaign stating that the United States may bomb Hadithah Dam. The concern was if the Iraqi military were to blow the dam it would flood southern Iraq and cause a huge humanitarian catastrophe and major problems for 3rd Infantry Division pushing north to Baghdad (slide 3).

B Company received the mission to seize Objective Lynx and ensure the dam wasn't rigged to be blown. The enemy situation stated that the dam was heavily guarded with 100–200 enemy personnel, numerous armored vehicles including T-55 battle-tanks and in excess of 50 antiaircraft artillery (AAA) pieces (slide 4). Within four hours, the commander established a plan, issued his orders, and conducted rehearsals. First Platoon's mission would be to secure the western flank to allow 2nd Platoon to clear the inside of the dam and allow our breachers to confirm the dam was not at risk (slides 5 & 6). As the sun began to set on March 31, we departed our ROD site for a 31km infiltration to Objective Lynx.

About 2km out from the objective, one of our ground mobility vehicles (GMVs) broke all four bolts on the steering

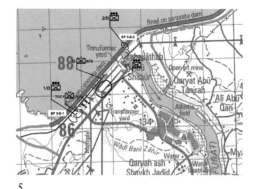

5

## TASK ORGANIZATION

| B/3/75 | BN CONTROL |
|---|---|
| 1/B/3/75 | TOC II (-) |
| 2/B/3/75 | -BN XO |
| 3/C/3/75 | -BN FS NCO |
| 2 X SNP TM | -BN ETAC |
| 3 X | -BN COMMO CHIEF |
| 2 x 120mm | -RTO |
| BN CCP (-) | |
| BN CSM | |

Vehicles:
14 GMVS
4 CARGO HMMWVs

| Major Weapon Systems: | |
|---|---|
| 7 X M2 | |
| 7 X MK19 | **TOTAL - 154** |
| 7 X JAVELIN CLU | |

*75 RANGER*

6

7

8

box, disabling it. The mechanic, with the assistance of four of my men, removed one bolt from three other vehicles, removed the threaded portions left inside the frame on the broken vehicle, and replaced three of the four bolts in 22 minutes.

The company moved in and, surprisingly, began the assault with no resistance. I was tasked to lead one of my squads with a M-240 machine-gun team up a small hill and clear a building on the left-hand side of the road. This was about the time the entire company realized we had already driven up about one-third of the way of the dam. The 3rd Platoon, C Company, were turning their vehicles around to find an alternate route to the main power facility at the base of the dam. My 1st Squad detained two guards immediately after arriving in position. I began to move my 3rd Squad with control of the M-240 to the crest of the small hill to begin clearance of the building. As soon as I got into position, the complexity of this mission became apparent.

We looked around and could see the entire dam structure. Until this point we didn't appreciate how large it actually was. The top of the hill, where our platoon's objective was, did not have the single structure we had planned for. It had 12 large concrete buildings. I immediately requested a second squad from the platoon leader to assist in clearing the objective. I ordered the 3rd Squad leader to begin clearing the first building and establish a foothold on what was the key terrain on the dam. The gun team leader set his machine gun in to isolate the remainder of the hilltop. Third squad began clearing the building; it was empty with all doors locked. We had most of this building cleared when 3rd Platoon, C Company, made contact down in front of the main dam structure at the power relay station (slide 7). It was a short engagement – some small arms and a couple .50-caliber bursts.

Once the building was secure, I moved the M-240 team to the roof to cover our movement. I began alternating the two squads between buildings across the objective. Everything was still pretty quiet at this point. Once we cleared to the far side of the hill to allow heavy guns to secure the southern flank, I called for all the vehicles to move up. It was about this time when my second squad moved across a 25m open area to a huge concrete mural of Saddam Hussein, when everything went crazy (slide 8).

All at once the lip of the hill opened up with small-arms, machine-gun and rocket-propelled grenade (RPG) fire. I believe the Iraqis had moved out of the buildings to survivability positions at the base of the hill when they heard the coalition aircraft and were moving back up the hill when they began firing. Further out, more than ten different

9

10

11

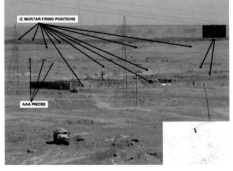

12

mortar tubes began engaging the hill almost simultaneously. Amazingly, no one had been injured.

The platoon immediately returned fire and began what turned out to be a four-hour battle to push the enemy forces back at least 1,200m out of RPG range. The platoon leader and radio-telephone operator (RTO) began using aerial platforms to engage the mortar positions that now had our position zeroed in on. I quickly got all of our vehicles up in positions where the heavy gunners were barely over the crest of the down slope in front of us and began engaging the close-in mortars with the MK-19 40mm grenade launcher and .50-caliber machine guns (slide 9).

About 30 minutes into the firefight, my 1st Squad leader came up to me and pointed out an island he thought had a mortar tube firing on our location (slide 10). As we both looked, the tube fired. I could not believe it. Due to the range of the island I secured an anti-tank gunner with a Javelin missile and he used it to engage the position that was dug into the island with rocks piled up in the front. We received no additional fire from the island. About 45 minutes later, we serviced the island with two 1000lb bombs just to ensure destruction.

As this fight continued into the morning light, it continued to show more and more problems. The vast, open desert in front of us was nothing but interconnected trench lines and bunkers for as far as the eye could see. Approximately one hour after daylight, one of our battle positions reported a GMV heading south away from the dam. We called and received a report that it was Tactical Operations Center (TOC) 2's vehicle moving to link up with 3rd Platoon, C Company. They had missed their turn, pushed down the road and had turned back to find it. On their way back they had stopped in front of two buildings that were in front of us. We began to refer to these buildings as CAS 1 (slide 11) and 2 (slide 12).

The Iraqi forces continued to maneuver to and from these buildings. We had more than 20 bombs dropped on both buildings by the end of the first three days. Immediately after the bombing stopped, one of the personnel had gotten out of the vehicle, turned around, and began running back to the vehicle and directly behind them from our location they were engulfed in small-arms fire. They sped back to our location. The problem was that the road headed directly back towards us, so we were unable to return fire to help them get out of there without possibly hitting them. As soon as the road turned right, three of my positions opened fire on the ambush site.

My medics quickly moved to where the vehicle was coming up, expecting the worst. When the vehicle made it to our location it had been hit pretty bad and was crippled. The engine

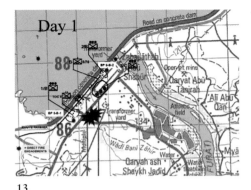

13

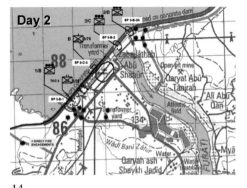

14

15

16

was barely running and the transmission was severely leaking fluid. One Ranger, who had moved out of the back seat, was hit four times in his back plate, but was uninjured. The driver had taken a round through the vehicle which had hit his right foot. The two remaining Rangers in the vehicle were unscathed. As the medics began treating the driver, we moved the vehicle up into a firing position before it was deadlined.

As the day continued, the enemy forces would consolidate in groups of 50 to 100 approximately 6–8km from our location. We used 120mm mortars to prevent their consolidation. They would then disperse and come at us in human waves of 10–15 personnel. This continued throughout the next few days. During the evening we began to fortify our positions as we tracked their movements with our thermal imagers. The first attempt the Iraqis made to move into our location that night was – I am sure – quite a shock to them. As they approached with weapons slung over their shoulders as if they were just going to walk right up on us, we engaged them about 600 to 800m out. After this, they never tried to walk right up to us again – they maneuvered. These human waves continued for the next two days, with at least one of our positions in contact every 30 minutes. These attempts made establishing a sleep plan very difficult.

Meanwhile, 2nd Platoon, B Company, had finished clearing the dam complex by mid-afternoon of Day One. They had two attempts to assault their battle point (BP) by vehicles. By the end of the first day the company had captured nine enemy prisoners of war and detained 25 civilian dam workers. During one of the attempts by the Iraqi forces on the eastern side of the dam, an Iraqi soldier was shot and rolled down one level of the earthen portion of the dam. Second Platoon was under intense fire from an Iraqi 23mm machine gun in the low ground to the front (slide 13). The 2nd Platoon sergeant and regimental command sergeant major maneuvered down the front of the dam under direct fire to assist the wounded Iraqi soldier. Unfortunately, this Iraqi soldier passed away a few hours later. Another wounded Iraqi had lost his lower jaw due to a .50-caliber bullet and our medics were able to save his life.

During the evening and throughout Day Two, the Iraqi forces continued attempts to retake the dam. Around mid-afternoon, one of my positions reported a kayak heading towards us. The gunner gave the kayak a warning shot. The Iraqi continued to head for a small island to the northwest of the dam. The kayak departed after about three to four hours and headed for the shore. Believing this was obviously an attempt to gather intelligence, the platoon leader and I decided to have the kayak engaged. With one burst from the .50-caliber, my gunner sank the kayak and the Iraqi began to swim

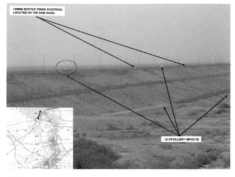

17

18

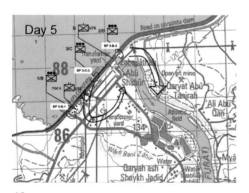

19

20

in to the shore. I dispatched a fire team to secure the prisoner and search him. The Iraqi was uninjured and did in fact have a number of sketches of our positions (slide 14).

Day Three, around 1100 hours, an artillery shot came from the southwest impacting about midway down the dam on the front slope. This caused great concern since until this we had only received mortar fire. The men were smart enough to get a back azimuth to the artillery shot and our Air Force combat controller began calling in aircraft to find the gun tubes. We received an additional two rounds that day from what we had determined to be 155mm artillery. As the artillery rounds came in on the dam, all the Iraqi forces moved to the city in the south, Hadithah proper. They then loaded approximately 20–30 vehicles and fled further south. This was the last attempt by dismounts to assault our locations. We began to plan for the Iraqis to use a combined arms attack after slamming us for a few days with artillery.

At first light on Day Four, the 2nd Platoon, B Company battle point (BP) began to be hit hard by an artillery gun from the southwest, an artillery gun from the northeast, and heavy mortars from just south of the dam. Within minutes, all three pieces had zeroed in on 2nd Platoon and forced it to withdraw back inside the dam. The Air Force controllers quickly brought in aircraft and located and engaged the artillery piece to the north. We never received any more fire from the north.

My platoon began engaging the mortar position to the south with heavy guns, and we were quickly answered with artillery directed at our location. Within minutes the artillery was impacting inside our perimeter. Throughout the day, artillery continued non-stop, moving from one BP to another up and down the dam. During this barrage, we received more than 100 artillery rounds within the perimeter and more than 350 on the entire dam.

Later on Day Four, as our position was getting hit, an artillery round went over our position and impacted directly in front of the mortar firing position. I remember seeing one of the mortarmen flying up in the air from behind a concrete wall the mortar crew were using for cover. I immediately called for my driver and medics to prepare to move down to their location. The mortar crew began motioning for a medic and we expected the worst as we moved out. The Iraqi observers must have seen this also as they began firing additional rounds right on the mortar's location.

I stopped our GMV about 50m short of the location and had everyone dismount. The driver and gunner moved away from the vehicle up against the concrete wall. My medic, another Ranger we had cross-trained to augment the platoon

21

22

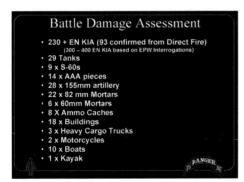

### Battle Damage Assessment

- 230 + EN KIA (93 confirmed from Direct Fire)
  (300 – 400 EN KIA based on EPW Interrogations)
- 29 Tanks
- 9 x S-60s
- 14 x AAA pieces
- 28 x 155mm artillery
- 22 x 82 mm Mortars
- 6 x 60mm Mortars
- 8 X Ammo Caches
- 18 x Buildings
- 3 x Heavy Cargo Trucks
- 2 x Motorcycles
- 10 x Boats
- 1 x Kayak

RANGER

23

medic, and myself moved up to the wounded Ranger. The two medics began to work on the Ranger who was unconscious and severely wounded. Every time we heard the artillery fire, we would hug the ground and a split-second later it would impact somewhere around us. My medics quickly stabilized him and we loaded up on a cargo vehicle to move him to the battalion casualty collection point at the center of the dam.

Once we moved from the mortar's position, the artillery began focusing on the hill where my platoon was located. I got my medics and immediately moved back to the BP. On the way back, I got a report from the platoon leader that one of the vehicles had nearly taken a direct hit. The Iraqis had a position dug out to protect a vehicle. We used this to our advantage by pulling one of our gun jeeps into it. My weapons squad leader, a heavy gunner and forward observer manned this position. A 155mm artillery round impacted right on the top lip of the position. The over pressure of the round blew all three men to the rear of the hole and moved the GMV about 2ft sideways. All three were extremely shaken up and a little hard of hearing, but other than that just fine (slides 15 to 18).

On Day Five we didn't receive any artillery rounds. We all believed the aircraft had finally found the gun pieces firing on our location. Around mid-day the platoon received orders to move down and clear CAS 1 and 2 (slide 19). Once we arrived at the location it was obvious why the Iraqi forces continued to move to these buildings. Inside we found 12 rooms (slide 20) containing arms and ammunition caches (slide 21). Due to the amount of weapons and ammunition we were only able to clear one of the two buildings that day.

On Day Six the artillery began again. This was extremely demoralizing to the platoon. We all were extremely worn out. Dodging artillery rounds all day and digging all night was really starting to take its toll. Only a few rounds came in this day. Later in the afternoon, we received two M-1 Abrams tanks. They would pass over the dam and continue operations to the north (slide 22). We also received orders to prepare for B Company, 3rd Platoon, to relieve us that evening and we'd fly back to the airfield we left seven days prior.

After the week was over, B Company had used direct fires, 120mm mortars, and various aerial platforms to kill or capture more than 230 enemy, 29 T-55 tanks, three heavy cargo trucks, two motorcycles, nine S-60s, 4 ZSU 23-2s, 14 various AAA pieces, 28 155mm artillery pieces, 22 82mm mortars, six 60mm mortars, eight ammo caches, ten military boats, and one kayak (slide 23).

As the US is engaged in a war against terrorism, nebulous in geography and time, the 75th Ranger Regiment continues its tradition as an excellent fighting unit. Very little information is available to the general public, and the Regiment probably is the closest to maintaining the dignity of "The Quiet Professionals."

(Slides courtesy of the 75th Ranger Regiment)

Combat actions at night around the Hadithah Dam. (75th RR)

The regular Army benefits greatly from former Rangers as they elevate the standards throughout their new units, and this common bond can only help the Army at large while waging a permanent war. As the Regiment analyzes its combat operations in Afghanistan, Iraq, and elsewhere, it behoves the decision makers to remember that Rangers are an elite light infantry unit that also does Special Operations missions (see page 257 for an official description of the modern Rangers). During Operation *Iraqi Freedom*, Strykers, 19-ton wheeled, armored vehicles available in a variety of configurations, were added to the Ranger Table of Equipment and Organization:

> The 75th Ranger Regiment will receive Stryker vehicles based on a validated Request for Forces based on the requirement for this capability in support of current operations in the CENTCOM AOR. This RFF is not associated with any other mobility initiative. Key to ARSOF unit capabilities is the ability to move operationally and tactically in an urban environment while being protected from mines, small arms, and blast/fragmentation threats. The Stryker vehicles bring unique capabilities to the battlefield which are not found with current mobility platforms. To conduct operations more effectively in the CENTCOM AOR, the 75th Ranger Regiment requires this capability immediately. The 75th Ranger Regiment will receive Stryker vehicles in third quarter, FY05. They will receive 6 vehicles first and shortly thereafter, 10.[231]

The addition of Stryker vehicles to the Ranger TOE may be a positive element, but surely it changes the intrinsic nature of Rangers – soldiers ranging on foot. Also, the Stryker has been heavily criticized for its overall poor performance in combat.

The most damning of all aspects of the Stryker report (see opposite) is not so much the quality of the actual vehicle but the sycophancy and groupthink throughout the Army. As Rangers progress in their careers one can only hope

# THE STRYKER PROGRAM

*Stryker Brigades versus the Reality of War: Fundamental Concerns About The Stryker's Capabilities in Combat When Evaluated Against Lessons Learned from the Conflicts in Afghanistan, Iraq And Elsewhere.* Written by Victor O'Reilly for Congressman Jim Saxton, D21 Aug 22, 2003.

## Executive summary: key facts about the Stryker

There are the strongest arguments for the Stryker program to be curtailed and the Stryker Mobile Gun System to be cancelled. The Stryker Concept reflected the vision of the previous Chief of Staff of the Army, General Shinseki, who argued that the existing force was either too heavy to be deployed quickly (tanks and infantry fighting vehicles) or too light to be effective (airborne or light infantry). He attempted to solve a deployment problem by buying more hardware instead of restructuring the force to make it more agile, and by talking to the Air Force and the Navy about lift. The 8 wheeled Stryker Light Armored Vehicle was selected (under debatable circumstances) to be the basis of a series of 6 Stryker Brigades targeted at global deployability in 96 hours. Stryker Brigades were to be the US Army's intervention force pending the development of a new force, the Objective Force, which was to be fielded in 2008 (an optimistic figure). General Shinseki's vision came from a period during which the future of the Army seemed to lie, in the main, with peacekeeping – Operations Other Than War. He did not change it after 9/11 although the requirements changed dramatically because the United States was, is, and will continue, to be at war. The Stryker program was supposed to be, in effect, "off the shelf." They could not stand up to heavy machine gun fire and were still entirely vulnerable to Rocket Propelled Grenades – RPGs – and the weight of their increased armor impacted negatively on speed, reliability and off road performance. The disturbingly high operational costs are not included. All Strykers are too heavy to be C-130 deployed for any tactically useful distance. None can roll-on, roll-off combat ready. All are vulnerable to RPG fire. All are particularly vulnerable in the wheel well area. All are proving to be extraordinarily expensive both to buy and operate. The process has been corrupted to an extent which is terrifying and it raises the most serious questions about the integrity of the Army Leadership, the effectiveness of civilian defense control and the oversight role of Congress. The purchase of the wrong items or flawed vehicles is likely to result in the unnecessary death of American soldiers. A seriously disturbing aspect of this entire Stryker exercise has been the lack of intellectual honesty and moral courage that has pervaded the process. The Army Leadership made it clear from the beginning that this project was going to be pushed through regardless of any data indicating it should be stopped, or careers would be destroyed. That is exactly what has happened. Negative findings have been suppressed or massaged; negative reports have been re-written; concerned Army personnel have been broken or cowed; worried contractors have been dismissed or paid off; simulations have been re-run with more positive assumptions; tests have been rigged. The reality is that the Army culture, where the Officer Corps is concerned, interprets "Duty," in the main, as unquestioning loyalty to one's immediate superior, regardless of the issue. There is the right way, the wrong way, and your superior's way. There is a strong careerist element as well based upon the practical fact that an officer's promotion is virtually entirely dependent upon the good graces of one's superior and a zero defect mentality. In short, the system dictates, or can dictate, near mindless obedience; and precedent over decades shows again and again the unpleasant consequences of questioning the Army culture. This system has fostered careerism amongst Army officers to an extent where it is becoming detrimental to National Security. "An officer of the US Army will sacrifice his life for his country, but rarely his career." In practice, since the Army is not a democracy, a great deal depends upon the tone set from the top – or, what is known as the "Command Climate." If the Command Climate crushes dissent, dissent will be crushed. Such was the case when General Shinseki was Chief of Staff.

Rangers and fighting vehicles don't mix – might as well join the Stryker Brigade. (75th RR)

that they will recall the Articles of War and the Ranger Creed. When Rangers start to question orders or circumstances that may challenge them ethically, these age-old guidelines ought to prevail – for every man must hold himself accountable for his actions.

## RANGER CASUALTIES IN OPERATION *IRAQI FREEDOM*

| Soldier | Battalion | Date KIA |
| --- | --- | --- |
| SSG Nino D. Livaudais | 3-75 | 3-Apr-03 |
| SPC Ryan P. Long | 3-75 | 3-Apr-03 |
| CPT Russell B. Rippetoe | 3-75 | 3-Apr-03 |
| CPL Andrew F. Chris | 3-75 | 26-Jun-03 |
| SGT Timothy M. Conneway | 3-75 | 28-Jun-03 |
| PFC Nathan E. Stahl | 2-75 | 21-Sep-04 |

A Stryker, soon to join the 75th Ranger Regiment. (DoD)

# THE MODERN 75TH RANGER REGIMENT

As we move into the 2000s, how is the modern 75th Ranger Regiment structured, trained, and equipped to deal with the new world order? Here is the official view from the USASOC Public Affairs Office:

The 75th Ranger Regiment is the U.S. Army's premier light infantry unit.

With a primary mission of planning and conducting special missions in support of U.S. policy and objectives, the regiment is headquartered at Fort Benning, Georgia, and consists of three Ranger battalions. The geographically dispersed battalions are:

1st Battalion, 75th Ranger Regiment – Hunter Army Airfield, Georgia

2nd Battalion, 75th Ranger Regiment – Fort Lewis, Washington

3rd Battalion, 75th Ranger Regiment – Fort Benning, Georgia

Since the advent of the Global War on Terrorism after Sept. 11, 2001, the 75th Ranger Regiment has conducted combat operations with almost every deployed special operations, conventional, and coalition force during both Operation *Enduring Freedom* and Operation *Iraqi Freedom*. The Ranger Regiment participated in a wide range of diverse operations that included airborne and air assaults into Afghanistan and Iraq, mounted infiltrations behind enemy lines, complex urban raids and rescue operations. Throughout this period, the Rangers have continued to train in the United States and overseas in order to prepare for future no-notice worldwide combat deployments. The regiment also continues to recruit, assess, and train the next generation of Rangers and Ranger leadership. More than 70 percent of current Rangers have conducted multiple combat deployments and many are on their fifth or sixth rotation since 9/11 in support of America's efforts during the Global War on Terrorism.

3/75 Rangers conducting training exercise at Fort Benning, Georgia. Note the lane markers/target identifiers. (Author's collection/Camera 1)

3/75 Rangers conducting training exercise at Fort Benning, Georgia. Note the lane markers/target identifiers. (Author's collection/Camera 1)

Typical Ranger missions are:

*Airfield Seizures*
To establish air-landing capabilities for follow-on forces
To establish trans-load sites for precious cargo
Conducted using both special operations and light infantry tactics, techniques, and procedures

*Special Operations Raids*
Strategic assets – high payoff targets
Destruction or recovery missions
Routinely operate within restrictive rules of engagement

*Urban Combat*
Advanced Military Operations in Urban Terrain techniques and breaching capability
Precision marksmanship
Advanced combatives (hand-to-hand) training

The Army maintains the Regiment at a high level of readiness. Each battalion can deploy anywhere in the world with 18 hours notice. Because of the importance the Army places on the 75th Ranger Regiment, it must possess a number of capabilities. These capabilities include:

*Direct Action Force*
Provides critical light infantry capability and skills
Routinely complements or supports other Special Operations Forces capable of executing platoon through Regimental-sized operations
Resourced for exceptional proficiency, experience, and readiness

*Specialized Infantry*

Increased lethality and agility due to habitual Special Operations Forces relationships and specialized equipment

Resourced and trained for deep, precise operations on hardened targets – in one cycle of darkness

Rapidly deployable and ready strike force

To maintain readiness, Rangers train constantly. Their training encompasses arctic, jungle, desert, and mountain operations, as well as amphibious instruction. The training philosophy of the 75th Ranger Regiment dictates the unit's high state of readiness. The philosophy includes performance-oriented training, emphasizing tough standards and a focus on realism and live-fire exercises while concentrating on basics and safety. Training at night, during adverse weather or on difficult terrain, multiplies the benefits received by Rangers in training events. Throughout their training, Rangers are taught to expect the unexpected.

All officers and enlisted soldiers in the Regiment are four-time volunteers – for the Army, for airborne training, for the 75th Ranger Regiment and for the U.S. Army Ranger Course. Those volunteers selected for the 75th Ranger Regiment must meet tough physical, mental, and moral criteria. All commissioned officers and combat-arms noncommissioned officers must be airborne- and Ranger-qualified and must have demonstrated a proficiency in the duty position for which they are seeking.

Upon assignment to the Regiment, both officers and senior NCOs attend the Ranger Orientation Program to help integrate them into the Regiment. ROP familiarizes them with Regimental policies, standing operating procedures, the commander's intent and Ranger standards. Junior enlisted soldiers assigned to the Regiment must first go through the

3/75th Rangers preparing to enter a hostile area during a training exercise at Fort Benning, Georgia. (Author's collection/Camera 1)

Ranger Indoctrination Program. RIP assesses Rangers on their physical qualifications and emphasizes basic Regimental standards. Soldiers must pass ROP or RIP to remain assigned to the 75th Ranger Regiment.

Junior enlisted soldiers assigned to the regiment who are not yet Ranger-qualified must attend a Pre-Ranger course, which ensures they are administratively, physically, and mentally prepared before they attend the U.S. Army Ranger Course. The result of this demanding selection and training process is a Ranger who can lead effectively despite enormous mental and physical challenges.

Each Ranger battalion is authorized 660 personnel, which are assigned to three rifle companies and a headquarters company.

Ranger battalions are equipped to be light, deployable, and high-tech. Equipment designers develop state-of-the-art warfighting equipment for the Regiment. Rangers are often the first in the Army to test and field many new systems.

Current Ranger weapons and equipment include:
M-4 Carbine
84mm Ranger Antitank Weapons System
60mm, 81mm and 120mm Mortars
M240B Machine Guns
Mark 19 RP MM Grenade Launcher
Javelin Portable missile system
Unmanned Aerial Vehicles
Ground Mobility Vehicle-R
Tactical Internet
All-terrain Vehicles
Grenadier Brat

When Soldiers leave the Ranger Regiment for other Army units, they take with them enhanced combat skills, expertise in joint, special operations and conventional arenas as well as new tactics, techniques, and procedures.

3/75 Rangers conducting training at Fort Benning. Note the sandbags around the vehicle. (Author's collection/Camera 1)

# FUTURE WARRIORS

The 75th Ranger Regiment has high standards and leads the way at home and on foreign soil. It draws its soldiers from a wide cross-section of America and like most combat arms tends to be homogenous, but no matter the racial or religious background of its Rangers, one is reminded by Jonathan Kirsh in *God Against the Gods* of the Crusaders who after years of toil returned to Europe from the Holy Land and brought with them the remnants of Classical Greece and Rome that had been preserved by Islam.[232] Some Crusaders were learning from the Arabs and the Jews and from this fruitful and positive cooperation a new intellectual life was born in Europe. May the Rangers who return from their overseas duties lead the way...

# Appendices

## Appendix A
*(Source: G. Rottman, US Army Rangers & LRRP Units 1942–87)*

| KOREAN WAR ERA RANGER INFANTRY COMPANIES (AIRBORNE) | | | | | |
|---|---|---|---|---|---|
| **Ranger Co.** | **Activation Date** | **Subordination** | **Duty Station** | **Inactivation Date** | **Inactivation Station** |
| 1st | Oct 28, 1950 | 2nd Infantry Division | Korea | Aug 1, 1951 | Chaun-ni, Korea |
| 2nd | Oct 28, 1950 | 7th Infantry Division & 187th ARCT | Korea | Aug 1, 1951 | Chiach'on-ni, Korea |
| 3rd | Oct 28, 1950 | 3rd Infantry Division & I Corps | Korea | Aug 1, 1951 | Ch'orwan, Korea |
| 4th | Oct 28, 1950 | 1st Cavalry Division* | Korea | Aug 1, 1951 | Chunchon, Korea |
| 5th | Nov 20, 1950 | 25th Infantry Division & I Corps | Korea | Aug 1, 1951 | Chajang-ni, Korea |
| 6th | Nov 20, 1950 | Seventh Army | Kitzingen, West Germany | Dec 1, 1951 | Kitzingen, West Germany |
| 7th | Nov 20, 1950 | Ranger Training Command | Fort Benning, Georgia | Nov 5, 1951 | Fort Benning, Georgia |
| 8th | Nov 20, 1950 | 24th Infantry Division and IX Corps | Korea | Aug 1, 1951 | Sanyang-ni, Korea |
| 9th | Jan 5, 1951 | Third Army | Fort Benning, Georgia | Nov 5, 1951 | Fort Benning, Georgia |
| 10th | Jan 5, 1951 | 45th Infantry Division | Camp Polk, Louisiana | Oct 15, 1951 | Camp Crawford, Japan |
| 11th | Jan 5, 1951 | 40th Infantry Division | Camp Cooke, California | Sept 21, 1951 | Camp Matsushima, Japan |
| 12th | Feb 1, 1951 | Fifth Army | Camp Atterbury, Indiana | Oct 27, 1951 | Camp Atterbury, Indiana |
| 13th | Feb 1, 1951 | Second Army | Camp Pickett, Virginia | Oct 15, 1951 | Camp Pickett, Virginia |
| 14th | Feb 27, 1951 | 4th Infantry Division | Camp Carson, Colorado | Oct 27, 1951 | Camp Carson, Colorado |
| 15th | Feb 27, 1951 | Third Army | Fort Benning, Georgia | Nov 5, 1951 | Fort Benning, Georgia |
| 8213th AU (Ranger) | Aug 25, 1950 | 25th Infantry Division & IX Corps | Korea | Mar 28, 1951 | Chajong-ni, Korea |
| 8245th AU (Raider) | Nov 12, 1950 | 3rd Infantry Division & 8227th Army Unit | Korea | Apr 1, 1951 | Sollim, Korea |

*The 4th was a "floater" and sometimes attached to the 187th Abn Regimental Combat Team, 1st Marine Division, IX Corps.

# Appendix B

## LONG RANGE PATROL COMPANIES AND DETACHMENTS

| Unit Designation | Major Command | Period of Service |
| --- | --- | --- |
| Co. E, 20th Infantry (LRP) | I Field Force Vietnam | Sep 25, 1961–Feb 1, 1969 |
| Co. F, 51st Infantry (LRP) | II Field Force Vietnam | Sep 25, 1961–Feb 1, 1969 |
| Co. D, 151st Infantry (LRP) | II Field Force Vietnam | Dec 26, 1968–Feb 1, 1969 |
| Co. E, 50th Infantry (LRP) | 9th Infantry Division | Dec 20, 1967–Feb 1, 1969 |
| Co. F, 50th Infantry (LRP) | 25th Infantry Division | Dec 20, 1967–Feb 1, 1969 |
| Co. E, 51st Infantry (LRP) | 23rd Infantry Division | Dec 12, 1968–Feb 1, 1969 |
| Co. E, 52nd Infantry (LRP) | 1st Cavalry Division | Dec 20, 1967–Feb 1, 1969 |
| Co. F, 52nd Infantry (LRP) | 1st Infantry Division | Dec 20, 1967–Feb 1, 1969 |
| Co. E, 58th Infantry (LRP) | 4th Infantry Division | Dec 20, 1967–Feb 1, 1969 |
| Co. F, 58th Infantry (LRP) | 101st Airmobile Division | Nov 10, 1968–Feb 1, 1969 |
| 71st Infantry Detachment (LRP) | 199th Infantry Brigade | Dec 20, 1967–Feb 1, 1969 |
| 74th Infantry Detachment (LRP) | 173rd Airborne Brigade | Dec 20, 1967–Feb 1, 1969 |
| 78th Infantry Detachment (LRP) | 3rd Brigade, 82nd Abn, Division | Dec 15, 1968–Feb 1, 1969 |
| 79th Infantry Detachment (LRP) | 1st Brigade, 5th Mech Division | Dec 15, 1968–Feb 1, 1969 |

## RANGER COMPANIES

| Unit Designation | Major Command | Period of Service |
| --- | --- | --- |
| Co. C (Ranger), 75th Infantry | I Field Force Vietnam | Feb 1, 1969–Oct 25, 1971 |
| Co. D (Ranger), 151st Infantry | II Field Force Vietnam | Feb 1, 1969–Nov 20, 1969 |
| Co. D (Ranger), 75th Infantry | II Field Force Vietnam | Nov 20, 1969–Apr 10, 1970 |
| Co. E (Ranger), 75th Infantry | 9th Infantry Division | Feb 1, 1969–Oct 12, 1970 |
| Co. F (Ranger), 75th Infantry | 25th Infantry Division | Feb 1, 1969–Mar 15, 1971 |
| Co. G (Ranger), 75th Infantry | 23rd Infantry Division | Feb 1, 1969–Oct 1, 1911 |
| Co. H (Ranger), 75th Infantry | 1st Cavalry Division | Feb 1, 1969–Aug 15, 1972 |
| Co. I (Ranger), 75th Infantry | 1st Infantry Division | Feb 1, 1969–Apr 7, 1970 |
| Co. K (Ranger), 75th Infantry | 4th Infantry Division | Feb 1, 1969–Dec 10, 1970 |
| Co. L (Ranger), 75th Infantry | 101st Airborne Division | Feb 1, 1969–Dec 26, 1970 |
| Co. M (Ranger), 75th Infantry | 199th Infantry Brigade | Feb 1, 1969–Oct 12, 1970 |
| Co. N (Ranger), 75th Infantry | 173rd Airborne Brigade | Feb 1, 1969–Aug 25, 1971 |
| Co. O (Ranger), 75th Infantry | 3rd Brigade, 82nd Abn, Division | Feb 1, 1969–Nov 20, 1969 |
| Co. P (Ranger), 75th Infantry | 1st Brigade, 5th Mech Division | Feb 1, 1969–Aug 31, 1971 |

264 • SHADOW WARRIORS

## LONG RANGE RECONNAISSANCE PATROL (PROVISIONAL)

| Unit Designation | Period of Service |
|---|---|
| 173rd Airborne Brigade (Separate) LRRP (Provisional) | May 1965–Dec 20, 1967 |
| 1st Brigade, 101st Airborne Division, LRRP (Provisional) | July 1965–Jan 10, 1968 |
| 1st Infantry Division, LRRP (Provisional) | Oct 1965–Dec 20, 1967 |
| 1st Cavalry Division, LRRP (Provisional) | Sep 1965–Dec 20, 1967 |
| 4th Infantry Division, LRRP (Provisional) | Sep 1966–Dec 20, 1967 |
| 9th Infantry Division, LRRP (Provisional) | Jan 1967–Dec 20, 1967 |
| 25th Infantry Division, LRRP (Provisional) | Mar 1966–Dec 20, 1967 |
| 196th Infantry Brigade (Separate), LRRP (Provisional) | Jan 1967–Dec 20, 1967 |

# Appendix C

# 75th Ranger Regiment Lineage and Honors

*(Source: US Army, 1 July 2003)*

Organized 3 October 1943 in the Army of the United States in the China-Burma-India
Theater of Operations as the 5307th Composite Unit (Provisional)

Consolidated 10 August 1944 with the 475th Infantry (constituted 25 May 1944 in the
Army of the United States) and consolidated unit designated as the 475th Infantry

Inactivated 1 July 1945 in China

Redesignated 21 June 1954 as the 75th Infantry

Allotted 26 October 1954 to the Regular Army

Activated 20 November 1954 on Okinawa

Inactivated 21 March 1956 on Okinawa

Reorganized 1 January 1969 as a parent regiment under the Combat Arms Regimental
System

Reorganized 1 July 1984 with Headquarters at Fort Benning, Georgia

Consolidated 3 February 1986 with the former 1st Ranger Infantry Battalion, 2d Infantry
Battalion, and 3d, 4th, 5th, and 6th Ranger Infantry Battalions (see ANNEXES 1–6)
and consolidated unit redesignated as the 75th Ranger Regiment; concurrently
withdrawn from the Combat Arms Regimental System and reorganized under the
United States Army Regimental System


ANNEX 1

Constituted 27 May 1942 in the Army of the United States as the 1st Ranger Battalion

Activated 19 June 1942 in Northern Ireland

Redesignated 1 August 1943 as the 1st Ranger Infantry Battalion

Disbanded 15 August 1944

Reconstituted 1 September 1948 in the Army of the United States as the 1st Infantry
Battalion and activated in the Canal Zone

Inactivated 4 January 1950 in the Canal Zone

After 4 January 1950 organic elements underwent changes as follows:

Company A redesignated 25 October 1950 as the 1st Ranger Infantry Company and
allotted to the Regular Army; activated 28 October 1950 at Fort Benning, Georgia;
inactivated 1 August 1951 in Korea

Company B redesignated 2 November 1950 as the 5th Ranger Infantry Company and
allotted to the Regular Army; activated 20 November 1950 at Fort Benning, Georgia;
inactivated 1 August 1951 in Korea

Battalion redesignated 24 November 1952 as the 1st Ranger Infantry Battalion and
allotted to the Regular Army (former organic elements concurrently redesignated)

Consolidated 15 April 1960 with the 1st Special Service Force (activated 9 July 1942),
the 2d Infantry Battalion (see ANNEX 2), and the 3d, 4th, 5th, and 6th Ranger
Infantry Battalions (see ANNEXES 3, 4, 5, and 6) to form the 1st Special Forces, a
parent regiment under the Combat Arms Regimental System

Former 1st Ranger Infantry Battalion, 2d Infantry Battalion, and 3d, 4th, 5th, and 6th Ranger Infantry Battalions withdrawn 3 February 1986, consolidated with the 75th Infantry, and consolidated unit redesignated as the 75th Ranger Regiment (remainder of the 1st Special Forces – hereafter separate lineage)

ANNEX 2

Constituted 11 March 1943 in the Army of the United States as the 2d Ranger Battalion

Activated 1 April 1943 at Camp Forrest, Tennessee

Redesignated 1 August 1943 as the 2d Ranger Infantry Battalion

Inactivated 23 October 1945 at Camp Patrick Henry, Virginia

Redesignated 29 July 1949 as the 2d Infantry Battalion (Companies E and F concurrently disbanded)

Activated 15 September 1949 in the Canal Zone

Inactivated 4 January 1950 in the Canal Zone

After 4 January 1950 organic elements underwent changes as follows:

Company A redesignated 25 October 1950 as the 2d Ranger Infantry Company and allotted to the Regular Army; activated 28 October 1950 at Fort Benning, Georgia; inactivated 1 August 1951 in Korea

Company B redesignated 2 November 1950 as the 6th Ranger Infantry Company and allotted to the Regular Army; activated 20 November 1950 at Fort Benning, Georgia; inactivated 1 December 1951 in Germany

Company C redesignated 27 February 1951 as the 14th Ranger Infantry Company, allotted to the Regular Army, and activated at Fort Benning, Georgia; inactivated 27 October 1951 at Camp Carson, Colorado

Company D redesignated 27 February 1951 as the 15th Ranger Infantry Company, allotted to the Regular Army, and activated at Fort Benning, Georgia; inactivated 5 November 1951 at Fort Benning, Georgia

Company E reconstituted 15 December 1950 in the Regular Army as the 9th Ranger Infantry Company; activated 5 January 1951 at Fort Benning, Georgia; inactivated 5 November 1951 at Fort Benning, Georgia

Company F reconstituted 15 December 1950 in the Regular Army as the 10th Ranger Infantry Company; activated 5 January 1951 at Fort Benning, Georgia; inactivated 15 September 1951 in Japan

Battalion redesignated 24 November 1952 as the 2d Ranger Infantry Battalion and allotted to the Regular Army (former organic elements concurrently redesignated)

Redesignated 14 June 1955 as the 2d Infantry Battalion

Activated 1 July 1955 in Iceland

Inactivated 11 March 1960 at Fort Hamilton, New York

ANNEX 3

Constituted 21 July 1943 in the Army of the United States as the 3d Ranger Battalion; concurrently consolidated with the 3d Ranger Battalion (Provisional) (organized 21 May 1943 in North Africa) and consolidated unit designated as the 3d Ranger Battalion

Redesignated 1 August 1943 as the 3d Ranger Infantry Battalion

Disbanded 15 August 1944

After 15 August 1944 organic elements underwent changes as follows:

Company A reconstituted 25 October 1950 in the Regular Army as the 3d Ranger
Infantry Company; activated 28 October 1950 at Fort Benning, Georgia; inactivated
1 August 1951 in Korea

Company B reconstituted 2 November 1950 in the Regular Army as the 7th Ranger
Infantry Company; activated 20 November 1950 at Fort Benning, Georgia;
inactivated 5 November 1951 at Fort Benning, Georgia

Company C reconstituted 15 December 1950 in the Regular Army as the 11th Ranger
Infantry Company; activated 5 January 1951 at Fort Benning, Georgia; inactivated
21 September 1951 in Japan

Company D reconstituted 15 December 1950 in the Regular Army as the 12th Ranger
Infantry Company; activated 1 February 1951 at Fort Benning, Georgia; inactivated
27 October 1951 at Camp Atterbury, Indiana

Company E reconstituted 15 December 1950 in the Regular Army as the 13th Ranger
Infantry Company; activated 1 February 1951 at Fort Benning, Georgia; inactivated
15 October 1951 at Camp Pickett, Virginia

Battalion reconstituted 24 November 1952 in the Regular Army as the 3d Ranger
Infantry Battalion (former organic elements concurrently redesignated)

ANNEX 4

Constituted 21 July 1943 in the Army of the United States as the 4th Ranger Battalion;
concurrently consolidated with the 4th Ranger Battalion (Provisional) (organized 29
May 1943 in North Africa) and consolidated unit designated as the 4th Ranger Battalion

Redesignated 1 August 1943 at the 4th Ranger Infantry Battalion

Disbanded 24 October 1944 at Camp Butner, North Carolina

After 24 October 1944 organic elements underwent changes as follows:

Company A reconstituted 25 October 1950 in the Regular Army as the 4th Ranger
Infantry Company; activated 28 October 1950 at Fort Benning, Georgia; inactivated
1 August 1951 in Korea

Company B reconstituted 2 November 1950 in the Regular Army as the 8th Ranger
Infantry Company; activated 20 November 1950 at Fort Benning, Georgia;
inactivated 1 August 1951 in Korea

Battalion reconstituted 24 November 1952 in the Regular Army as the 4th Ranger
Infantry Battalion (former organic elements concurrently redesignated)

ANNEX 5

Constituted 21 July 1943 in the Army of the United States as the 5th Ranger Battalion

Redesignated 1 August 1943 as the 5th Ranger Infantry Battalion

Activated 1 September 1943 at Camp Forrest, Tennessee

Inactivated 22 October 1945 at Camp Myles Standish, Massachusetts

ANNEX 6

Constituted 16 December 1940 in the Regular Army as the 98th Field Artillery Battalion

Activated 20 January 1941 at Fort Lewis, Washington

Converted and redesignated 26 September 1944 as the 6th Ranger Infantry Battalion

Inactivated 30 December 1945 in Japan

## 75th Ranger Regiment Honors
*Campaign Participation Credit*

World War II: Algeria–French Morocco (with arrowhead); Tunisia; Sicily (with arrowhead); Naples–Foggia (with arrowhead); Anzio (with arrowhead); Rome–Arno; Normandy (with arrowhead); Northern France; Rhineland; Ardennes–Alsace; Central Europe; New Guinea; Leyte (with arrowhead); Luzon; India–Burma; Central Burma

Vietnam: Advisory; Defense; Counteroffensive; Counteroffensive, Phase II; Counteroffensive, Phase III; Tet Counteroffensive; Counteroffensive, Phase IV; Counteroffensive, Phase V; Counteroffensive, Phase VI; Tet 69/Counteroffensive; Summer–Fall 1969; Winter–Spring 1970; Sanctuary Counteroffensive; Counteroffensive, Phase VII; Consolidation I; Consolidation II; Cease-Fire

Armed Forces Expeditions: Grenada (with arrowhead); Panama (with arrowhead)

*Decorations*

Presidential Unit Citation (Army) for EL GUETTAR
Presidential Unit Citation (Army) for SALERNO
Presidential Unit Citation (Army) for POINTE DU HOE
Presidential Unit Citation (Army) for SAAR RIVER AREA
Presidential Unit Citation (Army) for MYITKYINA
Presidential Unit Citation (Army) for VIETNAM 1966–1968
Valorous Unit Award for VIETNAM – II CORPS AREA
Valorous Unit Award for BINH DUONG PROVINCE
Valorous Unit Award for III CORPS AREA 1969
Valorous Unit Award for FISH HOOK
Valorous Unit Award for III CORPS AREA 1971
Valorous Unit Award for THUA THIEN – QUANG TRI
Valorous Unit Award for GRENADA
Valorous Unit Award for MOGADISHU
Meritorious Unit Commendation (Army) for VIETNAM 1968
Meritorious Unit Commendation (Army) for VIETNAM 1969
Meritorious Unit Commendation (Army) for VIETNAM 1969–1970
Meritorious Unit Commendation (Army) for PACIFIC AREA

## 1st Battalion, 75th Ranger Regiment Lineage

Organized 3 October 1943 in the Army of the United States in the China-Burma-India Theater of Operations as an element of the 5307th Composite Unit (Provisional)

Consolidated 10 August 1944 with Company C, 475th Infantry (constituted 25 May 1944 in the Army of the United States), and consolidated unit designated as Company C, 475th Infantry

Inactivated 1 July 1945 in China
Redesignated 21 June 1954 as Company C, 75th Infantry
Allotted 26 October 1954 to the Regular Army
Activated 20 November 1954 on Okinawa
Inactivated 21 March 1956 on Okinawa
Activated 1 February 1969 in Vietnam
Inactivated 25 October 1971 in Vietnam

Redesignated 31 January 1974 as Headquarters and Headquarters Company, 1st Battalion, 75th Infantry, and activated at Fort Stewart, Georgia (organic elements concurrently constituted and activated)

Headquarters and Headquarters Company consolidated 3 February 1986 with former Company A, 1st Ranger Infantry Battalion (see ANNEX); 1st Battalion, 75th Infantry, concurrently redesignated as the 1st Battalion, 75th Ranger Regiment

ANNEX

Constituted 27 May 1942 in the Army of the United States as Company A, 1st Ranger Battalion

Activated 19 June 1942 in Northern Ireland

Redesignated 1 August 1943 as Company A, 1st Ranger Infantry Battalion

Disbanded 15 August 1944

Reconstituted 1 September 1948 in the Army of the United States as Company A, 1st Infantry Battalion, and activated in the Canal Zone

Inactivated 4 January 1950 in the Canal Zone

Redesignated 25 October 1950 as the 1st Ranger Infantry Company and allotted to the Regular Army

Activated 28 October 1950 at Fort Benning, Georgia

Inactivated 1 August 1951 in Korea

Redesignated 24 November 1952 as Company A, 1st Ranger Infantry Battalion

Consolidated 15 April 1960 with the 1st Company, 1st Battalion, 1st Regiment, 1st Special Service Force (activated 9 July 1942), and consolidated unit redesignated as Headquarters and Headquarters Company, 7th Special Forces Group, 1st Special Forces

Consolidated 6 June 1960 with Headquarters and Headquarters Company, 77th Special Forces Group (activated 25 September 1953), and consolidated unit designated as Headquarters and Headquarters Company, 7th Special Forces Group, 1st Special Forces (organic elements constituted 20 May 1960 and activated 6 June 1960)

Former Company A, 1st Ranger Infantry Battalion, withdrawn 3 February 1986, consolidated with Headquarters and Headquarters Company, 1st Battalion, 75th Infantry, and consolidated unit redesignated as Headquarters and Headquarters Company, 1st Battalion, 75th Ranger Regiment (remainder of 7th Special Forces Group, 1st Special Forces – hereafter separate lineage)

## 1st Battalion, 75th Ranger Regiment Honors

*Campaign Participation Credit*

World War II: Algeria–French Morocco (with arrowhead); Tunisia; Sicily (with arrowhead); Naples–Foggia (with arrowhead); Anzio (with arrowhead); Rome–Arno; Normandy (with arrowhead); Northern France; Rhineland; Ardennes–Alsace; Central Europe; New Guinea; Leyte (with arrowhead); Luzon; India–Burma; Central Burma

Korean War: CCF Intervention; First UN Counteroffensive; CCF Spring Offensive; UN Summer–Fall Offensive

Vietnam: Counteroffensive, Phase VI; Tet 69/Counteroffensive; Summer–Fall 1969; Winter–Spring 1970; Sanctuary Counteroffensive; Counteroffensive, Phase VII; Consolidation I

Armed Forces Expeditions: Grenada (with arrowhead); Panama (with arrowhead)

*Decorations*

Presidential Unit Citation (Army) for EL GUETTAR

Presidential Unit Citation (Army) for SALERNO

Presidential Unit Citation (Army) for POINTE DU HOE

Presidential Unit Citation (Army) for SAAR RIVER AREA

Presidential Unit Citation (Army) for MYITKYINA

Presidential Unit Citation (Army) for CHIPYONG-NI

Presidential Unit Citation (Army) for HONGCHON

Valorous Unit Award for VIETNAM – II CORPS AREA

Valorous Unit Award for GRENADA

Republic of Vietnam Cross of Gallantry with Palm for VIETNAM 1969–1970

Republic of Vietnam Cross of Gallantry with Palm for VIETNAM 1970–1971

Republic of Vietnam Civil Action Honor Medal, First Class for VIETNAM 1969–1971

## 2d Battalion, 75th Ranger Regiment Lineage

Organized 3 October 1943 in the Army of the United States in the China-Burma-India Theater of Operations as an element of the 5307th Composite Unit (Provisional)

Consolidated 10 August 1944 with Company H, 475th Infantry (constituted 25 May 1944 in the Army of the United States), and consolidated unit designated as Company H, 475th Infantry

Inactivated 1 July 1945 in China

Redesignated 21 June 1954 as Company H, 75th Infantry

Allotted 26 October 1954 to the Regular Army

Activated 20 November 1954 on Okinawa

Inactivated 21 March 1956 on Okinawa

Activated 1 February 1969 in Victnam

Inactivated 15 August 1972 in Vietnam

Redesignated 1 October 1974 as Headquarters and Headquarters Company, 2d Battalion, 75th Infantry, and activated at Fort Lewis, Washington (organic elements concurrently constituted and activated)

Headquarters and Headquarters Company consolidated 3 February 1986 with former Company A, 2d Infantry Battalion (see ANNEX); 2d Battalion, 75th Infantry, concurrently redesignated as the 2d Battalion, 75th Ranger Regiment

ANNEX

Constituted 11 March 1943 in the Army of the United States as Company A, 2d Ranger Battalion

Activated 1 April 1943 at Camp Forrest, Tennessee

Redesignated 1 August 1943 as Company A, 2d Ranger Infantry Battalion

Inactivated 23 October 1945 at Camp Patrick Henry, Virginia

Redesignated 29 July 1949 as Company A, 2d Infantry Battalion

Activated 15 September 1949 in the Canal Zone

Inactivated 4 January 1950 in the Canal Zone

Redesignated 25 October 1950 as the 2d Ranger Infantry Company and allotted to the Regular Army

Activated 28 October 1950 at Fort Benning, Georgia

Inactivated 1 August 1951 in Korea

Redesignated 24 November 1952 as Company A, 2d Ranger Infantry Battalion

Redesignated 14 June 1955 as Company A, 2d Infantry Battalion

Activated 1 July 1955 in Iceland

Inactivated 11 March 1960 at Fort Hamilton, New York

Consolidated 15 April 1960 with the 4th Company, 2d Battalion, 1st Regiment, 1st Special Service Force (activated 9 July 1942), and consolidated unit redesignated as Headquarters and Headquarters Company, 10th Special Forces Group, 1st Special Forces

Consolidated 30 September 1960 with Headquarters and Headquarters Company, 10th Special Forces Group (activated 11 June 1952), and consolidated unit designated as Headquarters and Headquarters Company, 10th Special Forces Group, 1st Special Forces (organic elements concurrently constituted and activated 20 March 1961)

Former Company A, 2d Infantry Battalion, withdrawn 3 February 1986, consolidated with Headquarters and Headquarters Company, 2d Battalion, 75th Infantry, and consolidated unit redesignated as Headquarters and Headquarters Company, 2d Battalion, 75th Ranger Regiment (remainder of 10th Special Forces Group, 1st Special Forces – hereafter separate lineage)

## 2d Battalion, 75th Ranger Regiment Honors

*Campaign Participation Credit*

World War II: Algeria–French Morocco (with arrowhead); Tunisia; Sicily (with arrowhead); Naples–Foggia (with arrowhead); Anzio (with arrowhead); Rome–Arno; Normandy (with arrowhead); Northern France; Rhineland; Ardennes–Alsace; Central Europe; New Guinea; Leyte (with arrowhead); Luzon; India–Burma; Central Burma

Korean War: CCF Intervention; First UN Counteroffensive (with arrowhead); CCF Spring Offensive; UN Summer–Fall Offensive

Vietnam: Counteroffensive, Phase VI; Tet 69/Counteroffensive; Summer–Fall 1969; Winter–Spring 1970; Sanctuary Counteroffensive; Counteroffensive, Phase VII; Consolidation I; Consolidation II; Cease-Fire

Armed Forces Expeditions: Grenada (with arrowhead); Panama (with arrowhead)

*Decorations*

Presidential Unit Citation (Army) for EL GUETTAR

Presidential Unit Citation (Army) for SALERNO

Presidential Unit Citation (Army) for POINTE DU HOE

Presidential Unit Citation (Army) for SAAR RIVER AREA

Presidential Unit Citation (Army) for MYITKYINA

Valorous Unit Award for III CORPS AREA 1969

Valorous Unit Award for FISH HOOK

Valorous Unit Award for III CORPS AREA 1971

Valorous Unit Award for GRENADA

French Croix de Guerre with Silver-Gilt Star, World War II for POINTE DU HOE

Republic of Vietnam Cross of Gallantry with Palm for VIETNAM 1969

Republic of Vietnam Cross of Gallantry with Palm for VIETNAM 1969–1970

Republic of Vietnam Cross of Gallantry with Palm for VIETNAM 1970–1971

Republic of Vietnam Cross of Gallantry with Palm for VIETNAM 1971–1972

Republic of Vietnam Civil Action Honor Medal, First Class for VIETNAM 1969–1970

## 3d Battalion, 75th Ranger Regiment Lineage

Organized 3 October 1943 in the Army of the United States in the China-Burma-India Theater of Operations as an element of the 5307th Composite Unit (Provisional)

Consolidated 10 August 1944 with Company F, 475th Infantry (constituted 25 May 1944 in the Army of the United States), and consolidated unit designated as Company F, 475th Infantry

Inactivated 1 July 1945 in China

Redesignated 21 June 1954 as Company F, 75th Infantry

Allotted 26 October 1954 to the Regular Army

Activated 20 November 1954 on Okinawa

Inactivated 21 March 1956 on Okinawa

Activated 1 February 1969 in Vietnam

Inactivated 15 March 1971 in Vietnam

Redesignated 2 October 1984 as Headquarters and Headquarters Company, 3d Battalion, 75th Infantry, and activated at Fort Benning, Georgia (organic elements concurrently constituted and activated)

Headquarters and Headquarters Company consolidated 3 February 1986 with former Company A, 3d Ranger Infantry Battalion (see ANNEX); 3d Battalion, 75th Infantry, concurrently redesignated as the 3d Battalion, 75th Ranger Regiment

ANNEX

Constituted 21 July 1943 in the Army of the United States as Company A, 3d Ranger Battalion; concurrently consolidated with Company A, 3d Ranger Battalion (Provisional) (organized 21 May 1943 in North Africa), and consolidated unit designated as Company A, 3d Ranger Battalion

Redesignated 1 August 1943 as Company A, 3d Ranger Infantry Battalion

Disbanded 15 August 1944

Reconstituted 25 October 1950 in the Regular Army as the 3d Ranger Infantry Company

Activated 28 October at Fort Benning, Georgia

Inactivated 1 August 1951 in Korea

Redesignated 24 November 1952 as Company A, 3d Ranger Infantry Battalion

Consolidated 15 April 1960 with the 1st Company, 1st Battalion, 2d Regiment, 1st Special Service Force (activated 9 July 1942), and consolidated unit redesignated as Headquarters and Headquarters Company, 13th Special Forces Group, 1st Special Forces

Withdrawn 14 December 1960 from the Regular Army and allotted to the Army Reserve (organic elements concurrently constituted)

Group activated 1 March 1961 with Headquarters at Jacksonville, Florida

Headquarters and Headquarters Company inactivated 15 April 1963 at Jacksonville, Florida (organic elements inactivated 21 January 1966)

Former Company A, 3d Ranger Infantry Battalion, withdrawn 3 February 1986, consolidated with Headquarters and Headquarters Company, 3d Battalion, 75th Infantry, and consolidated unit redesignated as Headquarters and Headquarters Company, 3d Battalion, 75th Ranger Regiment (remainder of 13th Special Forces Group, 1st Special Forces – hereafter separate lineage)

# 3d Battalion, 75th Ranger Regiment Honors

*Campaign Participation Credit*

World War II: Algeria–French Morocco (with arrowhead); Tunisia; Sicily (with arrowhead); Naples–Foggia (with arrowhead); Anzio (with arrowhead); Rome–Arno; Normandy (with arrowhead); Northern France; Rhineland; Ardennes–Alsace; Central Europe; New Guinea; Leyte (with arrowhead); Luzon; India–Burma; Central Burma

Korean War: First UN Counteroffensive; CCF Spring Offensive; UN Summer–Fall Offensive

Vietnam: Counteroffensive, Phase VI; Tet 69/Counteroffensive; Summer–Fall 1969; Winter–Spring 1970; Sanctuary Counteroffensive; Counteroffensive, Phase VII

Armed Forces Expeditions: Panama (with arrowhead)

*Decorations*

Presidential Unit Citation (Army) for EL GUETTAR

Presidential Unit Citation (Army) for SALERNO

Presidential Unit Citation (Army) for POINTE DU HOE

Presidential Unit Citation (Army) for SAAR RIVER AREA

Presidential Unit Citation (Army) for MYITKYINA

Valorous Unit Award for BINH DUONG PROVINCE

Valorous Unit Award for MOGADISHU

Republic of Korea Presidential Unit Citation for UIJONGBU CORRIDOR

Republic of Korea Presidential Unit Citation for KOREA 1951

Republic of Vietnam Cross of Gallantry with Palm for VIETNAM 1969

Republic of Vietnam Cross of Gallantry with Palm for VIETNAM 1969–1970

Republic of Vietnam Civil Action Honor Medal, First Class for VIETNAM 1969–1970

## Appendix D

# Ranger Citations – Operation *Enduring Freedom*

## AWARDS AND CRITERIA FOR EACH

Courtesy of the Department of Defense

### Silver Star

For gallantry in action. The required gallantry, while of a lesser degree than that required for the award of the Medal of Honor or Distinguished Service Cross, must, nevertheless, have been performed with marked distinction.

### Bronze Star Medal with "V" device

For acts of heroism not involving participating in aerial flight, which are of lesser degree than required for the award of the Silver Star.

### Bronze Star Medal

For meritorious service or achievement, not involving participation in aerial flight. Awards may be made to recognize single acts of merit or meritorious service. The required achievement or service, while of lesser degree than that required for the award of Legion of Merit, must nevertheless have been meritorious and accomplished with distinction.

## CITATIONS

Courtesy of the 75th Ranger Regiment

The President of the United States of America, authorized by an Act of Congress, July 9, 1918, has awarded the

### Silver Star

STAFF SERGEANT ARIN K. CANON
UNITED STATES ARMY
FOR GALLANTRY:
in action against the enemy during the period of 3 March 2002 to 4 March 2002, in support of Operation Enduring Freedom. Staff Sergeant Canon's valorous actions while in direct contact with enemy forces and in the face of extreme duress during the successful rescue of Special Operators contributed immeasurably to the success of the mission and to the saving of additional lives. Staff Sergeant Canon led the support element during the initial assault on an enemy fortified position. His leadership was instrumental in suppressing the objective and protecting the assault enemy. Immediately following this action, he coordinated the defense of the entire objective, placing personnel and key weapon systems that enabled the platoon to defeat two enemy counterattacks. The gallantry displayed by Staff Sergeant Canon during 18 hours of combat is in keeping with the highest standards of valor. Through his distinctive accomplishments, Staff Sergeant Canon reflected credit upon himself, the United States Army, and the Department of Defense.

The President of the United States of America, authorized by Executive Order, 24 August 1962 has awarded the

## Bronze Star with "V" device
SPECIALIST CHRIS M. CUNNINGHAM
UNITED STATES ARMY
FOR EXCEPTIONALLY MERITORIOUS SERVICE:
while serving as a squad automatic weapon gunner during Operation Enduring Freedom. Specialist Cunningham's valorous actions, in particular during a battle on 4 March 2002, contributed immeasurably to the tremendous success of a Task Force. Specialist Cunningham was an integral member of the assault force that attacked a fortified enemy position to relieve the pressure on Chalk 1, who had been fighting the enemy for over two hours. Specialist Cunningham was instrumental in providing security for the aid and litter teams and facilitated the consolidation of all casualties to a safe area. The gallantry displayed by Specialist Cunningham during 18 hours of combat is in keeping with the highest standards for valor. Specialist Cunningham's accomplishments reflect great credit upon him, this command and the United States Army.

The President of the United States of America, authorized by Executive Order, 24 August 1962 has awarded the

## Bronze Star with "V" device
SPECIALIST OSCAR J. ESCANO
UNITED STATES ARMY
FOR EXCEPTIONALLY MERITORIOUS SERVICE:
while serving as a M203 gunner during Operation Enduring Freedom. Specialist Escano's valorous actions, in particular during a battle on 4 March 2002, contributed immeasurably to the tremendous success of a Task Force. Specialist Escano was an integral member of the assault force that moved over 2 hours through arduous terrain to destroy an enemy fortified position and relieve the pressure on Chalk 1. Additionally, Specialist Escano assisted in providing security for aid and litter teams during two counterattacks by enemy forces. The gallantry displayed by Specialist Escano during 18 hours of combat is in keeping with the highest standards for valor. Specialist Escano's accomplishments reflect great credit upon him, this command and the United States Army.

The President of the United States of America, authorized by Executive Order, 24 August 1962 has awarded the

## Bronze Star with "V" device
SERGEANT PATRICK GEORGE
UNITED STATES ARMY
FOR EXCEPTIONALLY MERITORIOUS SERVICE:
while serving as a team leader during Operation Enduring Freedom. Sergeant George's valorous actions, in particular during a battle on 4 March 2002, contributed immeasurably to the tremendous success of a Task Force. Sergeant George moved for two hours with Chalk 2 over arduous terrain at an extremely high altitude and under enemy fire. Sergeant George led the assault on an enemy fortified position to relieve the enemy

pressure on Chalk 1. Additionally, he played a critical role in securing the objective and consolidating the casualties. The gallantry displayed by Sergeant George during 18 hours of combat is in keeping with the highest standards for valor. Sergeant George's accomplishments reflect great credit upon him, this command and the United States Army.

The President of the United States of America, authorized by Executive Order, 24 August 1962 has awarded the

## Bronze Star with "V" device
PRIVATE FIRST CLASS DAVID B. GILLIAM
UNITED STATES ARMY
FOR EXCEPTIONALLY MERITORIOUS
SERVICE:

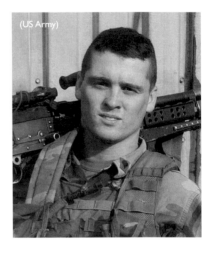

(US Army)

while serving as a M240B machine gunner during Operation Enduring Freedom. Private First Class Gilliam's valorous actions, in particular during a battle on 4 March 2002, contributed immeasurably to the tremendous success of a Task Force. Private First Class Gilliam immediately exited the aircraft and suppressed the enemy. He was able to suppress the fortified enemy bunker while a four-man element assaulted the position. Private First Class Gilliam played an integral role in the entire operation by providing suppression on enemy positions to facilitate the capture of the high ground, the defeat of two enemy counterattacks and the consolidation of friendly wounded. His gallantry during 18 hours of combat is in keeping with the highest standards for valor. Private First Class Gilliam's accomplishments reflect great credit upon him, this command and the United States Army.

The President of the United States of America, authorized by Executive Order, 24 August 1962 has awarded the

## Bronze Star with "V" device
SPECIALIST RANDY J. PAZDER
UNITED STATES ARMY
FOR EXCEPTIONALLY MERITORIOUS
SERVICE:

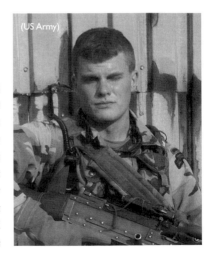

(US Army)

while serving as a M240B machine gunner during Operation Enduring Freedom. Specialist Pazder's valorous actions, in particular during a battle on 4 March 2002, contributed immeasurably to the tremendous success of a Task Force. Specialist Pazder moved with Chalk 2 over arduous terrain at an extremely high altitude and under heavy enemy fire to relieve enemy pressure on Chalk 1. Specialist Pazder suppressed the enemy fortified and facilitated the assault on the enemy position. The gallantry displayed by Specialist Pazder during 18 hours of combat is in keeping with the highest standards for valor. Through his distinctive accomplishments, Specialist Pazder's actions reflect great credit upon him, this command and the United States Army.

The President of the United States of America, authorized by Executive Order, 24 August 1962 has awarded the

## Bronze Star with "V" device
SPECIALIST JONAS O. POLSON
UNITED STATES ARMY
FOR EXCEPTIONALLY MERITORIOUS SERVICE:
while serving as a squad automatic weapon gunner during Operation Enduring Freedom. Specialist Polson's actions, in particular during a battle on 4 March 2002, contributed immeasurably to the tremendous success of a Task Force. Specialist Polson moved under direct and indirect enemy fire to link up with Chalk 1, which was under enemy fire for over two hours. As part of the Assault Force, he moved over arduous terrain at an extremely difficult altitude to provide integral suppressive fires on the enemy. The gallantry displayed by Specialist Polson during 18 hours of combat is in keeping with the highest standards for valor. Specialist Polson's accomplishments reflect great credit upon him, this command and the United States Army.

The President of the United States of America, authorized by Executive Order, 24 August 1962 has awarded the

## Bronze Star with "V" device
SPECIALIST OMAR J. VELA
UNITED STATES ARMY
FOR EXCEPTIONALLY MERITORIOUS
SERVICE:
while serving as an M240B assistant gunner during Operation Enduring Freedom. Specialist Vela's valorous actions, in particular during a battle on 4 March 2002, contributed immeasurably to the tremendous success of a Task Force. Specialist Vela moved with Chalk 2 to relieve the enemy pressure on Chalk 1. The assault force movement culminated in an assault on an enemy fortified position where Specialist Vela was integral to suppressing the enemy. Specialist Vela assisted the

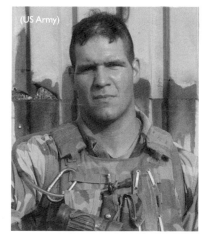

(US Army)

aid and litter teams and provided security under a withering enemy counterattack. The gallantry displayed by Specialist Vela during 18 hours of combat is in keeping with the highest standards for valor. Specialist Vela's accomplishments reflect great credit upon him, this command and the United States Army.

The President of the United States of America, authorized by an Act of Congress, July 9, 1918, has awarded the

## Silver Star
SERGEANT MATTHEW LAFRENZ
UNITED STATES ARMY
FOR GALLANTRY:

in action against the enemy during the period of 3 March 2002 to 4 March 2002, while serving as a Platoon Medic in support of Operation Enduring Freedom. Sergeant LaFrenz's valorous actions while in direct contact with enemy forces and in the face of extreme duress during the successful rescue of Special Operators contributed immeasurably to the success of the mission and to the saving of additional lives. In five separate occasions, Sergeant LaFrenz exposed himself to enemy fire while providing medical support to casualties. Sergeant LaFrenz was able to consolidate all casualties within four hours providing aid to nine casualties in an exhausting frigid environment. The gallantry displayed by Sergeant LaFrenz during 18 hours of combat is in keeping with the highest standards of valor. Through his distinctive accomplishments, Sergeant LaFrenz reflected credit upon himself, the United States Army, and the Department of Defense.

The President of the United States of America, authorized by an Act of Congress, July 9, 1918, has awarded the

## Silver Star
SPECIALIST AARON LANCASTER-TOTTEN
UNITED STATES ARMY
FOR GALLANTRY:

in action against the enemy during the period of 3 March 2002 to 4 March 2002, while serving as a Squad Automatic Weapon Gunner in support of Operation Enduring Freedom. Specialist Lancaster-Totten's valorous actions while in direct contact with enemy forces and in the face of extreme duress during the successful rescue of Special Operators contributed immeasurably to the success of the mission and to the saving of additional lives. While exiting the aircraft, Specialist Lancaster-Totten was severely wounded by shrapnel. With total disregard for his well being, Specialist Lancaster-Totten continued to engage the enemy from a covered and concealed position. His ability to provide suppressive fire enabled the assault element to break contact from the enemy. The gallantry displayed by Specialist Lancaster-Totten during 18 hours of combat is in keeping with the highest standards of valor. Through his distinctive accomplishments, Specialist Lancaster-Totten reflected credit upon himself, the United States Army, and the Department of Defense.

The President of the United States of America, authorized by an Act of Congress, July 9, 1918, has awarded the

## Silver Star
CAPTAIN NATHAN E. SELF
UNITED STATES ARMY
FOR GALLANTRY:

in action against the enemy during the period of 3 March 2002 to 4 March 2002, while serving as a Platoon Leader in support of Operation Enduring Freedom. Captain Self's valorous actions while in direct contact with enemy forces and in the face of extreme duress during the successful rescue of Special Operators contributed immeasurably to the success of the mission and to the saving of additional lives. While exiting the aircraft, Captain Self was severely wounded in the thigh. With total disregard for his well being, he fought to the first covered and concealed position, engaged the enemy with his weapon, gathering remaining combat effective Rangers, and began calling close air support on enemy locations. The gallantry displayed by Captain Self during 18 hours of combat is in keeping with the highest standards of valor. Through his distinctive accomplishments, Captain Self reflected credit upon himself, the United States Army, and the Department of Defense.

The President of the United States of America, authorized by an Act of Congress, July 9, 1918, has awarded the

## Silver Star
SERGEANT ERIC W. STEBNER
UNITED STATES ARMY
FOR GALLANTRY:

in action against the enemy during the period of 3 March 2002 to 4 March 2002, while serving as a Squad Leader in support of Operation Enduring Freedom. Sergeant Stebner's valorous actions while in direct contact with enemy forces and in the face of extreme duress during the successful rescue of Special Operators contributed immeasurably to the success of the mission and to the saving of additional lives. Sergeant Stebner organized an assault against an enemy fortified position. He led all aid and litter teams under withering enemy counterattack fire during consolidation of all casualties. This action took over four hours during which Sergeant Stebner personally exposed himself to enemy fire at least five times in order to save his fellow comrades. Through his distinctive accomplishments, Sergeant Stebner reflected credit upon himself, the United States Army, and the Department of Defense.

The President of the United States of America, authorized by an Act of Congress, July 9, 1918, has awarded the

## Silver Star

SERGEANT JOSHUA J. WALKER
UNITED STATES ARMY
FOR GALLANTRY:

in action against the enemy during the period of 3 March 2002 to 4 March 2002, while serving as a Fire Team Leader in support of Operation Enduring Freedom. Sergeant Walker's valorous actions while in direct contact with enemy forces and in the face of extreme duress during the successful rescue of Special Operators contributed immeasurably to the success of the mission and to the saving of additional lives. Sergeant Walker immediately exited the aircraft and destroyed an enemy soldier who was shooting at his aircraft. He was able to suppress the enemy with his M4 carbine, an M249 squad automatic weapon, and an M203 grenade launcher. Sergeant Walker was an integral part of a four-man assault force that moved up a deep slope, in knee-deep snow, through a hail of enemy fire in broad daylight. The gallantry displayed by Sergeant Walker during 18 hours of combat is in keeping with the highest standards of valor. Through his distinctive accomplishments, Sergeant Walker reflected credit upon himself, the United States Army, and the Department of Defense.

The President of the United States of America, authorized by an Act of Congress, July 9, 1918, has awarded the

## Silver Star

STAFF SERGEANT HARPER WILMOTH
UNITED STATES ARMY
FOR GALLANTRY:

in action against the enemy during the period of 3 March 2002 to 4 March 2002, while serving as a Squad Leader in support of Operation Enduring Freedom. Staff Sergeant Wilmoth's valorous actions while in direct contact with enemy forces and in the face of extreme duress during the successful rescue of Special Operators contributed immeasurably to the success of the mission and to the saving of additional lives. Staff Sergeant Wilmoth coordinated the linkup with Chalk 1 over arduous terrain, at an extremely high altitude, and

(US Army)

under enemy direct and indirect fire. After the linkup, Staff Sergeant Wilmoth organized the assault on an enemy fortified position. The gallantry displayed by Staff Sergeant Wilmoth during 18 hours of combat is in keeping with the highest standards of valor. Through his distinctive accomplishments, Staff Sergeant Wilmoth reflected credit upon himself, the United States Army, and the Department of Defense.

## Appendix E

# Organization and Equipment –
# Introduction to the Ranger Regiment

Ranger Regiment

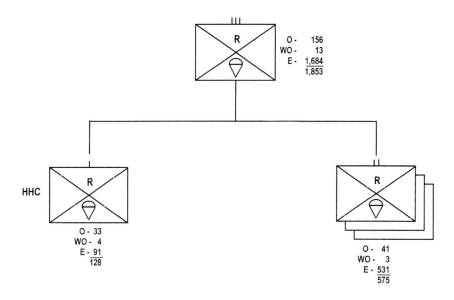

Ranger Regimental HHC

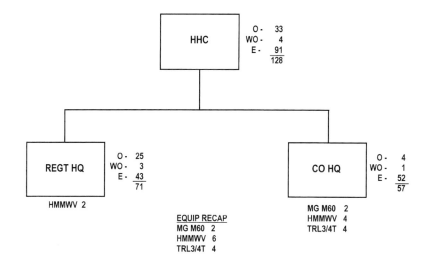

## Ranger regimental staff

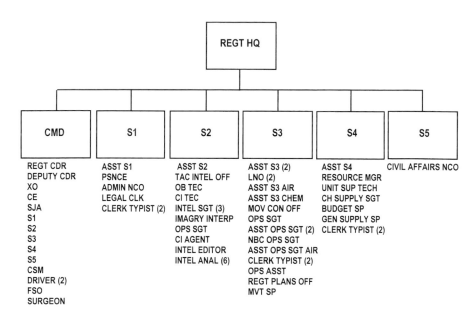

**REGT HQ**

| CMD | S1 | S2 | S3 | S4 | S5 |
|-----|-----|-----|-----|-----|-----|
| REGT CDR | ASST S1 | ASST S2 | ASST S3 (2) | ASST S4 | CIVIL AFFAIRS NCO |
| DEPUTY CDR | PSNCE | TAC INTEL OFF | LNO (2) | RESOURCE MGR | |
| XO | ADMIN NCO | OB TEC | ASST S3 AIR | UNIT SUP TECH | |
| CE | LEGAL CLK | CI TEC | ASST S3 CHEM | CH SUPPLY SGT | |
| SJA | CLERK TYPIST (2) | INTEL SGT (3) | MOV CON OFF | BUDGET SP | |
| S1 | | IMAGRY INTERP | OPS SGT | GEN SUPPLY SP | |
| S2 | | OPS SGT | ASST OPS SGT (2) | CLERK TYPIST (2) | |
| S3 | | CI AGENT | NBC OPS SGT | | |
| S4 | | INTEL EDITOR | ASST OPS SGT AIR | | |
| S5 | | INTEL ANAL (6) | CLERK TYPIST (2) | | |
| CSM | | | OPS ASST | | |
| DRIVER (2) | | | REGT PLANS OFF | | |
| FSO | | | MVT SP | | |
| SURGEON | | | | | |

## Ranger regimental headquarters company

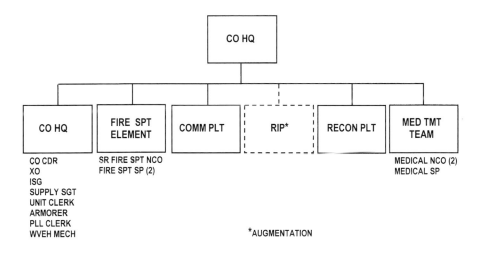

**CO HQ**

| CO HQ | FIRE SPT ELEMENT | COMM PLT | RIP* | RECON PLT | MED TMT TEAM |
|-------|------------------|----------|------|-----------|--------------|
| CO CDR | SR FIRE SPT NCO | | | | MEDICAL NCO (2) |
| XO | FIRE SPT SP (2) | | | | MEDICAL SP |
| ISG | | | | | |
| SUPPLY SGT | | | | | |
| UNIT CLERK | | | | | |
| ARMORER | | | | | |
| PLL CLERK | | | | | |
| WVEH MECH | | | | | |

*AUGMENTATION

# Ranger regimental communications platoon

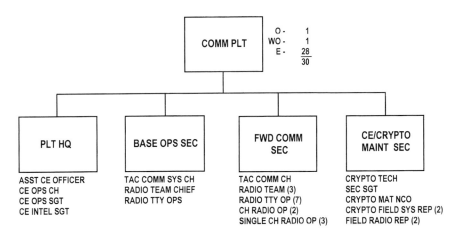

# Ranger regimental reconnaissance platoon

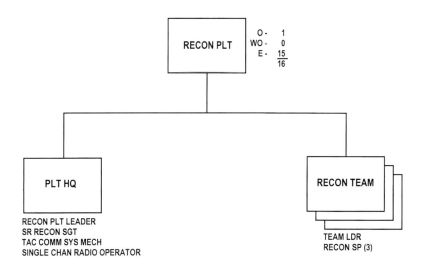

## The Ranger battalion

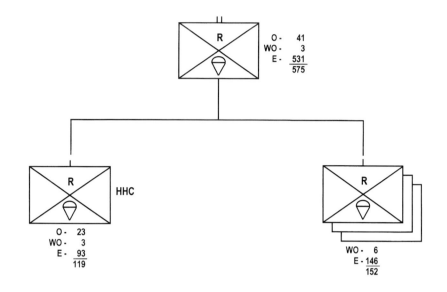

## Ranger battalion HHC

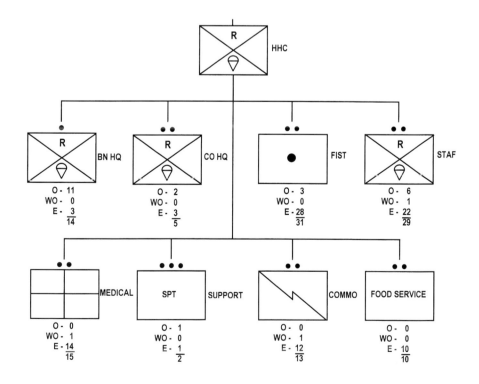

## Ranger rifle company

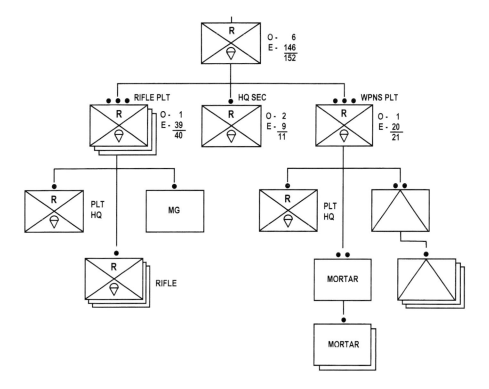

## Ranger rifle platoon

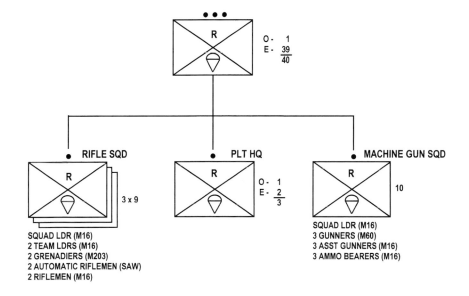

## Ranger weapons platoon

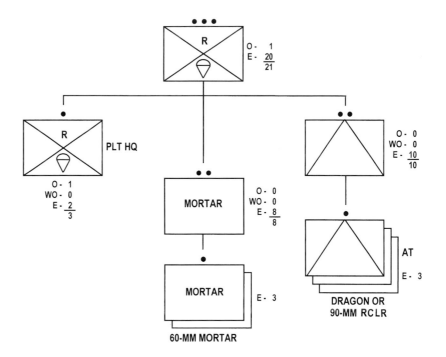

O- 1
E- 20
21

PLT HQ

O- 1
WO- 0
E- 2
3

MORTAR

O- 0
WO- 0
E- 8
8

O- 0
WO- 0
E- 10
10

MORTAR

E- 3

60-MM MORTAR

AT

E- 3

DRAGON OR
90-MM RCLR

# Appendix F

As the regiment consolidated its position within the special operations community, Rangers wanted to avoid being misused in future combat operations and thus created the Ranger Doctrinal Statement, reproduced here courtesy of the 75th Ranger Regiment.

# Ranger Doctrinal Statement

## I. GENERAL
A.   The Ranger Regiment is a light infantry unit composed of highly trained and motivated Airborne/Ranger qualified soldiers. Every effort will be made to insure that the Ranger Regiment is the best military unit in the world. The Regiment will have the highest priority for all types of Army support to insure that it is under no burden which would detract from its outstanding image.

## II. EMPLOYMENT CONSIDERATION
A.   The Ranger Regiment can be rapidly deployed to any location in the world where U.S. military presence is required. The unit can infiltrate by air, land and sea and is capable of independent operations for short periods of time (normally 5 days maximum).
B.   The Ranger Regiment requires an austere Table of Organization and Equipment (TOE) to give it maneuverability and adaptability. All essential equipment must be man portable to facilitate rapid deployment and to provide an operational capability on any terrain or climactic condition. Augmentation and tailoring of Ranger units with non-TOE personnel and equipment should be considered a normal practice for each mission. When required, each battalion must also have the capability for limited duration conventional infantry operations. It should not be misunderstood; the ideal use for Ranger Battalions is in the conduct of swift, daring missions, which are of time sensitive and strategic nature.
C.   The Ranger Regiment must have priority for issue of new equipment. New man portable weapons, lightweight clothing and equipment, improved rations, the latest communications equipment, and STABO devices should be supplied to Ranger units as soon as such items are ready for issue.
D.   The unit training of Ranger Battalions must take advantage of select characteristics of the unit and ensure maximum individual cross-training in all organic weaponry and communications equipment to provide the highest degree of proficiency.
E.   In the accomplishment of their missions, the Ranger units must be trained to conduct small unit landing force/amphibious operations; capable of communicating with and effectively directing the tactical employment of Navy and USAF close air support.

## III. TRAINING
A.   What makes the Ranger Battalions capable of conducting special military operations? Training. The Ranger Battalions train twelve months of the year. Ranger Battalions have no post support requirements; no police or guard details; and no personnel on special duty (SD). Training is continuous except for two, two weeks of block leave each year. During these breaks, two weeks in the summer and two weeks

during the Christmas/New Year holidays, every Ranger is given the opportunity to take leave. Block leave serves as a safety valve to relieve the pressure of the demanding pace of training and also assures the commander that he will have a full complement of personnel for training.

B.    The result of having maximum personnel available for training and few external distractions is numerous off post deployment exercises. The battalions conduct arctic, jungle, desert, and mountain training periodically. Amphibious training is also conducted. The individual Ranger is exposed and challenged by every imaginable type of terrain and climactic conditions. He is tested by elements, his peers, and evaluators.

C.    Emergency Deployment Readiness Exercises (EDREs) and Joint Readiness Exercises complete the wide array of Ranger Training.

D.    All Ranger training is conducted as performance oriented training. Realism in training and a sense of accomplishment are the commander's stated goals. Training isn't conducted that does not improve either individual or collective skills. No single ingredient plays a more important role in honing and developing battlefield skills than stress conditioning. Army Research Institute (ARI) studies corroborate this finding.

   1.  ARI Findings
      a.  Soldiers who have not been trained under stressful conditions do not react well when confronted with antagonistic situations. They tend to compromise critical or sensitive situations.
      b.  The phenomenon of training under stress is that each successive antagonist or stress situation is more easily overcome than the preceding situation.
      c.  Highly motivated soldiers trained under exacting and stressful conditions have proven that they reach relatively higher levels of performance and retain these skills longer than those not exposed to similar conditions.

E.    Complementing the stress conditioning developed during daily training is the stress created by the battalions' intensified readiness posture during the periods of Ranger Ready Force (RRF). The 1st, 2nd, and 3rd Ranger Battalions alternate periods of responsibility for RRF with each other throughout the year. One of the three battalions is poised to respond to an emergency at all times. While the Battalion is on RRF, all of its troops and its equipment can be assembled, loaded and ready for deployment within 18 hours. Each time a no-notice alert is initiated, every Ranger knows that what may appear to be a readiness exercise may actually be a response or a build up to a deployable maintenance level. The unit and every individual Ranger is either ready or he's not. The state of mind that exists in the Ranger Battalion is that we are ready NOW.

F.    There is no secret formula for the success of the 75th Ranger Regiment. It is very simply a matter of:

   1.  Individual soldiers are 4 time volunteers (volunteer for the Army, for Airborne School, the Ranger Regiment, and Ranger School).

   2.  The Ranger Indoctrination Program (RIP) further prepares the soldiers coming to the 75th Ranger Regiment to assume their missions as Rangers. The program was initiated in 1978 at the 1st Ranger Battalion based on a need to continuously receive, integrate, and train new personnel for the battalion regardless of where the battalion might be. RIP is a three-fold program that accomplishes these tasks:

      a.  Administratively in-process newly assigned junior enlisted personnel into the Regiment. Then prepare them physically and mentally for a smooth integration into their respective Ranger Battalion.

b. Familiarize newly assigned leaders with the battalion missions, standards, and staff functions; and prepare them for their leadership position.

c. Prepare Rangers mentally, physically, and academically for attendance to the U.S. Army Ranger School.

3. Officer experience is the highest available. All platoon leaders are (1st) Lieutenants and have served as Platoon leaders. All Company Commanders have had prior successful commands, as has the Battalion Commander. Key Staff Officers have also had prior experience in their respective positions. No Officer serves in the Regiment to learn a job. Rather, he brings successful experience in that position to the Regiment.

4. The maximum number of soldiers are available for training because of the block leave concept.

5. Training is conducted in all environments (arctic, jungle, desert, and amphibious).

6. Excellent training in specialized skills throughout each company (HALO, SCUBA, Sniper, Demo, Pathfinder, etc.).

7. Multiple Emergency Deployment Readiness Exercises (EDRE) each year.

8. Multiple Joint Readiness Training Exercises each year.

9. The capability of the commander to summarily eliminate from the Regiment any soldier who fails to meet Ranger standards.

G. Very simply, highly motivated and experienced soldiers are given all the necessary time and resources with which to train toward clear cut objectives and goals. Unfortunately, the two elements of the highly skilled soldiers and training time are precious commodities, the shortage of these prevent most Army units from achieving Ranger standards.

# IV. OPERATIONAL CONCEPTS

A. The 75th Ranger regiment is a flexible, highly trained, and rapidly deployable light infantry force with specialized skills that enable it to be employed against a variety of targets. Typical Ranger special operations missions include:

1. Raids against high value targets.

2. Recovery of selected personnel and equipment.

3. Interdiction of lines of communications.

4. Attack of command, control, and communications facilities as well as support, combat support, and combat service support facilities.

5. Demonstration of U.S. presence or resolve by participation in military activity which serves U.S. interests.

6. Performance of other combat missions to assist ground command in the accomplishment of the mission.

B. Ranger battalions are rapidly deployable to any location in the world where immediate U.S. military presence is required. The units infiltrate a hostile area by air, land, or sea, and are capable of independent operations when adequately supported. Missions assigned to Ranger battalions should be of such significance that the success of the mission will enhance the Commander-in-Chief's campaign plan.

C. Ranger operations normally take two forms: quick response and deliberate operations.

1. Quick response operations rely on the readiness of Ranger units to achieve mission accomplishment before an enemy can react to the presence of Rangers in the area.

2. Deliberate operations rely on meticulous planning for every phase; detailed reconnaissance and surveillance of target area; deceptive countermeasures and absolute secrecy; through preparation and rehearsals; and decisive action characterized by surprise, speed, precision, and audacity.

3. Both types of mission require that the mission be completed and the unit extracted before the enemy can react in strength.

D.   Command and control of the Ranger Regiment is normally at a level where the unit's capabilities can be fully employed on a world wide and theater wide basis.

1. The command echelon to which the Ranger Regiment is assigned or attached provides necessary resources to employ it properly and must possess or be augmented with an operational staff capable of employing Ranger forces. The staff has immediate access to required national level intelligence, sufficient communications for control, and other support assets such as aircraft or tactical mobility assets.

2. In the NATO environment, Ranger forces are commanded by the Special Operations Force Command and placed in support of the unified command or other forces as directed.

E.   New members of the Ranger Regiment require an extensive training period to develop necessary skills and experience. Because of this extended training period, mission selection should balance the strategic significance of the target against anticipated casualties. If Rangers sustain heavy casualties, it will require extensive time to reconstitute them before they are an operational asset.

F.   Rangers are capable of extraordinary performance based on their exceptional training requirements; however, malemployment stemming from a lack of understanding of their fighting capabilities as fighting units will guarantee their early demise. Inherent in the basic Ranger-type operation is high risk and the potential for a high casualty rate. On the other hand, Rangers should not be committed to impossible tasks or be expected to accomplish tasks in a conventional role which are beyond the capability of a large sized, more heavily armed conventional unit. In the past, Ranger units have disappeared from the force structure when their ranks were depleted because casualties and suitable replacement system was lacking. Therefore, Ranger units must be committed, "appropriate, tactically or strategically significant operations which will produce substantive results."

# Appendix G
# The 75th Ranger Regimental Reconnaissance Detachment

The RRD has three missions: active reconnaissance, surveillance, and direct action. The RRD is fully integrated into Ranger operations and is comprised of proven performers and leaders from the 75th Ranger Regiment. These positions are not open to entry level soldiers.

The RRD was created with the formation of the Regimental Headquarters in 1984. The RRD has participated in six military operations: Operation *Just Cause*, Panama; Operation *Uphold Democracy*, Haiti; Operations *Joint Endeavor*, *Guard and Forge*, Bosnia; Operation *Joint Guardian*, Kosovo; Operation *Enduring Freedom*, Afghanistan; Operation *Iraqi Freedom*, Iraq.

Rangers must complete a 20-week course before assignment as a RRD team member. During the course, they complete military free-fall parachute training, the Survival, Evasion, Rescue and Escape course, advanced training in navigation, infiltration and exfiltration, communications, and imagery. They graduate with medical, reconnaissance, fieldcraft, and expert marksmanship skills. Additionally, RRD students participate in live-fire, fire support, and mission-planning exercises.

## Appendix H

# Global War on Terrorism Medals

Courtesy of the Department of Defense

## EXPEDITIONARY MEDAL

**Obverse**

**Reverse**

1. Description: A bronze color metal disc 1³/₈in. in diameter, charged with a shield adapted from the Great Seal of the United States surmounting two swords hilts to base saltirewise enclosed within a wreath of laurel; overall an eagle, wings displayed, grasping in its claws a serpent. On the reverse, the eagle, serpent and swords from the front of the medal with the encircling inscription "WAR ON TERRORISM EXPEDITIONARY MEDAL."

2. Symbolism: The shield and eagle represent the United States. The swords denote readiness and the resolve to fight international terrorism, which is symbolized by the serpent crushed in the eagle's claws. The wreath denotes honor and achievement.

3. Ribbon: The ribbon is 1³/₈in. wide and consists of the following stripes: ⁵/₃₂in. Bluebird 67117; ³/₃₂in. Old Glory Blue 67178; ¹/₁₆in. White 67101; ³/₃₂in. Old Glory Blue 67178; ¹/₁₆in. Bluebird 67117; ¹/₁₆in Golden Yellow 67104; ¹/₁₆in. Bluebird 67117; ³/₁₆in. Scarlet 67111; ¹/₁₆in. Bluebird 67117; ¹/₁₆in. Golden Yellow 67104; ¹/₁₆in. Bluebird 67117; ³/₃₂in. Old Glory Blue 67178; ¹/₁₆in. White 67101, ³/₃₂in Old Glory Blue 67178; ⁵/₃₂in. Bluebird 67117.

4. Criteria:

a. Authorized to be awarded to soldiers who deploy abroad for service in the Global War on Terrorism Operations on or after 11 September 2001 to a date to be determined. Initial award is limited to soldiers deployed abroad in Operations Enduring Freedom and Iraqi Freedom in the following Department of Defense designated specific geographic areas of eligibility (AOE): Afghanistan, Bahrain, Bulgaria (Bourgas), Crete, Cyprus, Diego Garcia, Djibouti, Egypt, Eritrea, Ethiopia, Iran, Iraq, Israel, Jordan, Kazakhstan, Kenya, Kuwait, Kyrgyzstan, Lebanon, Oman, Pakistan, Philippines, Qatar, Romania (Constanta), Saudia Arabia, Somalia, Syria, Tajikistan, Turkey (East of 35 degrees east longitude), Turkmenistan, United Arab Emirates, Uzbekistan, Yemen, that portion of the Arabian Sea north of 10 degrees north latitude and west of 68 degrees longitude, Bab El Mandeb, Gulf of Aden, Gulf of Aqaba, Gulf of Oman, Gulf of Suez, that portion of the Mediterranean Sea east of 28 degrees east longitude, Persian Gulf, Red Sea, Strait of Hormuz and Suez Canal.

b. To be eligible for the award, a soldier must be assigned, attached or mobilized to a unit participating in designated operations for 30 consecutive days or for 60 nonconsecutive days in the AOE, or meet one of the following criteria: 1) Be engaged in actual combat against the enemy and under circumstances involving grave danger of death or serious bodily injury from enemy action, regardless, of time in the AOE. 2) While participating in the designated operation, regardless of time, is killed or wounded/injured requiring medical evacuation from the AOE. 3) Soldiers participating as a regularly assigned air crew member flying sorties into, out of, within, or over the

AOE in direct support of Operations Enduring Freedom and/or Iraqi Freedom. Each day that one or more sorties are flown in accordance with the criteria shall count as one day towards the 30 consecutive or 60 nonconsecutive day requirement.

c. The medal may be awarded posthumously to any soldier who lost his/her life while, or as a direct result of, participating in Global War on Terrorism Operations, without regard to length of such service, if otherwise eligible.

d. Only one award of the GWOTEM may be authorized for any individual. A message will be transmitted at a later date by the Military Awards Branch to address battle stars/service stars.

5. Components: The following are authorized components and related items:

a. Medal (regular size): MIL-DTL-3943/307. NSN 8455-01-506-7144 for set which includes regular size medal and ribbon bar.

b. Medal (miniature size): MIL-DTL-3943/307. Available commercially.

c. Ribbon: MIL-DTL-11589/579. Available commercially.

d. Lapel Button (ribbon replica): MIL-DTL-11484/295. Available commercially.

6. Background:

a. On 20 September 2002, the Office of the Assistant Secretary of Defense, requested the Institute provide suggested designs. This was accomplished and the design was selected on 7 January 2003. Executive Order 13289, dated 12 March 2003, signed by President Bush, established this medal.

b. In order of precedence, the GWOTEM will be worn before the GWOTSM and both shall directly follow the Kosovo Campaign Medal (KCM) (i.e., KCM, GWOTEM, GWOTSM, KDSM, etc.).

c. Soldiers may receive both the Global War on Terrorism Expeditionary Medal (GWOTEM) and the Global War on Terrorism Service Medal (GWOTSM) if they meet the requirements of both awards; however, the same period of service establishing eligibility for one cannot be used to justify service eligibility for the other.

d. Order of precedence and wear policy for service medals awarded to Army personnel is contained in Army Regulation (AR) 670-1. Policy for awards, approving authority and supply of medals is contained in AR 600-8-22. The policy for display of campaign streamers on guidons/flags and supply of streamers is contained in Chapter 9, 840-10.

# SERVICE MEDAL

**Obverse**

**Reverse**

1. Description: A bronze color metal disc $1^3/_8$in. in diameter, charged with an eagle, wings displayed, with a stylized shield of thirteen vertical bars on its breast and holding in dexter claw an olive branch and in sinister claw three arrows, all in front of a terrestrial globe with the inscription above "WAR ON TERRORISM SERVICE MEDAL." On the reverse is a laurel wreath on a plain field.

2. Symbolism: The eagle and shield, adapted from the Great Seal, represent the United States. They protect the globe above and behind, symbolizing American resolve to combat and overcome global elements of international terrorism. The laurel wreath represents the drive for peace. The three arrows signify vigilance, resolve and peace.

3. Ribbon: The ribbon is $1^3/_8$in. wide and consists of the following stripes: $^5/_{32}$in. Old Glory Blue 67178; $^1/_8$in. Golden Yellow 67104; $^1/_8$in.

Scarlet 67111; ¹/₁₆in. Old Glory Blue 67178; ¹/₁₆in. White 67101; ⁵/₁₆in. Old Glory Blue 67178; ¹/₁₆in. White 67101; ¹/₁₆in. Old Glory Blue 67178; ¹/₈in. Scarlet 67111; ¹/₈in. Golden Yellow 67104; ⁵/₃₂in. Old Glory Blue 67178.

4. Criteria:

a. Authorized to be awarded to soldiers who have participated in or served in support of Global War on Terrorism Operations outside the designated areas of eligibility (AOE) for the Global War on Terrorism Expeditionary Medal, on or after 11 September 2001 to a date to be determined. Initial award of the Global War on Terrorism Service Medal (GWOTSM) will be limited to airport security operations (from 27 September 2001 through 31 May 2002) and soldiers who supported Operations Noble Eagle, Enduring Freedom and Iraqi Freedom.

b. All soldiers on active duty, including Reserve Component soldiers mobilized, or National Guard soldiers activated on or after 11 September 2001 to a date to be determined, having served 30 consecutive days or for 60 nonconsecutive days are authorized the GWOTSM.

c. The medal may be awarded posthumously to any soldier who lost his/her life while, or as a direct result of, participating in Global War on Terrorism Operations, without regard to length of such service, if otherwise eligible.

d. Only one award of the GWOTSM may be authorized for any individual. A message will be transmitted at a later date by the Military Awards Branch to address battle stars/service stars.

5. Components: The following are authorized components and related items:

a. Medal (regular size): MIL-DTL-3943/308. NSN 8455-01-506-7170 for set which includes regular size medal and ribbon bar.

b. Medal (miniature size): MIL-DTL-3943/308. Available commercially.

c. Ribbon: MIL-DTL-11589/580. Available commercially.

d. Lapel Button (ribbon replica): MIL-DTL-11484/296. Available commercially.

6. Background:

a. On 20 September 2002, the Office of the Assistant Secretary of Defense, requested the Institute provide suggested designs. This was accomplished and the design was selected on 7 January 2003. Executive Order 13289, dated 12 March 2003, signed by President Bush, established this medal.

b. In order of precedence, the GWOTEM will be worn before the GWOTSM and both shall directly follow the Kosovo Campaign Medal (KCM) (i.e., KCM, GWOTEM, GWOTSM, KDSM, etc.).

c. Soldiers may receive both the Global War on Terrorism Expeditionary Medal (GWOTEM) and the Global War on Terrorism Service Medal (GWOTSM) if they meet the requirements of both awards; however, the same period of service establishing eligibility for one cannot be used to justify service eligibility for the other.

d. Order of precedence and wear policy for service medals awarded to Army personnel is contained in Army Regulation (AR) 670-1. Policy for awards, approving authority and supply of medals is contained in AR 600-8-22. The policy for display of campaign streamers on guidons/flags and supply of streamers is contained in Chapter 9, 840-10.

# Appendix I

# The Roles of MI NCOs in the 75th Ranger Regiment

by Sergeant First Class James A. Blacss

Providing tactical intelligence to the combat commander should be the goal of military intelligence units and organizations at both the tactical and strategic levels. The MI noncommissioned officer (NCO) can accomplish this through technical and tactical proficiency, understanding the needs of the user, accessing the right information from the best possible sources and disseminating that information as quickly and as accurately as possible. In this appendix, I will discuss how the MI NCOs and intelligence soldiers of the 75th Ranger Regiment accomplish the mission of providing tactical intelligence to the combat commander.

## INTELLIGENCE NCOS' MISSION AND ORGANIZATION

At the 75th Ranger Regiment, our mission is to plan and conduct special military operations in support of U.S. policy and objectives. The 75th Ranger Regiment's intelligence section is an integral element in determining the regiment's success. Our mission is to provide timely and quality intelligence support to the regimental commander, staff, and ranger battalions during the conduct of all Ranger operations while maintaining an 18-hour worldwide deployment capability.

The Rangers' unique mission and capabilities require the section to function with efficiency and tactical and technical proficiency without hesitation. The 32 intelligence NCOs and intelligence specialists assigned to the 75th Ranger Regiment and its three battalions play an essential role in this mission.

To fully understand the ranger intelligence NCOs' roles in the accomplishment of our mission, it helps to understand the organizational structure. The 75th Ranger Regiment consists of the Regimental Headquarters and 3d Battalion colocated at Fort Benning, Georgia; 2d Battalion located at Fort Lewis, Washington; and 1st Battalion located at Hunter Army Airfield, Georgia. To best support three separated battalions, the majority of the intelligence personnel are located at the headquarters with the Regiment's S2 and MI Detachment (MID), which consists of the analysis, communications, counter-intelligence, and weather sections. The regimental S2 maintains oversight of both the Regimental Reconnaissance Detachment (RRD) and the MID.

## PHASED SUPPORT FOR THE MID

The MID supports ranger operations in three distinct phases: pre-deployment, deployment, and employment. The functions of the detachment NCOs during these phases are addressed below.

**Pre-deployment Phase**. The most important task of our NCOs during this phase is ensuring the detachment's ability to deploy, with all available personnel, anywhere in the world within 18 hours of notification. This requires constant supervision to ensure that everyone is deployable, has personal matters in order, is weapons-qualified, and that all equipment is always ready and packed. It is the Ranger view that "you must first get to the war, before you can fight it." While accomplishing this task, the NCOs must also complete the equally important mission of providing intelligence support to the tactical military decisionmaking process that occurs in conjunction with every ranger deployment. Other day-to-day functions during this phase include developing the following products –

The Daily Read File, which provides current intelligence to the commander, selected staff members, and the battalions. It provides information on the intelligence interests of our higher headquarters to the analysis section and gives the analysts a basis on which to focus intelligence gathering. This product also exercises the intelligence systems with which we deploy.

The Country Workbook, which forms the core of the information the analyst will use in a deployment or crisis situation. It is designed as a ready reference so that the analyst will have access to information on a specific country if the need arises.

The Order of Battle Workbook, which is developed each time a situation or crisis occurs that leads the regiment to begin mission analysis and troop-leading procedures for possible ranger involvement.

The Weekly Bluebook, the primary method by which the detachment communicates current intelligence to the commander, staff, and non-deployed battalions.

The Weekly Intelligence Brief, the method used by the regional analysts to communicate current intelligence to the rest of the section. The dialog provides the MID Senior Intelligence Sergeant with the opportunity to provide feedback and guidance, allows the analyst to practice briefing techniques, and becomes an open forum of discussion on assessments.

The "Top Ten" Hot Country List, which provides a focus for potential hot spots to the commander, staff, and battalions and informs our higher headquarters of our focus. It also provides our analysts with a basis of information to focus intelligence gathering better.

**Deployment Phase**. During this phase, the MID coordinates the intelligence-gathering effort and produces its intelligence products in preparation for combat operations. The focus for the Ranger MI NCO during this phase is on intelligence preparation of the battlefield (IPB).

The detachment has very specific standard operating procedures (SOPs) that are employed during this process. The primary one is the Regimental Intelligence SOP, which draws heavily on low-intensity stability and support operations and special operations doctrine. It is the responsibility of the MID NCOs to produce the products and to supervise the IPB process. The Ranger intelligence NCOs are directly responsible for coordinating the activities of the analysis and collection management sections of the MID.

The Analysis Section conducts the initial intelligence preparation of the battlefield. It focuses on target-specific areas, using the intelligence processes of battlefield area evaluation, terrain and weather analysis, threat evaluation, and threat integration. The section uses FM 34-130, Intelligence Preparation of the Battlefield, as a guideline, but specifically tailors analysis to ranger operations. The Analysis Section produces paragraphs 3, 4, and 5 of the intelligence estimate[233] and provides all available intelligence to selected ranger battalions and regimental reconnaissance detachments in the most timely and efficient manner possible.

The Collection Management Section locates all available imagery products and maps, and establishes a dissemination plan. They compile a list of all needed and available imagery and map resources and analyze imagery in support of the IPB process.

**Employment Phase.** During the third phase, the MID provides the necessary and available intelligence to the commander, staff, and subordinate ranger battalions and to the Army Special Operations Task Force (ARSOTF). They perform the four critical tasks described below.

While conducting Regimental Main Command Post (R-MAIN) operations, the intelligence NCOs assist in orchestrating the intelligence effort as directed by the regimental commander. They must interface with the staff, battlefield operating system (BOS) representatives, subordinate ranger battalions, units, and attached elements to ensure proper information flow and coordination. Several products used in support of this task are the primary responsibility of the intelligence NCOs working in the R-MAIN and include the following:

A situation map (SITMAP) showing locations of enemy dispositions and friendly intelligence collection assets.

Significant events list.

Intelligence asset status.

Enemy battle damage assessment.

Priority target list.

Reconnaissance and surveillance communications schedules.

The second major task is liaison and support to command and control (C2) operations. Other NCOs provide Intelligence BOS representation to C2 nodes or liaison teams as dictated by the mission. The MID has sent NCOs on the C2 teams supporting every conflict since the activation of the regimental headquarters.

Intelligence production, the next task, is conducted by the Analysis Section during employment. The focus of this element is on monitoring the current battle, while preparing for the future battle. The Analysis Section is responsible for conducting the following actions:

Processing incoming message traffic.

Updating the SITMAP with current enemy information, light and weather data, enemy order of battle, and friendly forces disposition.

Preparing overlays.

Conducting terrain analysis and target research.

Preparing target folders for dissemination to subordinate ranger battalions and the RRD.

Preparing for briefings.

Producing intelligence summaries and Annex B to the Operations Orders for follow-on missions.

The Air Force Weather Section assists by providing accurate weather intelligence and forecasts for current operations as well as future operations.

The fourth task is collection management. Some of the responsibilities of these intelligence NCOs include ensuring the message flow is handled according to our SOP and submitting requests for support and requests for intelligence information to higher headquarters and echelons. In addition, they maintain the intelligence journal, Requests for Information (RFI) log, collection plan, and collection asset status board. Finally, they maintain an accurate inventory of all on-hand imagery and photographs, analyze imagery in support of the target development process, produce sketches of specific areas of importance, and order, maintain, and distribute maps to mission planners.

## CONCLUSION

To provide the combat commander with the greatest opportunity for success, we must ensure that our subordinates are prepared to deploy at very short notice, understand our SOPs, and are trained both physically and mentally to assume this responsibility. The intelligence NCO must provide the best available intelligence to the user and it must be in a format that is clear, concise, and to the point. Most importantly, it must fit the needs of the combat commander's mission. Good ground tactical intelligence will win our future battles. It is our job as MI NCOs at the tactical level to ensure that we never fail.

Sergeant First Class Blaess is currently assigned to the 75th Ranger Regiment as the MID Senior Intelligence Sergeant.

# Appendix J

# Ranger Citations – Operation *Iraqi Freedom*
Courtesy of the 75th Ranger Regiment

The President of the United States of America, authorized by an Act of Congress, 9 July 1918 (amended by act of 25 July 1963), has awarded the

## Silver Star
CAPTAIN DAVID S. DOYLE
UNITED STATES ARMY
FOR GALLANTRY:

in action against an armed enemy, while serving as company commander during Operation Iraqi Freedom from 31 March 2003 to 7 April 2003. Captain Doyle led his company superbly during several days of battle against a numerically superior force. Captain Doyle's heroism under fire and superior leadership directly resulted in the success of the battle. Captain Doyle's personal courage, tactical expertise and professional competence while under days of effective enemy direct and indirect fire contributed directly to saving the lives of countless Soldiers and the overall success of the mission. Through his distinctive accomplishments, Captain Doyle reflected great credit upon himself, a Task Force, and the United States Army.

The President of the United States of America, authorized by an Act of Congress, 9 July 1918 (amended by act of 25 July 1963), has awarded the

## Silver Star
SERGEANT FIRST CLASS JEFFREY A. DUNCAN
UNITED STATES ARMY
FOR GALLANTRY:

in action against an armed enemy, while serving as a Platoon Sergeant for a Task Force, from 31 March 2003 to 9 April 2003, in support of Operation Iraqi Freedom. Sergeant First Class Duncan directed accurate and deadly machinegun fire against enemy positions which helped his men move into a dominating position for rapid attack on advancing enemy Soldiers. While under intense attack, Sergeant First Class Duncan and his men saved a wounded enemy soldier and took several prisoners. Fearlessly he volunteered to return to the platoon's position by foot to coordinate return fire on the enemy. Sergeant First Class Duncan's courage, vision, and professional competence directly contributed to the overall success of the Task Force. Throughout his distinctive accomplishments, Sergeant First Class Duncan reflected great credit upon himself, the Task Force, and the United States Army.

## Appendix K

# Ranger Commanders

## HONORARY COLONELS OF THE REGIMENT
COL Herman W. Dammer  April 1985–June 1989
LTG Samuel V. Wilson  June 1989–September 1992
COL Francis W. Dawson  September 1992–January 1996
COL Ralph Puckett  January 1996

## HONORARY COMMAND SERGEANTS MAJOR OF THE REGIMENT
SMA Glen E. Morrell  June 1989–June 1992
SGM Warren E. Evans  June 1992

## COMMANDERS OF THE 75TH RANGER REGIMENT
COL W. O. Darby 1st Colonel of the Regiment September 1943–August 1944
COL F. D. Merrill 2nd Colonel of the Regiment October 1943–August 1944
COL W. A. Downing 3rd Colonel of the Regiment  July 1984–August 1985
COL J. S. Stringham 4th Colonel of the Regiment  August 1985–July 1987
COL W. B. Taylor Jr 5th Colonel of the Regiment  July 1987–June 1989
COL W. F. Kernan 6th Colonel of the Regiment  June 1989–July 1991
COL D. L. Grange 7th Colonel of the Regiment  July 1991–July 1993
COL J. T. Jackson 8th Colonel of the Regiment  July 1993–July 1995
COL W. J. Leszczynski Jr 9th Colonel of the Regiment July 1995–June 1997
COL S. A. McChrystal 10th Colonel of the Regiment June 1997–July 1999
COL P. K. Keen 11th Colonel of the Regiment July 1999–July 2001
COL Joeseph L. Votel 12th Colonel of the Regiment July 2001–August 2003
COL James C. Nixon 13th Colonel of the Regiment August 2003–Present

## COMMAND SERGEANTS MAJOR OF THE 75TH RANGER REGIMENT
CSM G. R. Carpenter   May 1984–August 1985
CSM A. Cobb   August 1985–June 1987
CSM G. D. Mock   August 1987–December 1988
CSM M. Leon-Guerrero  June 1989–November 1992
CSM J. Laye   November 1992–June 1994
CSM G. Ponder   June 1994–July 1996
CSM M. T. Hall   July 1996–April 2000
CSM W. E. Rakow  April 2000–July 2002
CSM H. A. Roberts July 2002–August 2003
CSM A. G. Birch April 2003–April 2005
CSM R. Inman April 2005–Present

# 1ST BATTALION, 75TH RANGER REGIMENT

## Past Commanders
COL W. O. Darby   World War II
COL J. Dobson World War II
LTC K. C. Leuer   January 1974–February 1975
LTC A. C. Stang, III   February 1975–July 1976
LTC E. O. Yaugo   July 1976–January 1978
LTC J. S. Stringham   January 1978–July 1979
LTC S. H. Williford   July 1979–July 1981
LTC J. T. Scott   July 1981–May 1983
LTC W. B. Taylor   May 1983–July 1985
LTC K. M. Nightingale   July 1985–July 1987
LTC W. F. Kernan   July 1987–December 1988
LTC R. W. Wagner   December 1988–June 1991
LTC K. W. Stauss (Killed in Training Mission) July 1991–October 1992
LTC J. M. Bednarek   October 1992–January 1993
LTC B. M. Pentecost   January 1993–March 1995
LTC P. K. Keen   March 1995–June 1997
LTC S. J. Hoogland   June 1997–August 1998
LTC J. L. Votel   August 1998–July 2000
COL Tony Thomas   July 2000–July 2002
LTC Michael M. Kershaw   August 2002–July 2004
LTC Richard D. Clarke   July 2004–Present

## Past Command Sergeants Major
CSM N. R. Gentry   January 1974–July 1975
CSM H. A. Caro (Killed in Training Mission) August 1975–November 1976
CSM G. E. Morrell   April 1977–June 1979
CSM J. Schalavin   June 1979–March 1982
1SG S. L. Fox (Acting)  March 1982–June 1982
CSM G. R. Carpenter   July 1982–May 1984
CSM M. Leon-Guerrero  July 1984–August 1985
CSM D. R. Dalton   August 1985–August 1988
CSM W. H. Acebes   August 1988–December 1989
CSM D. P. Lamica   December 1989–July 1992
CSM P. J. Sebay   July 1992–June 1993
CSM C. D. Baldridge   July 1993–March 1995
CSM J. J. Mellinger   March 1995–June 1997
1SG J. T. Taylor (Acting)  June 1997–October 1997
CSM W. Rakow   October 1997–April 2000
CSM D. Greenway   April 2000–July 2002
CSM H. Hance  July 2002–November 2003
CSM J. C. Hardy  July 2004–Present

# 2ND BATTALION, 75TH RANGER REGIMENT

## Past Commanders

LTC A. J. Baker   October 1974–July 1976
LTC G. H. Bethke   July 1976–May 1977
LTC W. A. Downing   May 1977–July 1979
LTC W. E. Powell (Killed in Training Mission) July 1979–September 1981
LTC J. E. Mace   October 1981–June 1983
LTC R. L. Hagler Jr.   June 1983–June 1984
LTC D. L. Severson   June 1984–January 1985
LTC J. J. Ellis   February 1985–May 1987
LTC J. J. Maher, III   May 1987–July 1989
LTC A. H. Maestas   July 1989–June 1991
LTC G. D. Speer   June 1991–June 1992
LTC R. L. Portante   June 1992–June 1993
LTC D. A. Barno   June 1993–June 1994
LTC T. A. Cole   June 1994–November 1994
LTC S. A. McChrystal   November 1994–June 1996
LTC J. M. Bednarek   June 1996–June 1998
LTC M. C. Okita   June 1998–Present
LTC Kevin C. Owens   June 2000–June 2002
LTC Jeffrey L. Bailey   June 2002–June 2004
LTC David B. Haight   June 2004–Present

## Past Command Sergeants Major

CSM W. E. Morgan   October 1974–August 1975
CSM R. E. Shaw   August 1975–Feburary 1976
MSG R. Rivera   March 1976–December 1976
MSG B. Pross   January 1977–Feburary 1977
CSM J. T. Gooden   February 1977–August 1978
CSM C. Barajas   September 1978–June 1980
CSM W. D. Stock   June 1980–June 1982
CSM J. E. Voyles   August 1982–January 1985
MSG Burrows   January 1985–August 1985
CSM M. Leon-Guerrero  August 1985–June 1989
CSM T. R. Duke   July 1989–June 1991
CSM J. G. Laye   June 1991–November 1992
CSM F. A. Magana   December 1992–Feburary 1996
MSG A. L. Eliefson   February 1996–April 1996
CSM J. L. McClain   April 1996–December 1997
1SG J. Du   January 1998–March 1998
CSM R. Rocco   March 1998–April 2000
CSM H. Roberts   April 2000–July 2002
CSM R. Inman   July 2002–April 2005
CSM D. O. Pallister April 2005–Present

# 3RD BATTALION, 75TH RANGER REGIMENT

## Past Commanders

LTC W. C. Ohl, II   October 1984–August 1985

LTC G. W. Hale   September 1985–July 1987

LTC R. M. Hensler   July 1987–March 1989

LTC J. F. Hunt   March 1989–July 1990

LTC J. T. Jackson   July 1990–July 1991

LTC J. T. Keneally (Killed in Training Mission) July 1991–October 1992

LTC F. H. Kearney, III   October 1992–Feburary 1993

LTC D. R. McKnight   February 1993–July 1994

LTC F. H. Kearney, III   July 1994–July 1996

LTC M. J. Ferriter   July 1996–July 1998

LTC D. B. Allyn   July 1998–June 2000

LTC J. C. Nixon   June 2000–June 2001

LTC S. J. Banach   June 2001–June 2003

LTC P. J. LaCamera   June 2003–July 2004

LTC J. G. Castles   July 2004–Present

## Past Command Sergeants Major

CSM A. J. Cobb   October 1984–August 1985

CSM S. L. Fox   August 1985–March 1987

1SG D. Purdy   March 1987–July 1987

CSM J. W. Jones   July 1987–November 1989

CSM G. E. Klien   November 1989–Feburary 1992

1SG J. Greer   February 1992–July 1992

CSM R. Salinas   July 1992–November 1993

CSM K. L. Holmes   November 1993–Feburary 1995

CSM R. R. Beam   February 1995–1999

CSM Kevin Connell   May 1999–December 2000

1SG Joshua Mitchell   December 2000–May 2001

CSM Jay Brimstin   May 2001–April 2002

1SG Hu Rhodes   April 2002–July 2002

CSM Alfred G. Birch   July 2002–July 2003

CSM Matthew Walker   July 2003–Present

## Appendix L

# Distinguished and Honorary Members of the 75th Ranger Regiment

The following individuals were inducted as Distinguished or Honorary Members of the 75th Ranger Regiment. Members are listed by the year of induction.

Since 1989, the tradition of Distinguished and Honorary Members of the Regiment has recognized those who have served the Ranger Regiment with excellence and distinction. Individuals recognized as Distinguished Members of the Regiment have served in the 75th Ranger Regiment and are designated to help maintain the *élan* and *esprit de corps* of the Regiment by their personal example. Individuals recognized as Honorary Members of the Regiment, although never assigned to the Ranger Regiment as active military members since 1974, have nonetheless made a significant contribution to the Ranger Regiment and its mission.

**1989**
BG Wesley B. Taylor, Jr
LTC(P) John J. Mahr, III
MG Wayne A. Downing
LTC Samual V. Wilson
BG Joseph H. Stringham

SMA(R) Glenn E. Morrell
MAJ Daniel V. Wright
CSM(R) Dave Dalton

**1990**
COL Henry Koren, Jr

General John P. Abizaid — stuck with the tough task of defeating the insurgency campaign in Iraq. He is a Grenada raider of 2/75, Hoover Institution alumnus, and fluent Arabic speaker. (DoD)

COL Robert W. Wagner
LTC James T. Jackson
MG(R) Kenneth L. Leuer
MG(R) Milton A. Pilcher
COL(R) Herman W. Dammer

**1991**
CSM Gary R. Carpenter
CSM George D. Conrad
COL(P) William F. Kernan, Jr
COL(R) Robert Black
SMA(R) Julius W. Gates
HON John O. Marsh, Jr
Mr Jim Altier
Mr Robert I. Channon
Mr Phil Piazza
Mr Rex Sharp
Mr Fran Cogglin
**1992**
CSM(R) Leon-Guerrero

**1993**
COL Wayne M. Barth
CSM William H. Acebes
COL John T. Keneally
1SG Harvey L. Moore, Jr
COL Gary D. Speer
LTC Kenneth W. Stauss
COL David L. Grange
CPT(R) Richards O. Stewart, Jr
COL(R) Ralph Puckett

**1994**
CSM Jesse G. Laye
LTC David W. Barno
CSM Autrail Cobb
LTG(R) Carmen J. Cavezza
COL(R) Francis W. Dawson
CSM(R) Warren G. Evans
MSG Roy Matsumoto
Mr George C. Ward

**1995**
LTC Brian M. Pentecost
CPT(R) Michael M. Davis
CW4 William Donovan
CSM Steve R. England
MG Jared L. Bates
CSM Michael I. Lampe

1SG Glenn L. Harris

**1996**
LTC James T. Scott
COL John J. Ellis
COL(R) Glynn W. Hale
COL(R) Roy A. Murray
LTC Francis H. Kearney, III
CSM George D. Ponder
CSM(R) Francisco Magana
CPT(R) Kevin Egan

**1997**
COL Stanley A. McChrystal
CSM Donald E. Purdy
Mr Duke Dushane
CSM Sam B. Spears, III
Mr Grant Hravayski
Mr Ray A. Fuller
Mr Rick Ehrler
CSM Neal R. Gentry
LTC P. K. Keen
CSM Stanley L. Fox

**1998**
LTC Michael Ferriter
LTC(R) Rex G. Masters
CSM Jeffrey J. Mellinger
CSM Jerry L. McClain
MSG Matthew Berrena
1SG(R) Arthur J. Silsby
Mr Emmett Fike
Mr Thomas W. Biggs
Mr William Carter

**1999**
BG William J. Leszcynski, Jr
COL Thomas Sittnick
COL Mick Bednarek
COL Steve Hoogland
LTC Francis J. Wiercinski
CSM Ralph R. Beam
CSM(R) Mike Martin
MSG Jimmy R. Pickering
MG Carl F. Ernst
COL James Oeser
LTC (Dr) Larry Lewis
MSG(R) Gil Berg
Ms Lola Brunson

Mr Leon Chapman
Ms Linda Davis
Ms Sheila Dudley
Ms Debra Hearne
Mr Thomas Herring
Mr William Mason
Mr Sumner R. Moore

## 2000

LTG Lawson W. Magruder, III
MG John R. Vines
MG John P. Abizaid
MG William P. Boykin
MG John M. Le Moyne
MG James M. Dubik
MG Geoffrey C. Lambertt
BG John C. Scroggins
BG Thomas R. Turner, II
COL Joseph L. Votel
COL Michael C. Okita
COL Daniel B. Allyn
CSM Michael T. Hall
CSM(R) Ralph Rocco, IV
LTG William P. Tangney
LTG Michael A. Canavan
Ms Jeanette M. Tapio
Mr Jerry D. Cooper

## 2001

COL Luke S. Green
COL Thomas A. Cole
COL James A Pfaff
COL Eric D. Hutchings
LTC James C. Nixon
LTC Brian P Stephenson
CSM Gerald E. Klein
CSM(R) Kevin P. Connell
CSM(R) Walt D. Stock
CSM Henry A. Caro
Mr William J. McDermott
Mr Raymond C. Wornica
Mr Osgood D. Murdaugh
Ms Penny Neff

## 2002

MG Eldon A. Bargewell
BG Bruce Barlow
COL James H. Schwitters
COL Raymond A. Thomas

LTC George D. Martin
LTC Mark L. Ritter
LTC Kevin C. Owens
LTC Vance J. Nannini
CSM Walter E. Rakow
CSM Douglas M. Greenway
CSM Richard W. Shuck
CSM(R) James E. Voyles
COL Al Aycock
COL(R) Gary R. Greenfield
LTC George D. Seaman
Mr Lucky Caswell

## 2003

MG Dell L. Dailey
BG Mark T. Kimmitt
COL Bernard S. Champoux
COL(R) Ralph Hagler
COL(R) Robert L. Click
LTC Campbell P. Cantelou
LTC Stefan J. Banach
CSM Michael A. Kelso
CSM Hugh A. Roberts
CSM Frank A.Grippe
CSM(R) George Horvath
1SG(R) David Mark Keith
SFC Robert Miller
BG Howard W. Yellen
COL Thomas F. Spellissy
Mr Randal Collinsworth
Mr H. Ross Perot
Mrs Carol Darby

## 2004

MG Dorian T. Anderson
COL Jeffery L. Bailey
COL K. K. Chinn
CSM Rafael Colondres
CSM Michael T. Etheridge
COL William K. Fuller
COL Michael M. Kershaw
LTC Paul J. Lacamera
CSM Charles L. Raper
CSM James W. Redmore
CSM Charles W. Thompson
CSM Richard L. Davis
COL(R) Henry L. Kinnison
Ms Sandee Rouse
Mr Greg Vogel

## Appendix M

The following two press releases are provided by the Department of Defense and the 75th Ranger Regiment Public Affairs Office. Unfortunately, all of the Rangers' combat operations are classified and very little light is shed on their accomplishments during the Global War on Terrorism.

# Ranger Battalion awarded Combat Streamer

DATE POSTED: APRIL 13, 2005
By Kim Laudano
75th Ranger Regiment Public Affairs Office

FORT BENNING, Georgia (USASOC News Service, April 13, 2005) – The 3rd Battalion, 75th Ranger Regiment was awarded a combat streamer for their contributions in support of the Global War on Terrorism during a ceremony here April 7.

Combat streamers recognize a unit's actions and contributions during combat, explained Command Sgt. Maj. Matthew Walker, 3rd Battalion, 75th Ranger Regiment. The streamer will be carried with the battalion colors and company guidons for a year when operations in support of the Global War on Terrorism conclude.

Each company was also awarded a combat streamer. This marked the third combat streamer for Company B, 3rd Ranger Battalion since 1984. Company B was previously awarded a combat streamer for contributions in support of operations in Somalia.

Outgoing regimental Command Sgt. Maj. Alfred Birch presented the unit streamer to Walker. Birch also presented each company's streamer to their first sergeants.

Walker said it was fitting that Birch presented the streamer to the battalion and to its companies because Birch led 3rd Ranger Battalion as command sergeant major during the battalion's first deployment in support of Operation *Iraqi Freedom*.

This was only the second time the entire battalion was awarded a combat streamer since the unit's inception in 1984. The first combat streamer was for contributions in support of Operation *Just Cause* in Panama.

USASOC

# 2005 Awards to Rangers

A Ranger team sergeant was presented the Bronze Star with Valor device for actions during a mission in support of Operation *Enduring Freedom*. According to his award citation, the Ranger's leadership under fire helped defeat a coordinated enemy attack on an objective.

A Ranger team leader was presented an Army Commendation Medal with Valor device for actions during a mission in support of Operation *Enduring Freedom*. According to his award citation, the Ranger's actions and courage under direct enemy fire assisted his fellow comrades to defend their position against a numerically superior force. His decisiveness and quick actions ensured that the Rangers will never leave a fallen comrade.

A Ranger was presented an Army Commendation Medal with Valor device for actions during a mission in support of Operation *Enduring Freedom*. According to his award citation, the Ranger's action and courage under direct enemy fire assisted his fellow comrades to initiate accurate and lethal fire into an unsuspecting numerically superior enemy force.

During another awards ceremony, Staff Sergeant Justin Viene and Staff Sergeant Jesse Walker stood on a stage at Fort Lewis, Washington before hundreds of 2nd Battalion, 75th Ranger Regiment comrades-in-arms just months after making critical decisions during an attack instigated by Afghani insurgents.

Their individual performances led to General Bryan Brown, the commanding general of U.S. Special Operations Command, to award a Silver Star to Viene and a Bronze Star with Valor device to Walker.

"These awards are not expensive to buy," said Brown, "but they are really expensive to earn – they are huge in their significance."

By choosing to show courage instead of fear when ambushed by enemy mortars and rocket-propelled grenades, they led squads of fellow Rangers to victory and safety.

"Fear is a reaction," said Brown. "But they made a decision of courage."

Years of Ranger training all culminated in one event where the two men used their collective skills to survive and defeat the enemy.

While out on patrol near the Pakistani border, the two squad-team leaders and their Rangers had to react to an ambush – something they had done many times in training.

But this time, the opposing forces weren't using blanks.

Although Walker had experienced an intense battle before during his earlier combat

The presentation of combat streamers to the 3rd Battalion, 75th Ranger Regiment. (75th RR)

deployments, Viene said it was the first time in five deployments he had been in a big firefight.

"It was kind of surreal for a minute – it didn't really sink in that it was happening. It all happened really fast," said Viene.

"To see the dirt kicking up beside you and realize that they're shooting at you. The training just took over," he said. "Time just slowed down."

While Viene grabbed two of his men and vaulted up a hill firing a squad automatic weapon at the enemy, Walker took care of wounded soldiers, set up security and worked the radios to communicate their situation.

"I grabbed the rest of the guys we had there and got them on the machine guns, suppressing the enemy so Viene could move up the hill," said Walker.

"I did what we were trained to do," he said.

And that's the advice both he and Viene give to younger Rangers in preparation for similar situations – excel at marksmanship, battle drills, medical training, and physical fitness.

All four elements combined to protect the Rangers' lives, and that emphasis on training is something family members use for reassurance when their sons, husbands, and brothers deploy to a combat zone.

Repeatedly denying that they did anything special and continually insisting that they only did their job, both Viene and Walker contribute their leadership success to daily training and the men who served with them.

"We didn't do it to get an award," said Viene. "It's just icing on the cake.

# Endnotes

1   René Chartrand, *Colonial American Troops 1610–1774 (3)*, Men-at-Arms 383 (Oxford, Osprey Publishing, 2003), p.21.

2   Author unknown, *Rangers Past and Present* (1st Battalion, 75th Ranger Regiment, Hunter Army Airfield, Savannah, Georgia, 1999), p.6. (This document draws its some of its history from Field Manual No. 21–50, Headquarters, Department of the Army, Washington 25, DC, 20 August 1957, pp.213–226, Colonial through Korea.)

3   Ibid.

4   Ibid.

5   Gary Zaboly, *American Colonial Ranger: The Northern Colonies 1724–64*, Warrior 85 (Oxford, Osprey Publishing, 2004), p.5.

6   http://www.army.mil/cmh-pg/documents/RevWar/revra.htm.

7   Gary S. Zaboly, *A True Ranger: the life and many wars of Major Robert Rogers* (New York, Royal Blockhouse LLC, 2004), p.7.

8   Stephen Brumwell, *White Devil* (Cambridge, Da Capo Press, 2005), p.49.

9   Robert Rogers, *Journals of Major Robert Rogers* (London, J Millan, 1765), pp.60–70. On microfilm at UC Berkeley.

10  http://www.archives.gov/national_archives_experience/charters/print_friendly.html ?page=declaration_transcript_content.html&title=NARA%20%7C%20The%20 Declaration%20of%20Independence%3A%20A%20Transcription.

11  *Rangers Past and Present*, pp.9–10.

12  http://www.army.mil/cmh-pg/documents/RevWar/revra.htm.

13  *Rangers Past and Present*, p.10.

14  http://en.wikipedia.org/wiki/Francis_Marion.

15  http://www.benning.army.mil/rtb/Hall_of_fame/HallofFame2/brigadier_general_fr ancis_marion.htm.

16  Philip Katcher, *The American Provincial Corps 1775–84*, Men-at-Arms 1 (Oxford, Osprey Publishing, 1973), pp.36–37.

17  Ibid, p.38.

18  http://www.royalprovincial.com/military/rhist/jrng/jrnglet1.htm.

19  *Rangers Past and Present*, p.11.

20  Ibid, p.12.

21  http://www.benning.army.mil/rtb/Hall_of_fame/Halloffame1/president_lincoln.htm.

22  This chapter is based on information given in *Rangers Past and Present*, pp.12–14.

23  Robert Black, *Rangers in World War II* (New York, Ballentine Books, Random House, 1992), p.14.

24  William Darby and William H. Baumer, *Darby's Rangers: We Led the Way* (California, Presidio Press, 1980).

25  Black, *Rangers in World War II*.

26  Ibid.

27  Jean Yves-Nasse, *Green Devils! German Paratroopers 1939–1945* (Paris, Histoire & Collections, 1997), pp.116–17.

28  Joseph A. Springer, *Black Devil Brigade: An Oral History* (New York, ibooks, 2001).

29  75th Ranger Regiment PAO document, *The American Ranger*.

30  *Rangers Past and Present*, pp.16, 20.

31  Stephen Ambrose, *D-Day: June 6, 1944: The Climatic Battle of World War II* (New York, Simon & Shuster, 1994), p.430.

32  David W. Hogan, *U.S. Army Special Operations in World War II* (Washington DC, Department of the Army, CMH Publication 70–42, 1992).

33  Joseph H. Ewing, *The 29th Rangers* (Washington, Infantry Journal Press, date unknown).

34  75th PAO document (1996).

35  Ibid.

36  *Rangers Past and Present*, pp.24–27.

37  David W. Hogan Jr, *Raiders or Elite Infantry? The Changing Role of the US Army Rangers from Dieppe to Grenada* (Greenwood Press, 1992), p.202.

38  Ross Hall interview/email (October 25, 2004).

39  Hogan, *Raiders or Elite Infantry*, p.185.

40  Phil Piazza interview.

41  75th PAO document (1996).

42  Personal interview (August 13, 2004).

43  Personal interview (August 25, 2004).

44  John D. Lock, *To Fight With Intrepidity: The Complete History of the US Army Rangers 1622 to the Present* (New York, Pocket Books, 1998), p.448.

45  Lee E. Russell and M. Albert Mendez, *Grenada 1983*, Men-at-Arms 159 (Oxford, Osprey Publishing, 1985), p.14.

46  Ibid, p.16.

47  Ronald H. Cole, "Operation Urgent Fury. The Planning and Execution of Joint Operations in Grenada 12 October–2 November 1983" (Washington, Office of the Joint Chiefs of Staff, Joint History Office, 1997), p.42.

48  Ibid, p.14.

49  Capt Todd Bearden, *Operation Urgent Fury*, IOAC Seminar paper (Fort Benning, GA, USAIS Library, October 1983), pp.25–28.

50  Capt Jonathan Tugman, "The Seizure of Rio Hato Airfield, Operation Just Cause, Bravo Company, 3rd Battalion, 75th Ranger Regiment 0103 hrs, 20 Dec 89" (Fort Benning, GA, USAIS Library).

51  Ronald H. Cole, *Operation Just Cause: The Planning and Execution of Joint Operations in Panama, February 1988–January 1990* (Washington DC, Joint History Office, Office of the Chairman of the Joint Chiefs of Staff, 1995).

52  Ibid.

53  http://en.wikipedia.org/wiki/Iran-Contra_Affair.

54  Ranger interview.

55  Senate report and Bill Gertz, "Aspin's decision on tanks was political," in *The Washington Times* (October 3, 1995); http://www.netnomad.com/powell.html.

56  75th PAO document (1996).

57  Interviews with anonymous Delta Force trooper (2000), and Delta Force Officer (1999); also mentioned by two TFR Rangers in separate interviews (1999).

58  http://wwwa.house.gov/international_relations/108/Pow042204.htm; http://www.cnn.com/2004/WORLD/africa/04/06/rwanda.amanpour/.

59    SOCOM, *United States Special Operation Command History* (USSOCOM, MacDill AFB, Florida, 1999), p.52.

60    Chalmers Johnson, *Blowback: The Costs and Consequences of American Empire* (New York, Metropolitan Books, 2000).

61    http://www.usatoday.com/news/washington/2004-04-09-alqaeda-memo_x.htm.

62    http://www.pbs.org/wgbh/pages/frontline/shows/knew/etc/cron.html.

63    Harvey Kushner, *Encyclopedia of Terrorism* (Thousand Oaks, CA, Sage Publications, Inc., 2003), pp.20–24.

64    http://www.afa.org/magazine/Dec2000/1200airlift.asp.

65    http://www.ausa.org/transformation/article_secondyear.html.

66    *The American Heritage Dictionary of the English Language* (Boston, Houghton Mifflin, 1976), pp.124–125.

67    http://www.army.mil/features/beret/beret.htm; http://www.carson.army.mil/pao/media_relations/data_card.htm.

68    http://en.wikipedia.org/wiki/Beret.

69    Zaboly, *American Colonial Ranger*, p.60.

70    Robert Black, *Documented History of Ranger Headdress*, email (2001).

71    Gary Zaboly and Timothy Todish, *The Annotated and Illustrated Journals of Major Robert Rogers* (New York, Purple Mountain Press, 2002), p.311.

72    Ibid, pp.292–322.

73    http://www.army.mil/features/beret/beret.htm.

74    Carl Lehman, Darby Ranger, interview/email.

75    http://www.army.mod.uk/para/history/northafrica.htm.

76    Robert Black, "The Ranger Beret" in *Gung Ho Magazine* (October 1984), pp.32–33.

77    http://www.army.mil/features/beret/beret.htm; http://www.carson.army.mil/pao/media_relations/data_card.htm, Roy Boatman interview.

78    Tommy Franks, *American Soldier* (New York, Harper Collins, 2004), p.362; Bob Woodward, *Plan of Attack* (New York, Simon & Schuster, 2004), p.292.

79    http://www.nationalreview.com/babbin/babbin081403.asp; http://www.pbs.org/wgbh/pages/frontline/shows/invasion/interviews/fallows.html; http://www.bostonphoenix.com/medialog/2004/10/kerrys-missed-opportunities.asp.

80    http://www.newyorker.com/archive/content/?030407fr_archive04.

81    http://www.pbs.org/wgbh/pages/frontline/shows/pentagon/interviews/vanriper.html.

82    http://www.cnn.com/2004/ALLPOLITICS/04/28/lautenberg.kerry/.

83    Ahmed Rashid, *Taliban: Militant Islam, Oil & Fundamentalism in Central Asia* (New Haven, CT, Nota Bene Yale University Press, 2001), pp.22, 25.

84    http://www.whitehouse.gov/news/releases/2001/10/20011007-8.html.

85    http://www.defenselink.mil/transcripts/2001/t10202001_t1020jcs.html.

86    Charles H. Briscoe et. al., *Weapon of Choice* (Fort Leavenworth, KS, Combat Studies Institute, 2003), pp.97–98.

87    Ibid, p.114.

88    Ibid, p.114.

89    Ibid, p.114.

90    Ibid, p.111.

91    Ibid, p.111.

92   Ibid, pp.114–115.

93   Ibid, p.112.

94   Ibid, p.113.

95   Naylor phone call with author (April 1, 2005).

96   Briscoe, *Weapon of Choice*, p.113.

97   http://www.defenselink.mil/transcripts/2001/t10202001_t1020jcs.html.

98   Briscoe, *Weapon of Choice*, p.141.

99   Ibid, p.141.

100  Ibid, p.143.

101  Ibid, p.143.

102  Ibid, p.144.

103  Ibid, p.144.

104  Mir Bahmanyar, *Afghanistan Cave Complexes 1979–2004*, Fortress 26 (Oxford, Osprey Publishing, 2004), p.26.

105  Peter Smucker, *Al Qaeda's Great Escape* (Brassey's Inc, 2004).

106  Carl Conetta, *Strange Victory: A critical appraisal of Operation Enduring Freedom and the Afghanistan war* (Cambridge, MA, Commonwealth Institute Project on Defense Alternatives Research Monograph #6, 30 January 2002); Originating website – http://www.comw.org/pda/0201strangevic.html.

107  Kershaw Speech (January 16, 2003).

108  Ibid.

109  Sean Naylor, *Not a Good Day to Die* (New York, March Berkley Caliber, 2005), p.67.

110  http://www.insidedefense.com (Inside Washington Publishers, August 12, 2004).

111  Department of Defense, Executive Summary (May 24, 2002).

112  Robert H. McElroy, "Afghanistan: Fire Support for Operation Anaconda" in *Field Artillery* (September–October 2002).

113  Briscoe, *Weapon of Choice*, p.277.

114  McElroy, "Afghanistan: Fire Support for Operation Anaconda."

115  Naylor, *Not a Good Day to Die*.

116  Ibid, pp.86, 152–153.

117  Ibid, pp.120–135.

118  Ibid, p.104.

119  Briscoe, *Weapon of Choice*, p.282.

120  Naylor, *Not a Good Day to Die*, pp.156–7.

121  Department of Defense, Executive Summary (May 24, 2002).

122  Dave Moniz, "Soldiers Describe '18-Hour Miracle,'" http://www.usatoday.com (March 7, 2002).

123  Ibid.

124  Esther Schrader, "Simple Mission Became 18-Hour Fight. Afghanistan: Flawed intelligence may have put unit in line of enemy fire" in *Los Angeles Times* (March 8, 2002).

125  Briscoe, *Weapon of Choice*, pp.286–88.

126  Department of Defense, Executive Summary (May 24, 2002).

127  Briscoe, *Weapon of Choice*, p.290.

128  Department of Defense, Executive Summary (May 24, 2002).

129  Naylor, *Not a Good Day to Die*, p.264.

130  Ibid, pp.150–153.

131  Ibid, p.306.

132  Ibid, p.286.

133  Briscoe, *Weapon of Choice*, p.134.

134  Naylor, *Not a Good Day to Die*, p.306.

135  Ibid.

136  Department of Defense, Executive Summary (May 24, 2002).

137  Briscoe, *Weapon of Choice*.

138  Ibid, p.297.

139  Naylor, *Not a Good Day to Die*, p.306.

140  Department of Defense, Executive Summary (May 24, 2002).

141  Briscoe, *Weapon of Choice*, p.298.

142  Naylor, *Not a Good Day to Die*, p.313.

143  Briscoe, *Weapon of Choice*, pp.298–300.

144  Department of Defense, Executive Summary (May 24, 2002).

145  Naylor, *Not a Good Day to Die*, pp.306–316.

146  Andrew Exum, *This Man's Army* (New York, Gotham, 2004), p.164.

147  Email forwarded by Steve Waterman, author unknown (summer 2001).

148  Department of Defense, Executive Summary (May 24, 2002).

149  Department of Defense, News Briefing (May 24, 2002).

150  Interview, member SOF (date unknown).

151  Briscoe, *Weapon of Choice*, p.302.

152  Ibid, p.302.

153  Ibid, p.302.

154  Naylor, *Not a Good Day to Die*, p.326.

155  "Pope Combat Controller Awarded AF Cross" in *AF Print News Today* (January 13, 2003).

156  Briscoe, *Weapon of Choice*, p.302.

157  Repeated calls to the PAO of NAVSPECWAR went unanswered regarding the authenticity of this document. Independent research could only confirm that Slabinski was the teamleader.

158  Department of Defense, Executive Summary (May 24, 2002).

159  Naylor, *Not a Good Day to Die*, pp.339–340.

160  Ibid, pp.37–38.

161  Senior Military Official, Department of Defense Background briefing on the Report of the Battle of Takur Ghar (May 24, 2002).

162  Briscoe, *Weapon of Choice*, pp.302–303.

163  Department of Defense, Army Special Operations Briefing (July 17, 2002).

164  Department of Defense, Executive Summary (May 24, 2002).

165  *US Army Ranger Handbook*, SH 21-76 (April 2000).

166  Kevin Vance, debriefing, Bagram Air Base (2002).

167  http://www.af.mil/factsheets/factsheet.asp?fsID=187.

168  Department of Defense, News Briefing (May 24, 2002).

169  Ibid.

170  Department of Defense, Executive Summary (May 24, 2002).

171  Department of Defense, News Briefing (May 24, 2002).

172  Briscoe, *Weapon of Choice*, p.304.

173  Vance, debriefing (2002).

174  Briscoe, *Weapon of Choice*, p.304.

175  Ibid, p.304.

176  Ibid, p.304.

177  Vance, debriefing (2002).

178  AFSOC PA by Tech. Sgt. Ginger Schreitmueller (May 29, 2002).

179  Vance, debriefing, 2002.

180  Department of Defense, Executive Summary (May 24, 2002); Briscoe, *Weapon of Choice*, p.305.

181  Vance, debriefing (2002).

182  Briscoe, *Weapon of Choice*, p.307.

183  Ibid, p.306.

184  Vance, debriefing (2002).

185  Ibid.

186  Naylor, *Not a Good Day to Die*, p.345.

187  Briscoe, *Weapon of Choice*, p.307.

188  Ibid, p.307.

189  Department of Defense, Executive Summary (May 24, 2002).

190  http://www.af.mil/factsheets/factsheet.asp?fsID=174.

191  Briscoe, *Weapon of Choice*, p.308.

192  Ibid, pp.308–309.

193  Ibid, p.309.

194  Ibid, p.309.

195  *Takur Ghar*, Discovery Channel (Dec 2004).

196  Department of Defense, Executive Summary (May 24, 2002).

197  Briscoe, *Weapon of Choice*, p.309.

198  Ibid, p.310.

199  Vance, debriefing, 2002.

200  Ibid.

201  Bradley Graham, "Bravery and Breakdowns in a Ridgetop Battle" in *The Washington Post* (May 24, 2002).

202  Vance, debriefing, 2002.

203  Department of Defense, Executive Summary (May 24, 2002).

204  Ellen R. Stapleton, "Louisville Airman Awarded Silver Star" (November 2, 2003), http://www.enquirer.com/editions/2003/11/02/loc_ky-airman.html.

205  C. Ray Hall, "123rd Special Tactics" in *The Courier Journal* (2003), http://www.courier-journal.com/localnews/2003/11/02ky/met-front-medal-6816.html.

206  Sean Naylor, "An act of courage: Surrounded by death, a young pararescueman chose to save lives – and lost his," *Air Force Times* (date unknown).

207  Vance, debriefing (2002).

208  Ibid.

209  Hall, "123rd Special Tactics."

210  Department of Defense, Executive Summary (May 24, 2002).

211  Bradley, "Bravery and Breakdowns in a Ridgetop Battle."

212  Vance, debriefing, (2002).

213  Public Affairs Office, HAAF (January 30, 2003).

214   Naylor, *Not a Good Day to Die*, p.352.

215   Exum, *This Man's Army*, p.171.

216   http://www.csis.org/isp/pcr/040514_barno.pdf.

217   http://www.doctorswithoutborders.org/publications/other/afghanistan_press conference_7-28-2004.shtml.

218   http://www0.un.org/apps/news/story.asp?NewsID=12573&Cr=afghan&Cr1=.

219   Interview with returning Special Forces operator (date unknown).

220   Woodward, *Plan of Attack*, p.292.

221   http://edition.cnn.com/2004/ALLPOLITICS/01/10/oneill.bush/.

222   Woodward, *Plan of Attack*, p.292.

223   Sean Naylor, *Army Times* (August 16, 2002).

224   Ibid.

225   http://www.jfcom.mil/newslink/storyarchive/2002/no091702a.htm.

226   Department of Defense.

227   Department of Defense.

228   http://www.pbs.org/wgbh/pages/frontline/shows/pentagon/interviews/vanriper..html.

229   http://www.usatoday.com/news/world/iraq/2003-02-25-iraq-us_x.htm.

230   http://www.globalsecurity.org/military/ops/iraq_orbat.htm.

231   Email from USASOC PAO (February 25, 2005).

232   Jonathan Kirsh, *God Against the Gods*, pp.280–281.

233   Paragraphs 3, 4, and 5 of the Intelligence Estimate are "Enemy Situation," "Enemy Capabilities," and "Conclusions," respectively.

# Bibliography and Further Reading

I should like to recommend several books that I found particularly useful as they tend to be rather honest and straightforward. These volumes should satisfy anyone interested in those particular time periods. Gary Zaboly's magnificent *A True Ranger; the life and many wars of Major Roger Roberts* has established him as the preeminent historian on Rogers' Rangers. Burt Loescher's multi-volume set on Rangers is a must have as well. James Altieri's *The Spearheaders* and James Hopkins' *Spearhead* present vivid eyewitness accounts of the Rangers' great campaigns, Darby's and Merrill's respectively. *Black and Gold Warriors: U.S. Army Rangers during the Korean War* by David Robert Gray is a great addition to the Ranger library. On the modern front, Mark Bowden's *Black Hawk Down* is still the best volume on the battle of the Black Sea and Sean Naylor's tremendous account of Operation *Anaconda*, entitled *Not a Good Day to Die*, sets an unprecedented standard in combat journalism.

## BOOKS

9/11 Commission, *The 9/11 Commission Report* (New York, W.W. Norton & Company, 2004)

Adkin, Maj Mark, *Urgent Fury, The Battle for Grenada* (Lexington Books, 1989)

Adleman, Robert H. and Walton, Col George, *Devil's Brigade* (The Chilton Books, 1966)

Altieri, James T., *Darby's Rangers* (Missouri, Ranger Book Committee, 1977)

Altieri, James T., *The Spearheaders* (Washington, Zenger Publishing Company, 1979)

Bahmanyar, Mir, *Aghanistan Cave Complexes 1979–2004*, Fortress 26 (Oxford, Osprey Publishing, 2004)

Bass, Robert D., *Swamp Fox* (Sandlapper Publishing Company, 1989)

Beckwith, Charlie, *Delta Force* (Dell, 1983)

Black, Robert, *Rangers in Korea* (New York, Ivy Books, Random House, 1989)

Black, Robert, *Rangers in World War II* (New York, Ballentine Books, Random House, 1992)

Bob, Joel and Wright, J. R., *Special Men and Special Missions, Inside American Special Operations Forces 1945 to the Present* (Greenhill Books, 1994)

Bolger, Daniel P., *Death Ground, Today's American Infantry in Battle* (Novato, CA, Presidio Press, 1999)

Bowden, Mark, *Black Hawk Down* (New York, Atlantic Monthly Press, 1999)

Breuer, William H., *Operation Torch* (New York, St. Martin's Press, 1985)

Breuer, William H., *The Great Raid on Cabanatuan* (New York, John Wiley & Sons, 1994)

Briggs, 1st Lt Clarence E., *Operation Just Cause, Panama December 1989, A Soldier's Eyewitness Account* (Stackpole Books, 1990)

Briscoe, Charles H. et al, *Weapon of Choice* (Fort Leavenworth, KS, Combat Studies Institute, 2003)

Burford, John, *LRRPs in Action* (Carrollton, TX, Squadron/Signal Publications, 1994)

Callahan, North, *Daniel Morgan: Ranger of the Revolution* (New York, AMS Press, 1973)

Center of Military History, *US Army, Merrill's Marauders* (Washington, DC, US GPO, 1990)

Cole, Ronald H., *Operation Just Cause: The Planning and Execution of Joint Operations in Panama, February 1988–January 1990* (Washington DC, Joint History Office, Office of the Chairman of the Joint Chiefs of Staff, 1995)

Cornum, Rhonda, *She Went to War* (Presidio Press, 1993)

Cuneo, John R., *Robert Rogers of the Rangers* (New York, Richardson & Steirmna, 1987)

Darby, William O. and Baumer, William H., *Darby's Rangers: We Led The Way* (California, Presidio Press, 1980)

Delauter, Jr, Roger U., *McNeill's Rangers* (Virginia, H. E. Howard, 1986)

DeLong, Kent and Tuckey, Steven, *Mogadishu! Heroism and Tragedy* (Westport, CT, Praeger, 1994)

Edited, *Combat and Survival, What It Takes to Fight and Win*, Vol I (H. S. Stuttman Inc, 1991)

Edited, *Commando Operations, The New Face of War* (Time-Life Books, 1991)

Edited, *Special Forces and Missions, The New Face of War* (Time-Life Books, 1990)

Ericson, Don and Rotundo, John, *Charlie Rangers* (Ivy Books, 1989)

Exum, Andrew, *This Man's Army* (New York, Gotham, 2004)

Field, Ron, *Ranger: Behind Enemy Lines in Vietnam* (London, Military Illustrated, 2000)

Flanagan, Lt Gen Edward M., *Battle for Panama, Inside Operation Just Cause* (Brassey's (US) Inc, 1993)

Foley, Dennis, *Special Men, A LRP's Recollection* (Ivy Books, 1994)

Grossman, Lt Col Dave, *On Killing, The Psychological Cost of Learning to Kill in War and Society* (Little, Brown, 1995)

Hackworth, Lt Col David H., *Hazardous Duty* (William Morrow, 1996)

Henderson, William Darryl, Cohesion, *The Human Element in Combat* (NDU Press, 1985)

Herbert, Anthony B., *Soldier* (Dell, 1973)

Hogan, David W. Jr, *U.S. Army Special Operations in World War II* (Department of the Army, Washington DC, CMH Publication 70–42, 1992)

Hogan, David W. Jr, *Raiders or Elite Infantry? The Changing Role of the US Army Rangers from Dieppe to Grenada* (Westport CT, Greenwood Press)

Hopkins, James E. T. and Jones, John M., *Spearhead: A Complete History of Merrill's Marauder Rangers* (Baltimore, MD, Galahad Press, 1999)

Hunter, Col Charles Newton, *Galahad* (Texas, The Naylor Company, 1963)

Hunter, Stephen, *The Day Before Midnight* (Bantam Books, 1989)

Ingersoll, Capt Ralph, *The Battle is the Pay-off* (New York, Harcourt Brace & Company, 1943)

Jenner, Robin and List, David, *The Long Range Desert Group*, Vanguard 36 (London, Osprey Publishing, 1983)

Joint Chiefs of Staff, *US Dept of Defense Dictionary of Military Terms* (ARCO, 1988)

Jones, Virgil C., *Ranger Mosby* (Virginia, EPM Publications, 1987)

Jorgenson, Kregg, *Acceptable Loss* (Ivy Books, 1991)

Kershaw, Michael, *Integration of Special Operations and General Purpose Forces* (Naval Post-Graduate School, 1994)

King, Dr Michael J., *Rangers: Selected Combat Operations in World War II*, No.11, Leavenworth Papers (Fort Leavenworth, KS, Combat Studies Institute, 1985)

Koons, James, *US Army Rangers* (Capstone Press, 1996)

Kushner, Harvey, *Encyclopedia of Terrorism* (Thousand Oaks, CA, Sage Publications, Inc., 2003)

Kyle, James H., *The Guts to Try* (New York, Orion Books, Crown Publishing, 1990)

Ladd, James, *Commandos and Rangers of World War II* (New York, St. Martin's Press, 1978)

Landau, Alan M. and Freida W., *Airborne Rangers* (Motorbooks International,1992)

Lane, Ronald L., *Rudder's Rangers* (Manassas, VA, Ranger Associates, 1979)

Lanning, Michael Lee, *Inside the LRRPs, Rangers in Vietnam* (Ivy Books, 1988)

Linderer, Gary, *Eyes Behind the Lines* (Ivy Books, 1991)

Linderer, Gary, *The Eyes of the Eagle* (Ivy Books, 1991)

Linderer, Gary, *Six Silent Men*, Book III (Ivy Books, 1997)

Lock, Major John D., *To Fight with Intrepidity: The Complete History of the US Army Rangers 1622 to the Present* (New York, Pocket Books, 1998)

Loescher, Burt, *The History of Rogers' Rangers*, Vol I–III (Burlingame, CA, self-published, 1969)

Maguire, Steve, *Jungle in Black* (Bantam Books, 1992)

Martinez, Reynel, *Six Silent Men*, Book I (Ivy Books, 1997)

McConnell, Malcolm, *Just Cause* (St Martin's Press, 1991)

McManners, Hugh, *The Scars of War* (Harper Collins, 1993)

McRaven, William H., *Spec Ops* (Novato, CA, Presidio Press, 1995)

Military Intelligence Division, *Merrill's Marauders* (US War Department, 1945)

Miller, Kenneth, *Six Silent Men*, Book II (Ivy Books, 1997)

Mosby, Colonel John S., *Mosby's Memoirs* (Nashville, TN, J.S. Sanders & Co. 1995)

Naylor, Sean, *Not a Good Day to Die* (New York, March Berkley Caliber, 2005)

Ogburn, Charlton Jr., *The Marauders* (Harper & Brothers, 1956)

Padden, Ian, *US Rangers* (Bantam Books, 1985)

Peers, William R. and Brellis, Dean, *Behind the Burma Road* (Boston, Little, Brown, 1963)

Randolph, John, *Marksmen in Burma* (Missouri, University of Missouri-Columbia, 1990)

Rashid, Ahmed, *Taliban: Militant Islam, Oil & Fundamentalism in Central Asia* (New Haven, CT, Nota Bene Yale University Press, 2001)

Reynolds, Quentin, *Raid at Dieppe* (Avon, 1943)

Roberts, Kenneth, *Northwest Passage* (Fawcett, 1964)

Rottman, Gordon, *Panama 1989–90*, Elite 37 (Oxford, Osprey Publishing, 1991)

Rottman, Gordon, *US Army Combat Equipments 1910–1988*, Men-at-Arms 205 (Oxford, Osprey Publishing, 1989)

Rottman, Gordon, *US Army Rangers & LRRP Units 1942–87* Elite 13 (Oxford, Osprey Publishing, 1987)

Russell, Lee E. and M. Albert Mendez, *Grenada 1983*, Men-at-Arms 159 (Oxford, Osprey Publishing, 1985)

Santoli, Al, *Leading the Way, How Vietnam Veterans Rebuilt the U.S. Military, An Oral History* (Ballantine Books, 1993)

Schauer, Harmut, *US Rangers* (Stuttgart, Germany, Motorbuch Verlag, 1992)

Seagrove, Gordon S., *The Burma Surgeon Returns* (New York, W. W. Norton, 1946).

Shapiro, Milton, *Ranger Battalion: American Rangers in World War II* (New York, Julian Messner, 1979)

Springer, Joseph A., *Black Devil Brigade* (New York, ibooks, 2001)

Stanton, Shelby, *Rangers at War, LRRPs in Vietnam* (Ivy Books, 1992)

Taylor, Col Thomas H., *Rangers Lead the Way* (Turner Publishing Co., 1996)

US Army, *Merrill's Marauders* (Washington D.C., Center of Military History, 1944)

US Army, *Small Unit Actions* (Washington D.C., Center of Military History, 1982)

Walker, Greg, *At the Hurricane's Eye* (Ivy Books, 1994)

Waller, Douglas C., *The Commandos, The Inside Story of America's Secret Soldiers* (Simon & Schuster, 1994)

War Department, Historical Division, *Small Unit Actions* (Center of Military History, 1982)

Watts, Joe C., *Korean Nights, The 4th Ranger Infantry Company (Abn) 1950–1951* (St. Petersburg, FL, Southern Heritage Press, 1997)

Wert, Jeffry D., *Mosby's Rangers* (New York, Touchstone, Simon & Schuster, 1990)

Woodward, Bob, *Bush at War* (New York, Simon & Schuster, 2002)

Woodward, Bob, *The Commanders* (Pocket Books, 1991)

Woodward, Bob, *Plan of Attack* (New York, Simon & Schuster, 2004)

Zaboly, Gary, *American Colonial Ranger*, Warrior 85 (Oxford, Osprey Publishing, 2004)

Zaboly, Gary and Todish, Timothy, *The Annotated and Illustrated Journals of Major Robert Rogers Fleischmanns* (New York, Purple Mountain Press, 2002)

Zedric, Lance Q. and Dilley, Michael F., *Elite Warriors, 300 Years of America's Best Fighting Troops* (Pathfinder, 1996)

Zedric, Lance Q., *Silent Warriors of World War II, The Alamo Scouts Behind Japanese Lines* (Pathfinder, 1995)

## ARTICLES

75th Ranger Regiment, "The Battle of Hadithah Dam"

75th Ranger Regiment Association, "Ranger Companies of the Vietnam War Era 1969–1972," *First Ever Reunion* (1988)

Bearden, Capt Todd, "Operation Urgent Fury, The US Invasion of Grenada" (USAIS Library, Fort Benning, GA, October 1983), pp.25–28

Black, Robert, "The Ranger Beret" in *Gung Ho Magazine* (October 1984)

Cole, Ronald H., "Operation Urgent Fury. The Planning and Execution of Joint Operations in Grenada, 12 October–2 November 1983" (Washington, Office of the Joint Chiefs of Staff, Joint History Office, 1997)

Di Tomasso, Thomas, "The Battle of the Black Sea, Bravo Company, 3rd Ranger Battalion, 75th Ranger Regiment 3–4 October 1993" (USAIS Library, Fort Benning, GA)

Lechner, Capt James O., "A Monograph of Combat Operations in Mogadishu, Somalia conducted by Task Force Ranger" (USAIS Library, Fort Benning, GA, September 19, 1994)

McElroy, Robert, "Afghanistan: Fire Support of Operation Anaconda" in *Field Artillery* (Sept–Oct 2002)

McHugh, Jane, "17 Heroes" in *Army Times* (Military Times Media Group, January 2003)

Phillips, Noelle, "Honor and Valor" in *Savannah Morning News* (Savannah, GA, January 2003)

Schrader, Esther, "Simple Mission Became 18-Hour Fight. Afghanistan: Flawed intelligence may have put unit in line of enemy fire" in *Los Angeles Times* (March 8, 2002)

Tugman, Capt Jonathan E., "The Seizure of Rio Hato Airfield, Operation Just Cause Bravo Company, 3rd Battalion, 75th Ranger Regiment, 0103hrs, December 1989" (Fort Benning, GA, USAIS Library)

## WEBSITES

http://www.soc.mil/News

http://thebayonet.com

http://insidedefense.com

http://www.dtic.mil/doctrine/jel/jfq_pubs/issue35.htm

http://www.newyorker.com

http://www.defense.gov/transcripts

http://sftt.org

http://www.findarticles.com

http://www.guardian.co.uk

http://www.pjsinnam.com

http://www.ausa.org

http://armytimes.com

http://www.socom.mil

http://www.washingtonpost.com

http://www.defenselink.mil/transcripts

# GLOSSARY

| | |
|---|---|
| AO | Area of Operations |
| Bangalore torpedoes | Man-portable munitions device, effective against anti-personnel mines |
| Basic training | An eight-week course teaching the recruit basic soldiering skills |
| "Bob Marley" | Shredded BDU material worn on helmet for easier identification |
| Claymores | The M18 Claymore, a directional fragmentation mine |
| BDU | Battledress uniform |
| CAS | Close air support |
| Class As | Ranger dress uniform |
| CUP | 5307th Composite Unit Provisional |
| CW | Continuous wave i.e. Morse code |
| DLS | Desert landing strip |
| DMV | Desert mobility vehicle |
| Dragon | M-47 DRAGON Anti-Tank Guided Missile |
| DX | Direct Exchange, or, to discard, dispose of, or to kill someone |
| EPW | Enemy Prisoner of War |
| ETS | Estimated time of separation |
| FARP | Forward arming and refueling point |
| FEBA | Forward Edge of the Battle Area |
| FO | Forward Observer |
| FRAGO | Fragmentary Order |
| Gamma Goat | Six-wheeled trailer/truck combination |
| HALO | High Altitude Low Opening |
| HHC | Headquarters and Headquarters Company |
| HMMWV | High Mobility Multipurpose Wheeled Vehicle |
| Hooah | Supposedly derived from a Native American greeting, it means everything and anything |
| IG | Inspector General |
| JSOTF | Joint Special Operations Task Force |
| KP | Kitchen Patrol |
| LAW | Light Anti-tank Weapon |
| LCE | Load Carrying Equipment |
| Little birds | MH/AH-6 helicopters |
| LRRP/LRP | Long range units made famous during the Vietnam War |
| LZ | Landing Zone |
| M203 | M-4/16 with 40mm grenade launcher |
| MOUT | Military Operations on Urban Terrain |
| MTB | Motor Torpedo Boat |
| NCO | Non-Commissioned Officer |
| NCOIC | Non-Commissioned Officer in Charge |
| NVA | North Vietnamese Army |
| NVG | Night-vision goggles |

| | |
|---|---|
| OP | Observation Post or Operation depends on use |
| OpOrd | Operations Order |
| ORP | Objective Rally Point |
| PLF | Parachute Landing Fall |
| Psyops | Psychological Operations |
| Ranger School | A leadership school lasting 58 days |
| Ranger Scroll | The 75th Ranger Regiment's distinctive unit patch adopted from Darby's Rangers |
| Ranger Tab | The patch worn by graduates of Ranger School |
| Ranger Training Brigade | The unit responsible for running Ranger School |
| RIP | Ranger Indoctrination Program, three-week course |
| ROP | Ranger Orientation Program, three-week course to reorient Ranger-qualified soldiers prior to their return to a Ranger unit |
| RRF1 | Ready Reaction Force, a state of high alert for a Ranger Battalion |
| RTB | Return to base |
| RVN | Republic of Vietnam |
| SOCOM | Special Operations Command |
| SOF | Special Operations Force |
| SOP | Standard Operating Procedures |
| Spectre | a C-130 type gunship |
| STABO | Full-body rappel or extraction harness integral with web gear for infantry operations |
| Sua sponte | The Ranger Regiment's official motto, "of their own accord" |
| TOC | Tactical Operations Center |
| TOE | Table of Organization and Equipment |
| VC | Viet Cong |

# Index

# A

# B

# I

# J

# K

# L